W9-DBT-726

FROM A BARE HULL

REVISED EDITION

OTHER BOOKS BY FERENC MATÉ

The Finely Fitted Yacht
Waterhouses
Behind the Waterfall—a novel
Best Boats
Shipshape
The World's Best Sailboats

Illustrations by Candace Maté

First printing, First Edition 1975
First printing, Second Edition 1983
ISBN 0-920256-07-4

Published by Albatross Publishing House

4 5 6 7 8 9 0

DISTRIBUTED IN THE UNITED STATES
BY W.W.NORTON, 500 FIFTH AVE., NEW YORK

FROM A BARE HULL

REVISED EDITION

FERENC MATÉ

ALBATROSS PUBLISHING HOUSE

To My Dearest Friend, Candace,
without whose confidence and perseverance
I would still be dangling my feet
from a leaky old scow.

Acknowledgements

Some of the best designed and engineered boats come from the Beneteau yard in the small French coastal town of St. Hilaire-de-Riez. The family owned yard has been building boats for over a century. Because of their fine engineering and construction methods, I turned to them before revising *Bare Hull*. (Sadly enough, they don't offer boats for home completion.) A few of the photos are directly from their library, while much of the rest were taken in their yards. For almost a week they were the most gracious of hosts, sharing with me many of their highly guarded secrets. A reporter from a French magazine (without his camera gear) who was being given a guided tour was shocked and amazed to see me roaming around clicking photos of everything in sight.

'I don't know how you managed that,' he said, 'but I swear it's easier to get a tank into the Kremlin than to get a camera in here.'

Avec toutes mes gratitudes mes amis.

And a very special thanks to the celebrated French photographer M. Frédéric Allain who took the jacket photo and the two dozen best shots in this book.

And the specialest (is that a word?) of thanks to Big Red for doing all the illustrations and suffering through all my ranting and raving.

Contents

Introduction to Revised Edition

Eight years is a long time in our lives and just as long in the life of the sailboat industry which seems to grow by leaps and bounds in knowledge and in quality and even – dare I say it – good taste. A great many of the truly homely boats have disappeared as have many of the truly badly built ones, replaced in many cases by fine craft designed and built by honorable men, whose ideas and innovations make writing about boats a joy to be looked forward to.

To keep up with these men and their ideas, *From a Bare Hull* had to be revised, not only to show what is now available, but also to replace old notions with better new ones; some that help to make a better boat and others that save money, time and grief.

The one thing that has not changed in *Bare Hull* is the insistence that everything be done as well as possible, and if some people find this unnecessarily tasking I ask them to read elsewhere, and if some builders find this an obstruction to selling of their sub-standard products then all I can say is 'Hurray!' for that's half the reason for this book.

Paris, 1983.   *Ferenc Maté*

Introduction

It has been a long dream. I was thirteen when we used to gather in the basement of a friend to play billiards on a wobbly-legged table the size of an honest suitcase, with tiny clay balls so lumped and pitted that our games seemed more like exercises of faith and hope than displays of skill or concentration. The basement was home to a huge tin furnace that ate sawdust and wood and coal and thumb-wrinkled magazines. From one someone had torn a picture, a brown picture of a sailboat, a schooner I think, and nailed it to the rough inside of the cedar-siding. I don't know who put it there, it may have been I; but from that picture on I decided I was going to get that sailboat and just sail around the world for the rest of my life.

For most of the years since, I made no conscious effort towards this end. But somehow I had always been certain that sometime, probably any day now, I'd be stepping aboard my boat and doing whatever I needed to do to get her on her way and just go. The fact that I have had absolutely no money, not even enough to accumulate a single noteworthy debt, appeared to have very little bearing on the certainty of my future plans. On the other hand, I knew nothing about sailing boats or their costs so I was never threatened by the magnitude of the financial chasm between my brown paper schooner and me.

I did however, at the age of nineteen take a significant step. Upon a small, old, wooden scow with an irreparable starboard list, I built a smaller two room house. Its unlimited use of previously used material blended in splendidly with the tiny Vancouver bay and the surrounding junk.

It was a poor marina with sinking floats, stinking water, and sporadic bursts of electricity. But perhaps because of this lack of glamour it attracted a fleet of colorful, though sometimes rotting, old sailboats and a pack of sometimes rotting though still unfinished new ones. Their owners almost without exception were very friendly and extremely talkative individuals (hence possibly the reason for the condition of their vessels) who were a great source of information regarding every imaginable aspect of sailboat theory, construction, refurbishing and surprisingly enough, maintenance.

Aroused by their endless discourses about toggles, garboards, pintles, and baggywrinkles I took a further step with the purchase of a then thirty-two-year-old Flattie, to which egomaniac owners refer as a Geary 18. The price was $100, high, but I did manage to persuade a friend to assume half ownership for $75.

Sailing in the bay called False Creek was made

illegal to succour the endless parade of trawlers, tug boats, and scows. I did have a small nameless motor but it ran for only eight minutes after I bought it so I had to abandon the idea of motoring out to legal sailing grounds. But there was always the night. The boat parade eased after the end of the workday so after dusk I hoisted my once-white sails and lurched into the darkness. The bay was unlit but after a few outings I learned where most things were and only when the scows were shifted without my knowledge did I run very hard into some unseen wire rope and huge poly-line. But the forestay was strong and it held. The hull wasn't strong and didn't hold when one night we were run over by a stampeding log boom. She had to be destroyed.

My following four years were spent continuing my education; living and sometimes working on the wharves; prowling about sailboats; listening to the talkatives; hustling rides, sometimes across the bay and sometimes through the islands; and squatting on the float's end waiting for the miracle.

I then met someone who also wanted to sail. She was more practical than I, had sailed much longer journeys, had infinitely more drive and ambition, and was capable of actually organizing dreams. The other thing we had in common was no money. So we prowled together. Later we were married. Then we bought a sailboat . . . all in pieces.

1

To Find a Boat

I never wanted to build a boat. I always hated boat building. I actually hated people who were involved in boat building.

Most people will tell you that they do it because they love it, they love the accomplishment and they love doing things with their hands. I, however, never thought myself good with my hands. And if the thought ever entered my mind, my step-father chased it away with brief psychologically effective terms like 'Oaf,' 'Ox,' 'Clumsy Oaf,' and 'Put your hands in your pockets so they won't get in your way.' The only thing I was allowed to do during his numerous undertakings around the house was to pull rusty nails from rotting boards, not exactly the most fulfilling preoccupation; so my fear of building soon turned into hatred.

Others advocate that if you are to cruise you must build your own boat to know how everything was put together, so when something fails you know how to repair it. I always thought that if I left building my boat to someone who *knew* how to build the thing in the first place, I probably would never *have to* repair it.

When no arguments were left, the maniac builders threw out the greatest *raison d'être*: cost, and when I still said, 'No,' they said, 'Try it.'

They said that I would learn to love boat building and the giant project would be finished in no

time. That last part of it convinced me. I knew they were wrong. I knew I could never learn to love it and I also knew that I could learn to hate it so much that I'd finish it in record time because I couldn't stand doing it any more.

I bought a hull.

About the cost, they proved to be absolutely correct. A boat like ours when bought from the factory completely outfitted to the point that ours is, will run approximately $60,000. We have spent altogether, even with some additional hired out labor, no more than $29,000 (1975) and ended up with a boat with ten sails, Aries self-steering, all winches, windlass, teak interior, teak decks, teak exterior, the large Volvo MD3B engine, windlass anchor chain, compasses, all bronze portlights, and other things too numerous to mention. The potential for savings is obvious.

The decision to build a boat was derived from a long search for the *right boat*. The purchase of an old sturdy wooden sailing-ship seemed at first most reasonable. Some appeared to be financially within range and the traditional lines and romantic aura were difficult to resist. I should here explain briefly why I first excluded construction other than wood.

Used Fiberglass-Hulled boats, the few that could be considered structurally capable of offshore work, were all too new, consequently much too expensive for our means. I must say that we drooled over the Cheoy Lee built Offshore 40, the Swedish Mistral 33, the Canadian Spencer 35 that the Roths employed so successfully in their Pacific cruises, and the whole line of meticulously-tooled Nicholsons from 32 to 38 feet. But the oppressive fact of our poverty emerged triumphant. We turned away.

Aluminum Boats were unavailable under 40 feet (at least in the Pacific Northwest), and although there was someone starting hull production in of all places Squamish, British Columbia, we felt somewhat leery of the novicity of the operation. This experience was several years ago and if you're aluminum inclined you may consider further investigation.

We did fleetingly acknowledge the existence of a 36 foot steel-hulled ketch which was being marketed at the ludicrous 'sail-away price' of $13,000.00. But upon inspection the boat turned out to be poorly welded, under-constructed (the ribs were already showing, a characteristic one would be more accustomed to seeing on a thirty-year-old tug boat), and for some inexplicable reasons the builder chose to make his steel cabin with 5′ 9″ headroom, evoking emotions somewhat analogous to being in an iron lung. To support our skepticism of steel-hulled boats we had a friend who bought a beautifully sleek 48 foot sloop, peeled away the insulation from the inside of the hull, and found sunshine.

This problem of internal rusting in steel boats will be encountered not only behind the insulation but also in the myriad of inaccessible nooks and crannies found on all sail-boats, and even in seemingly innocent places like behind tanks and batteries where water may be trapped in some pocket and go undetected and be forever eating away at the hull. One need not have leaks to have this problem occur, for steel is its own worst enemy and *sweats*, through condensation, enough in a single cold night to drown the average horse.

For home completion, steel hulls are at a great disadvantage, for it is most difficult to attach anything to their frames, whereas in a wood hull pieces can be glued and screwed on, and in a fiberglass hull they can be bonded directly to the hull.

Ferro Cement was in irreconcilable turmoil, producing, aside from a few masterpieces, the most frightening herd of bestial mutations imaginable. Even the ones that were well built seemed to deteriorate very rapidly. In the boatyard next door I often found cement boats holed unbelievably badly from relatively minor impacts with rocks and pilings or even after just tipping over in a cradle, holings which would not have occurred in any decent fiberglass boat. Ferro cement is very brittle stuff. As if that wasn't enough, it's also very stiff being much less elastic than steel, which in turn, is only $1/30$th as elastic as fiberglass.

Multihulls are scary. Although they are somewhat less expensive to build than monohulls because they don't require ballasting, they do have four drastic disadvantages:

(a) They can break up more readily in wild seas than a monohull because of the tremendously varying forces exerted on their broadly spread hulls by the movement of the waves. The long spars connecting the hulls act in effect like lever arms, multiplying the force of the seas – as if the ocean needed any help.

(b) If flipped they stay flipped.

(c) They are vicious things to maneuver in tight harbors, and

(d) They are almost impossible to find moorage for.

But they do have two marvelous characteristics as well: they can go into the shallowest of bays and cruising grounds *and* they go like the proverbial bat out of hell. The latter point has not gone unnoticed by those vying for speed; in the 1983 Trans-At Race, forty-four out of the fifty-four starters were multihulls.

But back to the search for *the* boat.

Our first affair was with an ancient, world-proven Tahiti ketch. Hanna created a craft of fabulously simple design which in most cases is extremely heavily built, often proudly maintained, frequently available in differing degrees of refinement (therefore cost) but agonizingly slow under sail. Some with the more ambitious Marconi rig are almost tolerable but the majority still flaunt the gaff main and this rig to windward is practically a joke. I'm not yearning to fly, if I did I would, but the number of additional days tacked onto already lengthy ocean crossings require additional space for water, stores, and above all somewhere to stretch one's self, none of which is available on this sturdy little ship.

Its sluggishness makes island-hopping tedious, often necessitating use of the engine, an occurrence which I detest. Some of course will say that when cruising, one should not have to worry about time, but there has to be a limit to how much slow sailing one can stand and my threshold is just above a Tahiti ketch. Apart from its slovenliness, its accommodations are marginal. The main cabin is almost adequate but with very little storage and only slouch-encouraging headroom. The forecastle with its ghastly ventilation and no headroom is utilised as a sail locker only.

The rest of the ship has some fine points. The double-ender to me is the most seakindly craft. The displacement and beam provide a stiff comfortable boat, the small cockpit is ideal for mean breaking waves and the aft-hung rudder is large and brutal. While not quite indestructible, it is very accessible for repair. Prices ranged between ten and fifteen thousand dollars up and down the west coast. The largest selection was in San Pedro.

Initially the cost seemed attractive but when complimented by expenses for the usually-needed new suit of sails, rigging improvements, engine replacement (most have gasoline engines which I dread), enlargement of fuel and water capacity, and some interior modifications; apart from caulking, painting, etc. the sum to be expended climbed effortlessly beyond the $20,000 point.

Preoccupation with somewhat more recent and faster designs followed. We fell in love with a 36 foot cruiser-racer yawl named Chica, memories of which still haunt me occasionally. She was a beautifully designed ship with slight tumblehome, not too fine an entry, and a graceful yet not excessive overhang. She was built in 1956. Her mahogany hull was immaculate, but the varnished house needed some care. The rigging was stainless, the spruce spars spotless, and the herringbone teak decks and brightwork below made us forget about our newly realized poverty. With its traditional skylight, varnished dinghy, and masterfully crafted cockpit, she was all we could dream of. BUT:

The forepeak was damp and dingy and tiny: the engine was a sputtering gas Atomic Four complete with a shockingly low fifteen gallon fuel capacity and no room for expansion. Her sail inventory was made up of a seventeen-year-old main, a middle-aged jib, and Noah's canvas mizzen. To aid us in our rationalizing, she displaced $22,000. But God she was a beautiful sight. I hope the varnished skylight leaks all over the new owner.

We began to overreact and immediately found the perfect substitute: a sleek looking 34 foot sloop built in 1945 and maintained in Bristol fashion by her original owner. Her price of $11,000 made us forget the gasoline engine, huge cockpit, and 7' 10" beam because of which (we were told by a knowledgeable and reliable friend) she would sail constantly on her ear into the wind causing a most uncomfortable ride; and her deep, heavily ballasted keel would result in a ceaseless pendulum-like roll downwind. Our attention was also brought to the mast which to me seemed to have a frighteningly fragile head supported by a ghastly number of struts, jumpers, and uncountable tiny bronze turnbuckles, all of which were dying to separate of fatigue at the first given opportunity. In short we were told that she would make an ideal island-hopper but only insanity could compel one to take her offshore.

I may at this point appear unreasonably picky but I lived around many disenchanted sailors who through their fallen dreams served as a perfect example of people insufficiently selective in their choice of boats resulting in harbor-bound fixers, rebuilders, reriggers, sellers, neurotics, and potential suicide victims instead of mariners sipping coconut juice under a faded African Queen in green Tahitian waters.

Indeed I have so far refrained from mentioning a resurging fear which I attempted resolutely to suppress, but which accompanied me to every wood boat viewing: ROT.

Three good acquaintances purchased seemingly sound, thoroughly surveyed, and unquestionably approved wooden cruising boats during the time we lived in our float house. Their prices hovered around $15,000; with old gas engines, galvanized rigging, and very basic though efficient construction they could definitely not be considered bargains. At any rate, within a few months of purchase all three found extensively dry-rotted areas.

The couple in the Tahiti ketch, after remodeling the entire interior, decided to install new stanchions and found the bulwarks rotted. They had planned to go cruising shortly, but instead tore apart the topsides, replaced the rot, got a divorce, and sold the boat. A lesser acquaintance bought a 36 foot Alden, I think it was. After passing the survey with flying dollars her stern post was found to be so rotten that the rudder was about to fall off. Repairs cost $2,700.

A closer friend bought a beautiful 36 foot gaff ketch with a mahogany hull. It was only twenty years old, beamy, freshly-painted, spotless, and I turned green with envy. After installation of a diesel engine they were going off on a hand-to-mouth cruise for a long time. When he took out the old galvanized tanks to have the galvanizing removed for the new diesel, he found a rotten fir plank in the cockpit. Three weeks later he had finished tearing out the entire rotten mess of an aft deck and replaced it with fiberglass over ply-

wood. Then he found rot in the starboard aft corner of the cabin, then in the port aft, then in all the corners, and then in the cabin top just aft of the main mast.

This mess resulted in innumerable weeks of labor, a lot of dead-cheap red wine drinking, a badly needed skylight aft of the mast, and seemingly inexhaustible drunken discussions on the potential merits of musk-ox ranching in the Northwest Territories or perhaps Alaska.

I'm not faulting the buyers' choices in any of the three cases. Blame lies only with the incompetent surveying, although all three surveys were by reputable people. The point I'm trying to make is that our indecisiveness and indulgence in extensive wharf shopping were enhanced by this fear of rot, which seemed ominously unavoidable.

It is certainly a problem which cannot be dismissed and to treat it tenuously is indeed the epitome of folly.

Here I will humbly make a note to the intransigent woodboat maniac who is reading this book for the solitary purpose of fortifying his arguments against all fiberglass boats and who will, regardless of rot or toredo worms or the plague, purchase a wooden one.

Take care. After the surveyor has completed his olympic-record-shattering dash through your future headache, find a knife, a flat pointed one that doesn't leave much of a mark, then find at least two hollow days to crawl, creep, slither, and weave over every inaccessible square inch of wood, and poke the knife into it. There's no need for a back swing, just poke gently; if there is rot the knife will penetrate with little effort. When you have found the rot take the flat pointed knife and sink it to the hilt into the villainous marine surveyor. Take a *giant* back swing.

To the topic. The Tahiti ketch, the Swedish cruiser, and the sleek weekender are only three of about forty wood boats we viewed for possible purchase, but these three seemed to traverse the range of the type of boat we had in mind. We looked at no boat under 30 feet for we felt they were too cramped for extensive cruising, and we considered nothing over 45 feet for with the increase in size come the increased problems of large-sail handling, the cost of maintenance, and the cost of repairs which escalate disproportionately. Most of all we did not want to rely on outside crew; we had enough difficulty tolerating each other without intensifying the charged atmosphere with a third victim.

Our following mania centered on new fiberglass cruisers built in the Orient. The possibility of taking delivery of a boat there with the then valuable American dollar seemed very promising. The boats appeared of excellent craftsmanship (mainly joiner work); the designs were so varied that one's choice was practically unlimited; and of course the prices made them seem almost attainable. We went into deep research regarding different designs and different companies and became involved even to the extent of exchanging a few night letters regarding delivery dates, modifications, color of cockpit cushions, etc. Then we began to hear horror stories. Most of them I'm certain were untrue, but they sufficed to demoralize us long enough to discover our present boat.

For the stories. Apparently we were then at the acme of the Oriental boat explosion, the world demand for them having become very intense. According to one story, one of the large manufacturers expanded from 200 to 1,300 employees in one year resulting in chaos, the hiring of inexperienced labor, and a fleet of substandard, hurriedly mass-produced craft, not to mention endless lineups at the john.

A smaller company was said to have cut back on their consumption of expensive fiberglass roving for hull construction, replacing it with somewhat more traditional burlap. Another was said to have been even more liberal and now used newspapers, the quality of which is rather low in the Orient to start with. Companies which were known to turn out hand layup fiberglass of four to six laminations were now using chopper

gun, the undesirability of which will be discussed later. The quality of stainless steel used for fittings and tangs was much below acceptable and the Sitka spruce used for masts had become scarce resulting in either green or warping Sitka lumber or knottier and heavier fir.

As I mentioned these rumors were all stories, few of them substantiated and even fewer first hand. I did however see one boat which had begun to expose its chopper-gunned hull by shedding its blue gelcoat in palm-sized flakes, an occurrence which struck me as somewhat unappealing in a boat only four months old, and I did see a boat that had a hundred thousand deck leaks and when the rubrails and caprails were removed it was found that not a drop of bedding compound had been used to place them.

Apart from flying over and examining the factories to disprove the claims of the talkers we could do little else but dismiss the idea of an Oriental craft.

At this time we heard about independence and thought about building our own. We even considered lofting the hull ourselves. Many of our neighbors had done just that and some beautiful results were turned out in fiberglass, wood, foam-sandwich, and of course the inevitable ferro cement. Designing one's boat to one's needs seemed attractive; building our own boat would be fulfilling and the final cost could be kept quite low. But there was one great frightening factor: the only boat which was anywhere near completion had taken its owner four years to build. He had an ideal system; four months of hoarding money on a freighter in the Arctic then eight months of twelve- to fifteen-hour days working on his William Garden designed Porpoise.

The results were enviable, but four years is much too long a time for someone as unstable as myself to maintain interest, even if I could become familiar with the myriad of skills needed to accomplish completion. And four years was record time. A sobering example was our next-float neighbor living in a then seven-year-old concrete cave of a hull with a polyethylene deck and huge icicles in their main non-cabin for decoration. I didn't have the nerve to begin.

The only remaining alternative was buying a completed fiberglass hull and struggling on from there.

The beamy, large-transomed hull of a modern sailboat. The flaps in the transom open up and jettison the inflatable liferaft. The boat is a Beneteau 38.

2

To Find a Hull

I shan't rave about our specific choice – William Atkin's Eric redesigned for fiberglass by naval architect W. I. B. Crealock and built by Westsail, but I will mention the points which we found favorable

Being a double ender, as I mentioned in connection with Hannah's thirty footer, makes our boat very seakindly. She offers little resistance to following seas, thus will not be pushed to dangerously high speeds with the possible eventuality of diving into a trough. The pointed end will split large following seas while a transom stern is likely to disturb them and cause them to break. Excessive speed may cause any wave to break but I feel that every ounce of help is worthwhile. John Letcher, who sailed his little 20 foot *Island Girl* to Hawaii and back found only one thing that he disliked about her and that was the transom which took brutal pounding from following seas. When he designed his next boat *Aleutka*, the biggest change he made was to make her a double ender.

Some people argue that double enders lack stern buoyancy, and thus tend to get pooped easily. This point of view is quite valid if the stern is lean and pointed, so be certain the one you choose is full and rounded.

The rudder is easily accessible, and like a Tahiti ketch more than sufficiently affixed with

three hefty sets of gudgeons which have been known to withstand two whole days of the boat being thrashed against rocks by 6 to 8 foot surf. The rudder did eventually begin to wear away so it was removed.

The beam is eleven feet which for a boat of only 27½ foot LWL yields vast amounts of living space below, that can be utilized in various, very functional layouts.

The bow and stern are full and buoyant. The ample beam along with 7,500 pounds of ballast gives good stability, and although she will heel somewhat early if not reefed, she will at a point become stiff and settle into a fast comfortable ride with the long keel holding a steady course. This stiffness and the long keel gives the helmsman a feeling of complete control without having to fight and struggle with the rudder. I have sailed on too many light, fin-keeled fiberglass boats which were prone to burying the rail and sometimes the cabin side, and although they never succumbed to a complete knockdown, they suffered a loss of rudder whereupon the boat would swing up into the wind. This of course makes for an exhilarating sail among islands and can be tremendous fun offshore with a good sized crew allowing for frequent relief at the helm, but for a small crew on a long voyage one of the most disheartening things is fatigue and if one has to spend most of one's time fighting the rudder, fatigue will certainly come sooner than on a more stable boat.

Apart from providing incomparable directional stability and pleasant turns at the helm, the long full keel has other advantages; it facilitates self-steering and eases the task of dry-docking either on ways or on the shore beside pilings without threat of damage or danger of the boat falling onto her side. If the latter should occur, the large beam will maintain her in a sufficiently safe position until refloating on the next tide without the threat of cabin-flooding or wave-damage to the topside. One boat did run aground in Mexico and had to await the tide change. She suffered no damage.

Now the French have some great ideas. This old gaff-cutter carries its own cradle wherever it goes, in the form of two poles that bolt to the gunwale and hold the boat upright. You can beach your boat anywhere anytime in mud or sand, or with the use of blocks even on a rocky bottom, and to hell with shipyards.

The modern application of this system on a new French sailboat. A heavy bronze casting bolted to hull to take the pole. The top hole is threaded to take a bolt while the bottom one just takes a pin to keep pole from moving. Heavy walled aluminium pipe can be substituted for wood poles. Since the poles would be 8 or 9 feet long on most modern cruisers, it might be wisest to cut the poles in half, thread the ends and use a common threaded coupling to re-unite them. Then you'd have four short poles which could be stowed in a sailbin without difficulty.

The Ideal Boat

But one would have to be very narrow-minded to pretend that this double-ender is a perfect hull. I'm not sure the perfect hull exists, but there are certainly many that outperform this one in both speed and maneuverability, and this is where one has to clearly establish one's priorities and decide just how much comfort in the way of motion one is willing to give up to gain extra speed, quicker helm response, and ease of handling in tight quarters, all of which can be had on a shorter keeled, lighter displacement boat.

And here we need not form two intransigent groups and start hurling stones at each other's glass houses, for the possibilities no longer lie only at two extremes as they did some years back, when, if one wanted a really well built boat he'd be restricted to the traditional full-keeled, full-bodied heavy displacement cruiser like an Ingrid or a Westsail, for in those days most manufacturers were involved in building weekend scat-abouts which had the offshore capabilities of a fiberglass outhouse. If one wanted anything in between he was pretty well forced to take the bus. But today most boats are of decent construction and moderate design, with moderate hull forms, moderate displacements, and some sort of a short keel often with a skeg to help prevent rudder stall and to add structural support to the rudder as well.

Advocates now exist for the widely ranging schools concerning design, and most arguments from all schools have logic to back them, so as I said the choices have to be based primarily on personal preference. But let us look at a few basic arguments.

Speed

As mentioned in the introduction this is *not* a book for experts – if it were I probably couldn't read it much less write it – so we'll leave obscenities like prismatic co-efficient, surface tension, and drag-induced-stall out of here. If you want to talk dirty, read stuff like Baader's *The Sailing Yacht* and the like. Anyway let's talk speed. Basically there are three major indicators of just how fast a boat will travel; Wetted Surface, Displacement, and Sail Area.

1. Wetted Surface

First, your speed will be determined by how much stuff you've got hanging below the water, i.e. the more stuff you've got hanging, the more power (sail *and* diesel) you will need to move you, *or* the more stuff you've got hanging the slower you will go. The term relating to this is *wetted surface*. To clarify and illustrate the principle, you can do a first hand experiment the next time you're in the tub. If you stick only your pinky under water you can move it along no problem, *but*, if you stick your whole hand or, for the more brutal, your whole arm under water and try to move *it* along, you can feel that now you've got yourself a brand new ballgame. *That's* wetted surface.

The amount of wetted surface can be reduced by cutting down on the displacement of the boat and by cutting away much of the keel which contrary to common belief is *not* all filled with ballast. In an interesting *sailing* test that Steve Davis, the very fine marine illustrator, did on a computer once, a given hull with a full keel was compared to the same hull modified to a fin keel and found that overall performance windward (speed plus angle of heading) was improved by almost 20 per cent.

To get a basic, very rough notion of the difference in the wetted surface between a heavy-displacement long-keeled boat and a light-displacement fin-keeled boat, look at the underwater areas of the illustrations of the Westsail and the Santa Cruz 40, in which they are both scaled down to roughly the same length. This of course is a *very* rough measure, for because of the way the bottom of the Westsail is designed you see almost every square inch of its underbody, while most of the *flat* bottom of the Santa Cruz doesn't show up on a profile drawing. Anyway, the formula for determining exactly how much wetted surface a boat has is exceedingly complicated and the novice might make an error in the calculations, so I feel it's infinitely safer and wiser just to guess.

2. Displacement

The second factor that influences a boat's speed is *how much* mass will have to be moved through the water. Now you can readily grasp the notion that something light like a small balloon will sail along more easily than something heavy, like a brick, and if you want to know just how much more easily, you can use a simple formula to figure it out.

$$\text{Displacement to length ratio} = \frac{\text{D (in long tons, 2,240 lbs)}}{(0.01\,\text{LWL})^3}$$

Who developed this fine little tidbit is a good question, but it is a good formula and it does work and it does give reliable, easy to compare figures such as that an Ingrid has a LWL/Displacement ratio of about 400 and the Santa Cruz about 100. Now whether this means that the Santa Cruz cruises four times faster than an Ingrid, or not, is something I don't want to even begin to contemplate for life is just too short for such frivolities, but it certainly means something so let's just leave it at that. Anyway what we're basically talking about here is density and as we all know the denser something/someone is the slower it/he will move. Which I guess means that complete denseness means no movement at all, which is an enviable state as far as I can tell, for then one can justifiably sit on a fine sandy beach, physically inert, virtually comatose, save for the small movement needed to slowly sip away at a barrel of old rum.

3. Sail Area

Comparing a boat's sail-area-to-displacement ratio is the last measure of performance that will help you compare boats.

$$\text{Sail-area to displacement ratio} = \frac{\text{Sail area}}{(\text{Displacement})^{2/3}}$$

For a boat of 12,000 pounds displacement and 597 square feet of sail area, the formula works like this: First the displacement in the brackets must be in cubic feet so we divide by 64 (sea water weighs 64 lbs/cu. ft.) and get 187.5. Now we have to carry this to the $2/3$ power. If you have only a basic calculator don't despair. First square the number (multiply it by itself) and you'll get 35,156. Next you'll have to rough-guess the cube root of this number or at least of 35, and that's not hard because we all know that the cube root of 27,000 is 30 ($3 \times 3 = 9$ and $3 \times 9 = 27$) so we have to guess higher and guess 33 which gives us 35,937 which is pretty close, so we guess a bit lower say 32.8 which gives us 35,287 which is as close as we need to be to 35,156. So now we have Ratio $= \frac{597 \text{ sq. ft.}}{32.8} = 18.2$.

Judging by its complicity, this formula was arrived at by the same mind as the first. The relationship we get could be described as square feet of sail per pound of boat. Modern consensus has it that anything that has a sail-area-to-displacement ratio of less than 15 might as well have stayed at home, while on the other hand anything over 20 will have to be reefed when the first whitecap is sighted.

The Performance Cruiser

Armed with all this information what can we do now? If we do it cautiously we can probably come up with some ideal notions of what a fast moving cruising boat can be.

First we should cut away as much of the underbody as decency permits so long as it doesn't jeopardize: (a) directional stability – the ability to stay on course as if she were riding on a rail, (b) the security of the rudder, and (c) the possibility of safe careening in some out-of-the-way place.

This probably means a medium-sized fin keel like that of Bill Crealock's Crealock 37 or Robert Perry's Reliant 37, with a skeg to support the rudder, as the same two boats have.

Careening a boat like this will of course be less secure than careening say a Tahiti Ketch with its slab-like bottom but then you've got to give up something someplace.

The displacement per length can be more accurately sought out in as much as the formula gives us firm numbers to go by. Most designers, even the hardened advocates of ultra-lights, admit that the heavier a boat is the more gentle and more kind will be its motion and the less fatiguing and less wearing will be its effect on the crew. Most will argue over exactly where this line of comfort lies, but it is generally acknowledged that any boat with a ratio below 250 will require a lot of quick, tiring body movements to adjust to its quick motion. The ideal cruiser should be around 300.

It has been common practice to guess the price of a boat by its weight, for boatyards would often rough-quote by the pound, and this is still generally true for similarly crafted yachts, that is to say similar quality boats will be of similar cost per pound. One can then quickly deduce that the lighter the boat the less it will cost and this is generally true until one gets to the other end, where ultra-lights require labor intensive specialized construction. But generally speaking one can save money by buying a lighter boat, for not only will he be saving on obvious things like construction materials, sailing gear (lighter boats are driven by smaller sails hence shorter rigs, smaller winches, smaller blocks etc.) and of course engines and fuel tanks, but he'll be paying much less for very expensive labor, for less

A Frers designed 42 with broad side-decks and vast foredeck, roaring along under reefed main and spinnaker.

labor will be required to put the less material together.

You should not jump to the conclusion here that you would be losing strength for every ounce you lose in weight, for that just is not so. An obvious example is of course the ballast, for assuming that your ballast-to-displacement ratio stays the same, then 35 to 50 per cent of your total reduction will always be in ballast, which adds about as much strength to your boat as a millstone does to your neck. Much of the to-be-discarded weight can be whittled from non-structural members like cabinetry, overlays, trim and liners.

The weight of the hull itself can be greatly reduced by getting the stiffness required from things other than thickness; either by using light cores such as Airex foam or balsa, or by using a system of longitudinal or lateral (or both) beams to reinforce a thinner skin. I exclude here the notion of using exotica like Kevlar and carbon-fiber for strength, for these things are just too costly for the average yachtsman.

Both reinforcing methods – coring and stiffening – will result in a boat that will under most circumstances have the longevity of thicker skinned cousins, for the hull can be just as stiff and hence just as resistant to twisting, oil canning, panting etc; all those things which through movement will eventually cause a boat to come apart. The one thing one will definitely be losing with a thinner skin is abrasion resistance. In other words if your boat runs onto a beach and lies on its side with the waves hammering at it, the consequent abrasion against sand or rock will wear through a thinner skin more quickly than a thick one. I'll give you a bit of cold comfort by telling you that in many cases such an occurrence would most likely take place in a storm, and any storm worth its salt will wear through *any* fiberglass hull in a few hours, so the real question is not whether you'll suffer a hole or not, but *how big* will the hole be, and *that* is hard to say. Now you must realize that here I'm not talking about hull thickness in the keel area; just the general hull itself and I'll elaborate more about this under the ballast section. The only boats that seem to last out storms in these wash-ashore cases are the steel or aluminum ones, whose malleable skins collapse and sag but seldom puncture. We were in Cabo San Lucas in last year's pre-Christmas storm that washed out a lot of Baja, Mexico, and washed ashore close to thirty boats in Cabo, and the only one that truly survived was a steel hulled boat, although there was talk that a Valiant 40 might be salvageable too.

At any rate, a good solid boat can be had even with traditional construction around the 300 point, and of course much lighter hulls can be built with coring or ribbing.

The last part, the displacement-to-sail-area ratio is a good guideline to have, and all things being equal, a boat around 16 or 17 should make a very well performing cruiser. Now you can of course say that any boat can achieve that ratio regardless of how massive its displacement, by increasing the height of the rig hence the size of its sails. This is true, but you will be getting larger, more expensive gear to pay for a heavy and already expensive boat, and that somehow sounds like throwing good money after bad, especially when the same performance could

have been had at a lesser cost by keeping the boat's displacement down in the first place. Besides, the larger the sails the harder they are to handle and the less likely are they to be changed and trimmed, just because 'it's too much trouble,' so all in all, the worse your boat will sail.

A few minor points regarding hull design are also worth discussing, just to give you a notion on what to look for during your search.

1. Entry
Speed of a boat, especially windward, is not determined only by its lightness and the size of its underbody. If a boat is to have good penetration into headseas, it must have a fine entry, and here again the word *compromise* comes to mind. On a racing boat the fineness of the bow is limited only by the rating rules, whereas on a cruising boat too fine a bow will often mean an uncomfortably wet ride. It could also produce problems with stowing such beastly items as anchors and chains, which on a boat doing long distance cruising would mean many hundreds of pounds, which could easily throw too fine a bow out of trim. Here again the more moderate approach of Chuck Paine and Bill Luders should be studied.

On the other hand, too full a bow can be a problem as well (everything seems to be a problem in this damned game), for then the boat will have trouble making as good a headway to weather as it should, so care should be taken not to end up with too *cheeky* a beast.

2. Beam
A beamy boat will not only be a stiffer boat that will stand up better to her sails but also a boat with more volume for stowage and living belowdecks. This seems an almost moot point since most of today's boats are endowed with ample beam, so one need not search too far.

3. Fairings
The final factor that will help a boat perform is

A well designed bow will penetrate the water easily yet won't bury itself even when driven hard.

the fairing of parts of the underbody. The surface finish is important of course, but even more so is the deadwood area around the propeller (if a cut-out is used) and the fairing of the skeg or keel to the rudder.

Ideally the deadwood area, that is the area just forward of the propeller should be tapered to as fine an aft section as possible with whatever size bulge necessary left for the cutlass bearing and shaft. Too many boats (ours included) have just a piece left out of the stern without any tapering, with the result that a broad flat deadwood area exists. Not only does this cause great drag when the boat is under sail, but it also produces great turbulence around the prop under power, meaning that the propeller will be spinning in messy, multidirectional eddies instead of biting into good *hard* water as it should. This can cause cavitation which causes vibration which rattles the eyeballs out of their sockets.

The keel-to-rudder or skeg-to-rudder fairing is the other vital area. Ideally the skeg or keel should overlap the rudder with tapered little fins closing off the opening as much as possible. If this is done, the water can flow smoothly without separation and drag, right from the bow to the trailing edge of the rudder, which incidentally need be no finer than the average razor blade.

Note excellent fairing between the skeg and rudder of this Beneteau motor-sailer. The deadwood ahead of prop could be faired better above and below the shaft. The stainless rod between keel and skeg keeps lobster-trap lines from catching on the prop.

Comfort

It is perhaps true that most people who spend tremendous piles of money and many years of their lives to get a fine cruising boat, do so with shockingly little sailing, not to mention cruising experience. There is basically nothing condemnable about this, and thank God that most of us approach sailing in different ways, for if we didn't there'd be a whole seafull of bitty cruising clones out there, as undistinguishable and as unpalatable as those famous hamburgers of you know who.

Yet I am often made sad by going aboard boats either factory finished or skipper completed, whose owners have done their sincerest best to buy or build the right thing to achieve their goal of a safe and comfortable yacht, yet all they really ended up with was an interestingly decorated though somewhat cramped family-room along the nautical theme, with a wetbar below, a little porch out back for sunning, and a bunch of ropes and stuff dangling from above. Well Merciful-Mary-Mother-of-Jeezus, why didn't these people think of *what* a boat *is* and what it's meant to *do* under varying and often unpredictable circumstances *before* they built in lounge chairs on the aft deck, Lazy-Boys below, and before they spent most of their time searching and pondering, measuring and arguing about which cabinet or corner would be best for the TV.

Perhaps the greatest single villain in this whole mess is the word *comfort*, for people bring aboard notions instilled in them by years of land-living and daydreaming and wearing out their shoes at boatshows, which are invariably in cozy colosseums or mausoleums, with lots of heat and lots of light and soothing elevator music, and restaurants and toilets for diversion, and above and beyond all not a single one of these brothels-for-the-mind ever heel, or pitch, or roll a single bloody inch.

Well. If you really want to get ideas that will help you plan your dreamboat, you should by-pass boatshows altogether and start visiting two totally different but infinitely more enlightening cultural establishments: rodeos and strip-joints.

Rodeos are the mandatory training grounds for sailors: bronco riding gives you an idea of what it's like changing down to stormsails with your legs wrapped around the bowsprit; calf-roping is the first step in trying to tie your shoe-laces belowdecks in a storm; bull wrestling will teach you how to dowse a genny filled with 30 knots of wind, and the chuck-wagon race is a virtual replica of a man running downwind with much too much sail up, genny-sheet in one hand, main-sheet in the other, knees slightly bent and both feet firmly rooted, and his mind in a state of confused panic trying to decide whether it's best to fill his pants up, or just give up on the whole thing and go completely blind.

Strip-joints are a must too – and here I speak of places showing skills of fine young acrobats not

some old deary parading with worn feathers – for to change your clothes at sea you'll have to learn to do it during back-flips and nip-ups and knee bends and the splits, while the stage sinks and rises and undulates about.

So when one talks about comfort at sea, one should talk about *surviving* as best one can, and that means being thrown across the cabin as infrequently as possible, spilling mulched-up canned-mush no more than once a day, and indulging in man-overboard fun no more than once an ocean. *That* is comfort at sea.

Motion

This is one factor that's almost impossible to correct on a boat once the hull has been molded, because out of the four main factors that control motion – Displacement, Balance, Beam, and Ballast positioning – three are forever designed and cast into the hull, unless you are uncommonly handy with a chainsaw.

1. Displacement

Displacement will, to a great degree, determine the *quickness* of a boat's motion – roll, pitch and yaw – and the greater the displacement the slower and more comfortable will the motion be. This is a simple thing to grasp and is easily observable if one looks at how a styrofoam *log* bobs, compared to the gentle movement of a real log made of wood.

2. Balance

Balance designed into the hull will also have a great effect on just *how* a boat will move. The best movement would be provided by a perfect double-ender whose bow and stern are formed about the same, hence they will both plunge and halt at about the same rate. The least even motion will probably be had on a modern ocean racer with a very fine entry and a stern that has almost all of the beam carried completely aft and down low, so that the boat looks like a double-ender sawn in half. These two are extreme designs of course, neither of which would make an ideal cruising boat for if the stern of a double-ender would be as fine as its bow *should be*, then the stern wouldn't have enough buoyancy to keep from being forever pooped by following seas, whereas the broad flat stern of the modern racer tends to come down with a jarring uncomfortable bang. So, look for moderation. The designer Chuck Paine seems to extract well balanced hulls in most of his beautiful designs.

3. Beam

Beam we've already touched on and of course the beamier the boat — all things being equal — the less she'll ride way down on her ear, and the easier life will be both above decks and below. A well beamed boat also yields the most comfortable, wide side-decks which allow for better weight shifting hence safer walking out on deck. An old fashioned meter-type hull on the other hand will sail much on her ear, and if the cabin were of a decent width, you'd have such narrow side-decks that you'd need a year of tight-rope lessons if you were to move with any speed at all.

Hulls of narrow beam (under 9 feet) should be carefully studied and measured up for accommodations. For although the designs may indicate a spacious tri-cabin layout with dinettes and lounge areas, upon evaluation one may find room for two quarter berths and a deep breath.

A pretty hull with lots of tumblehome and small stern. For emergency propulsion it uses a sweep that sits in the oarlock you see to port. Now why any one Frenchman would name his sailboat after an American TV western is beyond me.

4. Ballast Distribution

Ballast distribution is the one thing that can to a limited degree be altered on a boat, for indeed trim ballast can be added, especially in the form of anchor chain, or sometimes in the form of lead pigs, but that really isn't the subject here. In general a boat whose ballast is spread along the bottom of a long keel will have more gentle, smoothly pitching movements than one with its ballast concentrated in the bottom of a deep fin.

Deck

The second determinant of how *comfortable* one will feel aboard a boat will be determined by how *comfortable* the boat is to handle, that is to say how *safe* one is moving around and managing the sails.

The foredeck moves the most on a boat (save for a bowsprit) and much hurried headsail changing and anchor handling will have to be done here, so it should be free of obstructions like bulky hatches or gawking vents, all those things you could snag, or trip and fall over. The side-decks should be wide, and it's hard to lay down exact parameters, but anything less than 16 inches is getting narrow especially if the cabin-sides are steep and even more so if the cabin-sides are high, for then once you're on a heel you'll find it impossible to walk on the lee-side of the boat. This can be demonstrated by an exaggerated example as in the drawing, showing a boat with a 16 inch wide deck with a 16 inch high cabin; the side deck nearly vanishes on a 35 degree heel. Now you can say you'll seldom be on a 35 degree heel but a slight decrease in deck width or a slight increase in cabin height will have the same effect on much lesser heels. All these problems can easily be gotten rid of by getting a boat with a flush deck or a near flush deck like a Swan or a Spencer 1330, but on other types of deck designs beware.

Bulwarks and toerails are vital on all boats, and to a point the higher the better, but if too high they're ugly and if too low then they're useless. So. The Bristol Channel Cutter and the Ingrid and the Westsail all have good-sized bulwarks an ideal height being 3 to 6 inches if they are to provide any safety and look good at the same time. The very low aluminium toerails are of little value, for many are just the right height to trip over and that's all. Some boats have no toerails at all and this is downright idiotic, for once your foot begins to slide, there'll be nothing to slow it much less stop it, from going all the way overboard. Britain's RYC which hosts the Fastnet race, drew up new requirements after the thirteen lives were lost in 1979, and one of the new changes was to require *all* boats to have a toerail of at least 1 inch in height. This of course is precious little but then I guess even a little is better than nothing.

I must admit that a huge cockpit with comfortable seat-backs, upholstered cushions, and room for at least four to lie about in undisturbed stupor has its decadent attractions. Yet when cruising, the need to survive overwhelms the urge to satisfy one's perversions; thus the lounge-pit must give way to a thimble-sized hole sufficiently long for four erect adults, sufficiently narrow for the helmsman to brace his legs in stiff winds, and sufficiently shallow to hold no more than a few hundred pounds of ocean when brimmed. Dimensions of 50 inches by 30 by 18 inches deep seem to me none too puritan; when one considers that a structure of such escetic dimensions holds almost 1,000 pounds of water, one becomes very reluctant to add even an inch in any direction.

While on the subject of the cockpit, another feature may be looked for. In most instances the engine and possibly the fuel tanks will be located somewhere below and around the cockpit area. To have the cockpit sole removable yet absolutely watertight seems to me an excellent idea. Marine diesels, reliable as they are, do break down and when they do so, they might have to come out, and when they have to come out they should do so by merely lifting the cockpit sole instead of ripping out the sink, sledgehammering the toilet

These two photos show how important a clean unobstructed foredeck is, for large often unruly sails will have to be wrestled with here.

If you don't think it's important to have a strong bow pulpit just look at this picture.

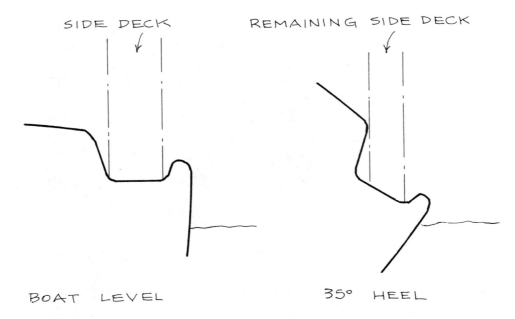

SIDE DECK

REMAINING SIDE DECK

BOAT   LEVEL

35°   HEEL

How a narrow side-deck becomes even narrower on a heel. Carried to an extreme with narrow deck and high house, the deck could become unusable on a severe heel.

bowl, disassembling the icebox and extracting the engine through the fourth drawer of the chart table, nut by bolt.

If the cockpit sole is truly removable, demanding no more than a few minutes of labor, then it is pleasant to have the sole out if one is to spend any length of time tinkering in the engineroom, for work is much more pleasant in any airy, lighted place.

But back to cockpit comfort. A backrest nicely angled (about 15 degrees) is essential for comfort as well as safety, for then one can brace oneself with little effort. On our boat nothing like this exists, and although this opens up the aft deck for lying about, it also allows for much sliding about, and to feel secure one must drape oneself over the lifelines like wet laundry. Get a backrest.

Details like proper places for winch-handles, charts, binoculars and the placement of winches and cleats all make for a safer boat especially for shorthanded sailing, for then in case of necessarily quick decisions, the helmsman won't have to scramble about to manage the yacht, but can do it from the relative safety of an organized cockpit.

Now to you this may look like the world's most boring shot, but actually it's full of goodies that all boat designers should think about. Starting from top: (1) Tiller extension lets helmsman move well outboard for better vision of headsails and view of road ahead; (2) Lazarette hatch has recess below it to allow hand to fit in and lift. This saves much time which you would otherwise be spending glueing your fingernails back on; (3) Teak slats for seat: warmer, better looking and much less slippery than raw fiberglass; (4) You have to look hard for this one but the fore-and-aft seats rise at their inboard edge as the helmsman's seat curves. This gives you a nice grip just behind your knees making the seats safe and secure on a heel; (5) What looks like a white garbage bag is actually the tip of the iceberg. It's an inflatable life raft of which only one-quarter is showing. You just lift up the helmsman's seat and out it comes. Nothing to untie, unchain or unlock; (6) Right beside the raft is a nice small propane tank in a molded cavity. If it leaks it runs into the raft-pit which drains overboard. The raft-pit is the path for the cockpit water to drain through; (7) Open spaces below seat slats make great daytime stowage; (8) Cockpit grate is beautiful and the world's best nonskid. This is the cockpit of the French Beneteau 35. And you thought this was a boring shot.

A very pretty cockpit with curved seat and curved cockpit sole for helmsman. Note intelligently recessed cleats below winches, to keep the little buggers from ramming you in the back.

Lines led aft can aid greatly in this respect. If halyards and reeflines and furling-gear lines are led aft to the cockpit, one will increase one's comfort as well as one's chances of staying aboard. This could also cut down on the number of winches needed, for with the use of stops as many as three lines could be managed with one winch. The one thing I do dislike about this system is that it usually means lines strung out over the cabin top which makes tying in reefs, and dowsing the main somewhat more treacherous, but then that's the trade-off. Personally I like the lines up forward because I enjoy swash-buckling about, raising and lowering sails and

hauling down on ropes and all that other stuff one does around the mast and foredeck.

The design of the whole rigging – both running and standing – is of great importance to the comfort of a boat's crew. If the standing rigging is well designed; for example, if inboard shrouds are done so as to leave a decent passage either out or inboard of them, if the backstay is so located (either well back or split or yoked to allow the helmsman to stand comfortably beneath it), and if the running rigging is kept out of the way of the crew's movement but winched well and safely around the cockpit, and if proper stowage is provided for the reams of

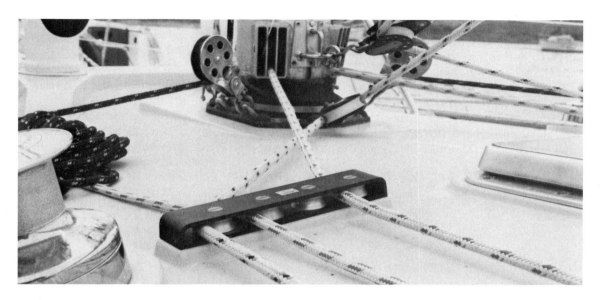

Set of turning blocks nicely engineered into a Beneteau deck. Note also blocks snapped into mast-collar, and raised section of fiberglass deck on which cowl-vent sits. They are actually built-in Dorade boxes and they vent below through more than one hole.

Close look at mast collar. Note that the eyes in it swivel. Note also problem with extrusions that have slots in them for track; they make perfect aquaducts for rainwater. This was a brand new boat and the neoprene boot had caulking all over it in a futile attempt at stopping the deluge. What is to be done?

line that end up heaped on the cockpit sole, then one can feel much safer and much more comfortable aboard, and things will go more smoothly and the boat will be sailed better and faster, and life will be much more fun, and *that* is comfort on a sailboat out at sea.

So the above things are the things to look for in a well designed yacht. The discussions here are abbreviated because unlike *Best Boats* this is not a book on boat design.

Now many will say that the criteria used, the constant worry over extreme conditions, the constant vigilance for danger and discomfort are the views of a pessimist, but nothing could be further from the truth. I've been a dreamer all my life and I'll always stay a dreamer, but I've learned that one must *do* things to get close to the dreams and that something involves feeling and seeing and *thinking* about yourself and your boat and the sea around you.

Everyone has his own phobias and intransigent beliefs even about sacred things like cruising boats. With kind permission of their authors, W. I. B. Crealock, N.A. and Herb David, N.A., we enclose their essays of thoughts regarding the *ideal* cruising boat. Somewhere between their varied point of view you should discover *your* cruising boat.

I'm sure you'll immediately notice the high toerail needed to keep the crew aboard, and the non-skid tape you'll have to put on large slippery surfaces like the plexiglass forward hatch to make them safe. And don't bother writing me; I don't have either of their numbers.

A Boat For Distant Waters

by W. I. B. Crealock, Naval Architect

'A man who goes to sea for pleasure,' said Samuel Johnson, 'would go to hell for a pastime.' And indeed we should devote as much foresight to the embracing of the one as to the avoiding of the other.

Those who wander across oceans in small boats will encounter hardship and discomfort enough, however sturdy their craft or great their expertise, so they should, at least, do what they reasonably can to reduce hardship and possible danger.

I am not discussing the boat intended primarily for local cruises of days or weeks or even months – though she will be well enough suited to that too – or even the boat for a single long passage, at the end of which lies a refit or retirement.

I am dealing with a boat for the increasing number of people who plan to voyage and live aboard for several years, usually on a frayed budget and far from normal facilities for repair and replenishment. These are the sailors who will, I believe, enjoy the greatest experience life has to offer.

It is tempting to be pedantic and to trot out one's own little preference as though it is perfection, but you may often judge the depth of a man's experience at sea by his reluctance to extol a particular type or feature as the ideal. There are simply too many variables in man and boat and sea. Some travel only to arrive, others for the journey itself; some to a time table, other to a whim.

What sort of boat, in broadest terms, are we seeking for these gypsies of the sea? After talking with many in the ports of the world and across my office desk, I believe that the majority want, very simply, a boat in which they can place absolute trust to overcome whatever the sea may offer and which will carry them with reasonable comfort and efficiency.

Most boats will survive 99 per cent of the hazards of the sea – for the boat usually outlasts the man. But, then, if you fall from a tenth floor window you'll be in pretty good shape for 99 per cent of the way; it is that last 1 per cent which may have you worried.

There was a time when 'Thou shalt be uncomfortable' seemed to be the unwritten commandment of the salty cruising man, and he was content to travel at the bottom of a damp, dark wooden hole, waging an exhausting no-win war against mildew and weeping seams.

Since fatigue is, I believe, a principal source of danger, we should require a boat with a kindly motion which will steer herself with or without a windvane, a boat which can be handled by a quarter of her crew under most conditions and provide them with dry, comfortable rest.

Though we are not discussing specific interior layouts here, I want to stress that word *dry*. One might imagine that a cruising boat would surely have one attribute above all others – watertightness – yet it is, in fact, one of the rarest qualities. Instead you will find fatuous little forehatches depending on a rubber gasket and a Sunday-afternoon fitting and skylights of traditional design which seem almost to beckon a wave below.

Clearly the first question to be settled is that of size. Length overall is an unsatisfactory criterion, although the mean between overall and waterline lengths would be some improvement. Displacement is a more accurate basis on which to judge practicability.

Let's be realistic on this question of displacement. There have been many long passages made by light displacement craft which were no less seaworthy, though unusually more tiring, than their more burdensome sisters. However, one cannot put a camper body on a Ferrari and expect to have a live-aboard sports car.

The cruising sailor wants to carry many months' food and water, extra fuel to make him independent of the substances he may be offered in a distant port, engine spare parts, three or four anchors plus a pile of chain and extra line, tools, perhaps some lumber for emergencies (surprisingly difficult to find in some parts), sail cloth, all the books he can accumulate, etc.

To carry all this without a whimper, his boat should have a displacement of 8,000 to 10,000 pounds per person; less than 7,000 pounds would mean some sacrifice and a lack of air space in the tropics, while 20,000 would push building and maintenance costs high and provide a handful for the crew to sail unless the boat were specifically rigged for the job.

Remember, too, that there is a considerable difference between a 25,000 pound boat designed for 20,000 or less, and a 25,000 pounder intended for that displacement and having suitable proportions and ratios. Displacement is no excuse for poor performance.

While suggesting adequate displacement, we should not be too greatly influenced by the traditional workboats and many world cruisers of the past. The cruising man was often short of funds and bought the heavy cumbersome cruiser because it was older and cost less.

Heavy-timbered workboats have a beauty and fascination of their own, but they were intended for quite a different purpose and their very massiveness was often planned to withstand the rigors of being pinned between laden hulls in port rather than conditions at sea. With, of course, numerous exceptions, they were husky but unrefined in performance and balance, and the faulty impressions which came from them and from the earlier cruisers somehow perpetuated themselves and survive to some extent today

To convert displacement to length we may use a displacement/length ratio of 360 to over 400, depending on type of construction, tankage required and so on, and since there seems to be considerable interest in boats of somewhat more than 40 feet in overall length, I am using as an example a 42 footer with a cruising displacement of about 32,000 pounds.

Displacements and measurements by themselves mean little. I recall a friend who used to boast that his girlfriend had the same displacement and leading dimensions as Marilyn Monroe. And no doubt she had, but one had only to see both of them under short canvas to realize that there had been some subtle rearrangement of prismatic and block coefficients.

The choice of coefficients for the underbody need not concern us here, but it should be mentioned that the long-distance cruiser is often shorthanded and seldom involves a large wardrobe of light sails. For this reason and because under power miles-per-gallon is much more important than miles-per-hour, it is unrealistic to provide a high prismatic giving best efficiency at the top of the boat's speed range. Better to have a hull shape that affords good performance over a wide range of speeds.

I suspect that the the reverse sheer is the most efficient for a cruiser, providing as it does freeboard and space where it is most useful, in the shoulders rather than the bow. But, then, a female weightlifter with a degree in economics would probably make the most efficient wife. Perhaps in some matters one must also let emotion rule and I choose the conventional sheer.

Bow shape offers considerable variety. The straight stem without flam or flare provides a truly comfortable motion, but to remain dry it needs too much freeboard and it provides a poor base for the sail plan. The long overhang is miserably wet, and the bluff bow is, of course, hard to drive to windward and causes a spastic motion in a head sea.

The bow with moderate and carefully matched overhang and flare offers us the best compromise.

In looking at the stern of an offshore cruising boat, think of it as a potential bow. When the weather gods have tired of watching you heave-to and insist on bare poles, it is the stern which must bear the brunt of the seas as you run with warps trailing.

Under such conditions I have seen a following wave strike the helmsman so hard that he bent the heavy bronze spindle of the steering wheel.

The possibility of such forces must be taken into account when considering the wide flat transom which affords maximum boat for the length. Almost as important is the considerable effect that the design of the stern has on the motion of the hull. The blending of these two factors thus contributes to the seakindliness which is a basic requirement.

The long counter and the very wide transom are the sterns which appeal to me least for deep sea work, the former for its slamming potential and the latter because it presents too broad a rump to an impetuous sea. The well tucked-up transom, however, is a good, inexpensive sea-going stern, especially on a boat under 30 feet, but it does little towards easing the motion.

The double-ender has gone to sea since the dawn of sail and is the ideal of many. It is simple and strong, and its outboard rudder is easily cared for where tiller steering is feasible. It is at its best in a short, steep following sea which no doubt explains why it is often used on work-boats which must cross a bar when reentering port. The steeper run which it produces may disturb a following sea when the boat is running too fast, but this claim is hard to confirm.

This stern is, of course, a compromise as is everything which moves in the sea. The steeper run to the buttocks slightly reduces its upper speed limit and if too fine it may induce hobby-horsing and restrict cockpit space. I prefer the Norwegian to the *lifeboat* version, but either may increase weather helm.

My own choice for a sea-going after end is the canoe stern, offering as it does a compromise between the seakeeping qualities of the double ender and the efficiency of the short counter. It produces a better run than the former and presents a better face to a following sea than the latter. Moreover, the canoe stern blends well with almost any bow and has good pitch-dampening potential. In wood it is difficult and expensive to build, but in glass it is simple.

Large beam is the attribute most often requested by cruising men. Beam gives not merely space and carrying capacity, but power to stand up to sail in a blow and an indefinable but real feeling of security when the wind is rising. Sailing on one's beam becomes tiring after a few weeks and complicates the routine chores below.

Here again we must control our appetite. The cruising hull does not lend itself to the more efficient wedge shape with its finer entry as readily as does the racing hull, and thus extreme beam brings with it a bluffer bow which takes more driving into a head sea and may cause a mutiny in the forecastle. Too much beam will usually lead to sluggishness in light and moderate airs and in larger boats it may cause too jerky a roll, although I consider this a much exaggerated danger.

In our example, because I considered 13 feet to be too great a beam for our standard of performance and handling, and 12 feet to be the minimum for adequate power, 12' 8" was chosen. As a rough guide for cruising boats in this size range, I believe that the ratio of waterline length to overall beam should lie between 2.65 and 2.85 unless there is a strong reason for doing otherwise.

Draft is very much a function of purpose. Too deep a draft will naturally restrict entrance to some of the quieter anchorages. In addition, it may give the boat too much grip on the water and she may be tripped and rolled by a large sea instead of giving a little to leeward. Adlard Coles in his excellent book, *Heavy Weather Sailing*, points out that, when a deck structure is damaged in heavy weather, it is often on the lee side because it has been rolled and hurled against an unyielding bank of water.

Deep draft, on the other hand, does promote steadiness on the helm and gives a boat the ability to tuck its head under its wing and heave to placidly, both absolutely vital attributes of the offshore cruiser.

Too little draft, apart from its effect on ultimate stability, is a serious detriment when you are battling off a lee shore. Remember that in a strong wind the surface water itself is moving quite rapidly to leeward – perhaps at one or two knots. The greater the penetration of the keel through that surface layer, the better the chance of clawing off. This explains the particular disadvantage of a small boat under such conditions. For all these reasons I chose a moderate draft of 5' 8".

Distribution of draft is also important. The boat we are considering should have a length of keel close to half its LWL so that it can take the ground safely and promote steadiness and the ability to heave to.

Having considered our hull, how do we propel it? A cruising friend of mine dreamed of banks of comely females at the oars, but Women's Lib has put that power source out of reach and we must be content with a more prosaic rig. Whether the boat should have one mast or two is a question with no certain answer. We have a tendency to choose the rig which has served us well before.

I have cruised many thousands of miles under cutter, ketch, and staysail schooner and I doff my hat to each. They will all serve well although I admit a slight personal prejudice towards the ketch rig.

Two masts in a 30 footer provide unnecessary complication though a lot of fun, and a sloop or cutter of 45 feet will be the upper limit for the average couple to handle. It is generally agreed that a mainsail of 400 to 600 square feet is as large as most couples can handle, depending on their strength and experience.

The cutter offers greater simplicity, lower initial cost, a less cluttered cockpit and increased windward efficiency.

The ketch offers a slight added safety factor if the masts are independently stayed. Smaller individual sails, great flexibility, the occasional convenience of being able to lope along under mizzen and headsails, and the oft referred to, but seldom used, mizzen staysail are the other usually cited advantages of the ketch rig.

I like the assistance in steering one can get from the mizzen and the convenient first reef that lowering the mizzen provides.

The ketch rig, per se, need not be as grossly inefficient as its foes claim. Several ocean racers manage to stagger along successfully under it. However, too often one sees a mizzen being stifled by a mainsail leech a few inches ahead of it. One gains a few extra square feet on paper, but the thrust per square foot is more important. Remember, too, that the average cruiser, frisking round the trade wind belts, will probably spend no more than five per cent of its time close hauled. Safety and pleasure demand, however, that it be able to step out to windward when asked to do so.

I am, of course, assuming a Marconi rig. It is more efficient with the wind forward of the beam, and it is simpler and cheaper. And yet, somewhere beneath the veneer of civilization, never mentioned without a penitential beating of the breast, I admit to a lingering addiction to the gaff.

If modern and properly proportioned the gaff rig does not fall far behind in efficiency for a cruising hull, and I suspect that for some hull shapes it might even prove superior. While I do not quite go so far as to recommend the gaff, I have to admire its air of elegance, and it is a strong and forgiving rig, easily repaired. It also has two considerable advantages: the mainsail can be lowered under almost any conditions; and the topsail (without which I would not consider the gaff rig) provides an excellent first reef that can be handled by one man without calling the watch below. The gaff rig does, however, have one great drawback, the lack of a permanent backstay.

We are not considering trade wind rigs in detail here, except to say that they form an essential part of the cruiser's wardrobe. On a trade wind passage, one piece of gear may rub on its neighbor 1,500 times a day; and the trade wind rig, apart from its benefit to steering, may

well pay for itself by eliminating chafe. The most common fault of such a rig is insufficient area, and at least two-thirds of the working sail area should be available in a passage rig.

The layout of the deck will depend in part on the layout below, but a few comments might be made on the center-cockpit arrangement which I happen to have chosen.

I followed three main guidelines. First, those parts of the boat which are used least should occupy the less comfortable sections of the boat. Second, a cruising boat, in keeping with the overriding consideration of simplicity, should be kept as open as possible, for those little cabins which look so snug on paper can be a curse in a warm climate. Third, I consider it the height of luxury to be able to sit in comfort within and gaze at the weather without or watch the activities of a new anchorage over breakfast. This means the boat must have some raised seating even though it entails some compromise.

These considerations become even more important with a center-cockpit. It is tempting to permit the aft cabin to become too spacious at the expense of the main living areas. A main salon with nothing but a dinette for seating does not allow the watch below to spread out, and a gam with a visiting crew resembles a sardine convention.

Accommodation, influenced by a host of minor considerations, must be as much of a compromise as the rest of the boat, for there is no single solution to the boat for distant waters.

A questionnaire sent to over 150 experienced deep-water cruising men some years ago did show a trend towards the ketch of moderate form; but it showed even more strongly a wide diversity of preferences in all aspects of the cruising boat and its gear. That is as it should be, for if you find that your dream ship is the same as she was a few years ago, better add a touch of Cuprinol to your grog – dry rot may be setting in.

The Ideal Small Cruising Sailboat

by Herb David, Naval Architect
Reprinted by permission of Pacific Skipper Magazine

Over a long period of time I have spoken to a lot of people and potential boat owners always asking what their boat might look like and the desired features of their dream boat, making notes about the specifics and generalities. The compressed general characteristics of a close to ideal small offshore cruising sailboat were:

1. The boat should be trailerable! The prices for slips in the marinas and the long waiting lists to rent a slip are keeping many away.
2. The boat should be capable of riding out bad weather and be easily taken out single-handed. It should also be able to stay at sea for some time.
3. The boat should be reasonably priced; not everybody is able to pay 50,000 for a boat.
4. It should be comfortable below deck, have full headroom, and allow a certain amount of privacy for the crew.
5. It should sail well under all weather conditions and have all basic safety and rescue devices on board.
6. The rig should be safe and simple to operate!

Taking the basic design parameters, the physical dimensions of the boat are immediately evident; length overall 28 feet, beam 8 feet (trailerable boats under 8 foot beam need no special permit on the road), draft 21 inches, draft centerboard down 5' 6".

The next consideration is the rig. To make sail handling easy without leaving the cockpit all sails are to be furled. This rig allows extremely fine adjustment on all courses. The boat can sail with optimum balance because the center of effort for all sails can be changed at will and as weather conditions permit. Spinnakers require constant attention and a lot of work on the fore deck; therefore the double jib has been devised. This sail is boomed out on two poles which attach to the mast. This sail which is actually one piece furls around the roller furler right in front of the mast. Such a functional sailplan requires an absolute minimum of work. A completely new approach is the furling mainsail, so reefing can be done in seconds without even leaving the cockpit.

All sheets and hauling parts from the furling drums run aft to both sides of the sliding hatch where specifically formed trough-shaped holes take all loose ends. From here even a man taking the boat out single-handed can reef and adjust sails in a snap.

The cockpit is almost 7 feet long, self-bailing through an oversized cockpit drain which ends above the waterline. This system eliminates the back pressure which always occurs on the cockpit-drains that have a pipe system which exits elsewhere under water; this cockpit drains in seconds. The control panel for the engine is recessed so no clothing or sheet can tangle, and it can still be operated by foot. At the aft end of the cockpit is a 6-foot-long track for the mainsheet-traveller mounted on a sill. A rather ingenious solution is the storage of the life raft. Its permanent location is aft, where it is ready and overboard in a matter of seconds.

The rudder is balanced which makes steering easier over long watches. The silent helmsman shown might not be everybody's cup of tea, but anyone who has gone to sea with one would not want to miss it. Self-steering over long distances is more than just a convenience.

Power is a 15 hp engine with a hydraulic drive system. An outboard engine might be used as alternate solution.

Considering the size of the boat, the interior features have a rather comfortable layout. Forward are two berths which can be made with a wedge-shaped cushion in the middle into a large double-sized berth. To starboard is a hanging locker, to port a head with shower and self-contained toilet. The forward stateroom is separated by a door which allows privacy forward. On the port side of the salon is a raised dinette under which the centerboard trunk disappears. A hi-low table makes this dinette into a double berth. To starboard is the galley with sink and two-burner stove. Aft of the galley is the chart table. Navigation is easier and better done on its own table, rather than on coffee tables. The navigator sits facing forward on the quarter berth.

There is ample storage throughout the boat for every purpose and it would go beyond the space available in this article to describe everything.

Basically the boat is laid out for fiberglass construction. With slight modifications, the skilled amateur could also build the boat in plywood or multiple chines, or strip planked over laminated frames, or acquire hull and deck from the builder, several possibilities for owning the boat on a limited budget.

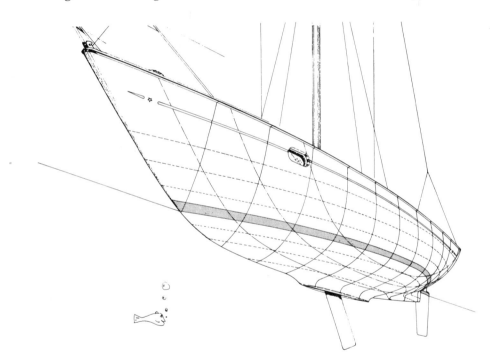

The Hull Form

The perspective lines drawing reveals very elegant lines, forward are sharp waterlines for windward performance. The boat is practically a double-ender under water, reducing resistance and wetted surface in the afterbody. The transom flares out above the waterline to add buoyancy aft and also to make room for a rather large cockpit.

A skeg which starts aft of the small keel will prevent crossflow and provide directional stability. The rudder is balanced which will make the helmsman's job a lot easier. In all, this hull will move without fuss through its element.

A fixed keel version is also planned, with a draft of 3' 9".

Downwind
The double jib of 215 square feet total is boomed out; these sails can be left unfurled in most weather conditions.

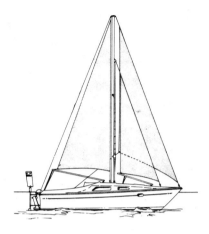

Light Weather
With jib, staysail, and mainsail, the sail area totals 358 square feet. The main is 147, staysail 72, the jib measures 139 square feet.

The Wind Increased
The jib is furled, the total sail area is now reduced to 215 square feet.

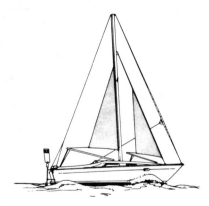

Storm
With the jib already furled, the mainsail and staysail are furled to a total of about 100 square feet and might be further reduced depending upon weather conditions.

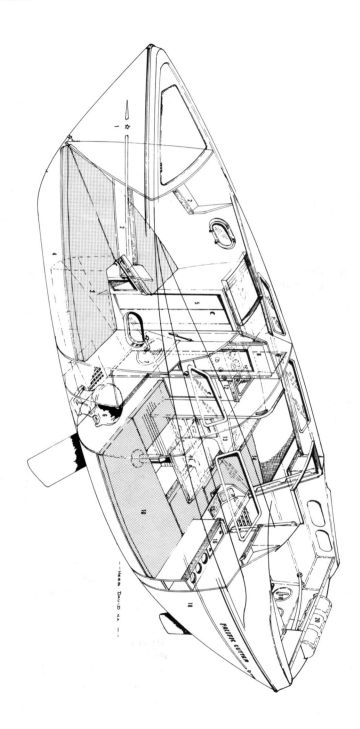

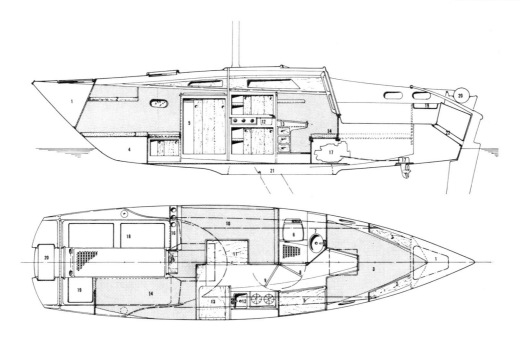

Interior Description by Numbers
(Consists of Perspective, Plan View and Starboard Elevation)

1. Chain Locker, Self Draining
2. Shelves over Berths
3. Berths
4. Storage under Berths
5. Hanging Locker
6. Self-contained Toilet
7. Formica Countertop and Stainless Steel Sink (mirror above)
8. Door to Head
9. Door separates Salon from Forward State-room
10. Dinette Storage under
11. Dinette Hi-Lo Table
12. Galley with Sink and Stove, ample storage above and below Camper Refrigerator fits under countertop
13. Chart table top folds up for chart storage below
14. Quarter berth also seat for navigator
15. Especially formed step to allow safe footing when boat is heeled
16. Storage for bottles and glasses
17. 15 hp engine with hydraulic drive
18. Storage under hatches
19. Watertight compartment with overboard drain for gas bottle on starboard
20. Life Raft
21. Centerboard trunk is hidden by dinettes riser of 7 inches
22. Location and route of oversized cockpit drain

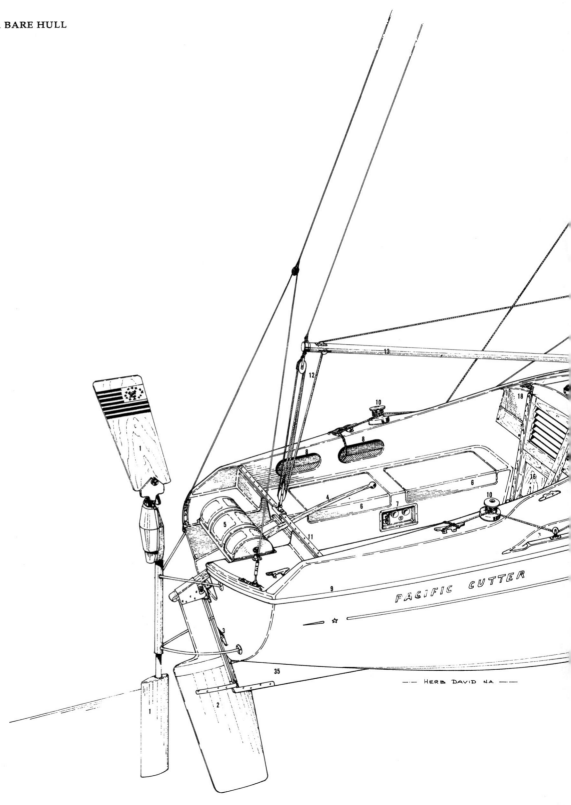

PACIFIC CUTTER

— HERB DAVID N.A. —

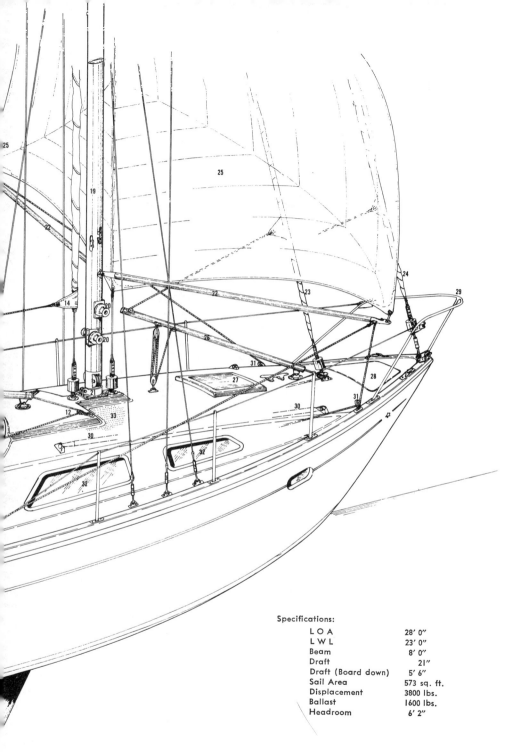

Specifications:

L O A	28' 0"
L W L	23' 0"
Beam	8' 0"
Draft	21"
Draft (Board down)	5' 6"
Sail Area	573 sq. ft.
Displacement	3800 lbs.
Ballast	1600 lbs.
Headroom	6' 2"

Overall Description by Numbers
(Perspective Drawing of Boat Outside)

1. Self steering
2. Balanced rudder
3. Oversized cockpit drain
4. Tiller
5. Life Raft
6. Hatches to storage lockers
7. Recessed control panel for engine
8. Storage on port and starboard for winch handles and small gear
9. Rubrail
10. Sheet winches
11. Mainsheet track
12. Main sheet
13. Main boom aluminum sheet and reefing line run inside
14. Mainsail shown in furled up position
15. Sliding hatch with compass on top
16. Two part doors, upper part vented
17. Recess for loose ends of sheets
18. Recess for loose ends of roller furling lines
19. Mast, aluminum profile
20. Light winches for halyards
21. Mast tabernacle casting
22. Outrigger booms aluminum or wood
23. Staysail shown in furled position
24. Jib shown in furled position
25. Double jib shown in outrigged position
26. Staysail boom
27. Hatch with translucent top
28. Hatch for anchor and chain locker
29. Bow pulpit with bow roller
30. Outrigger boom in position on deck
31. Outrigger downhaul
32. Tinted windows with metal frame around strong enough to stand on
33. Non-skid cover on all walking areas
34. Hydro dynamic shaped centerboard
35. Skeg

Construction

Regardless of how well a boat is designed, if it is sloppily or witlessly or greedily built, then all the best designing in the world won't have made it into a seaworthy yacht. And if the thing doesn't show its weaknesses now, then it certainly will later, for a boat is constantly working and moving even at a dock as wakes and winds move her, and every motion causes a little loosening and a little weakening. So whatever you buy and whatever you build had better be built well or it won't last long, and as the years go by you'll be spending more and more time fixing, and less and less time sailing, and that somehow seems very wrong to me.

1. Hull Layup

A cruising boat or any boat that is to last, must be of hand laid-up fiberglass, which is usually a mixture of woven cloth or roving, and some mat between the layers to pad the thickness for more stiffness. All of this is saturated with resin. To determine just how well a boat should be laid up is no easy task, that is to say to lay down a law about how many laminates should be used for a certain size of boat, is very hard indeed, for it depends to a great extent on exactly what will follow, or just how well the boat will be built thereafter. The laminate requirements will depend on whether the hull will be reinforced with ribs, or stringers, or by a special grid of bulkheads, or a foam core. For all those reasons I did give most of the layup schedules for the boats in *Best Boats*, so for a complete review of those different approaches please consult that volume. But of course there will be those who will want numbers (most of us need numbers to feel really comfortable) so I'll try and give a few. But please remember that these are personal things reflecting my own paranoias and my own years of sailing and research. So here it goes, and remember this is for a good capable cruising boat, and we are talking about *minimum* laminates in the topsides, not including reinforce-

ment in the keel area or stem, or stern, or at the chainplates. Up to 25 feet, 1 laminate of mat and cloth, plus 2 units (1 layer each) of 1½ ounce mat and 20 to 24 ounce roving. Up to 33 feet 1 laminate of mat and cloth, plus 3 units of mat and roving; up to 38 feet 1 laminate of mat and cloth plus 4 units of mat and roving, or 3 units *plus* reinforcement of coring or ribs. For the bigger boats use more.

Here I'd like to put in a point of view. It seems to me that from 35 feet up it would behoove the boat if structural reinforcements other than more laminates were used to stiffen the hull, like longitudinals and latitudinals (p. 279 *Best Boats*) or Airex or Balsa or similar cores (Chapter 23 and 25 *Best Boats*). Putting in more laminates will of course strengthen the boat just as much, but you are adding a lot of cost and a lot of weight. Remember for every 10 pounds you build into the boat you'll have to build in 7 to 10 pounds of ballast.

The minimum thickness you already have of almost ⅜ of an inch with the 3 units plus the cloth is quite sufficient skin thickness, so all you're really looking for is overall stiffness, and this can be better gotten from stiffeners other than more laminates. If you add a ⅜ or ½ inch core of Balsa, the gain in stiffness will be enormous, for you will indeed be creating a girder of sorts, much like girders in bridges and roof trusses, where two pieces are spread and stiffened by very light members in between. The argument over whether to use a synthetic coring like Airex or end-grain Balsa keeps going on and you'll have to do a lot of outside reading to make up your own mind. All I can say is that some of the best builders in the world use one and some the other, so it probably doesn't make an earth-shaking amount of difference. If anything should help you decide then maybe the fact that the resin can penetrate the Balsa a bit better, therefore creating a better bond and perhaps reducing the chance of delamination, will be enough to tip the scales.

The other method of stiffening, using latitudinals and longitudinals, is also an excellent system. Although it does nothing to insulate the hull against heat, or cold, or sound like a coring does, it does add tremendous strength, and the nice thing is that it can be used discriminately in areas that need reinforcement most – near bulkheads, chainplates etc. As a matter of fact a combination of the two might make for an excellent yacht, i.e. using a coring down to the waterline but not below, for in case of puncture of the lighter outer skin, repairing a hole would be a problem. From the waterline down a laminated ribbing could be used, especially if a fin keel with its tremendous torquing is to be reinforced. I must confess that one of my favorite boats from a construction point of view is the Frers 40 built by Tom Dreyfus at New Orleans Marine, and he used a single skin undirectional

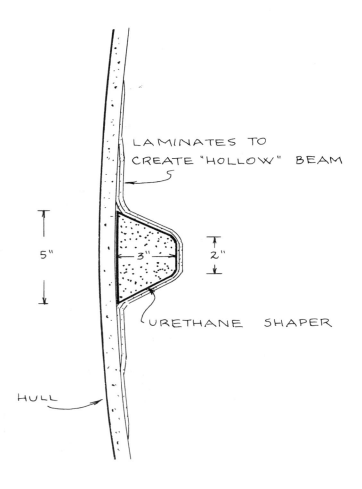

Cross section of stiffening beam. These measurements are not the word from the mount and can be altered somewhat. But remember the larger the beam the stronger it is.

roving construction with rib-type reinforcements, and apart from all the previous reasoning, the whole thing just *felt* and *looked* right. Besides, well placed ribs can and should be used as bases for major and minor bulkheads, for they will guarantee that the bulkheads leave no hardspots on the skin, weakening the hull and reducing the boat's life. Many builders just laugh at this, but if they had seen as many damaged boats as I have, and noted that in too many instances a bulkhead literally *broke* the skin in half, then they would immediately begin using foam behind their bulkheads.

The ribs are relatively cheap and simple to fabricate, see figure, cut as they are out of sheets of closed-celled urethane foam. If you cut the ribs with 45 degree angled sides then you'll have no waste, for every second piece can be flipped and used in full. The laminates over this core will be the actual structural members of the *beam*. They should be equal to one half of the number of laminates used in the hull's skin, e.g. if the skin is made up of 4 units of mat and roving, then 2 units of mat and roving should be used for the beam. The units of the laminates should be overlapped and tapered for the cleanest and strongest result. The first unit should overhang the beam's edges by at least 1½ inches with each successive layer overlapping the first layer by the same amount. This sytem of overlapping should be used whenever bonding anything to the hull, be it pads or bulkheads or beams.

The additional reinforcement should be added while the hull is *green*, that is the laminates have not yet fully cured. This green stage lasts up to three weeks. When bonding anything to a hull older than that, it is recommended that one wipe the surface thoroughly with acetone to soften it and clean it, and thereby insure better bonding.

While we're on the topic of these ribs or whatever they are (let's call them *ribs* because if we keep calling them *latitudinals* and *longitudinals* I'll run out of ink in no time) we may as well finish discussing how to make them, for it's not inconceivable that you may buy a hull and want to put in ribs to stiffen it. This might be a most intelligent approach anyway, for it would certainly broaden one's range of purchasable hulls, for then even a lightly built hull could be considered for purchase, and with a bit of reinforcement be turned into a respectable cruiser. So.

2. Reinforcing the Hull

Before you run out and buy enough urethane foam to cover the Houston Astrodome, stop and figure out what you're going to do with it all. The first intelligent step might be to give the naval architect who designed the boat a call and see if he has any suggestions. Actually any naval architect could be of help; the closer the better. Otherwise you could lay out your indestructible network of beams as follows:

- under all vertical bulkheads.
- under all horizontal bulkheads.
- in the form of a ladder to reinforce the keel (under the cabin sole)
- generally throughout the whole boat to form a grid with 18 to 24 inches between the centers of the ribs.

Whatever your grid looks like, make sure you continue it right into the stem (the leading edge of the bow) for it is the bow area that takes most of the pounding when going to weather in heavy seas. Now, do *not* start out by cutting up all the foam and piling it down below in a heap, and then mixing up 10 gallons of resin to bond it into place thinking you'll slap it all together in no time. You won't. First, measure in and mark all the places where the ribbing will go, and if you don't want to be that precise, at least lay out, very accurately, all the major bulkheads.

Next, cut some 3 inch wide by 8 inch long mat pieces and have them beside you with a board twice that size. You will be laying each piece on this board and wetting it out (cover and saturate with resin, using a 3 inch brush) as you go.

Next, mix a small batch of *cool* resin, and that means go easy on the hardener. Now, lay the first foam rib exactly into place and using a piece

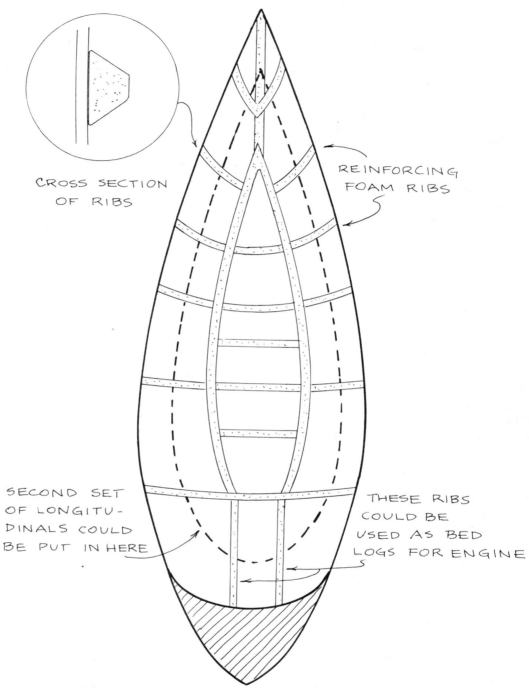

CROSS SECTION
OF RIBS

REINFORCING
FOAM RIBS

SECOND SET
OF LONGITU-
DINALS COULD
BE PUT IN HERE

THESE RIBS
COULD BE
USED AS BED
LOGS FOR ENGINE

Reinforcing a hull with foam-cored, laminate covered beams. These can stiffen a relatively thin hull to make it as seaworthy as a thick one without the great added weight and cost.

of mat every 18 inches or so, run it up, and over, and down, the foam rib extending out onto the hull, and thus tacking the foam rib into place. Make sure the back is dead flat against the hull.

It is advisable to work two different areas at a time, say the two sides of the bow, otherwise you'll keep nudging the piece you've just placed by trying to fit the next piece to it. If you work the two areas side by side, the *tacks* will have a bit more time to set. Once the tacks have set, check the beams for level and for placement. This is an excellent time to cut the tacks if the ribs have to be re-set. You can now see the folly of attempting to place a beam then bonding immediately completely over it a couple of times, for then if any shifting occurs you'd have one holy time cutting the beam loose and shifting it back into place. Anyway, once you've tacked into place a whole area like the forepeak, and checked it, go ahead and lay the first unit of bonding over this section.

Two words of warning: (a) Mix this batch of resin very *cool*, for if you mix it hot, the resin will go off quickly emitting a lot of heat, and if your hull is very thin to start with, this *hot-stripe* that you're placing on the skin can actually deform the hull. This does not mean you'll end up with a crushed Coors can but you might see the odd, not too pretty ripple. (b) For exactly the same reason lay on only one unit of bonding at a time, otherwise you'll get twice the resin, twice the heat, twice the warpage, etc.

Whatever you do, do a very fine job of laying in these bonds, and do a very fine job with anything you do, for the better the quality of your work in the beginning, the easier it will be for you to do the next step well.

A most important note: The hull should be in perfect, undistorted shape before the reinforcing is done, that is why it's best to have this done in the mold. If that's not possible, it's best to have the deck installed first to help hold the boat's shape.

Well, now that we've jumped way ahead of ourselves and discussed how to reinforce a hull,

perhaps we should go back a step and talk about how a hull should have been built in the first place, in other words: what to look for when you're shopping for a hull.

The argument that the thickness of the hull as an indicator of strength cannot be relied upon is to a point acceptable. A $^3/_8$ inch thick hull with only, say two layers of mat and roving (or much worse – cloth) is in fact weaker than another hull utilizing the same number of laminates of equal weight with an accumulated thickness of $^1/_4$ inch. It's obvious that the difference in thickness had to have been made up by resin which in itself has little strength. The strength of all fiberglass products comes from the tensile strength of the fibers of the mat, or roving, or cloth laid in the resin. (A simple experiment with a cube of set resin dropped from even a modest height onto a solid surface will, by shattering, demonstrate the above point.) But a well-squeegeed layup of three or four paired layers of adequate laminates like 2 ounce mat and 24 ounce roving will result in a solid dependable hull for up to a 38 foot cruising boat.

3. Mat, Roving, and Cloth

Mat – an unwoven conglomeration of loose, random length fibers laid upon each other.

Roving – long fibers woven into a thick but loose pattern.

Cloth – very tightly woven long fibers resulting in a much finer material than roving.

It is obvious that to attain maximum strength the strongest of the three materials should be used, putting cloth, because of its high density fibers, on the top of the list. But a hull of pure cloth is very expensive to lay up due to the number of individual layers required to achieve sufficient stiffness, so one has to use alternate layers of mat.

The next choice would then be a hull of pure roving, for it would give the rigidity required because of its sufficient resin holding ability due to its loose fibers. It would also, with its heavily textured surface, supply ensuing layers with a

Short-fibered chopped mat.

Diagonally woven heavy roving.

well-bonding, rough face. But it is because of this textured surface that roving must be combined with mat for an ideal bond. If one looks at roving one will see the surface riddled with hollows. If the following layer of unyielding-to-contour roving is added, the depth of these hollows is doubled and they will contain either unreinforced resin or much weaker air. When mat is alternated, its shorter fibers will easily conform and fill the hollows of the old layer of roving, as well as provide a supple base for the hard protrusions of the next layer, which must be applied before the resin in the mat has catalyzed.

4. Chopper Gun

People who advocate the chopper gun method of layup, base their argument on the fact that the chopped fiberglass strands, because of their poly-directionalness, are the strongest of the three reinforcing agents. This statement must be cautiously let out the other ear.

A hull containing by weight, less than 30 per cent reinforcing fibers is considered weak by most experts. Yet with the resin dependent chopper gun it is almost impossible to achieve a fiber content close to 30 per cent. At the same time a well squeegeed mat and roving hull can have up to 38 to 40 per cent glass content. A mistake which I myself tripped upon is to surmise that a difference of 8 to 10 per cent can hardly be considered significant. On closer examination one must realize that this 8 or 10 per cent actually makes up almost 30 per cent of the fiber content, thus resulting in a hull stronger or weaker by that percentage. Apart from actual strength, the short fibers will not provide the resilience and flexibility of hull supplied by the long fibers of cloth or roving.

5. Lamination Procedures

It may be worthwhile suggesting, to all those who will have a chance to inspect the incomplete hull of their future boat, that they look for proper laminating procedures. The obvious thing is to inquire into the weights and numbers of layers of material used. One should ascertain that full lengths of the material run the entire length or breadth of the hull. Although this procedure may slow production compared to a set-up where a number of short pieces are overlapped, it will, through the continuous fibers, add great strength as well as prevent difficult-to-work-around lumps in the hull.

The best method of laying up the hull, that is the method which will give the boat the greatest strength, involves laying unidirectional strands of roving diagonally. This method creates the web with the least give. Few builders use unidirectional roving, using instead *woven* roving which has strands woven into each other at 90 degree angles. The most common method of layup is to put a layer of mat next to the gelcoat followed by a layer of cloth and another layer of mat. These very low grained pieces allow a smooth hull finish, whereas if the coarse roving were put closer to the gelcoat, then the texture of the roving would *read* through the gelcoat, at best not being too pretty, at worst looking like a waffle.

The method of laying up subsequent units of mat alternated with roving is generally uniform through the industry. Long lengths of the roving and mat are laid into the mold longitudinally then *wetted-out* (saturated with resin), then the extra resin is rolled or squeegeed out. Some builders have improved upon this method choosing to alternate their runs of roving: one longitudinal layer followed by a transverse one. This should create a stronger *woven web* effect.

On flat-bottomed boats like modern racers, the athwartship (transverse) runs of cloth or roving can be run from sheer to sheer, but on cruisers with long deep keels with compound curves, full runs are almost impossible. So the thing to look for is that the builder has run the material a good 16 inches or more past the centerline. This will then create a bottom of double thickness, a bottom that is not merely thickened up by adding in extra layers, but that is an integrally interwoven part of the hull.

Generally speaking it's good to see a layer-over-layer overlap of about 6 inches.

Once the above has been confirmed one should check for the following:

Lumps. Although the exterior of a hull may be completely fair, bumps and lumps may be evident inside it, indicating an accumulation of resin either through poor squeegeeing or because of catalyzing before the excess could be effectively removed. Apart from what is obvious from the discussion of unreinforced resin, these spots could be areas of weakness because of the trapped air they may contain. Subsequent layers may hide the obvious air pocket, so if a suspicious lump is encountered one should tap it to ascertain whether or not a hollow exists. One should not look for tiny gnat-sized ripples, but a major lump, the size of half a plum should serve as a warning.

Gloss. Smooth glossy areas, unbroken by the contour of the fibers beneath, are also indication of poor squeegeeing or poor catalyst-resin mixing. Again, slight patches are bound to occur in any boat due to the sensitivity of the medium to any vacillation in temperature or humidity, but a frequent recurrence should at least prompt one to make serious inquiries. If the builder shrugs it off as irrelevant, interpret this reaction as a sign of ignorance which is likely to infect his entire product. Shop elsewhere.

White fibers. This argument is the last straw one can cling to with tenacity. They may be visible through the resin and again they are an indication of improper procedure with a resultant loss of strength. The cause of this occurrence

Chopped strand mixed with resin is shot over a layer of roving to wet it out and provide filler fibers before the next layer of textured roving is applied.

To get the excess resin out of a fiberglass laminate, one can either use a rubber squeegee or a bronze roller. The squeegee gets a bit more resin out, hence you'll get a bit higher glass-fiber-to-resin ratio, hence more strength.

Thoroughly wetted out fiberglass roving with all excess resin removed.

is probably shrewd and not poor judgement. A manufacturer may use very heavy fibers in long layers and may even end up with a beautifully textured, glossless, lumpless surface through which the white unsaturated fibers are visible. Visible white fibers are a result of too rapid catalyzing. While the mixture was *cool* enough to remain workable to a fair end result, it did go off prematurely, in a sense that all the fibers had *not* had sufficient time to be saturated. Premature catalyzation is done only to save waiting time, i.e. time during which a mold must be left unused awaiting catalyzing before the next layer can be applied. Since a manufacturer has only a limited number of costly molds, his motivation for accelerating catalyzation is obvious. To see the ridiculous extreme of what may result, take a piece of unresined fiberglass cloth and crumple it in your hand . . . not too seaworthy is it? I must note that the above occurrence would likely be encountered in a quality boat yard, one using heavy roving which is the most difficult to saturate.

6. Ballast

Here we go again. I read in the first edition of *Bare Hull* that, and I quote: 'If a fiberglass cruising boat is to last any length of time, the ballast should be internal.' Oh, youth! How nice it was to be so sure of things then, and if we weren't actually sure, we would somehow convince ourselves in no time. But as the years go by we learn so much, and the more we learn the more confused we get. So anyway, I'm not so sure anymore. I've kissed a few reefs in the past eight years, one of them rather passionately, and since then I've often thought that perhaps the next time I would rather hear the external lead keel scraping, than the bottom of a fiberglass hull. But the damage in the worst case of reef-kissing was only cosmetic – some gouges of about $1/32$ of an inch – so I calculated that at this rate I can afford to smack about thirty-two swarthy reefs before I actually suffer a holing, and I don't think even *I* am dumb enough to do that. And even if I

were, so what? What good is life without a few decent scars?

So I just don't know. I did contemplate putting some sort of *shoe* on the keel – a plate of steel or something – but then I figured that if I took all the time and effort this would involve and spread it over the next few years as bits of extra care with navigation, then I should be able to avoid reefs for about the next 200 years and after that I'll probably find some other hobby anyway. So.

Externally ballasted boats do have the one undeniable advantage: if they go aground lightly on rock or coral, the lead may get badly gouged but no structural damage will be caused. An internally ballasted boat may have part of its fiberglass hull ground away or badly abraded, necessitating very thorough repair.

If steel punchings or other rapidly oxidizing material is used for internal ballast, it is necessary that it be carefully sealed from air and water by either tar or, better yet, resin. If this precaution is not taken the entire inaccessible ballast may in a few years turn to rust. For details on the above procedure see the chapter on ballast installation. Some people advocate using concrete because it is less expensive than resin, but concrete is a mess and much worse, it retains moisture which softens the hull and rusts the steel, so just forget it.

I have purposely avoided involvement in lengthy discussion about ballast ratios and their distribution. The books of Eric Hiscock and D. M. Street attack the problem verbosely and thoroughly. My attempt to reword their findings would I believe be superfluous. It's enough to say that a ratio of less than 35 per cent ballast should be carefully looked at.

If a fin-keeled boat or an externally ballasted boat is chosen, one should look for four major points of construction: (a) a well reinforced bottom, (b) a well attached keel, (c) a well *fitted* keel, and (d) a well sealed keel.

Reinforcing the bottom is important for internally ballasted boats as well, so it is good to emphasize that the ballast area *should be twice as*

Four different ways of ballasting a fiberglass hull.

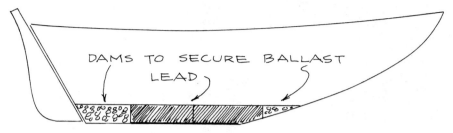

A. INTERNAL LEAD

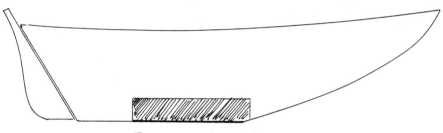

B. EXTERNAL JAMMED

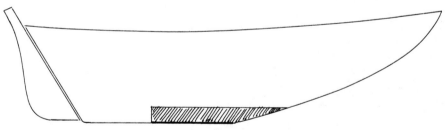

C. EXTERNAL FAIRED

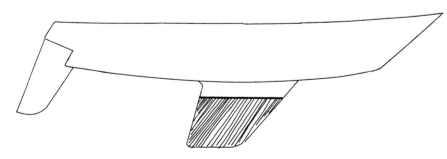

D. EXTERNAL FIN

Lead castings for internal ballast.

Large fin-keel ballast awaiting installation. The top of the casting should be trimmed to fit the bottom of the hull as perfectly as possible to avoid the need for great amounts of filler which can crack and fall out and loosen the keel.

thick as the rest of the bottom. These are Lloyds' specs and they are good specs indeed, but it's also good to note that this thickness should be carried past the immediate ballast area. Lloyds' rules call for a lapping of at least half the width of the keel before beginning tapering and fairing in. Most experts agree that there is nothing wrong with surpassing these minimums, especially on a deep fin-keeled boat where the torque generally (and in the case of a grounding particularly) is tremendous indeed. Almost all racers (Frers, Peterson, Santa Cruz) have an additional floor grid to reinforce their bottoms, and unless the bottom is monstrously thick, this should be done on any fin-keeled boat.

Attaching the keel well is the next step. The best system I have seen was on the Crealock 37, which used ten 1 inch diameter bolts, and the Beneteau 42 which used fourteen 20 mm. bolts (more than $^{13}/_{16}$ inch). The more bolts you use the less likely that all the torque will be put on one or a few bolts at any one time, and of course the larger the bolt the less likely it is to bend. Of course some say that at some point the bolts should bend or break, or they'll tear the bottom right out of the boat, but then you'd have to begin a brand new set of calculations to determine exactly when this tear-away keel should tear away.

The backup plates for the keel-bolts should be very substantial. Du Plessis in his excellent book *Fiberglass Boats,* calls for a backup-plate diameter

Paired up keel-bolts with back-up plates incorporated into reinforcing beams.

equal to three times the diameter of the bolt, and a backup-plate thickness equal to one-quarter of the diameter of the bolt.

The backup-plate should not be square or it will have four hard corners pressing on the hull. Some people advocate the use of a single plate built into the bottom to backup all the bolts, but I'm not sure this is such a great notion, for it is hard to keep a plate like this well bonded in a place like this. If water seeps in between the layers and softens the glass God knows what can happen. If you want the load more evenly distributed than the single-washer system allows, it might be wise to pair up the bolts, that is to say use one oblong washer for every two bolts.

Fitting of both internal cast keels and external cast keels is equally important. They both have to be ideally fitted, yet these *ideals* are diametrically opposed. An internal cast keel *must* fit loosely, in other words, it must not be wedging the hull apart as it is being set in place. If it does, not only will it forever keep trying to split the boat in half, but it can sit *up* in the keel leaving a nice hollow spot between itself and the keel's bottom. The hollow spot, because of its inaccessibility, might be left unfilled. This will definitely be a weak spot in case of grounding, for the bottom can puncture much easier if it is not backed up *directly* by the mass of the ballast working as a shock-absorber.

With an externally ballasted boat the opposite is true; the external casting should fit the hull as snugly as possible especially at the top of the casting. Here the looser the fit the harder it will be to seal, and the lower the fit the more likely later movement, and hence leakage, will occur. Unless it is financially impossible, the casting should be of lead, for then trimming the top or reshaping it with a torch will be possible. If however the casting is of steel, no such potential exists. You may shrug and say that one should just make a casting perfect to start with, but casting a 5,000 pound keel is no child's play, and to cast the thing so that it fits within ⅛ of an inch *or less* over the whole area is nearly impossible.

So avoid a steel keel and get a lead one and be sure it's trimmed and not just padded with junk, for the junk will eventually crack and float away and then everything will shift and rattle and leak.

Sealing of the keel-joint is the last important point. Some people use a resin putty or epoxy putty between the casting and the bottom of the hull, saying that the adhesive qualities of these will help to hold the keel on, but that sounds a little strange to me; I mean are we talking about glueing on 5,000 pounds of lead to a small surface with Crazy-Glue or what? Silly. The keel bolts should hold the keel on, and the keel should be embedded in something forever flexible such as polysulfide, for nothing is surer than that the keel will work some, then crack a hard sealant some, and then 'Look out Benny here comes the ocean!'

A note on internal ballast before we go on. Whether the ballast is cast or is of loose punchings embedded in resin, it must be sealed, that is bonded over thoroughly with mat and roving. This is important, first, to keep bilge water from seeping down into the ballast, and second, to make sure the ballast stays put in case you go turtle, and not go flying about the cabin like a canary in heat. Amen.

7. Bulkheads

If you are purchasing a completed boat the following item will definitely concern you. If you are acquiring a hull only, it is quite probable that you will have the main structural bulkheads installed. This procedure is a common one, inspired not by the human kindness of the manufacturer, but by the necessity of reinforcing the hull before it's extracted from the mold. Some companies use temporarily bonded in stiffeners obviating premature apprehension, for then you will install your own bulkheads and you will be able to do it properly.

Properly to me is a simple and inexpensive method that utilizes an angled piece of rigid polyurethane foam installed between the bulkhead and the hull, see figure. The foam serves

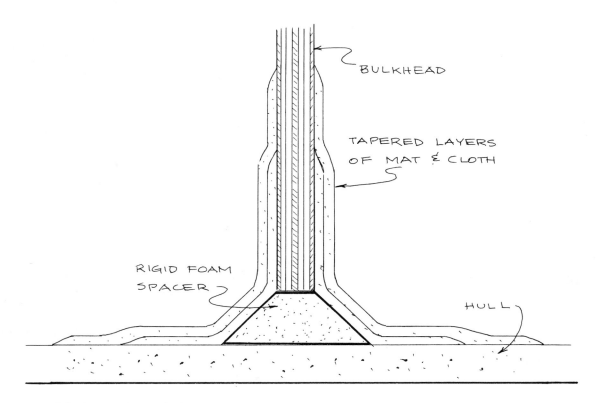

BULKHEAD

TAPERED LAYERS
OF MAT & CLOTH

RIGID FOAM
SPACER

HULL

I don't care what anybody says, this is still the proper way to install a bulkhead. It keeps the hard edge (and often hard point) of the bulkhead away from the hull, and the wide curve of the mat and cloth over the foam is a much stronger unit than a sharply turned 90 degree one which is what you would get without the foam.

three purposes. First, if it is cut on a 45 degree angle, the foam will create a gentle curve the lines of which will be easily followed by the bonding of mat, cloth, or whatever material comes on top. If the foam were excluded it is obvious that the bonding would have to make a sharp right-angular turn resulting in a brittle and delicate area.

Second, the foam will absorb sudden jolts imposed upon the hull by heavy seas and, along with the flexible section of bonding which covers its angled surfaces, it will prevent the transmission of these jolts to the stiff ungiving bulkhead.

Third, the constant undulation of the hull could bring about chafe between it and the bulkhead. Admittedly this motion will not cause immediate problems with almost any boat, but where two surfaces of unequal hardness are rubbing against each other, eventually something will begin to wear away. If the foam is inserted this process will in no way be halted, but the victimized member will be the non-structural foam instead of the bulkhead or the hull.

This is a simple necessity and if a boat yard deems it unnecessary, you and a small fee should have little trouble convincing them of its importance. If their appeal is that they've never used the method, show them this section. Charge a small fee.

The material most commonly used for bulkheads is plywood. It must be the highest quality marine grade, and it should be ¾ inch thick. Since in a fiberglass boat these bulkheads take the place of ribs, frames, and beams used in wood boats, the need for them to provide optimum stiffness and rigidity is obvious. Plywood less than ¾ inch thick is much too flexible; I recently almost became nauseated sitting in an Oriental 'cruising' boat watching the ⅜ inch bulkheads undulate gently.

The minor bulkheads can be much thinner of course and if you listen to Bill Lee, designer and builder of the Santa Cruz rocket-ships, then you'll be convinced that *all* bulkheads can be pared down to just over ¼ inch. But sure is sure, and unless lightness is a critical factor, keep the major bulkheads thick. The other bulkheads — berths, cabinets, etc. — can be cut down to Bill Lee's specs if you don't mind having to install knees and baffles to stiffen long ones. The nicest idea on any boat would be to have the gridwork of ribs in place first, then one wouldn't have to: (a) rely so much on the bulkheads for stiffness, and (b) fool around with putting foam behind each bulkhead because it would already be there.

Anyway, the bonding used to bond in bulkheads should be *half as thick as the hull itself*, and overlaps of 2 inches of the layers of laminate I would not consider too cautious.

On any thick bulkhead (and here is why it's nice to have thick ones), especially a teak one, it would be best to rout a 2½ to 4 inch wide strip about ⅟₁₆ to ⅛ inch deep out of the edges to be bonded. This is *structurally* important on teak plywood for teak is too oily a wood to make a proper bonding surface. On all other plywoods this is of cosmetic concern only, because all the bonds can be laid *within* the routed area, enabling one to do a very thorough filling, fairing and finishing, indeed.

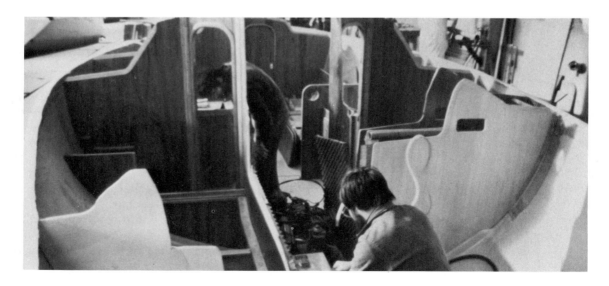

Most of interior is completed in the boat before the deck goes on.

8. Deck and Cabin Mold

Unless one is a completely self-sufficient boat builder, he should investigate further into the company whose hull is being considered for purchase. The major task in boat construction is, of course, the hull, and if you feel competent to continue on your own from this stage, fine; I hope the pages on decking will serve as an aid.

If, however, you require a more completed boat before you take command you should look thoroughly into a molded cabin deck, which most hull manufacturers offer. Apart from the basic esthetics of their design, which I will leave to your taste, you should consider the following points: cockpit layout, method of construction, bulwarks, hull to deck attachment, mast step support.

The cockpit we've already discussed so let's go on.

Method of Construction. To give glass reinforced plastic decks sufficient rigidity so that they will not whip and vibrate themselves to death, loosening deck fastenings, chainplates, hull-deck attachments, etc. in the process, a layer of sufficiently thick marine plywood or balsa or other coring should be laminated into them. On decks and cabin tops of boats below 40 feet, coring of ½ inch thickness is satisfactory although balsa is best at ⅝ inch.

Large, flat areas like decks, housetops and hatches should have balsa coring which gives stiffness and insulation without undue weight.

Which of these materials is best is a matter of choice, although I would now prefer balsa for it is: (a) lighter; (b) it is an insulator obviating the need of further insulation; and, (c) all things being equal, it should bond better to the glass laminates especially if the vacuum system (which literally *sucks* the resin into the coring) is used. The drawback of balsa is that you'll have to predesign your deck hardware layout and insert solid plywood where any fittings are to be bolted, for if you bolt through balsa, you'll be tightening the nut until the cows come home and all you'll be doing is crushing the deck or cabin top. Many builders prefer to do the whole foredeck in solid plywood, so any future shifting of cleats, chainpipes or windlasses will not be a major problem.

The plywood should not be thrown in as undisturbed sheets, but it should be tapered at the edges where the curves are to be encountered, to enable placement of a smoothly fitting bonding not threatened by the impossibility of 90 degree angles, see figure. The removal of sharp edges is also vital to eliminate the corners against which the flexing glass must work. An untapered edge will, in a disturbingly short period, crack the glass, if not to the extent of jeopardising the deck's structural integrity, then at least to the point where dreaded rain water may find its way to the plywood and causes dreaded rot.

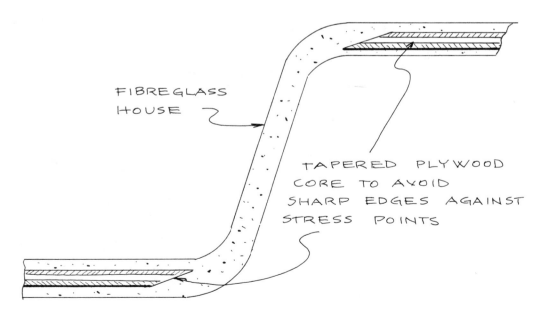

FIBREGLASS HOUSE

TAPERED PLYWOOD CORE TO AVOID SHARP EDGES AGAINST STRESS POINTS

If plywood coring is used in a house or deck for stiffening, the edges of the plywood should be tapered to avoid hard-edge stress points.

The quality of fiberglassing is just as vital here as it was in the hull. And although the thickness of the glass on either side of the plywood need not be nearly as heavy, it should still be made up of a well worked mat-and-roving or mat-and-cloth combination.

Another vital aspect of construction is the radius of the curves of cabin-top-to-sides, deck-to-cabin-sides and, if applicable (and it should be), deck-to-bulwarks. Although curves of a small radius appear to me more attractive partly because they're traditional, and mostly because they are fairly easy to overlay handsomely with teak decks, the practicality of this method structurally, must be questioned. A small-radius curve where the two adjoining planes approach 90 degrees with little transition, makes for a potentially weaker area than one with a larger radius which will, with its flexibility, transmit vibrations without having to drastically alter the form of the waves at one vulnerably angled point.

Again this philosophy may not be critical for a standard fiberglass boat which, designed partially for racing, is usually outdated and disposed of by the time the twentieth installment is paid, but for a cruising boat which hopes to establish a permanent relationship with its owner, any detail in design and construction that will increase its life expectancy must be considered a necessity.

One builder who likes to keep his racing-cruising decks light and strong inserts balsa coring into vertical surfaces as well, for example, in cabin-sides and cockpit sides. Putting coring into the cockpit area is very wise indeed, for not only does it allow a removable cockpit sole to be lifted by a mere human, but it also provides excellent sound insulation from the engine.

9. Bulwarks

Bulwarks are to a great extent considered a phobia of the traditionalists, but quite apart from this undeniable truth they have great practical value. Obviously they keep the deck a little drier; how much so depends of course on their height and the amount of freeboard. On a major heel they can provide a good walking surface, or if not high enough, at least a ledge against which one can wedge one's feet. In any rough sea the psychological comfort they provide through their visual massiveness, can be of value, unless of course it's dark out.

The best I have left for last, for the most vital service (and I am referring to the definition of vital: 'necessary to the existence, well-being and indeed continuance') the bulwarks can render, is to reinforce the stanchions. Stanchions bolted only into the deck will work loose even from everyday use, like visiting behemoths yanking them from their base when boarding. They will definitely not last long enough to keep a hurtling body from going overboard. If you insist on using stanchions of this kind to support lifelines onto which you may snap your safety harness in a storm, at least have the decency to leave your foul-weather gear and good rubber boots down below so someone else can use them in the morning when you're gone.

If your stanchions are just screwed into the deck, remember to unscrew them at the onset of a storm and hide them in a safe place until the winds die down.

With bulwarks of any height you have the opportunity to install stanchions that will actually serve some purpose. The stanchions can be so fabricated as to bolt through the bulwarks at well spread points, see figure. If for some reason this construction is not favored, a standard deck through-bolted stanchion can be sufficiently reinforced if a collar is attached to it at the top of the bulwarks. This reinforcement will shorten the treacherous lever arm and make the term *lifeline* less of a joke.

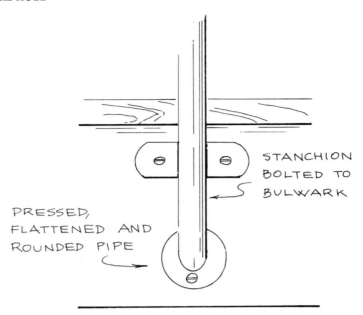

STANCHION
BOLTED TO
BULWARK

PRESSED,
FLATTENED AND
ROUNDED PIPE

A stanchion whose mounting bolts are nicely spread, guaranteeing a strong stanchion that will not be torn out. This, of course, requires the presence of a bulwark that's about 4 inches in height.

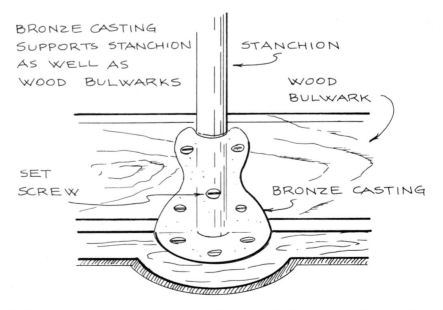

BRONZE CASTING
SUPPORTS STANCHION
AS WELL AS
WOOD BULWARKS

STANCHION

WOOD
BULWARK

SET
SCREW

BRONZE CASTING

A beautifully cast bronze stanchion base used on the Jason. *(See* Boat *section.) Free standing teak bulwarks are bolted to it leaving good deck drainage between the deck and the bulwark. I wonder if the stanchion holds the bulwark or vice-versa?*

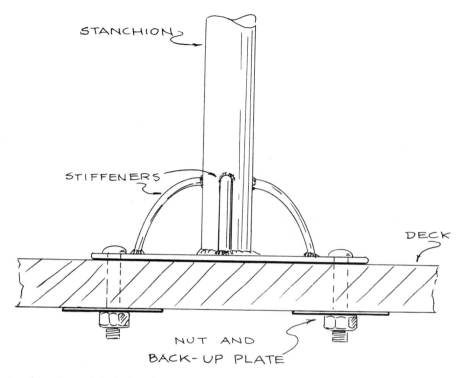

A stanchion through-bolted and properly backed up by good sized plate, not little washers. The stiffeners add to the life of the stanchion

A stanchion base that gets support from a bolt in the 2 inch high aluminum toerail.

10. Hull-to-Deck Attachment

Do not for an instant wrongly assume that because this heading appears late in this section it is of lesser importance. If this procedure is improperly executed, consequences may vary from the slightly annoying inaccessible leak to the most embarrassing habit of *deck popping*, one of which I have witnessed.

It was a squally, rainy, miserable day for a race, and the first boat came out of the downpour almost on her side with the great genny sheeted tight, and the whitecaps were blown apart but this guy just wouldn't luff, then there was a great loud crack, then a sound like a beer-can tearing and the next moment the sails were in the water and the deck was in the water but the hull floated upright, topless, a short distance away, blown slowly sideways by the wind, dragging mast and sail and half the crew behind her.

The deck had been pop-riveted to the hull. The rivet heads were small; with constant motion between hull and deck the rivet heads bore out the holes in the thin laminates. When the force was too great, the deck popped. The mast had been stepped through to the keel and it too had acted as a lever; so perhaps without this touch, then who knows.

Pop rivets are the fastest to install and most-to-be-avoided fasteners. They are sure to work loose in time or at least leak constantly.

Screws, if they are large, self-tapping, and used at short intervals in thick fiberglass, are of some value in tiny boats for a tiny time. If small and used in conjunction with thin fiberglass, take a lot of Bibles. Even for a small yacht this method is most treacherous for the drill bit has to be a perfect size. If it is too large the power of the screw gun will tear out the shallow threads the screw has cut in the glass and spin freely and hold nothing. If the bit is too small the screw will tighten prematurely and the heads will snap off. Some companies I've heard of who use this method seldom bother to drill out the broken screw and replace it. Anyway the whole thing is useless.

Sheer clamp. If a flange is absent on the hull, a sheer clamp of some hardwood may be attached to it with screws and mish-mash. The deck in turn can be screwed and mish-mashed onto this clamp. Since hardwoods hold screws well, this method should be fairly safe for some years. Mahogany would be ideal, for although it does not hold screws as well as oak, it is somewhat less prone to rot. If a caprail is installed over the seam, embedded well in polysulphide and maintained watertight, the life of the attachment may be prolonged, although moisture can condense on the inside of the hull around it and rot it anyway, so the whole thing in this day and age is rather a waste of time.

Bonding. A small flange may be located on the hull, and the deck set in place upon it. Then from below layers of mat and roving are laid over both, building up from narrow to wider strips. If sufficient laminations are used, well fitted, and well squeegeed this method could be excellent, for it will create a leak-proof monolithic structure, with even stress at every point. If well done, this attachment can be the slowest but the strongest of all. If not well done, and there are few things more difficult than bonding upside down sticky, droopy material, the thing is guaranteed to leak and is virtually impossible to repair. With high hollow bulwarks the method is an impossibility. Alajuela Yachts have used this method for many years and theirs is one of the most solid yachts in captivity. (See *Best Boats* chapter *Hallelujah*.)

One objection I do have to this procedure is that to achieve superlative bonding, the surfaces to be bonded should be *green*. That is, the fiberglass should have cured as little as possible. This *green* bonding is very infrequently done on production boats whose assembly system seems to require almost total completion of the interior, preceding the placement of the deck-cabin onto the hull.

Through-bolts, see figure. Through-bolting is a somewhat less delicate operation than bonding, but undeniably a demanding job if high, narrow bulwarks are encountered. The prerequisites are two extremely strong overlapping flanges. These flanges must be integral, i.e. turned over ends of laminates and not narrow little shelves added later on. If they are added later you might as well sew the things together with pink cotton thread. The turned over laminates must be perfect examples of fiberglassing, e.g. roving with mat and/or cloth, because the strain in these rather sharp angles will be severe.

Before the two flanges are laid together, a disgustingly huge, and shockingly costly amount of polysulphide (either black or white) should be laid onto the lower flange, but only after it, as well as the deck flange, have been carefully cleaned with acetone to remove dirt and dust. This procedure should eliminate most of the

leaks. The holes should again be of perfect diameter for the bolts to hold ideally. The bolts should be fairly large, at least 1/4 inch, and stainless steel. They should be flat head so that the tapered cheeks can prevent lateral movement, and they should be countersunk – just. You must fill each hole, just after drilling, with polysulphide and *then* insert the bolt.

On the lower end, a handsome sized stainless steel washer should be popped on, then either a lock washer or a lock nut. The nut should be tightened until it screams. This operation is nerve racking if one must hold a washer, lock washer, and nut between narrow shoulders of high bulwarks. It is definitely a two-man operation, for one person has to be outside with a screwdriver while the more unfortunate fellow is down below with nuts, washers, ratchets, etc.

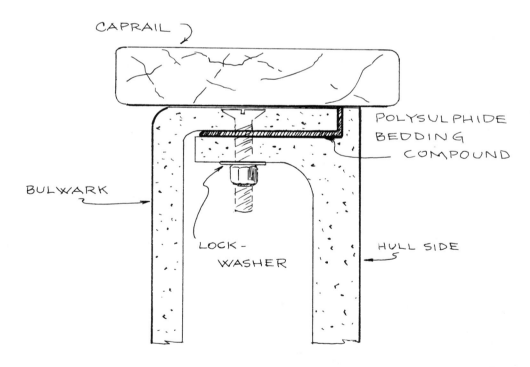

A very commonly used hull-to-deck joint, using bolts on 4 inch to 8 inch centers. Polysulfide bedding compound should be used instead of resin putty, for the resin can crack and open the way for water.

An interesting hull-to-deck joint which leaves both the bolt and the nut of the fastening exposed for future tightening.

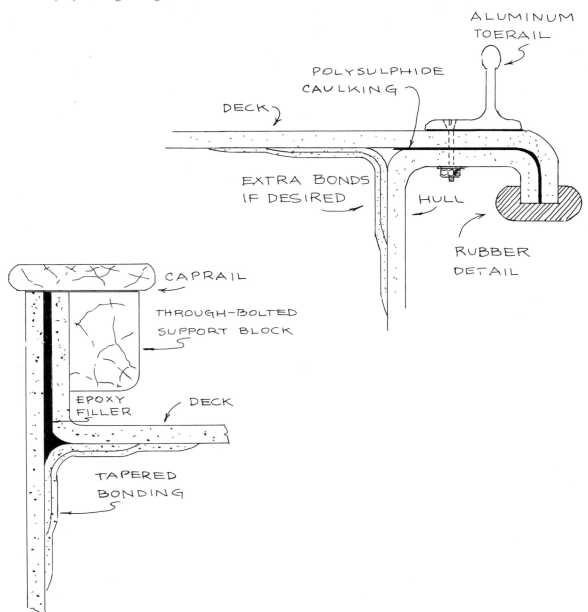

ALUMINUM
TOERAIL

POLYSULPHIDE
CAULKING

DECK

EXTRA BONDS
IF DESIRED

HULL

RUBBER
DETAIL

CAPRAIL

THROUGH-BOLTED
SUPPORT BLOCK

EPOXY
FILLER

DECK

TAPERED
BONDING

A first-class hull-to-deck joint that requires a perfectly fitting hull and deck, and many hands, for the epoxy has to be applied, then the deck slipped into place, then a clamp placed every foot or so, all before the epoxy sets up. The actual strength of the joint comes from the multiple fiberglass laminates laid in belowdecks.

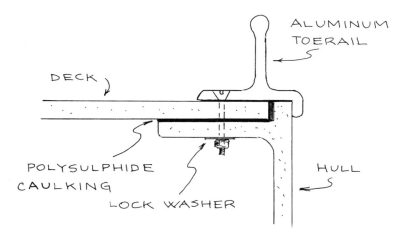

Probably the most common hull-to-deck joint used in boatbuilding today, that incorporates an aluminum toerail in conjunction with the through-bolts. Here the toerail makes a very good 'back-up plate' for the head of the bolt.

If performed as prescribed above with the bolts spaced no farther than 4 to 6 inches, it should be a good solid method leaving very few things to chance.

This bolting thing is by far the most common of today's methods and a happy thing it is too, for when *Bare Hull* was first written you could go deaf in most boatyards from the sound of rivet-guns popping, in a vain attempt to staple feeble hulls to feeble decks.

On many current boats, the aluminum toerail acts as an external backup-plate and of course this is much better than relying on a screw-head alone. Most rails are pre-drilled on 4 inch centers making for some very good hull-to-deck joints indeed. C & C and some other builders use a rubber molding instead of polysulfide. The protruding bead of molding then serves as a form of bumper.

Note: For plywood decks with glass overlay consult chapter on deck construction.

11. Mast Step

I include this item under the section on decks because a deck-stepped mast, *if well done*, is as good as a keel-stepped mast. Reasons: With aluminum as the most commonly used material for masts, the need for a completely snug footing above which the old wooden mast could indulge in a bit of bending and whipping is mostly eliminated. This theory does not imply that the mast should be footed on ball bearings, but rather it puts forth the idea that the major factor with the stiff aluminum mast is compression. As long as this force is transferred to the keel, the number of stages involved in the process (assuming of course that they are well designed and solidly constructed) will little imperil the integrity of the whole. Some people will never agree and will always insist on a keel-stepped mast and that's fine, but it is very difficult to seal around a mast with any success especially the newer ones which have grooves for sail-tracks

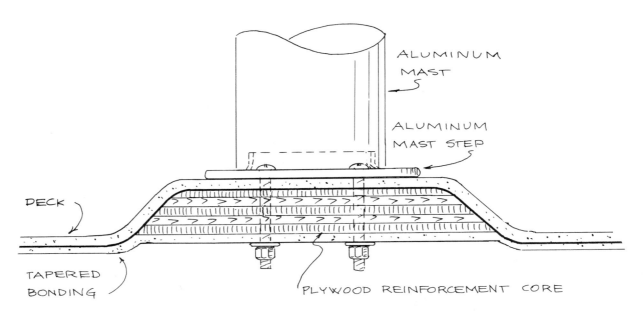

The cabin top has to be generously reinforced if the mast is to be stepped on deck, usually built up about 2 inch out of layers of plywood with bonding over. From this point down the mast must be tightly shored. See diagram.

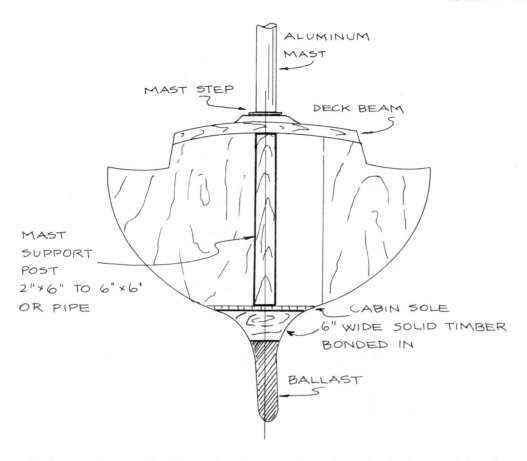

ALUMINUM
MAST

MAST STEP

DECK BEAM

MAST
SUPPORT
POST
2"×6" TO 6"×6'
OR PIPE

CABIN SOLE
6" WIDE SOLID TIMBER
BONDED IN

BALLAST

Deck-stepped mast and its support. Note: there must be continuous bracing (no spaces) from the top of the ballast right through to the mast. If the mast support can be attached to the main bulkhead, so much the better.

right down to the base.

For the conservatives who at this point are tearing the book in half, I provide a few basic requirements for deck-stepped masts which should meet with their approval.

First, the deck at the point of stepping should be repeatedly reinforced over an expanded area, to spread the load. Four laminated layers of ½ inch thick plywood 12″ × 24″ I would not consider pessimistic. With fiberglass on the cabin top, any sudden increase in load on a tiny area, regardless how brief the span of time

involved, will cause cracks that can lead to leaks and possibly delamination. A footing of this size will not only help eliminate this occurrence, but will also enable the tinkerer to move his mast slightly fore or aft to improve performance, ease or provide weather helm, or just pass the time.

Beneath this mast-step, structural bulkheads and deck beams are a necessity, as well as a stainless tie-rod which ties the deck to some very large floor member to keep the deck from *pumping*. Bulkheads should be installed as previously indicated. The beams will spread the load athwartships, and the bulkheads aid nicely in distributing some of the force over the hull as well as the keel on which they are based. To reinforce the deck beams and remove most of the load from the bulkheads, a solid post of steel, teak, oak, or other material of high load bearing capability should be installed directly under the mast step, see figure.

This post is no place to exercise frugality. Acquire a post of the most generous dimensions permissible spacially and esthetically, and make certain it fits snugly and evenly between the beams and the cabin sole. If at all possible this beam should be attached to one of the bulkheads to prevent play. The cabin sole must at this point be reinforced with monstrous floor timbers at least as wide as the post. These timbers in turn must be blocked up from the keel. If any of the above steps are excluded, you may as well forget the whole thing and stick the mast in a Christmas tree stand.

If you are buying a hull and deck, some of these problems will be of only minor concern to you, but you should ascertain the location of the main bulkheads and confirm the potential of completing the above procedure without insurmountable, pre-installed obstacles, such as a fiberglass cabin sole with a shower pan directly beneath the mast.

12. Inboard Shroud Bases

To argue against the fact that an inboard rig gives a far better windward performance than an outboard rig is sheer mush-mindedness. With an inboard rig a large headsail can be sheeted flat and the boat's pointing ability will increase dramatically. The only disadvantage one can possibly cite is that because the inboard rig has the port and starboard shrouds closer together the rig becomes a bit less stable than an outboard rig, but this can be compensated for by a bit of overbuilding at the shroud bases. In all, if one wants a performance cruiser with any beam, consideration of an inboard rig should be kept at the forefront of one's mind.

There seem to be an infinite variety of ways of basing inboard shrouds, and most good naval architects have worked out their own fine system, so let us just go over the three major ones.

Deck and Gusset Supported. Spencer boats of Vancouver, Canada, the builders of the Roth's now nicely aged *Whisper*, terminate the base of their shrouds at deck level and use underdeck plates which are reinforced by gussets that go something like this: At each upside-down T-plate (with the head of the T below the deck and the leg of the T protruding through the deck), a large double knee or gusset is laminated up to transfer the loading from the deck down onto the hull. Now, these plates have substantial 3" × 4" bases, and the whole thing is welded up out of $3/8$ inch stainless steel. The gussets for each plate are hand-laid-up fiberglass with a final thickness of $1/4$ inch. They reach 18 inches down the hull and are 10 inches deep. On one of their boats they actually use *two* of these (one port and one starboard) reinforced plates to lift the hull *and* deck *and* 5,000 pounds of internal ballast out of the mold. Now that is about a total of 10,000 pounds. Since the chainplates are $3/8$ inch thick, we can assume that each plate is making contact with the lifting pin on a $3/8'' \times 3/8''$ surface which is about $1/8$ of a square inch, and since each $1/8$ of a square inch is supporting 5,000 pounds then the loading is about 40,000 pounds per square inch which is about eight times the load put on a racing boat by its hydraulic system. Ought to hold.

Bulkhead Supported. Many inboard rigs use the main bulkhead as a base. This of course means that the bulkhead must be reinforced substantially. On a New Orleans Marine built Frers 40 ocean racer, the system works like this: The bulkhead is of $3/4$ inch plywood that is reinforced on both sides almost in its entirety with multiple layers of unidirectional roving that run well up onto the hull, and the housetop and sides. The laminates on either side are built up as thick as the hull itself. To this monolith they attach the chainplates made of $5/8$ inch thick

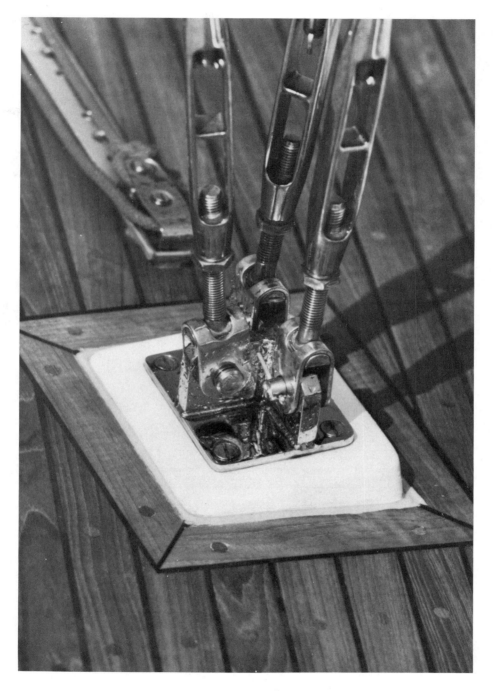

Open bodied turnbuckles joining a single inboard chainplate.

stainless steel, backed up on the other side of the bulkhead by a similarly shaped piece of 3/16 inch stainless. The plates are bolted to each other through the bulkhead with ten stainless steel bolts 5/8 inch in diameter. They've used this system on many extremely hard-pushed racers over the years and haven't had one fail yet. I wonder why.

A variation on this system is the one used by France's Beneteau yard as well as many other builders. This system is usually used because the main bulkhead isn't located where it can be used as a base, so a secondary, usually a longitudinal bulkhead is installed somewhere below or as part of settees. In the case of the Frers designed First 42, the laminates start up the hull about 18 inches from the edge of this bulkhead, then come down to the bulkhead, up one side then down the other, and continue along the hull for another 18 inches, see figure.

Self-Supporting Rigs. Perhaps the ideal system would be the *self-supporting* one used on some of the large ultra-lights like the Hunter and Santa Cruz boats. This system calls for a large

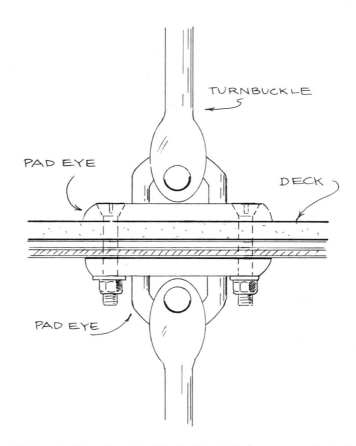

Inboard shroud fittings inside and outside of deck. Only the bolts penetrate the deck and these are easily sealable. The lower rod continues down to a fore-and-aft, low bulkhead. See next diagram.

fabricated beam of steel or aluminum to run athwartship (see photo p. 191 *Best Boats*). This beam is heavily glassed into the hull. The chainplates are integral to this beam, being either welded onto or bent from its ends. Next, to make things even better, the mast is stepped *onto* the center of this beam, and of course it's all tied together with the shrouds, so in a sense the mast is actually holding itself up.

To put it more accurately the beam cuts down on the forces that tend to want to pull the bilges *up*, and push the mast *down* through the center of the boat. The bonding of this beam into the hull is, of course, still a crucial point, and great care must be used here.

As you can see from the above, we've come a long way in a decade from the massive outboard rigs to the even more massive inboard ones.

On some inboard rigs there is no through-deck penetration by the shrouds themselves, instead there is a pad-eye type plate both above and below the deck bolted massively together, with a short stay going from the belowdeck plate to whatever bulkhead attachment has been

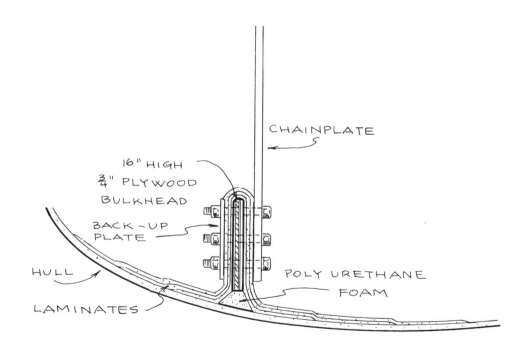

Low fore-and-aft bulkhead acts as base for inboard shrouds. The laminates over the bulkhead are as thick as the hull itself, and run well past the point of bulkhead–hull contact. The laminates are run over the bulkhead over its entire length, which should be from one athwartship bulkhead to another.

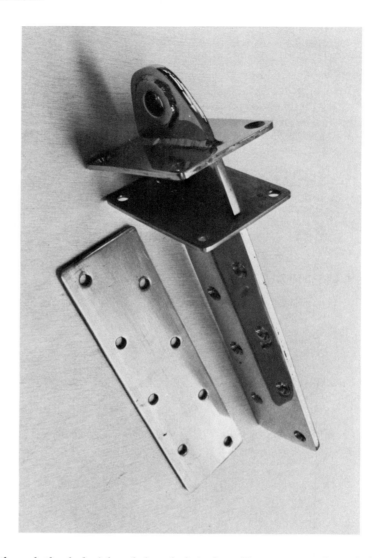

Another through-the-deck, inboard-shroud chainplate. The eye stays above deck while the chainplate comes through and is bolted to the main bulkhead. The other piece is a solid back-up plate which is used instead of washers.

arranged. This seems to be a better design than the shroud itself going through the deck with some sort of rubber boot around it to try to seal the water from going belowdecks, for the boots can very often wear or tear and can only be replaced if the end of the shroud is set completely free.

With all of the above methods it is most important that the reinforcement at the base of the shrouds be the strongest in the hull, for it is here that most of the torment will take place.

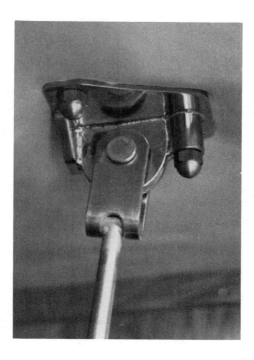

The belowdecks fitting of an inboard chainplate. It matches the shape of the plate on deck and the two are bolted together. Toggle and rod carry load down to a fore-and-aft bulkhead below the settee.

Apart from the foregoing I will recommend very little that will dangerously inhibit your boat buying freedom. But I must stress that the above points are most vital and uneliminatable factors which should not be taken lightly. Unfortunately the industry is still incurably infected by quick-buck artists whose knowledge is limited and ignorance unbounded, so that unless extreme scrutiny is exercised, one may belatedly realize that one has purchased a steaming pile of horse manure.

On the other hand many benignant people exist in the industry whose limitless good intentions are unfortunately equalled by their lack of taste and more alarmingly lack of expertise. Their convictions may sound pure and unquestionable but the material they work with is in its vulnerable infancy. So I must caution you to employ passionate analytics, ask the most embarrassing and personal questions available, and then if you are convinced that you have found the right boat, go somewhere else, just to be certain. Have patience . . . the Ark wasn't built in a day.

Design Aspects to Look for in Hull and Deck:
1. Fine Bow and Moderate Stern
2. Sufficient Beam
3. Long Keel or Fin *and* Skeg
4. Well Supported Rudder
5. Small Cockpit
6. Bulwarks
7. Wide Cabin and Wide Decks
8. Headroom in Forepeak
9. Radius of Deck to Hull Curves
10. Hull-to-Deck Attachment (most important)
11. Room to Sleep in Cockpit
12. Engine Room Access
13. Type of Through-Hull Fittings

Construction Aspects to Look for:
1. Hand Layup
2. Hull-to-Deck Attachment
3. Reinforcement
4. Quality of Laminations
5. Laminating Schedule (hull thickness and type of fibers used)
6. Thickness of Bulkheads
7. Installation of Ballast
8. Mast-Step Reinforcement
9. Rigidity of Cabin Sole
10. General Care and Attention to Details

General Things to Look for:
1. A Proven Design
2. Proven Construction (sailing history)
3. Manufacturer's Ability to follow up with parts, help and advice
4. Potential Marketability in case of resale

3

The Boats

This chapter is a list of the best sailboats built in Canada and the United States available in different stages of completion. I apologize to builders whom I was unable to track down.

Almost all of the following boats have a whole chapter written on them – their design, construction, with emphasis on outstanding ideas – in *Best Boats to Build or Buy*.

Marshall Catboats

It would be difficult to find a more ideal craft than a fine old catboat, for cruising the shoal areas of the east coast or the Bahamas. Its enormous beam gives it great stability and lots of room both above and below decks. The rig, with its single sail, is a dream to handle requiring minimal equipment, although because of the size of the sail one must keep a sharp eye on increases in wind speed.

The Marshall catboats range from the open 15 foot Sandpiper to the large Marshall 26 with an 18 footer and a 22 footer in between. Only the 26 has full headroom, but the others have enormous main hatches over the salon and galley, which open up the whole belowdecks in fair weather. Completion of the boats is straight forward with minimal cabinetry and just enough exterior trim to make the project fun. One thing should be kept in mind with these cats, and that is that even the 18 footer has a beam of over 8 feet so they are not readily trailerable.

Sanderling 18 — "Pop" Arnold

LOA—18'2"   Beam—8'6"   Draft—19"/4'4"   Displ.—2,200 lbs.   Ballast—500 lbs.   Sail Area—253 sq. ft.

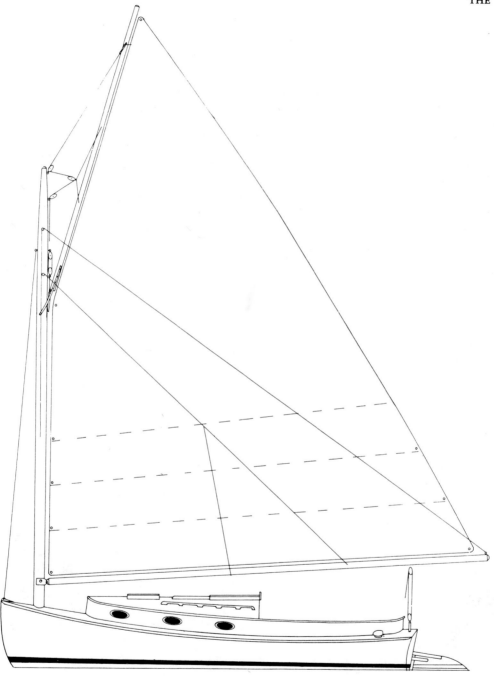

Marshall 26 — Breck Marshall
LOA—26'6'' LWL—25'0'' Beam—11'9'' Draft—2'6''/5'5'' Displ.—10,000 lbs. Ballast—1,200 lbs. Sail Area—540 sq. ft.

Flicka

Flicka has been described as a 'pocket cruiser' and a 'cruiser's dream' and she is indeed both those things, for in spite of her size of a mere 20 feet, she has a good-sized cockpit, excellent accommodations belowdecks with, amazingly enough, full headroom. Her designer Bruce Bingham should be heartily congratulated for achieving all that, and even more so for having managed all the while to keep *Flicka*'s lines moderate and eye-pleasing. The aft-hung rudder is strong and simple; the cockpit is comfortable; and the foredeck is fine although the side-decks are understandably narrow. She is available with two rigs – the more romantic (though slower windward) gaff-cutter, or the more practical and a little cheaper sloop. The boat comes with a full interior liner if you wish it, making home completion very facile but resulting in much wasted stowage space, extra weight, and more money. Anyway, the interior cabinetry is so simple that building it all out of plywood would not only be very easy but also great fun. And *Flicka* is cheap to boot.

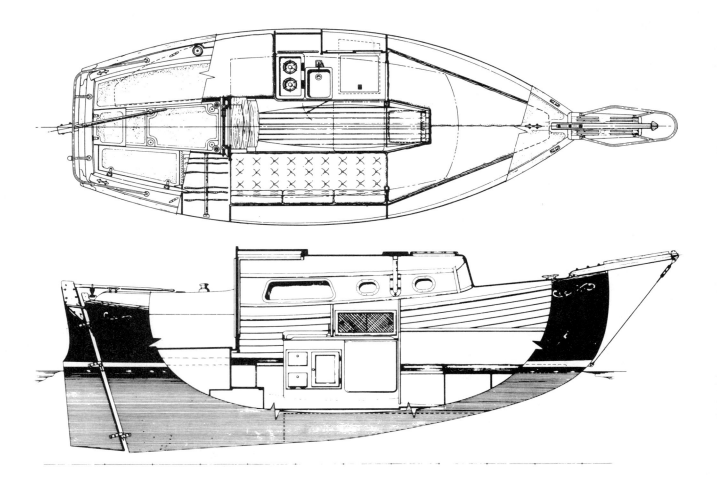

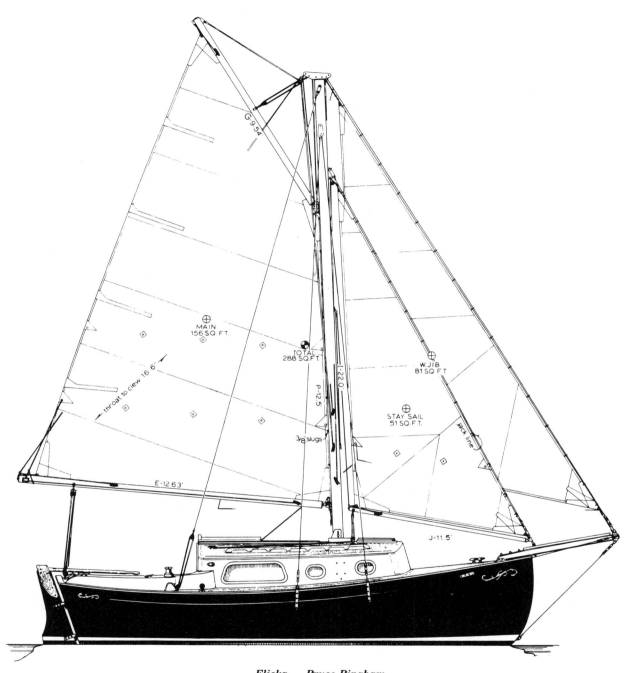

Flicka — Bruce Bingham
LOA—20'0'' LWL—18'2'' Beam—8'0'' Draft—3'3'' Displ.—6,000 lbs. Ballast—1750 lbs. Sail Area—Std: 250/Gaff: 288

Aleutka

The best thing about looking at boats year after year, is stumbling onto something new and unexpected and ingenious. John Letcher's *Aleutka* was just such a find. He designed her after spending many months aboard *Island Girl* a little twenty foot wooden cruiser, sailing from California to Hawaii to Alaska and back again. He drew *Aleutka* as a fine little double-ender with twin keels, that give her a draft of only 2' 9", which gives her access to many small bays and river deltas, and above all that, enable her to be beached in sand or mud at any time. She has an unusual raised flushdeck section amidships,

making for fine sitting belowdecks. Lots of light is provided by a skylight over each settee. Her entry is nicely moderated but her stern is full for good buoyancy. Her mast is of the tabernacle variety enabling her to navigate under low bridges and down underground rivers. As you can see from the plans there is no provision for an engine (although one can be easily fitted) for John believes firmly in silence, so he has used, and highly recommends, a pair of fine 8 foot sweeps which, with moderate effort, move the boat along at 1¼ knots. This is a fine speed for sight-seeing while getting a bit of exercise.

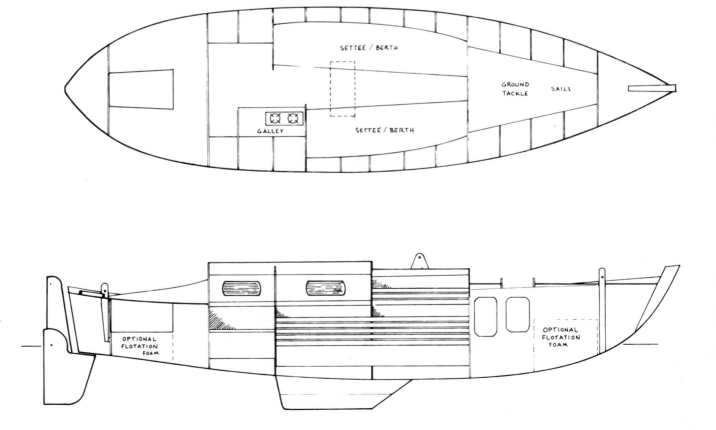

MAIN
130

TOTAL
251 SQ.FT.

FORE
47

JIB
74

Aleutka 26 — John Letcher

LOA—25'5''   LWL—22'6''   Beam—7'2''   Draft—2'9''   Displ.—5,500 lbs.   Ballast—1,500 lbs.   Sail Area—251 sq. ft.

The Friendship Sloops

It's always heartwarming to see a beautiful yacht of the past resurrected in modern materials, especially when the same care is being put into her construction as was decades ago by the original craftsmen. Two such little yachts are being built in Southwest Harbor, Maine, at the Jarvis Newman yards. The larger one is a 31 foot Friendship sloop based on the original *Dictator*, while the smaller one of similar lines is a 25 foot Friendship sloop after the original *Pemaguid*.

Both have graceful bows, lovely sterns, sweeping sheers, and pleasantly low deckhouses that continue perfectly into coamings that surround the whole cockpit. The ballast can be either exterior or interior which should satisfy both schools of thought . *Pemaguid*'s interior is a good example of economy and thoughtfulness, with two good seaberths aft, a trim athwartship galley and a large salon area forward, made possible by the location of the mast farther forward still.

Both boats have enormous cockpits making for excellent gathering places in sunny anchorages. In all, both are lovely crafts for loving and dedicated yachtsmen.

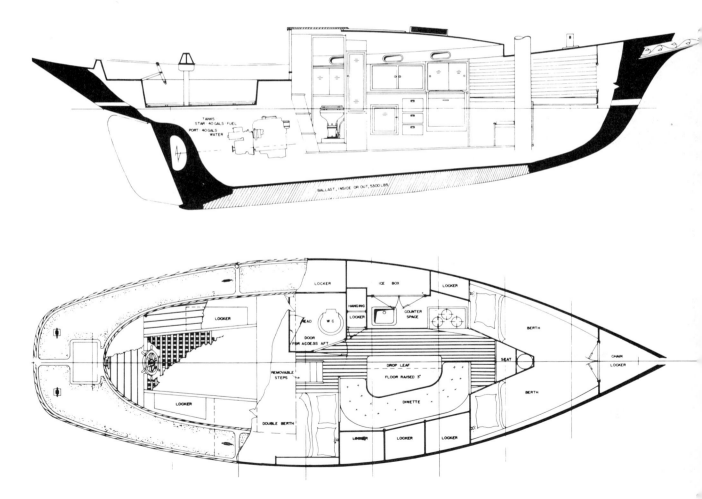

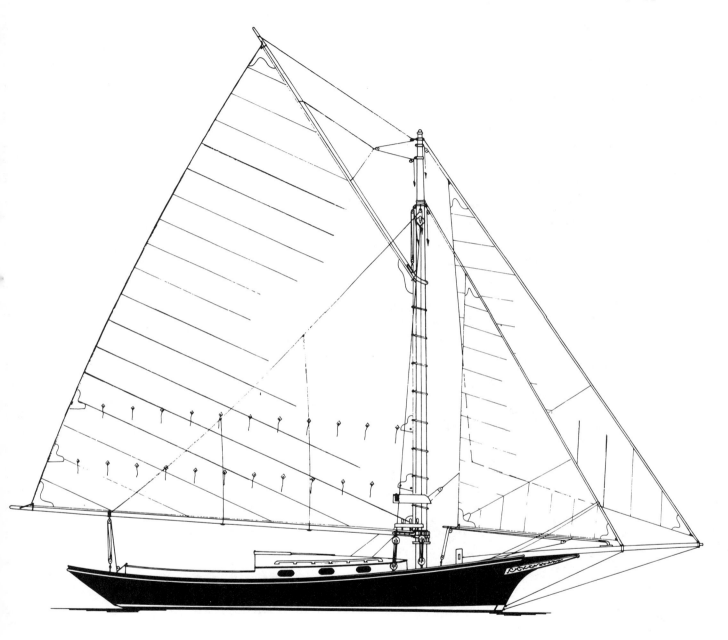

31' Friendship Sloop (Dictator)
LOA—30'10"   LWL—26'0"   Beam—10'8½"   Draft—5'0"   Displ.—17,500 lbs.   Sail Area—761 sq. ft.

The Bristol Channel Cutter

If you want a tough little boat that sails very well and looks as beautiful as any new yacht her size, this is the boat to get. Mr. Lyle Hess designed her along the lines of the Itchen ferry and Bristol pilot boats, and she looks just as handy and as seaworthy as her ancestors. Mr. Hess also designed the Pardy's *Seraffyn*, which sailed around the world in fine style, and without an engine at that, and that says a lot for the boat's sailing and handling abilities.

The Channel Cutter has a powerful stern, good beam and moderate entry, and a generous sail area of 584 square feet to move her nearly 7 tons. Her decks are generously broad with high, free-standing bulwarks that make fore-and-aft movement safe and comfortable. The cockpit-well is made cleverly small to hold very little water. The interior can be laid out in a variety of ways, but to me the best seems to be the one shown, with quarterberth and chart-table and galley aft, and an interesting forepeak with much stowage and a workbench and a head under a lid that works as a step to help you grope into the sailbin.

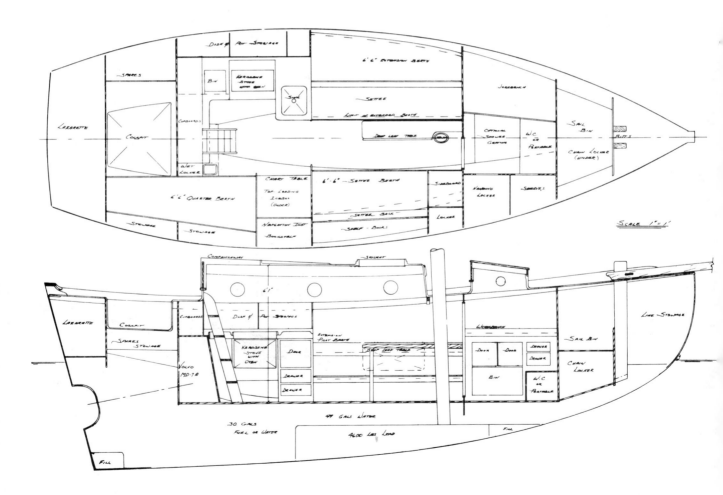

Bristol Channel Cutter — Lyle Hess
LOA—28'1"   LWL—26'3"   Beam—10'0"   Draft—4'7"   Displ.—13,800 lbs.   Ballast—4,600 lbs.   Sail Area—584 sq. ft.

Annie

Chuck Paine who designed *Annie*, has managed over the years to draw some of the trimmest and most timeless looking yachts. He is one of the very few new-generation designers with a fine eye and the strength to follow his own convictions. Boat-builder Tom Morris of Southwest Harbor, Maine, has chosen Chuck Paine designs for all his boats, and the two have worked well together, coming up with little yachts of high quality in both design and craftsmanship.

Annie is one of Chuck's earlier boats but she's certainly typical of most of his designs having a good entry, moderate beam and a fairly thin keel. The stern has good power without looking bulky and the sheer is as sweet as you can ask for. Tom Morris offers a variety of interiors of which only one is shown here. The most interesting however is one that has put the head aft across from the galley, lengthening the port berth and allowing the bulkhead to be cut well back. This opens up the whole boat into a large but still very cozy space. The decks are broad and the cockpit very spacious and the mast is keel-stepped. A true yacht.

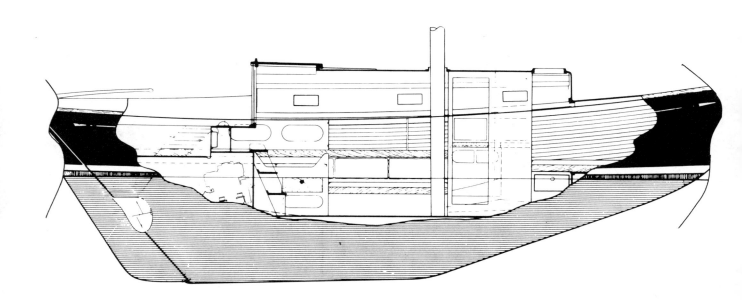

Annie — Chuck Paine

LOA—29'5"   LWL—24'6"   Beam—9'5½"   Draft—4'6"   Displ.—11,027 lbs.   Ballast—4.400 lbs.   Sail Area—456 sq. ft.

Leigh

A double-ender from Chuck Paine and Tom Morris. *Leigh* differs substantially from most double-enders in that she has fine ends, a modern hull-shape and a very thin and well cut-back keel. Her displacement is moderate and her ballast-to-displacement ratio very high, very close indeed to 50 per cent which makes up for the soft bilges that tend to lack initial stiff-ness. She is a beautiful sight and sails very well. Again Tom offers an infinite number of layouts, all of them with a myriad of little lockers and stowage spaces, and with Chuck's designs you need them, for as you can tell from the measurements (and see from the lines of his hulls on p. 99 of *Best Boats*) his boats are no floating elephants.

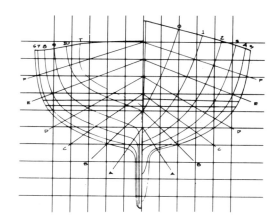

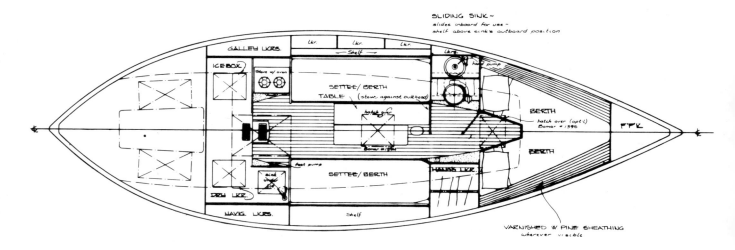

Leigh 30 — Chuck Paine
LOA—29'8"   LWL—23'4"   Beam—9'7"   Draft—4'7"   Displ.—9,100 lbs.   Ballast—4,400 lbs.   Sail Area—420 sq. ft.

Frances

I'm not sure why it is so, but small boats seem to excite me more than big ones; perhaps it's because I can sense all the thought and effort the designer had to put into the design to make everything work, normally a greater challenge than on a large boat where there is all sorts of space to toss the accommodation and deck layouts about without endangering the lines of the boat. Now there's a mouthful. Chuck Paine's little *Frances* is an admirable little boat with lines so graceful they could turn most large boats green with envy, and with her fine interior and spacious decks she could make an excellent little sailing ship and a friendly home for a small family for a few months' sojourn anywhere. Her draft of 3' 10" is shoal enough to give her access to most places, and her sail area of 337 square feet is easy to manage. Her ballast-to-displacement ratio is even higher than *Leigh*'s being just over 50 per cent and reports from owners indicate that she's remarkably stiff and will seldom bury her rail. Her interior has three good berths and, if desired, an enclosed head. She comes as a flushdeck or with a short deckhouse that ends just aft of the mast.

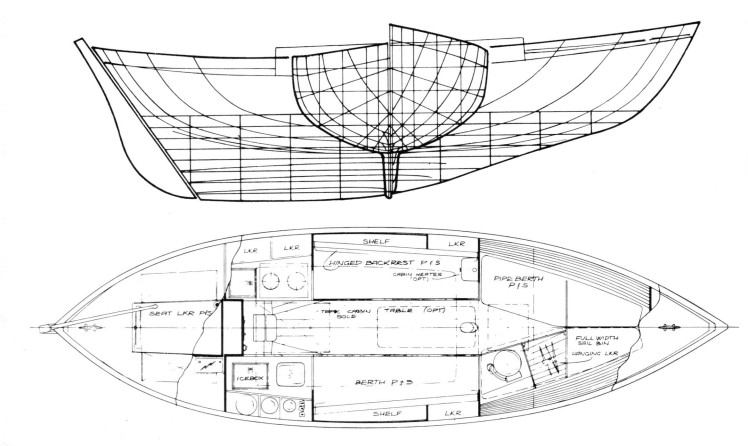

Frances 26 — Chuck Paine
LOA—26'0''   LWL—21'3''   Beam—8'0''   Draft—3'10''   Displ.—6,800 lbs.   Ballast—3,500 lbs.   Sail Area—337 sq. ft.

Naja

The French are a wonderful people who live and die for tradition. Thousands of them mill among the fish stalls and the fruit stalls and the cheese stalls, twice a week on the Boulevard Ménilmontant just behind our flat, searching for hours on end for the freshest and the ripest and the best, instead of running into a *supermarché* and quickly buying everything at once; and at the hour of *les grands répas* twice a day – noon and evening – everyone sits down and eats for uninterrupted hours, so much so that if you're anywhere outside a large city everything but everything is firmly shuttered up, yet when it comes to innovations in technique and design, the French thrive on ingenuity and novelty, sometimes I swear just for the sheer good fun.

They design the world's most outrageous clothes; they design cars that are like no others (we have a mid-engine fiberglass sports car that is a three-seater, and I mean three bucket seats side by side in front), and they design magnificent sailboats like the giant *Vendredi 13* and the small but very pretty *Naja*. She is built of cold molded plywood, on all wood frames (for photos and complete construction see Chapter 9 of *Best Boats*) and she comes in any stage of completion and she sails like a demon, and all the pieces are precut to such precision that she fits together like a jigsaw puzzle. And boy does she look beautiful with teak decks and varnished mahogany topsides.

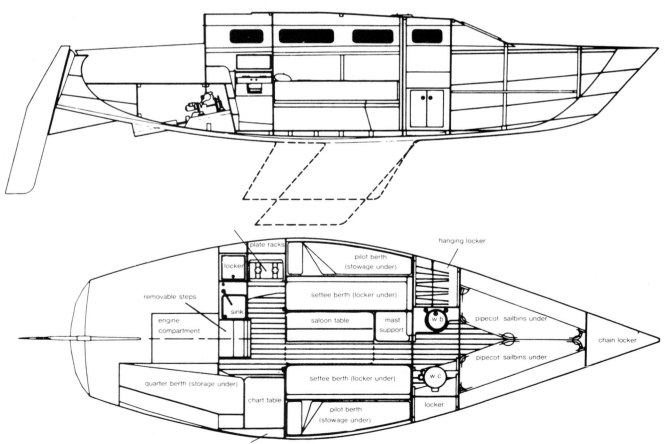

Naja 30 — S. Langevin
LOA—29'8"   LWL—27'2"   Beam—10'6"   Draft—5'9"/4'3"   Displ.—6,240 lbs.   Sail Area—355 sq. ft.

Whistler

The free-standing cat-rigs have certainly come into their own these last few years, mainly because of the success of the line of Freedom yachts, which have proved to be very easy to handle even with a small crew, and have shown good speed both off the wind and on it. The masts are self-supporting thus completely unstayed, which of course calls for the application of much reinforcement in the areas where they penetrate the deck. Whistler's masts are made of carbon-fiber (which is very strong and extremely light), and common fiberglass materials. The masts are tapered to keep their top ends light and are extremely flexible (see photo p. 126 *Best Boats*) which means they will tend to break less easily than their aluminum counterparts, because when hit by a hard gust the masts can *give* a little. There is no such built-in shock-absorber in an aluminum mast or its rigging. Whistler is a pretty center-boarder built in the Down-East tradition of excellent craftsmanship.

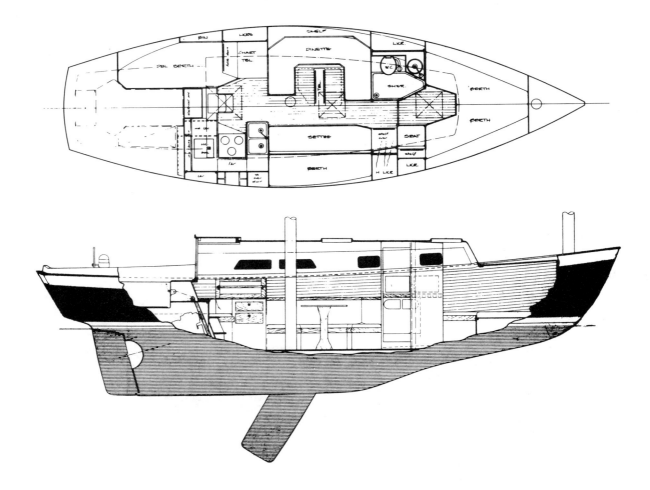

Whistler — Chuck Paine

LOA—32'½'' LWL—25'10'' Beam—10'6'' Draft—3'7''/7'6'' Displ.—11,986 lbs. Ballast—5,000 lbs. Sail Area—520 sq. ft.

Westsail 32

Even good old things can become better old things with the years. Since we got our 32, some intelligent changes have been made to both the hull and deck molds. The hull was modified to create a finer entry, the gudgeons and pintles have been streamlined and even the keel was thinned down a bit. The deck mold got a skylight engineered into it to provide badly needed light below, the hatch openings now have built-in coamings and the deck hardware has all been streamlined to hold better and snag less. Otherwise she's still a heart-warming sight, and without doubt one of the most comfortable cruising boats around. Oh yes, the rudder has been changed drastically since the drawings; there is now much more surface down at the bottom where it does the most good.

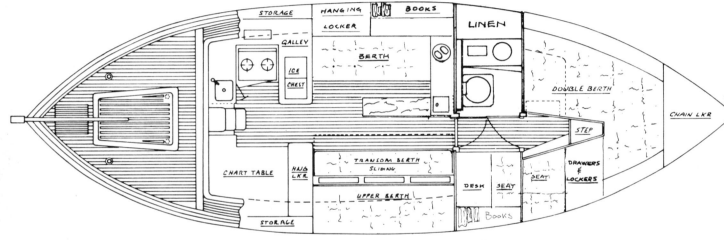

AUTHOR'S "WARM RAIN"

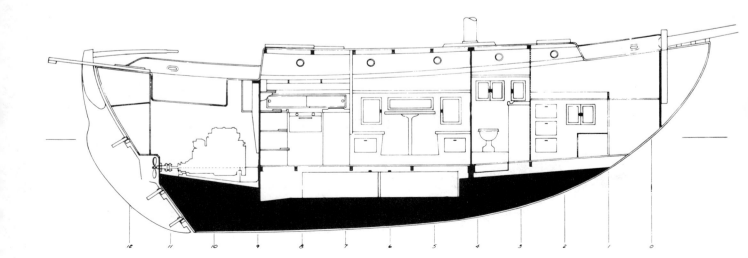

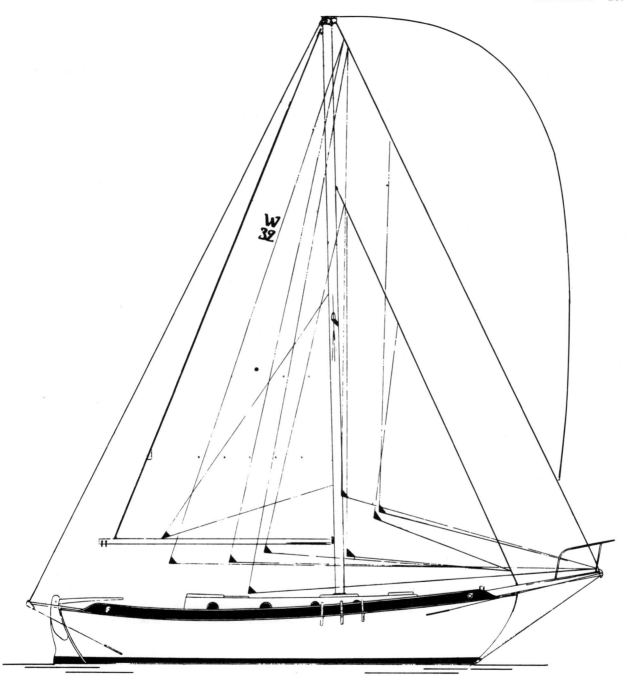

Westsail 32 — W. I. B. Crealock
LOA—32'0'' LWL—27'6'' Beam—11'0'' Draft—5'0'' Displ.—19,500 lbs. Ballast—7,000 lbs. Sail Area—663 sq. ft.

Raider 33

A handsome coastal cruiser from the boards of John E. Cherubini and the boatyard of his brother Joe. She has one of the prettiest modern hulls around, has good deckspace and a functional, straightforward interior. The drawings cannot show the very high quality of workmanship put into the boat in the totally family worked boatyard of the Cherubinis. A good little yacht at a very good price no matter at what stage of completion she's bought.

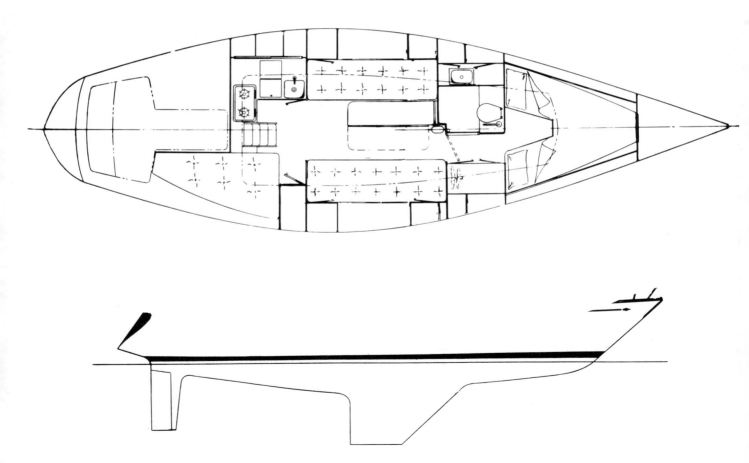

Raider 33 — John E. Cherubini
LOA—33'4" LWL—27'0" Beam—10'7" Draft—4'0"/5'8" Displ.—9,300 lbs. Ballast—4,100 lbs. Sail Area—498 sq. ft.

Luders 34

For what it's worth this is one of my favorite boats mostly because of her sensible and pretty lines. Bill Luders has been designing boats for over 40 years and without doubt he has two of the finest *eyes* for beauty among naval architects. And his boats also *sail* beautifully fast, some of his best known ones being the 12 meter *American*

Eagle, and the L-27 *Storm* which all but dominated racing for a decade around Long Island Sound.

The Luders 34 has a cut-back long keel, pretty overhangs, nicely proportioned deck house and an efficient ⅞th inboard rig. Her heavy displacement should give her a comfortable motion.

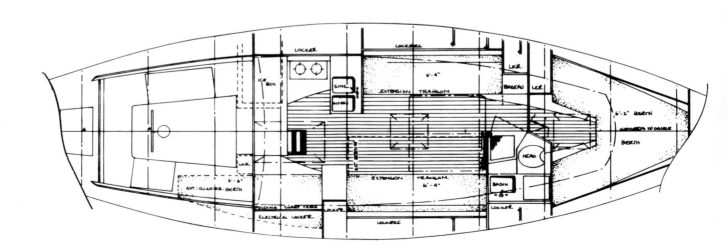

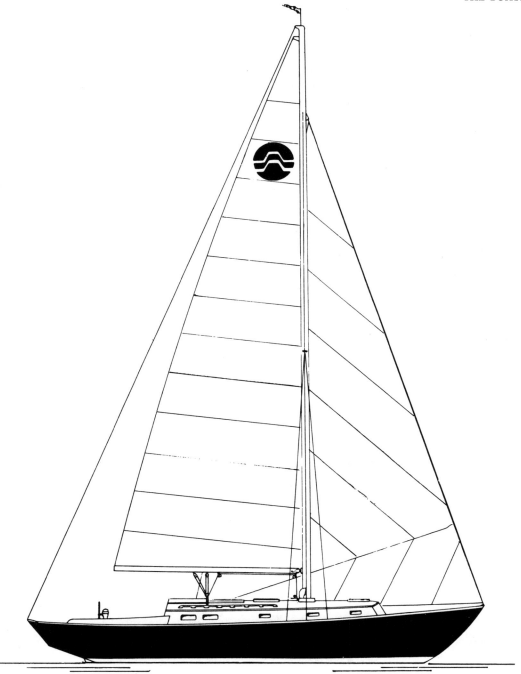

Luders 34 — Bill Luders
LOA—33'10½" LWL—24'0" Beam—10'3" Draft—5'0" Displ.—12,800 lbs. Ballast—5,000 lbs. Sail Area—532 sq. ft.

Jason 35

This is about as small a full-keel as you can get, with both ends of the keel cut and chewed away. Her cutter rig is all kept on deck – no problems here with boomkins and bowsprits – and her main is modern with a high aspect ratio. The cockpit well is very small but has very comfortable back-rests. She is built like a tank by Miller Marine which has a very good name in the one-off large racing boat field. She is an excellent boat for serious offshore cruisers.

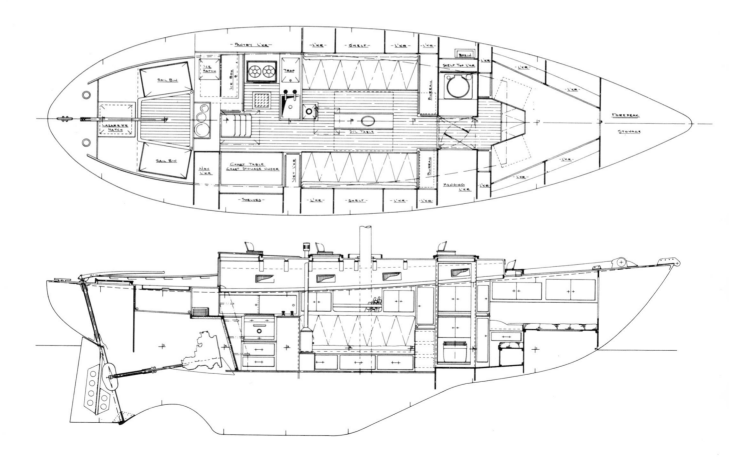

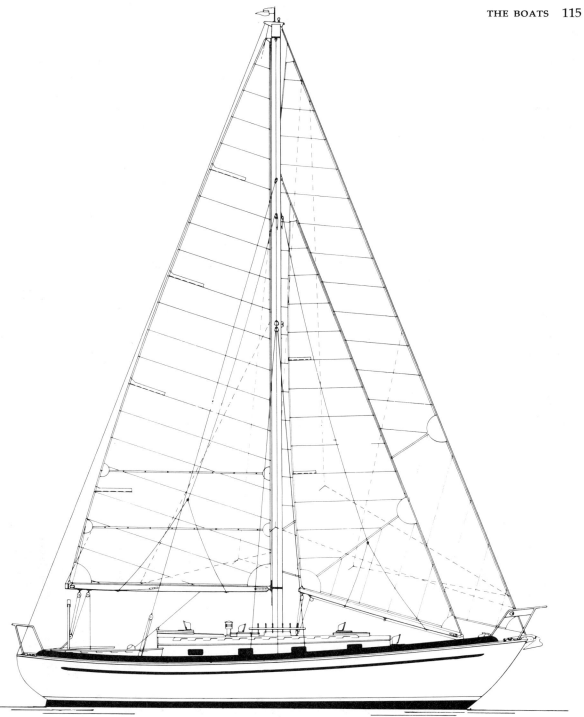

Jason 35 — Ted Brewer
LOA—34'6"   LWL—27'4"   Beam—11'2"   Draft—5'0"   Displ.—16,800 lbs.   Ballast—6,200 lbs.   Sail Area—634 sq. ft.

Peterson 35

If you want to win races, having a boat designed by Doug Peterson gives you a good start. This design is almost 10 years old, but has been updated over the years with a new cockpit, shorter house, new interior and more importantly new keel and rudder, and she still dominates her class in North-West racing. She has a very pretty hull (for lines see p. 187 *Best Boats*) and a completely modern rig with baby-stay and running-backs and hydraulics. But be warned. This is a thoroughbred requiring much attention on a fast, dead run. Windward she's a dream.

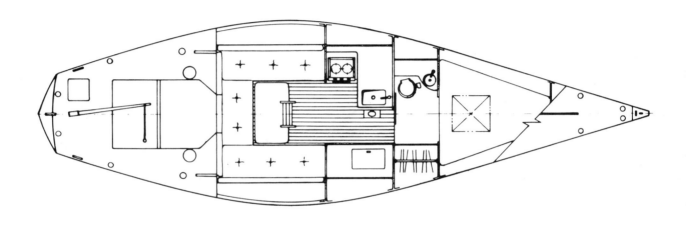

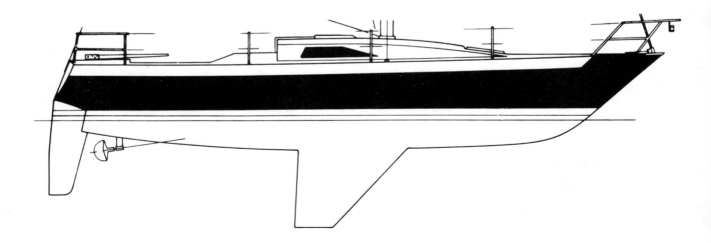

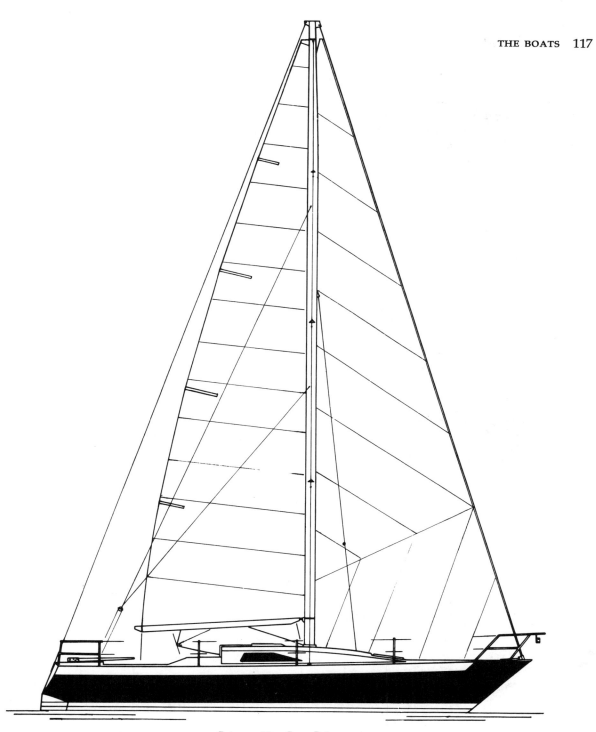

Peterson 35 — Doug Peterson

LOA—35'5''   LWL—28'6''   Beam—11'3''   Draft—6'3''   Displ.—13,200 lbs.   Ballast—6,500 lbs.

Sceptre 36

Another modern, well thought-out coastal cruiser/club racer, whose hull is much prettier in real life than on the drawings. With her length, her standard layout gives room for large berths and good stowage space. Built to very high standards by Hein Driehuyzen who is also the designer.

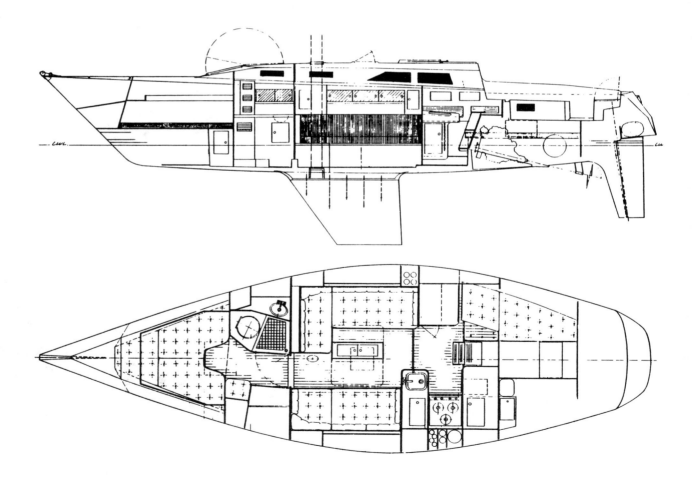

Sceptre 36 — Hein W. Drienhuyzen
LOA—35'6" LWL—29'1" Beam—11'5" Draft—4'11"/6'0" Displ.—12,000 lbs. Ballast—5,500 lbs. Sail Area—597 sq. ft.

The Cape George Yachts

If you want a hefty cruiser drawn along the lines of Bill Atkin's boats, and if you want a beautiful boat with a fiberglass hull and wood deck and wood house, and if you want a quality boat built like a Steinway piano, then get yourself a Cape George, built by Cecil M. Lange and Son in Cape George, Washington. They build boats like many old boats wish *they* had been built. The sizes are 31 feet, 36 feet, and 40 feet, and the 31 is probably the prettiest and the 36 the most sensible, but if you want a private state-room aft you'll have to get a 40. Whichever you get you'll be getting a true yacht.

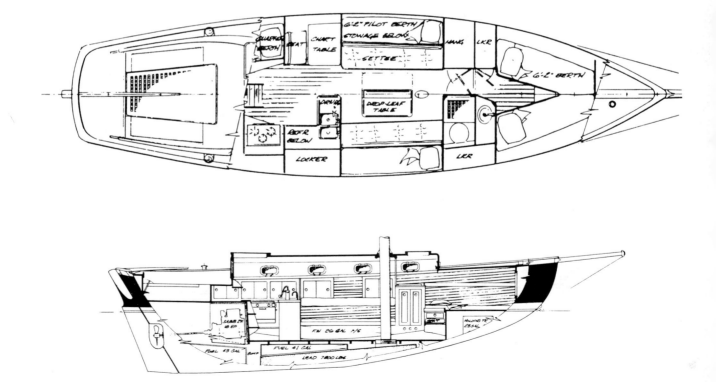

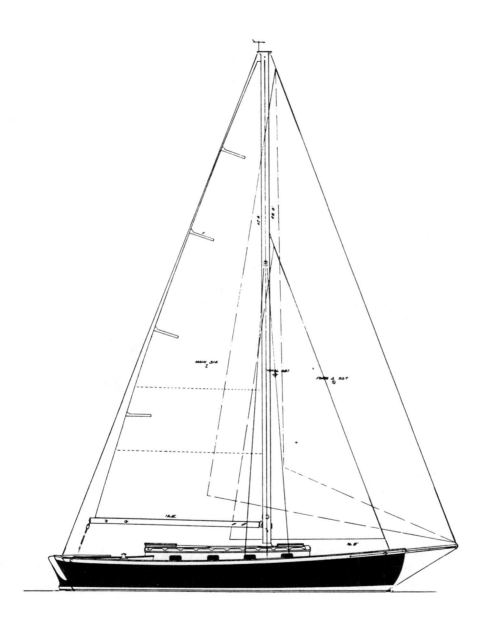

Cape George 31 — Wm. Atkin/T. J. Nolan
LOA—31'0'' LWL—27'6'' Beam—9'6½'' Draft—4'8'' Displ.—15,835 lbs. Ballast—7,000 lbs. Sail Area—681 sq. ft.

Crealock 37

The Crealock 37 may just be the embodiment of the *ideal* offshore cruiser, with sufficient displacement for comfort, excellent underbody for speed, a good rig for both handling and performance, and of course good looks. You may naturally ask, if it's such a modern cruiser, why is its rig not inboard; why does it have old-fashioned chainplates? The answer may lie in the fact that the 37 has a relatively narrow beam of only 10' 10". If you compare that to the 12' 6" beam of the Frers 40 a few pages hence, you can readily deduce that were the Crealock as beamy as the Frers, and were its rig left where it is now, it would actually *be* inboard by about 10 inches on either side. Now how is *that* for convoluted thinking? Oh yes, she comes as a cutter or a yawl.

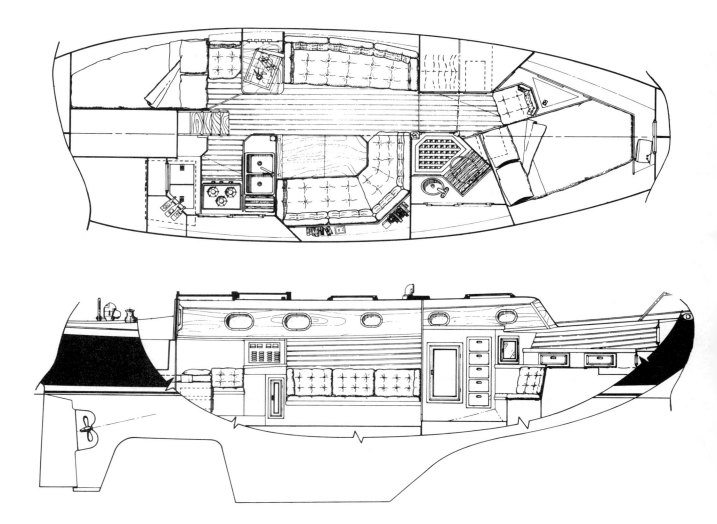

Crealock 37 — W. I. B. Crealock

LOA—36'11"   LWL—27'7"   Beam—10'10"   Draft—4'4"/5'5"   Displ.—16,000 lbs.   Ballast—6,000 lbs.   Sail Area—Cutter:758 Yawl:666

Ingrid and Alajuela

Now here's a classic. This is one of Bill Atkin's great achievements, which with a fined down entry and a very tall and modern cutter rig tends to go like a very manageable and comfortable bat out of hell (relatively speaking of course). Both boats are built to the highest standards with very heavy rigging and equally heavy gear. The Ingrid is available with a multitude of layouts while the Alajuela sticks doggedly to one, but that is a good one indeed with three good sea-berths, a huge chart-table and an enormous owner's cabin forward with a vast playpen of a double berth and why not; you only use a double in port anyway so it might as well be in the bow which can only be used for stowage and little else when at sea. To give you an idea of the construction, I'll just tell you that the hull of the Ingrid built in Washington State, has *seven* layers of roving in the topsides *plus* six extra layers down the stem and stern. Bring on the icebergs.

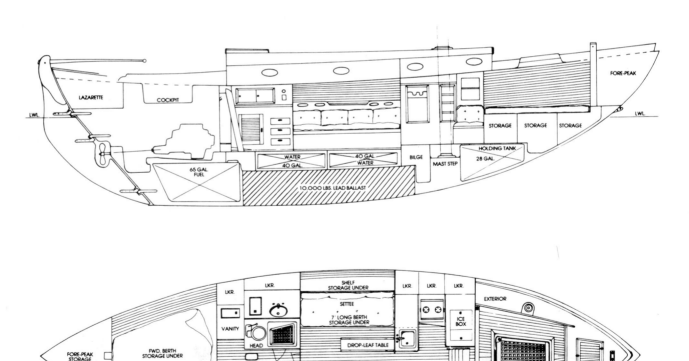

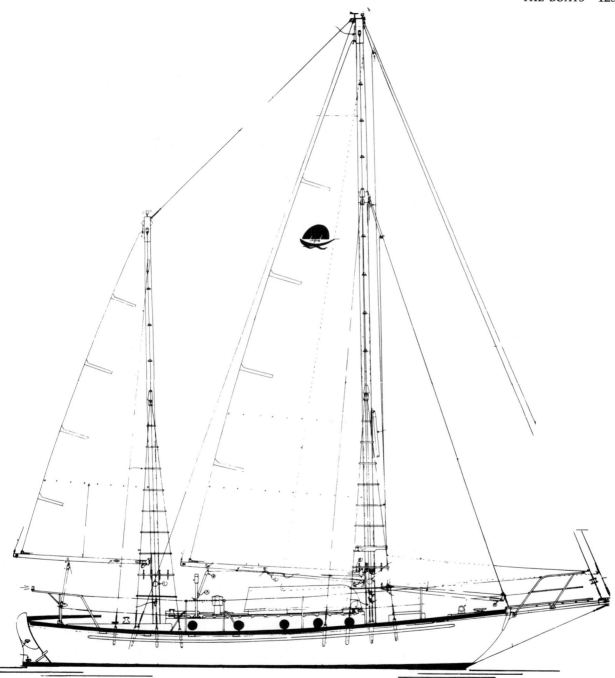

Ingrid 38 — Colin Archer/Wm. Atkin
LOA—37'8"   LWL—32'0"   Beam—11'4"   Draft—5'8"   Displ.—26,000 lbs.   Ballast—8,000 lbs.   Sail Area—848 sq. ft.

Gillmer 31 and 39

If you haven't had your fill of double-enders yet, here's a couple more. The 31 has its rudder hung aft and sports a conservative keel and a conservative rig of 447 square feet, with an equally conservative ballast-to-displacement ratio of under 33 per cent. The 39 has a modern rig, cut away underbody and a sail area of a whopping 835 square feet which gives her a sail-area-to-displacement ratio of 17.3 so hang onto your reeflines. The 39 has an interesting layout with the head aft on the port side, and the good-sized owner's cabin aft of that. The chart table is an excellent size, and as you can see the salon is comfortable indeed. The 31 has a straightforward interior with three good seaberths.

The engineering is very good on both boats especially the 39 which is newer, featuring things like an anchor-well designed so that a Danforth anchor fits in it like a glove, and a steering system whose moving parts are completely accessible from the cockpit, being laid out in a shallow fiberglass pan directly below the cockpit sole.

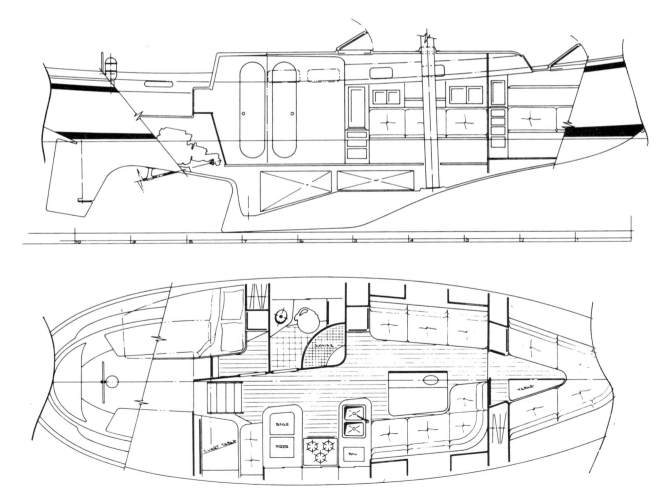

Gillmer 31 — Thomas Gillmer
LOA—31'0"   LWL—25'0"   Beam—9'6"   Draft—4'7"   Displ.—13,600 lbs.   Ballast—4,400 lbs.   Sail Area—447 sq. ft.

Frers 40

A state-of-the-art racer from the drawing board of German Frers, Jr., and New Orleans Marine. It wins races and goes like stink and costs a lot.

Many points about the advanced construction methods of this boat have been discussed in previous parts of this book.

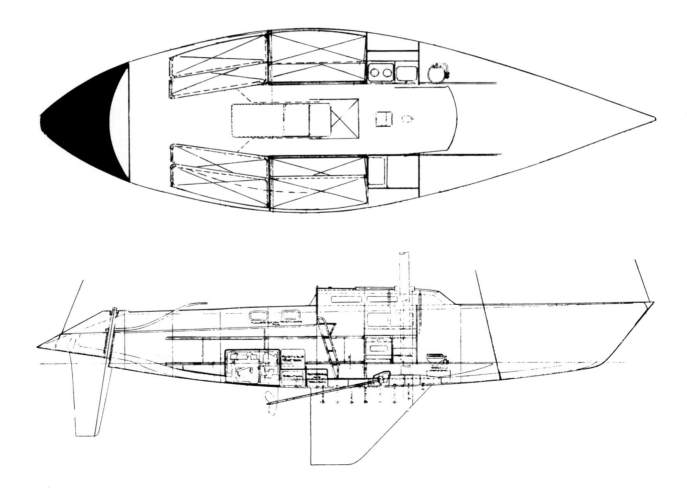

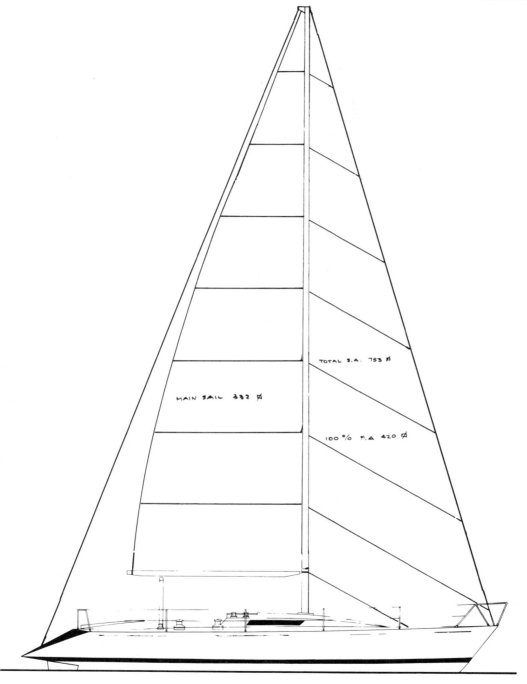

TOTAL S.A. 753 ☐

MAIN SAIL 332 ☐

100 % F.A 420 ☐

Frers 40 — German Frers

LOA—40'0''   LWL—34'0''   Beam—12'6''   Draft—7'6''   Displ.—15,000 lbs.   Sail Area—753 sq. ft.

Spencer 1330

A handsome boat along the lines of older Swans, with high freeboard and a nicely drawn low house. Her underbody is split but has a good size skeg. Her sail-area-to-displacement ratio of 17 means she'll sail very well indeed, and her moderate LWL/DISP ratio 250 means she'll still give a fairly comfortable ride. The volume belowdecks is enormous so what you put in her will be limited only by your imagination. The designer/builder is Spencer Boats, the same people who produced Hal Roth's *Whisper*. The workmanship is absolutely first class.

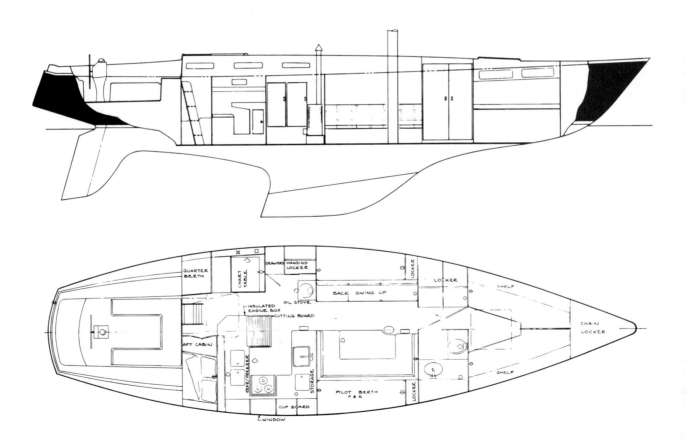

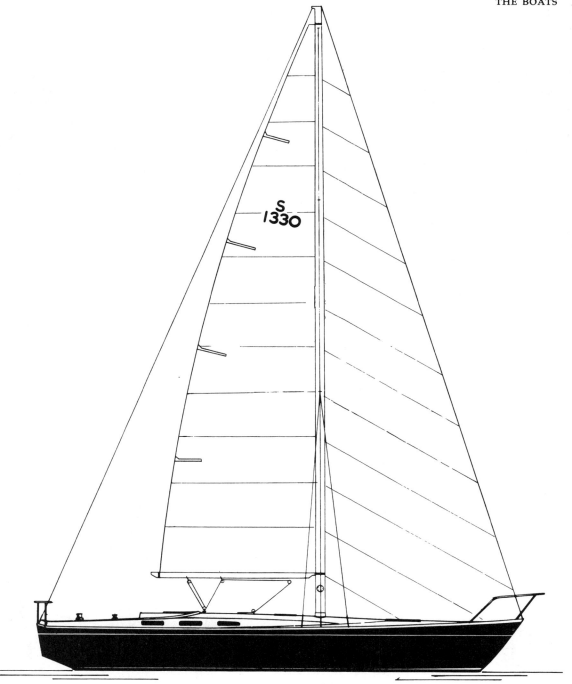

Spencer 1330 — John Brandlmayr

LOA—43'8'' LWL—35'0'' Beam—13'0'' Draft—7'0'' Displ.—23,000 lbs. Ballast—10,000 lbs. Sail Area—882 sq. ft.

Cherubini 44 and 48

Designer John E. Cherubini did a commendable job of scaling down L. Francis Herreshoff's *Ticonderoga* to a very manageable size and an almost affordable price. The 44 has a sail-area-to-displacement ratio of an astounding 19.67 and she flies. She was first overall in last year's Fort Lauderdale to Key West race. Performance aside, she's a joy to the eyes, probably surpassed in beauty only by her larger sister the 48 foot Cherubini schooner. They are both built in the same fashion as Cecil Lange's boats with fiberglass hulls and meticulously fabricated wood decks and wood houses. The construction is truly first class and the thought and engineering behind nearly every piece is close to remarkable. Perhaps these are today's ultimate yachts.

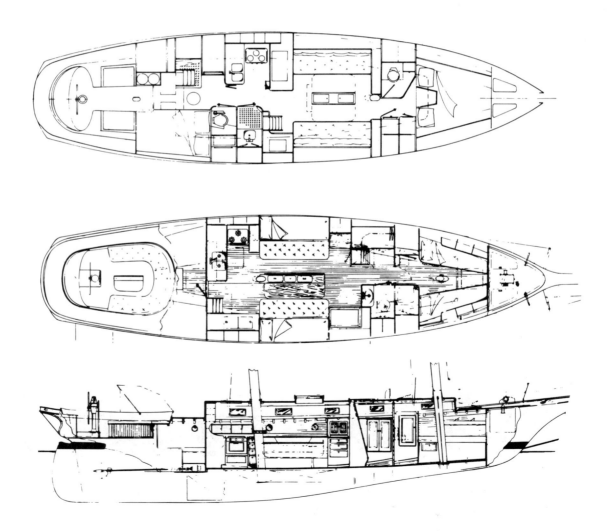

Cherubini 48 — John E. Cherubini
LOA—48'9"   LWL—44'0"   Beam—13'0"   Draft—5'0"   Displ.—37,000 lbs.   Ballast—16,900 lbs.   Sail Area—1,227 sq. ft.

Santa Cruz 40 and 50

Designer Bill Lee has a motto: 'Less is best,' and when you go belowdecks on one of his boats, the first question that'll pop into your mind is, 'Where's the rest of it?' He has managed, through scrupulous engineering, to keep the weight of a 50 foot boat down to 16,000 lbs. His whole line of boats is based on the very successful 66 foot *Merlin* which set a new Transpac record in 1977 averaging 11 knots. In the 1981 Transpac a number of Santa Cruz 50s averaged well over 9 knots without too much effort, i.e. none broke. If it's long legs you want look no further.

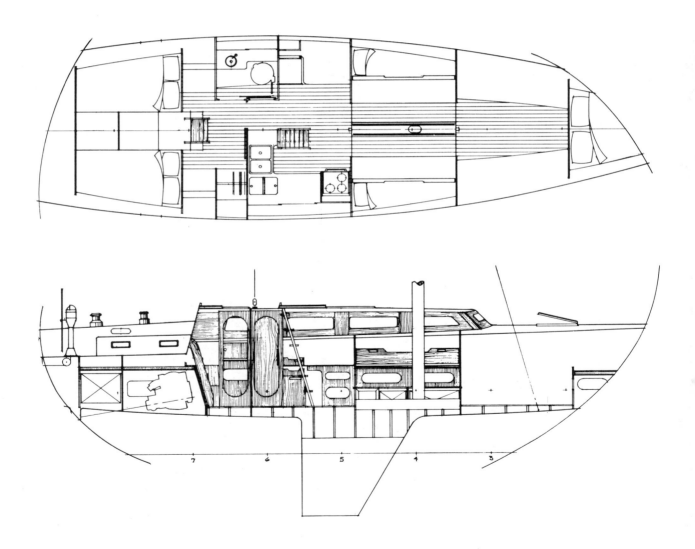

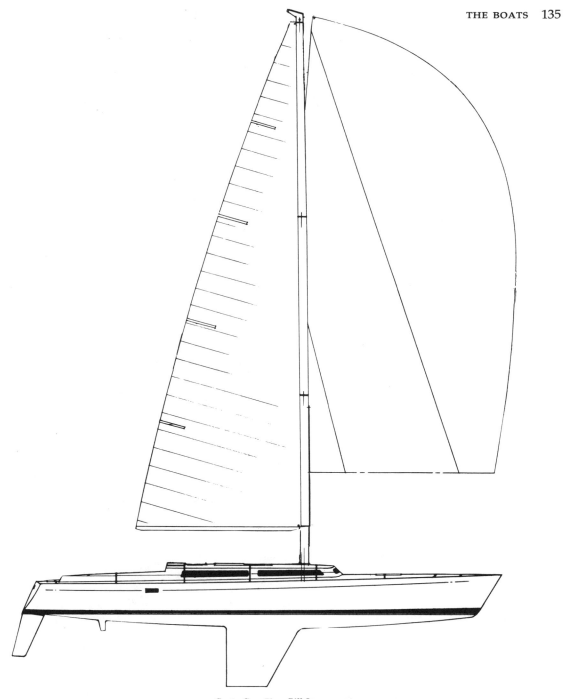

Santa Cruz 50 — Bill Lee
LOA—50'0'' LWL—46'5'' Beam—12'0'' Draft—8'0'' Displ.—16,000 lbs. Ballast—8,000 lbs. Sail Area—1,050 sq. ft.

The Nordic Tug

If you have to have a powerboat, here it is. It behaves exactly like a boat should, that is to say it doesn't leap, scream, thrash, or pound like so many powerboats of unlimited stupidness often do. And it even looks like a boat instead of a plastic submarine sandwich.

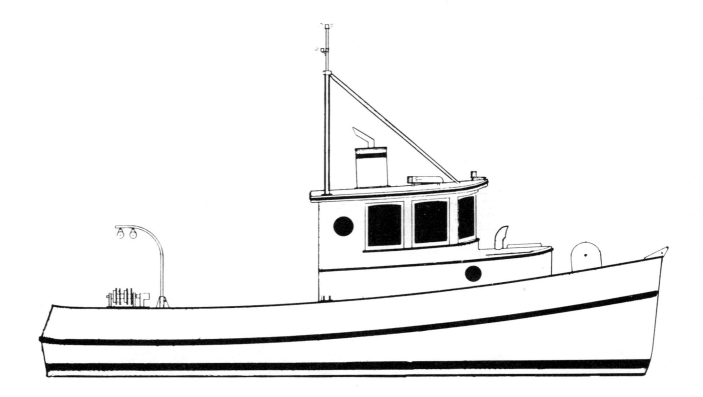

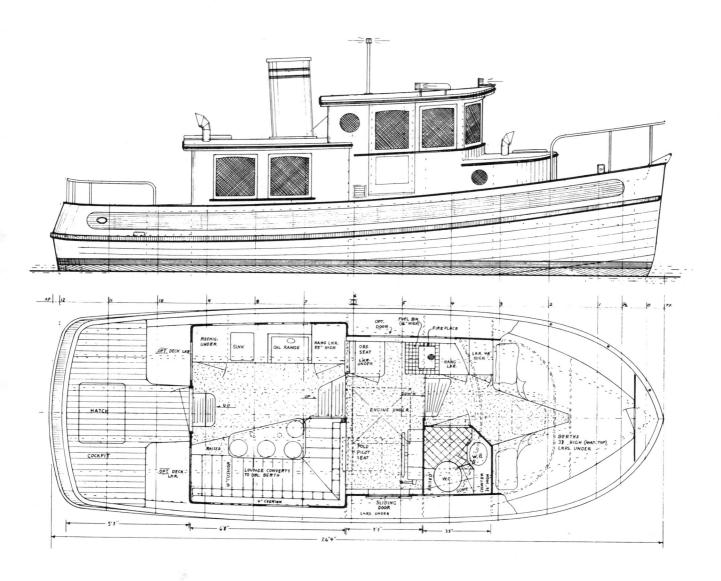

Nordic Tug — Lynn Senour

LOA—26'4"   Beam—9'6"   Draft—2'8"   Displ.—6,000 lbs.

4

Planning the Interior

It is best to keep work areas near an open, well-aired companionway. Seasickness occurs with greater frequency in stuffy, confined catacombs than in well-aired spaces. Also, communication with the helmsman is made easy. To be totally practical, I defy anyone to carry a cup of coffee from a galley located near the forepeak and arrive in the cockpit with more than ten drops. Besides, if working below makes you feel like heaving up, you won't have as far to go.

The salon, because we spend so many waking hours in it, is the focal point of the boat; therefore its layout shall not be treated lightly. That it must be in the center of the boat, the point of least motion, is obvious. That it must have totally comfortable seats in as many sea conditions as possible, is essential, and that it must provide an atmosphere of relaxation and emotional calm is critical. Beyond the salon, one must make room for a head, and also furnish sleeping or storage facilities, or both. The decision is difficult at best, but if one works on a combined assimilation of cruiser live-aboard, the finalizations come rather easily.

Chart Table

This work area should be next to the companionway to facilitate communication with the helmsman and to avoid carrying a very delicate sextant all the way forward or aft in rolling or choppy seas. In our boat it is next to the galley so that the chart table top can, in port, act as a second preparation area for large meals (i.e. for the opening of large cans). The aft section of the boat experiences less motion than areas further forward, thereby making it less difficult to do accurate plotting and calculations.

The surface should be at least 32" × 25" to give space for folded Admiralty charts; plus it should allow about 4 inch margins on top and on one side where one can place plotting tools while flipping or turning the charts. Chart flipping by means of the old tablecloth-off-the-table trick will simply not work here because you have to slip the tablecloth back under the plotting tools before they hit the table top.

The next decision you face after surface size is whether to make the chart table a sit-down or stand-up variety. I prefer the stand-up because it is easier to brace oneself in a rolling sea using legs and pelvis only, leaving both hands free. The desk type chart table is usually placed, by necessity, next to the curving hull. On an unfavorable heel you will slide on the athwartships seat right to the hull with nothing but your arm and shoulder to maintain your upright position. Plotting with one hand

Elegant chart table with large working surface, and much storage outboard as well as forward of the table. And it even has a nifty holder for pencils and compass.

(especially the wrong one) is no fun.

The stand-up table also saves storage space underneath the table top, into which you can install a number of chart drawers clear down to the cabin sole. If you don't use them all for charts, they make excellent drawers for small tools, odd screws, and numerous paraphernalia which can be very handy close to the companionway. They can be pigeon holed by building great numbers of dividers, so that the items in the drawer don't avalanche when the boat rolls. The lowest drawer possible should be used for this venture, for down low the boat's movement is minimized and so is the unavoid-able racket of what sounds like a million marbles rolling back and forth in a large tin can.

Some advocate that the sit-down table is infinitely superior, for one can get off one's feet while working out sights. True, but there should be numerous other places in the boat to perform this function. And to those who want to hide the chart table away from the weather-admitting companionway, I say a little rag can wipe a long way.

Salon

The center table, I think, is an absolute must for

An ideal salon with great comfortable settees around the center table, and a pilot berth on either side. A large skylight over table provides light. Cut-back bulkheads help open up interior. The 'planked' ceiling looks infinitely better than just acres of plastic tacked to the overhead.

a cruising boat. It is usually accompanied by two fore and aft berths which act as daytime settees. The backs should be slanted about 15 degrees to provide comfortable seating. The seats should be about 20 to 22 inches deep to provide luxurious seating, yet to be necessarily snug sea-berths.

We have found that 20 to 22 inches is a perfect compromise. Anything less than this dimension is useless as a berth and not quite comfy enough to slouch back into as a seat. Anything over 23 inches is too wide as a sea-berth (of course we're both built like toothpicks), for one is tossed about in rolling seas. As a seat, it will be also too

wide, for the edge will cut behind one's knee. I think also that the center table very nicely unites the salon, enabling conversation to flow athwartships from relaxed positions instead of the quarter-neck-twist that one is forced to practice from the straight-backed pews of a cramped dinette.

The back rests do not necessarily require upholstery or padding. It is easier to have doors opening to lockers if no upholstery is in the way. If the backs are sloped, they will prove to be comfortable; if they are not quite soft enough, toss cushions can be utilized.

As for the table itself, the number of varieties

is endless. Fully supported ones are extremely functional in rough seas, but they act as room dividers otherwise. Pole-less tables create a feeling of open space, but reinforcing them against hurtling bodies is a tremendous task.

One end of our table is attached to a bulkhead structure by means of a large multi-bolted angle iron, see figure. The other end is reinforced with welded steel rod and plate to provide optimum support, see figure. We made the table quite short, adequate for the two of us to eat from, in order to keep the unsupported part of the table as short as possible.

I have seen numerous collapsible and fold-up tables, but most of them folded up and collapsed at the most inappropriate moments. If you do

have a good idea though, try it. At worst, you'll have to build another one.

Design your salon as liberally as you like. You can be quite diversified, but be warned: most people who build their own cruising boats have never cruised before. Being unfamiliar with the reasons for the confined space of a small boat they spread out their settees and berths and end up with a storage-spaceless, grab-supportless barn with uncomfortably narrow outboard settees joined only by air. To imagine the consequences at sea you need only close your eyes and picture a barrel of about a 10 foot diameter being tossed about on 20 foot waves. You should not forget to picture yourself inside the barrel. Now just sit back and relax.

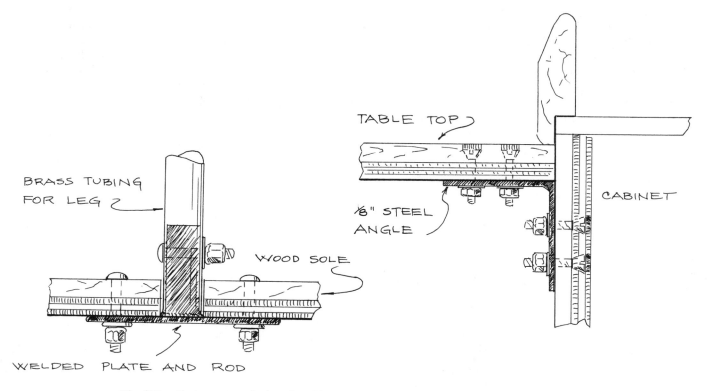

The fitting that supports the leg of a table can, with a little care, be nicely hidden from sight.

Attaching one end of a center table to cabinet or bulkhead. The steel angle should be 5 or 6 inches wide.

The Galley

If at all possible, the galley should be U-shaped with adequate body support for either tack. Concentration of sink, icebox, stove should be maximum. Once you're braced in a seaway, it's a shame and risky to have to let go just to pick up two cloves of cloves. The stove should, of course, be gimballed with a bar in front of it to prevent you falling all over the burners if the boat lurches. Beware of placing the stove too far amidships with deep cupboard space behind it. Few things are worse than a badly scorched armpit.

Sinks must be near the boat's centerline to enable them to drain on either tack. Most people feel strongly that sinks should be as gigantic as possible. For large families, perhaps. But for small ones, it will just invite days' old dirty dishes. A small double sink will function much better than a large single, because the baffle will keep water from gaining splashy momentum. You also have one extra sink in which to drip dry dishes.

The greater the depth, of course, the less chance of spillage. But care must be taken that you do not place the bottom of the sink lower than the water-line, for you will then have to have a bilge pump to pump it out. This procedure is acceptable, but it does present the new possibility of siphoning in water and flooding the boat if the pump fails.

I think that a fresh water manual pump in the galley is adequate. Pressure or gravity fed water is comfortable, but one tends to use more water than if one has to pump every drop by hand. If you must have self-transporting water, make it gravity fed. It has few moving parts.

Salt-water pumps, in my opinion, are totally absurd. You drill another hole in your hull and for what? The whole ocean is at your door step. All you need is a bucket. In the tropics, algae grow rapidly in a salt-water plumbing system, and every push of the pump will belch out air that smells like a pig farm. Anyway, it's more pleasant to wash your dishes on deck if the hot sun is beating down and you can't find enough fresh water to splurge on your dishes. On deck, a bucket functions marvelously well. If the weather outside is adverse, and pouring rain prevents you from exterior dishwashing, then you have more than enough fresh water to fill all your tanks, wash your dishes, and even paint some miniature watercolors. All you have to do is be ingenious enough to collect it. Collection can be done with awnings, large canvas funnels, and simplest of all, sails.

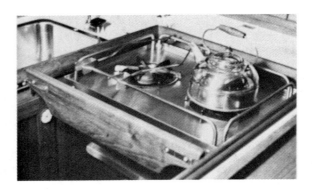

Protective bar in front of stove helps to keep cook secure.

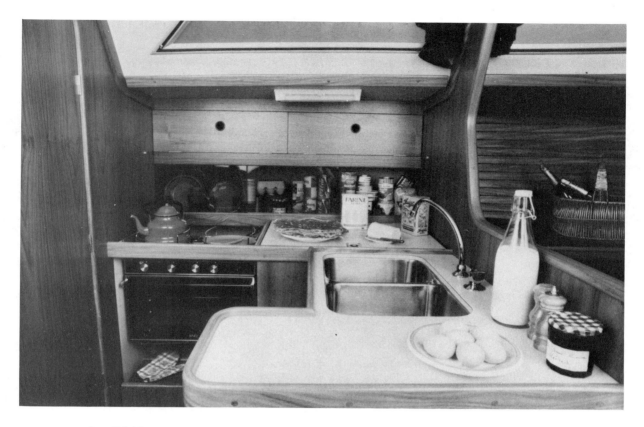

A well laid out, U-shaped galley with built-in safety bar in front of the stove, a good double sink and generous work-surfaces.

The icebox should be large enough to carry 50 pounds of ice and still leave at least 2 cubic feet for food. Insulating it is critical. If you can pour about 5 inches worth of two-part urethane foam all around, your two blocks of ice should last you up to three weeks. Pouring this foam takes tact. Although it looks totally harmless as it merrily bubbles away, it does have tremendous power through expansion.

We braced the outside shell as well as the inside fiberglass liner of ours when we performed the task, but the thing still warped and buckled a little. Therefore brace it well and beat the two parts with a drill motor and paint-stirrer (use only half a pint of each at a time). Pour in over a large surface if possible. If you pour the whole thing into a small corner, the outerlayer will harden first through contact with air and the lower layers will tend to blow the icebox apart. Wait until the first batch goes off and a tough skin is formed before you pour the second.

Icebox lids are best hinged. The variety that slides does so at the most awkward times. Front opening iceboxes are not recommended because the precious cold air spills out of them when the door is opened. To prevent loss of cold air in top loaders, put a loop in your icebox drain hose, see figure. Water will collect here and prevent the

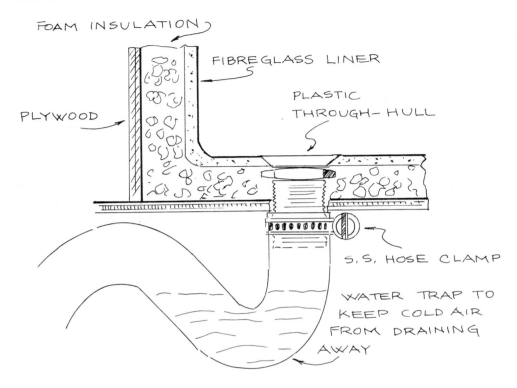

FOAM INSULATION

FIBREGLASS LINER

PLASTIC THROUGH-HULL

PLYWOOD

S.S. HOSE CLAMP

WATER TRAP TO KEEP COLD AIR FROM DRAINING AWAY

The hose that leads the melted ice out of the icebox should have a loop in it to hold a bit of water, or all the cold air will drain out too. Be sure the through-hull you use is a flush-fitting type otherwise you'll always have a little pond of stale water brewing and fermenting in the bottom of your icebox. Bubble, bubble, toil and trouble.

cold air from spilling out into the bilge. Arrange to have your ice water drain into a portable container that you can dump over the side. The smell of spilled milk gone sour in the bilge can foul your boat for days.

All cabinets should be shallow, or as partitioned as possible to avoid the need of lengthy searches. Compartmentalization is most desirable to prevent both spillage and the nerve wracking noise that cans and things make as they roll freely about. I see little need for storing all your pots and pans in cupboards. Copper

bottomed stainless steel pans are extremely functional and their either tarnished or polished bottoms are visually pleasing. They can be hung onto a bulkhead (bottoms out) and set into little gallows as shown in the figure. They will then become completely rattle-free and can be left exposed without need for a door which would only create a more confined feeling in the galley. If they are hung a few inches above the counter, the space below them can be utilized for food preparation.

A completed icebox awaiting spray-foaming at the Beneteau yard. Note the nicely compart-mentalized countertop and high searails.

Icebox lids should be as heavily insulated as the icebox itself.

Berths

I'm not sure if sleep is only a personal problem, but I must have seven hours of comfortable sleep or I'm a dish rag the following day. Thus berths offering total comfort and safety are an absolute must for me.

Good sea berths (as mentioned in the *Salon* section) should be no more than 22 inches nor less than 20 inches. Bunk boards that curve up at both ends are very comfortable in mild seas where they provide some shoulder support and security without the need for leeboards or straps. Bunk lengths should exceed the person's height by at least 4 inches, especially if the person sleeps on his stomach, thereby extending his toes.

Foot lockers and spaces like those described by Mr. Street and Mr. Hiscock at the foot of a bunk are advisable. They not only create functional storage spaces, but they give the bunk's occupant a feeling of home by allowing him to keep his personal possessions near his berth place.

I do prefer pilot berths for a similar reason. They are completely private and are not used for any other purpose but sleeping. Thus the occupant need not fear a foul-weather-geared derriere landing on his face, interrupting his dreams. The confinedness of most pilot berths tends to separate them from the rest of the cabin, creating a secure place that can most often be curtained off to allow undisturbed daytime rest. It can also be easily lee-boarded for a secure foul-weather rest. I always found the existence of a separate level in a boat intriguing; for although I may seldom use it, I know the possibility for refuge to 'another area' exists if I were ever to need it. Psychological reassurances can be of great help in a small space, especially at sea. (Especially if you're a little nuts.)

Sloped settee back with footwell at foot of berth. Footwell is excellent for daytime stowage of bedding.

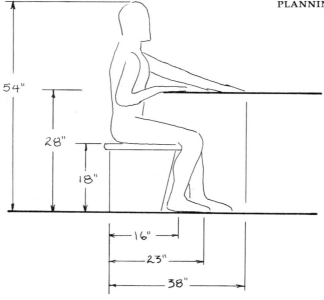

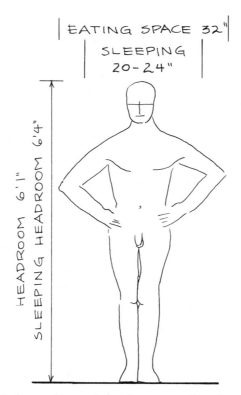

Ideal measurements for working and sleeping spaces. Keep in mind that berths can be made narrower at the foot – down to about 16 inches if need be – but it's nice to keep them wider so you can bend your knees a bit when sleeping on your side.

Another sea-berth considered as excellent as the pilot berth is a quarter berth. This berth can be placed well aft, part of it beside or above the diesel. Here the ride is comfortable in all sea conditions, and the berth does not take up otherwise valuable space. Because it is customarily wedged between the hull and the engine room bulkhead, it can be used without any weather boards. The forward end of the berth can, most often, act as a settee for a sit-at chart table if so desired, a commonly exercised procedure in many production boats, see figure.

The Griffith's *Awanhnee* has a unique quarter berth in that it is accessible from the cockpit and can therefore be used by the second person on watch until the helmsman requires his help.

The quarter berth has two drawbacks: (1) in hot climates it becomes the most stuffy of accommodations and (2) if the engine is being used, sleep is almost impossible. The solution to the first problem could be solved by installing a portlight in the cockpit side for ventilation. As for the second, don't use your engine.

Portlight in cockpit can provide good air and light into quarterberth, head, or whatever.

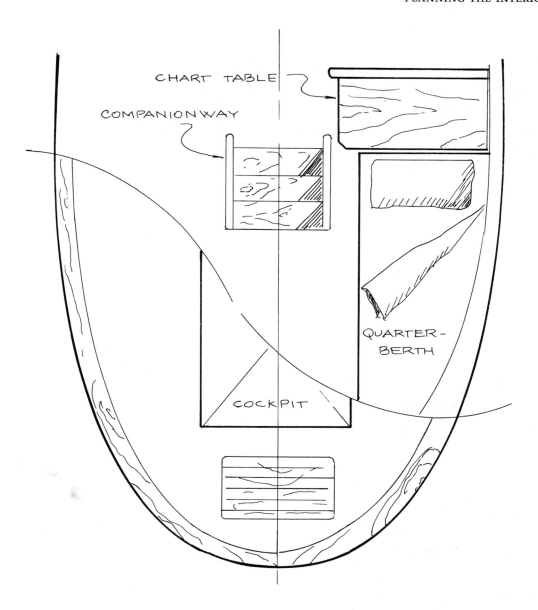

CHART TABLE

COMPANIONWAY

QUARTER-
BERTH

COCKPIT

The fabled quarterberth chart table combination. This berth is probably the most comfortable aboard a sailboat being well aft in the area of least motion. But at night you better let the navigator know you'll be sleeping there otherwise he may come belowdecks in the dark and use your head as a seat cushion.

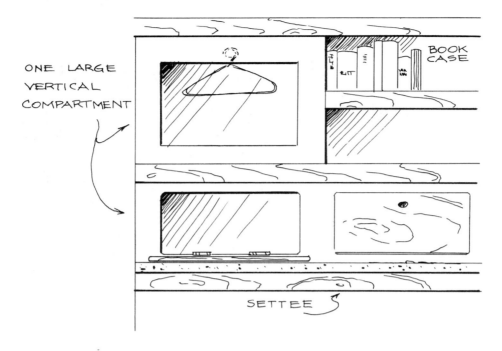

ONE LARGE VERTICAL COMPARTMENT

BOOK CASE

SETTEE

A hanging locker disguised as two separate units. Recommended only for those desperate for space for it's a bugger to use.

Seats and Settees

I find that I cannot built too many seats (in as many separated areas as possible) into a boat. Although Candace and I do get along sufficiently well (we have been together for over twelve years, almost twenty-four hours a day), it is comforting for us both to be able to go to another compartment, in this case the forepeak, and be able to sit down and read or write or just sit. Too many people concentrate only on a great number of berths and storage, thereby creating forepeaks in which you can either lie down or hang up your underwear. The inclusion of a seat does create the feeling of a private cabin where one can spend time creatively, productively, privately.

The seats need not be wide or long or enormous. They should be comfortable, and comfort can easily be yielded by a seat 28 inches long by 18 inches deep, especially if the curvature of the hull is used as the back rest. Light, both natural and artificial, should be generously provided in this area to make the seat more utilitarian.

Personally, I require a desk of my own for whatever writing I may do in the boat. The salon table or the chart table could not serve as acceptable substitutes because I need to sometimes leave notes and reference material undisturbed and uninterrupted by meals and course plottings, etc. This demand was rather selfish in a

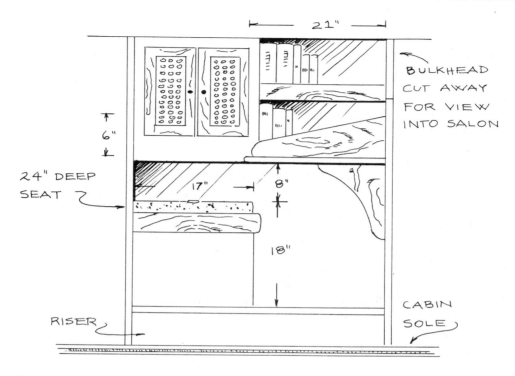

21"

6"

24" DEEP
SEAT

17"

8"

18"

BULKHEAD
CUT AWAY
FOR VIEW
INTO SALON

CABIN
SOLE

RISER

The plans and measurements for my study aboard Warm Rain. *These can be used for chart table plans as well although I would then add another 4 inches to the depth of the table top making it 25 inches deep.*

32 foot boat, but I managed to talk Candace into surrendering a 3' × 4' storage space (one hanging locker and four drawers) on the condition that we provide some substitutes elsewhere. The miniaturizing of a study into such confines proved quite successful, see figure. The seat serves as storage; the desk top lifts up to provide storage space; next to the hull is a bookcase and a small cabinet with shelves.

We had to replace the drawers that normally go in this space, so we built a structure in the forepeak next to the settee. Then we went on to disguise a hanging locker in the salon by putting doors over book shelf space and deleting the top of the bunks back rest, see figure. We now have a

ventilated locker that does not look like an enormous hanging locker, yet provides ample hanging space. The door in the back rest serves as access to the locker's bottom, where one can store foldable items, shoes, etc.

We worked many hours on the design of the study, adding ¼ inch here and ½ inch there. The measurements we came up with shown in the drawing have proved to be very comfortable.

Again I can only reinforce the importance of comfortable seating places dispersed as much as possible in the boat. Remember the boat is small and in time you'll be tired of every cranny. Familiarity breeds ennui; so try to make the layout as exciting initially as your creativity allows.

The Head

Little of importance can be said of the head except that I deem it foolish to allow it to take up too much valuable space. I have seen some boats where a very comfortable private cabin could have been installed in the huge space allotted for the head, in which the owners spent about ½ of 1 per cent of their total time.

Make the head sink small. You'll waste less water. The head sink can drain into the head to eliminate an additional through-hull and to help to keep the head clean. Vent the head well, for nothing is less comforting to seasickness than dubious odors. One 6 inch diameter port and a 4 inch cowl vent are minimum requirements.

It is most helpful to have the head fixture itself face fore and aft, confined between bulkheads, so that you can brace yourself on either tack. If you think the small space is claustrophobic, paint it white.

The Forepeak

Since most of one's life will be spent in port, a comfortable double berth in the forepeak should be available. A width of 48 inches should suffice, especially if some additional space for knees (for sleeping on one's side) is provided.

Placement of this berth is most critical. A good 34 inches should be available between the surface of the berth and the cabin top so that one can sit up in bed. I do not believe that one's intimate life should suffer just because one is mentally unbalanced enough to live in a sailboat. As I mentioned before, we placed a settee and some storage on the starboard side of our forepeak, but I have seen many boats utilize this space to very good advantage by installing a work bench or complete storage, etc. Discretion is yours. If you intend to have no company and single berths will prove adequate for your tastes, then you can convert the entire forepeak to sail stowage, a dark room, or whatever you need.

Stowage

I placed this section last because I think that it is the most overrated, overdiscussed topic on the boat. It is questionable that man can totally congest any volume of space no matter how vast if given enough time (see Earth). When I hear people rave about the wonderful amount of available storage space a boat has, I shudder. By the glare in the eyes I can see the caravan of unworthy hoardage ranging from collapsible golf carts to inflatable wading pools meandering into the boat. You do need as much stowage as possible, so plan to leave as much junk behind as possible. You will feel much freer.

Most stowage spaces should be top loading. Not only do top loading spaces hold more items per equal volume, they prevent their contents from escaping when the boat is heeling or rolling. Front loading spaces require a carefully constructed door, whereas the tops of top loading spaces can be of rough plywood since they are usually covered by cushions.

If you must have front loading storage, make the access hole as small as possible so that the walls surrounding the hole can act as baffles for the stored goods. On the other hand, consider what you will be stowing where and be sure to allow an adequate enough hole to get the gear inside. If you have shelves in any of your storage areas, be sure that they have searails of adequate height (about 2 inches), or everything is guaranteed to spill in your lap when you open the door on an unfavorable heel.

Most gear in a boat tends to be small. One extra large storage space should be left for awkwardly large items. But apart from that, the many compartments of old traditional boats seem an excellent idea. With this type of storage, one need not rummage through a mountain of goods to get to the tiny item that one is seeking. If you do require special storage for a number of large items though, be sure to plan it all before you start building. A drawing with a list of

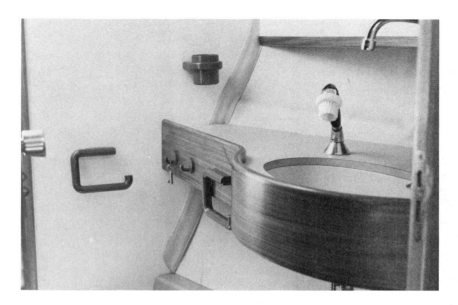

The elegantly designed head of a Beneteau. Note beautifully curved teak laminate and tastefully designed and very utilitarian cup and towel racks.

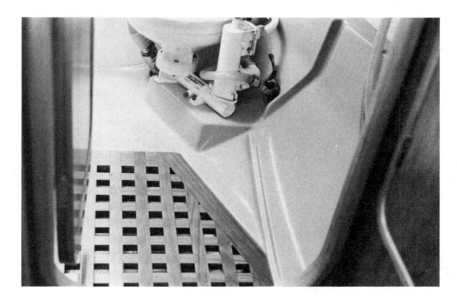

The advantage of a fiberglass liner is that it locates for you cabinet faces so you save some time in assembly, but you do pay for it in cost, extra weight, and inaccessibility to much of the hull. I'd do without a liner if it comes much higher than the cabin sole. Note handy seacock locations.

compartments that has a fairly good inventory of what each locker contains can save hours of search. Sail lockers, as well as wet lockers for foul weather gear, should be self-draining and well ventilated so that mildew cannot grow.

The Engine Room

This compartment has always been thought of as a greasy, slimy, dingy hole where you should venture only as a last resort. I see no reason for such a situation. A diesel is a simple, clean machine and its room can be kept immaculate with a little forethought. Do not try to utilize every square inch above and around the engine for storage. It is a good idea to have spare parts readily accessible, but you will have to get at every part of the engine sooner or later, so it is best to leave open space around it. If possible, leave room above the engine so that you can crawl over it and get to the stuffing box in any seas.

If you have unused areas under tank shelves, put slats across their fronts. You can then store spare parts, common tools, rags, etc. behind the slats and through spaces between them you will be readily able to see what you're looking for. It's good to have all of these items close at hand in the engine room, for once you are peacefully wedged in you will not want to crawl out for any reason.

Plan all your fuel shut-offs and engine intake seacocks so that they are *readily* accessible when you need them. The finest of seacocks can be of little value if it cannot be got at easily.

All the above planning will be of little use if you can't see anything once you are inside the engine room. If your engine is below the cockpit, install deadlights in the cockpit side or the cockpit sole to bring in the natural light. If your cockpit is small and the sole removable you can consider a heavy piece of plexiglass for your cockpit sole. The plexiglass should be at least 1 inch thick to make it rigid enough. This approach is a very expensive proposition, cost-ing approximately $250, but it does make for a beautifully lit engine room that's a pleasure to work in.

You might be able to save on cost by buying some surplus plexiglass that is badly scratched. Don't let the scratches scare you off. You should under no circumstances leave the plexiglass clear, but sand the surface lightly with 220 sandpaper. It will diffuse the sunlight and keep the engine room from becoming an oven. Sunlight is also most detrimental to fuel hoses, which will tend to have a much shorter life and break down sooner if direct sun gets onto them. Teak slats or grates over the plexiglass would be ideal; for even if sanded, plexiglass can become very slippery when wet.

Access to the engine room is also critical. You may have to get in very quickly. I've seen companionways that dismantle into pieces which, of course, fly about with great abandon in a seaways as soon as you remove them. I have even seen an arrangement where the galley sink was hinged upward and had to be flipped up before access to the engine room could be had. I'd feel singularly stupid if my engine stalled as I was roaring into a fuel dock and I had to pause for a moment to wash my dishes before I could remedy the malady.

The best solution is a ladder that hinges up and hooks to the cabin top. In the bulkhead a large hinged door will provide the most rapid, unobstructed access. Be sure to put hooks on the door to hold it in the open as well as the closed position.

Shelves should be so laid out in the engine room that batteries are right next to the entranceway. Since batteries should be checked daily for water level, as little crawling about as possible should be required. Fuel filters should be so laid out that they are also readily available and accessible, as should be the dip stick to check the oil in both the transmission and the engine itself.

Lighting and Ventilation

This topic has been very well covered by Mr. Hiscock and Mr. Street. As it has, I can only emphasize the importance of ample light and moving air below decks. All portlights should be opening and of a good diameter. Plastic portlights are inexpensive but they do have a tendency to warp and break down with heat. If they warp they will inevitably leak. Good solid bronze portlights are most advisable to use, the heavier the better, for then they cannot be warped out of shape and leak. Six inches in diameter is the smallest one should use. Anything smaller, like 4 inches, will provide very little light or air. Portlights on the forward face of the cabin should be of the deadlight variety, for here one will encounter heavy seaways and can be assured of an opening port leaking. Deadlights, deck-lights, and hatches are well covered in the construction chapters. Therefore, I will only say here that you should try to install as many as you can, but if you do use skylights be sure to get tempered glass. As costly as it is, it will not break easily. Odd sizes of glass are difficult to replace in out of the way harbors; therefore, it might be advisable to take spare pieces with you.

One final note: Personalize your boat as much as you like but if you have some doubts about keeping it forever, try to make it as unoutlandish as possible. Some things that hit you in the middle of the night as incredibly brilliant inventions may prove to be the cause of a lot of smirking and chuckles behind your back and make your boat almost unsellable. A friend who laid out a beautifully open-spaced sitting room type arrangement in his extremely strong very well equipped cruising boat has had trouble selling it for one year because his personal whims were put ahead of common sense and practicality. It's almost impossible to find a 'perfect' layout but I would say that Doug Peterson's Baltic 38 with a fine cabin below the cockpit should definitely get the layout of the year award.

The ultimate 8-inch portlight. The hinge on the left supports the solid cast cover which can be dogged shut over the glass in big gales and typhoons, while the hinge on the bottom supports the opening glass part.

Now we all know that cowl-vents are the best vents in the world, but we also all know they snag lines quicker than an octopus in heat, so it's best to design some sloped tubing around them. On this Beneteau it's right beside the companionway hatch so it serves as a grabrail as well.

A Goiot plexiglass hatch with built in vent. Not as efficient as a cowl-vent but it helps. Note hatch is triple pinned for strength.

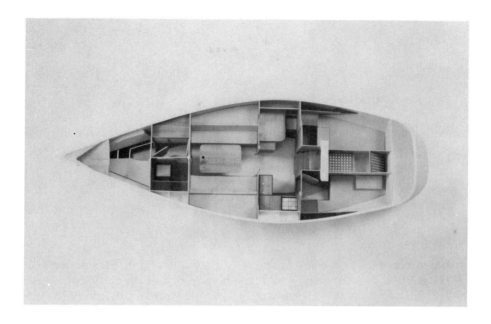

If you can get a hull model from your builder, you can lay out your interior to your heart's content and make sure it all works before you spend a fortune on the real thing.

5

Make or Buy

Since most manufacturers offer completed boats, as well as bare hulls and decks, one must decide at what stage to begin work oneself. Finishing aids, such as ballast, cabin sole, pre-cut plywood parts, rudder, etc. can be factory installed or factory bought. They can be either a great help or a monstrous inconvenience, depending on the individual's final goals.

I shall try to evalute each item for its merits and its disadvantages, discussing the factors such as cost, time involved, machinery or tools necessary. I will purposely exclude the question of ability, for I firmly believe that if one has the inclination and time he can easily eclipse the quality achieved by all manufacturers and many craftsmen. The amount of time to be sacrificed, of course, may be very great. But if time is not a factor, you do possess the interest, and you do want the best possible results, then do it yourself. Otherwise, I hope the following points will aid you in deciding your point of commencement.

Ballast

It's heavy. To lug six or seven thousand pounds of steel or lead up a scaffold is not my idea of self-fulfillment. If you are building an A-frame to install your engine, or if you have your boat under a roof with strong beams, your task will be eased. But the problem of getting the ballast to your boat in the first place still remains. The money saved by ballasting yourself is not a lot. With the mechanized methods of factory installation time is kept to the minimum, and although the hourly rate they charge may bottom out at $25, the total should not amount to more than $500, the price of a good wheelchair. Therefore, unless you have access to scrap lead which you can melt down yourself and you don't cringe at the thought of wearing a truss, by all means proceed. Only then will you be certain of what actually went into your ballast and how.

There are a few reasons for ballasting yourself. Should you subscribe to the alternate religion of your chosen boatbuilder with regards to location (centralized or evenly spread, see figure), you have a chance to resolve the conflict. If the builder doesn't supply all cast lead and you are a firm believer in lead as I am beginning to be, you can have it. Undeniably all lead will result in a stiffer boat with more bilge space, and above all it will not rust if gudgeons leak or stray water from inside finds its way down. On the other hand price-wise, steel is way ahead, costing as little as 6¢ a pound. Whereas, lead, even if creatively scrounged, will run 30¢ a pound minimum. You may also want to relocate some ballast

DETAIL OF BLOCK
(COULD BE FUTURE
MAINSHEET BLOCK)

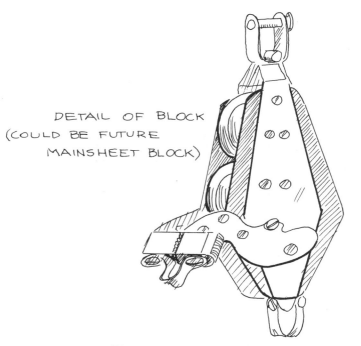

SELF-CLEATING FIDDLE BLOCK
WITH BECKET

TRACK
(FUTURE MAINSHEET)
THROUGH-BOLTED
TO FRAME

"A"- FRAME

BLOCK

PLYWOOD CHUTE

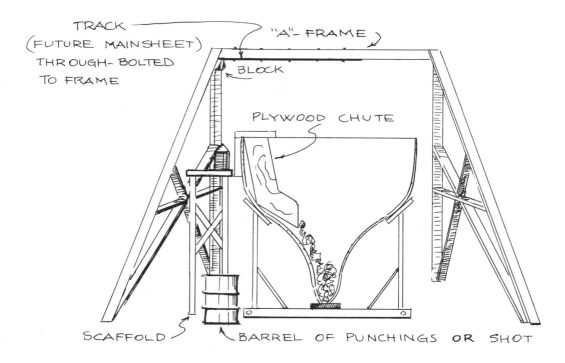

SCAFFOLD

BARREL OF PUNCHINGS OR SHOT

to compensate for changing the location of the engine or tanks (which may in instances be considered as ballast).

We had our ballast factory installed. Apart from a minor gudgeon seal problem, which they rapidly and promptly corrected, I have had no misgivings or regrets.

Home installation of external ballast keels, on the other hand, should be avoided like the plague, for they require fitting, trimming, refitting, jacking up and jacking down and only God knows what else, so by the time you have the casting delivered, jacks rented, and generally worried yourself sick, you may as well have had the factory install the beast in the first place. That solves that.

Cabin Sole

Most fiberglass boatbuilders offer a fiberglass cabin sole. If you have inbred prejudices for or against one, your life will be simple; otherwise, evaluate.

The cost of a glass sole factory installed, for a 30 to 40 foot boat, is close to $1,500.00. If you do your own, using mahogany sole timbers and marine plywood, your cost in materials should not exceed $350.

Even if you are financially independent, you should still consider the following. Most of these soles have raised faces or ridges as shown in the photo which (a) give it rigidity and (b) define the location of berths, cabinet faces and other furniture. If you are satisfied with the offered interior layouts, this sole could be a blessing, for you will be able to install your rough interior in very little time. If you plan minor changes only, the fiberglass sole is still acceptable. But if you have drastic divergences in mind, or are uncertain of your final plan, then certainly do a plywood sole yourself or have the factory install one for you; the ridges will only frustrate and inhibit you.

On the pro side, the fiberglass cabin sole will usually have a non-skid finish of sorts and color

that can serve as a final easy-to-maintain surface if you like that sort of thing. If, however, you're more traditional and want teak, oak, etc. for your sole, then you will have great difficulty engineering your wood over and around the ridges. I must admit, though, that where the cabin sole angles up to follow the curvature of the hull, the fiberglass surface there makes a very very nice bed into which a covering layer of wood can be screwed. Thus you wont have the annoying problem of having to laminate ribs to the hull to which you finally screw your wood cabin sole.

Apart from the above, the fiberglass sole can actually cut down available floor space, it may be installed in parts and therefore be horribly misaligned, and it will certainly have sloping ridge faces for the furniture (it has to, to facilitate removal from the mold). These surfaces may not offer the best positive methods of attachment.

But it will not rot, it may have a very handy built-in shower pan, it is practical in heads and galleys where water frequents, and it may have bilge hatch cut-outs with molded seating cleats, which are very strong and very handy. Choose.

If you do decide to get one, make certain that it has a plywood core for rigidity. Ascertain that this core is at least 1/2 inch thick; because if not, it will give too much, delaminate, and emit spine scratching noises at every step. If the manufacturer does not do so, make sure that you install a goodly number of knees at intervals to keep the thing from behaving like a trampoline.

Rudder

Factories usually charge around $1,000 for a rudder. High, perhaps, but to me it seems a ridiculously complex job to fabricate one (if plugs and molds have to be made). Therefore, if the design offered suits you and the construction appears acceptable, I would strongly encourage factory purchase. It will probably come with fitted pintles, gudgeons, and other items which would require considerable time if attempted on

The massive liner in place. Note great number of athwartship beams and the massive longitudinals, all of which stiffen the hull. A liner cannot be just a cosmetic cover. If it is it's much worse than nothing, for then cabinetry cannot be bonded directly to the hull; cabinetry which could add much reinforcement.

If a liner is used, its underside should be generously laden in the contact areas with great gobs of resin-putty, so when the liner is laid into the hull, good adhesion will be had and the liner will actually reinforce the hull instead of just hiding it.

a one-off basis.

The construction here, of course, is very important; one should look for very good fiber-glassing and a closed-cell core so that the thing doesn't fill with 300 pounds of water if a leak develops in a seam. If an open-cell foam is used, good construction is self-defeating. Although the foam will provide some rigidity and resilience on rock-banging, it will also act as an insatiable sponge if the glass cover fails. Also, look for a steel plate inside the rudder. If it is foam only, the rudder may be very buoyant, causing a genuine struggle if you are heeled, as it wants constantly to bob up like a fat lady.

If the rudder is outboard, it would be nice to have a straight following edge on it to facilitate a trim-tab installation. Speaking of installation,

one should consider having the factory perform this feat; for if your rudder is anything like ours, it will weigh 200 pounds. Aligning it and making gudgeon holes while holding the thing in your other hand is no easy task. Whether you or the factory install it, make sure, even if you have to bribe an employee, that the hull, gudgeons, and the pintles are well bathed with acetone before the polysulphide bedding is applied. The acetone removes mold-release wax, which is present for the following reason:

When installing an outboard rudder, it is common procedure to drill through the hull, install the bolts in place, then build a dam out of mish-mash or other filler material around the bolts. Installing the bolts first, allows you to drill through two 1 inch thick walls rather than a 4 inch thick wall. But if the mish-mash goes in after the bolts, mold-release wax or grease must be used on the bolts so that when the mish-mash has set the bolts can be removed. Then the gudgeons are bedded and rebolted. This wax or grease inevitably finds its way onto the hull and gudgeon. Mold-release wax is an excellent product and grease likewise, but if they remain on either of the above surfaces, you may as well throw two unopened tubes of $5 polysulphide into the garbage. It'll save you from getting goo all over your hands. More about gudgeons and pintles under *Rudder Installation*.

Engine

To choose a marine engine is a problem at the best of times. I was fortunate because our manufacturer offered only Perkins and Volvo diesels, therefore facilitating the choice. Of course, one can pick any marine engine and purchase it for any boat. But when a boatyard offers an engine, it usually means that they have a prefabricated engine pan (fiberglass molded pan designed especially for the specific engine mounts, supports, etc.) which, besides suiting the engine, fits the hull perfectly in a predestined spot.

The engine pan usually has a nice bilge of its own to collect oil drips and keep the gooey mess from getting into the boat's own bilge. The pan, above all, is a time-saving device for the buyer. The cost of ours installed (fitted and bonded to the hull) was $240. Other manufacturers charge somewhat close to that. A friend, choosing to install a Faryman for which no pan was available, spent almost a week designing and building a wood platform for the mounts and $90 worth of resin to bond the thing to the hull. So, if (a) you are happy with the type of engine offered, (b) you are satisfied with its location, (c) you can afford it; and (d) you don't know anyone who can get you a better deal somewhere else, you may as well buy one of the offered engines. At least have them install the pan, then set and

align the engine on it. They can't charge too much for that and it will save you hours of measuring, guessing, and lifting your engine back and forth on its mounts.

In the appendix I will elaborate on marine engines. For now I will mention only that we chose a Volvo MD3B, a diesel.

With the Volvo, the entire engine can be reworked from the top, i.e. you can change rings, pistons, etc. without having to haul the engine out of the boat. Automotive conversions like the Perkins have to be repaired and disassembled from the bottom.

Of course a diesel is heavier and much more expensive than its gas counterpart. But then it doesn't have an electric ignition system which usually fails when you most need it. And it doesn't have the stray fuel vapors which settle in the bilge, ignite, and blow the cabin and mast across the bay, leaving you seated in the head for all to see.

I must say, I don't know everything about engines. As a matter of fact, I don't know anything about them, but I do know that gasoline vapors explode at the slightest provocation and that diesel vapors don't, unless compressed. I know that blowers work and alarm systems work and sniffing works, but blowers fail and alarm systems die and noses catch cold or get drunk and that's when the cabin and mast go flying across the bay. Therefore, as long as the company offers a diesel, any diesel, and you're happy with the aforementioned points, have them install it. But definitely don't have them hook it up to tanks, batteries, exhaust, etc. If you are deadly afraid of doing it yourself, hire someone to help you. But be there with him all the time, and watch and help and ask questions. Remember the answers, so that when the emergency arises you will know exactly where to turn, what tool to use, and what procedure to follow.

Some solid arguments exist against getting an engine with the boat. The first one is usually financial. The fact does exist that it is unnecessary to have the engine sit in the boat for a year or two while the carpentry work is being done. It is only gathering dust and it is a large investment sitting there producing nothing. If there is structural work to be done in the engine room, for example the installation of tanks, shelves, etc., the engine could be a hindrance in that it will be in the way in a space which is usually too small in most boats.

The argument that later installation is difficult should not hold true, especially if the engine room is located below a removable cockpit sole. Hiring a truck crane for a couple of hours to install it should not exceed $60 to $80. Then of course, there is also the argument that while you are building the rest of your boat, you are very likely to discover a lot of facts and information about engines of all sorts which may enable you to make a wiser choice as well as spend a little time hunting around for bargains you may not have considered possible before. Whichever way you go, you should not encounter great difficulties. Whichever way you go, please get a diesel. In the appendix are specifications for the most commonly used marine diesels for 25 to 50 foot boats.

Tanks

Virtually the identical rule that applied for the fiberglass cabin sole is applicable here. If you are totally happy with the tanks' location, the quantity of them, and the installation method that the company offers, then perhaps purchasing their tanks is a good idea.

If you know a good sheet metal man, one who has worked with stainless or aluminum, then go to him, because from a few basic measurements supplied by even the chinziest of builders, he can build you a good tank. And, if you force some tears to your eyes and acclaim in a trembling murmur that the life of your wife and children will depend on the quality of his product, he can maybe build you a jewel of a tank.

If you are somewhat unsure of your final lay-

out, or if you question the location of the tanks even slightly, forget them for now and let them wait until you build some of the interior. Brilliant inspiration may somewhere come upon you.

1. Location

Tanks when full can be very heavy. Water weighs almost 10 pounds per gallon and diesel fuel is only slightly lighter. To place them as low as possible and as far inboard as possible in the boat is crucial. Some of mine are up high and far outboard, but then I didn't have a book such as this one to guide me.

Not only will this positioning make for a stiffer boat, but the area of least movement in the boat is down low and near the centerline. Even in the most disorganized seas, the tanks in this location will have fewer forces working on them, thereby increasing their life expectancy. The argument that you can firmly fasten and secure anything to anything is admirably naive. Some movement and working will always occur, regardless how miniscule. It will eventually result in great movement, greater working, and earlier fatigue on the tank, its fittings, and fastenings.

To have fuel tanks near the engine is good. The shorter the fuel line, the better. I've had friends whose flexible lines snake through cabinets and lockers only to be continually nicked and crimped by cans of sliced bananas or steel-lined heels of undiscardable cowboy boots. The less lines weave about, the less the chance of air locks, etc.

With water tanks, the idea of down low installation is still advisable. But it may be nice to have at least a 5 gallon tank above the galley counter height. This tank could be pumped full from the larger bilge tanks with a secondary bilge pump and provide gravity-fed water to the sink. It will not only free one hand (a vital aspect in any seas) but will eliminate the problem of a low-output galley pump that wears out and breaks down with monotonous predictability.

I believe the separation and division of both fuel and water tanks is a must. If one fuel tank is contaminated by water or dirt, it's nice to have a standby. If water goes foul in one tank, it's reassuring to have another that may have escaped calamity. If one set of plumbing lines fouls or breaks, it's good to be able to shut off the bypass, then use the other.

2. Material

It's almost unquestionable that water tanks should be made of stainless steel and diesel tanks of monel or black iron. Integral tanks are dangerously prone to some sort of salt water seepage. Sealing them, and still being able to gelcoat the interior to avoid the endless fiberglass taste and moisture absorption, is no small task. Some say that seepage is inevitable. Even though fiberglass tanks allow maximum use of given space, I do not favor them. Stainless steel for water is ideal. It's true that some plastic tanks have no flavor, but they may eventually harden, become brittle, and crack. If the hull manufacturer tries to tell you otherwise, don't believe him. Ask a plastic, then a stainless man and

draw your own conclusions.

For diesel fuel, I have been told the following by a man who has been supplying the boat manufacturers of Southern California for thirty years. The list goes from most ideal to least:
1. Monel
2. Aluminum
3. Black Iron
4. Stainless

The price of monel is almost double that of stainless or aluminum, making it almost out of the question. Stainless has the advantage of being somewhat easier to weld and solder than aluminum, but if the quality of stainless is low, or the quantity of sulfur in the fuel is high then pinholing can occur. If your hull man does not supply either of them, have your own built.

3. Construction

Even if you are satisfied with the suggested locations and happy with the material provided, please check the following vital items:

(a) Baffles. No section of tank should contain

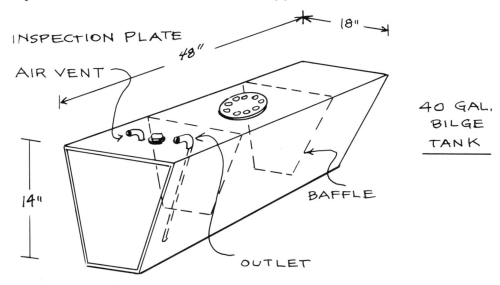

Steel or aluminum tank construction. Note large inspection plate for cleanouts, and note interior baffles. Tanks should not have more than fifteen or so gallons per compartment (between baffles) for in rough seas, sloshing fluids can build up great momentum and beat the tank apart from the inside.

more than 20 gallons without a baffle. If more is allowed, a half-full tank in a violent sea can throw about great amounts of liquid of not little weight, putting unnecessary strain on seams and fastenings. An acquaintance installed a 200 gallon tank (the size of a decent wading pool) without a single baffle. He insisted that the walls were thick, the welding fine, and the support adequate. Three weeks after launching he owned the world's largest sieve. They don't call him 'Old Nutso Anderson' for nothing.

(b) Fittings. Fittings should be mounted on top of the tanks. The fitting-to-tank attachment is usually the weak spot. To risk having this attachment or a shut-off valve fail and the contents drain unstoppably into the bilge is utter folly.

The fittings on stainless tanks should be brass. Some people, out of thoughtless false economy, install galvanized on diesel tanks. The coating eventually peels and clogs the injectors, which are replaceable at the cost of about $200 each. A brass fitting retails even today at no more than $6.00.

(c) Welding. The spot welding on stainless steel should be evenly spread (no more than an inch apart) and shallow enough not to penetrate the steel. The edges should be turned to accommodate soldering. The soldering in turn should deeply penetrate into the seam to make a long soft seal. My friend, the tank man, brought this procedure to my attention, showing me the end of a tank he had to shorten. To demonstrate the quality of his work, he clamped the welded, soldered seam into a vise and assaulted it with a large hammer until I almost went deaf. Then he showed me a piece of coiled and wrapped metal without the tiniest crack in any seam.

The baffles should also be spot welded, with welds occurring as frequently along them as at the ends of the tanks. The ends are sealed with solder and there is reason to assume that the welds on the baffles are at least as vulnerable; therefore, a spot of solder over each weld here should not be considered overkill.

If the hull manufacturer's tanks meet the above somewhat stringent demands then by all means buy them, but install them yourself. In all seriousness your life may one day depend on your tanks (a thorough mention of installation procedure will be made in a later chapter).

All tanks should have an inspection lid such as this, through which the tank can be cleaned without being torn out of the boat.

Fuel tanks should have 90 degree shut-off valves mounted immediately to the tank. This way if any leaks develop in the fuel lines, the fuel can be shut off completely.

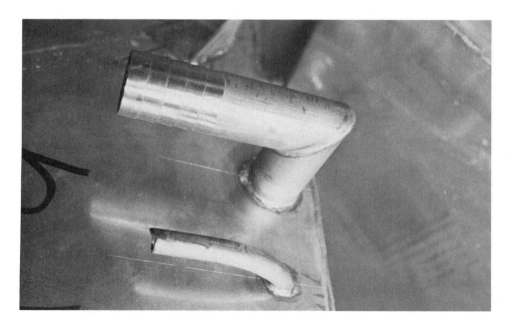

The fittings on tanks should be barbed to achieve a very positive and secure hose connection.

Precut Plywood Parts

One of the most time-saving items you can purchase is a precut plywood interior, see photo. Most companies offer either full-size paper templates or precut and roughly fitted plywood pieces that are numbered and coded. They are fairly easy to assmble if the routing is at least decent. Most pieces have to be scribed to the hull and perhaps trimmed, but overall the package still saves a tremendous number of hours compared to making and cutting templates, then saber-sawing the actual pieces from four by eight sheets of plywood.

We bought such a package. I must say I did have a few frustrations when I found some odd looking pieces that seemed to fit nowhere. But in the final analysis things worked out well, even though we modified about 40 per cent of the boat to some degree. The major criteria here is, of course, that you follow the original plans religiously. If you deviate or try to change more than about 20 per cent of the interior, you will lose too many of the original parts to make the precut worth your while.

An interior kit of this sort for a typical 30 to 35 foot boat can be fitted and assembled in about 160 hours at the most. This estimate is providing of course that (a) all the pieces are shipped together and (b) none of the pieces are viciously mis-cut.

The usual labor charge for routing and shipping an interior of this sort is about $600 – really not excessive when you consider how long it would take you to buy, load, unload, pattern, and cut out the pieces. Again, have the manufacturer provide you with an itemized list of pieces (see sample list in figures) and perhaps a set of diagrams, no matter how unpolished, depicting some semblance of the piece in its final position. These aids will give you a much clearer picture in attempting to guess where a piece that looks something like a cross between an octopus and a chicken should fit.

CHART TABLE PATTERNS
H-1   Chart table top – $\frac{1}{2}$ inch fir
H-2   Chart table face – $\frac{1}{2}$ inch mahogany plywood
H-3   Chart table face – $\frac{1}{2}$ inch mahogany plywood
H-4   Chart table divider – $\frac{1}{2}$ inch fir plywood
H-5   Chart table divider – $\frac{1}{2}$ inch fir plywood
H-6   Aft hanging locker (aft side) – $\frac{1}{2}$ inch mahogany plywood
H-7   Aft hanging locker face – $\frac{1}{2}$ inch mahogany plywood
H-8   Aft hanging locker (forward side) – $\frac{1}{2}$ inch mahogany plywood
H-9   Ends for chart table and galley (two of these) – $\frac{1}{2}$ inch mahogany plywood
H-10   Aft hanging locker top – $\frac{1}{2}$ inch fir
H-11   Chart table lid – $\frac{1}{2}$ inch fir
H-12   Aft hanging locker bottom shelf inside locker
H-13   Chart table lid – $\frac{1}{2}$ inch fir
H-14   Aft hanging locker back – $\frac{1}{2}$ inch mahogany plywood
H-15   Chart table cabinet – $\frac{1}{2}$ inch mahogany
H-16   Chart table and galley locker face (two of these) – $\frac{1}{2}$ inch mahogany
H-17   Chart table cabinet shelf – $\frac{1}{2}$ inch fir
H-18   Switch panel side – $\frac{1}{2}$ inch mahogany plywood
H-19   Switch panel front – $\frac{1}{2}$ inch mahogany
H-20   Chart table cabinet (aft face) – $\frac{1}{2}$ inch fir
H-21   Cabinet corner posts – $1\frac{3}{4}$ inch teak
H-22   Cabinet corner trim (forward) – $\frac{13}{16}$ inch mahogany
H-23   Post above hanging locker – $1\frac{3}{4}$ inch teak
H-24   Sea rail – $1\frac{3}{4}$ inch teak
H-25   Sea rail corner – teak
H-26   Grab rail support – $\frac{13}{16}$ inch mahogany
H-27   Cabin corner trim (aft) – $\frac{13}{16}$ inch mahogany
H-28   Bulkhead support knee

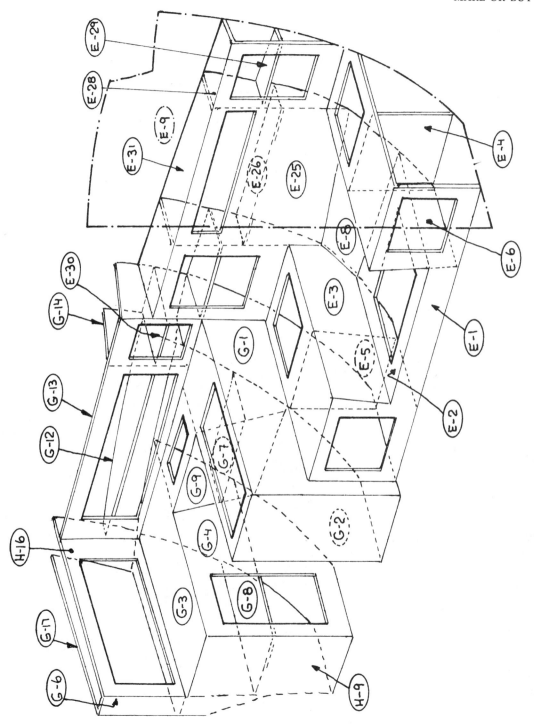

Again, I'll mention that if you consider buying this kit, be absolutely certain that the bulkheads the manufacturer provides are ¾ inch thick and the cabinets ½ inch thick.

The grade of plywood provided is, of course, to be seriously considered. I believe no real need exists for marine plywood in a fiberglass boat other than for the bulkheads. For the cost, all it really supplies is absolutely perfect pieces with no small voids like you will find in the much less expensive ABX grade ply. ABX is quite acceptable but you should get at least ABX, because it has one perfect side (that's the A), one very good side with no knots (B), and the laminating glue utilized is of exterior grade (X).

Other than the above points, the kit is a worthwhile proposition as long as you won't feel inhibited or restrained from attempting changes, believing that only the gods at the factory can devise the proper design or the proper cut. Hack, cut, and butcher all you like. The world isn't going to fall on your head and you'll wind up with an interior that you like or at least one that you created. If you do plan drastic changes, it may still be wise to buy full-size paper templates from the factory. They usually provide them for approximately $150. And here it's not quite as heartbreaking to throw away a few pieces of paper as it is to throw away a large piece of ½ inch mahogany ply.

Precut and numbered plywood interior makes assembly fast and easy if the pieces have been well cut to start with.

Finishing and Trim Kits

1. Metal parts

Most boatyards have stainless fittings custom-made for them in bulk; thus, they get a sizeable discount which they sometimes pass on to customers. Even if not, you will spend a tremendous amount of time and money getting a shop to custom make you a few pieces. Therefore, if the parts the boatyard offers are well welded and are guaranteed to be at least the 304 stainless or good bronze, then purchase your hull fittings, stanchions, chainplates, and tangs from the factory. The fittings should be of sufficient thickness to withstand the worse possible weather, even a good number of knockdowns and pitch-polings. Anything that is marginal has no place on a cruising boat.

If you know a machinist who is dying to build your part for the sheer joy, who is trustworthy, and who is willing to do it for little money, by all means don't deprive the man.

2. Wood parts

Often offered are teak or mahogany trim for interior and exterior as well as doors and drawers. These parts are milled, bull-nosed, etc. and are very convenient if you are going to follow the standard interior. But even if you think you will be, I would not purchase too many of these items. As you build you will surely find you'd like to change something and no matter how trivial the change may be, the thought of discarding even a few pieces of teak worth the price of gold will surely inhibit you.

I look upon these packages with great negativity for I know from experience that the most enjoyable parts of the boat are those we've conceived and created ourselves. To rob oneself of these tiny joys is being quite masochistic and defeats the main purpose of building a boat yourself, which is to create something to your own needs out of your own dreams and your own design and with your own hands. If you are willing to sacrifice the simple pride and quiet joy

arising from this, by all means go ahead. Buy every piece and fit 'A' to 'B' and 'X' to 'Y', but next time buy a big-saw puzzle. They're cheaper and they don't create such an unholy mess in the backyard. Of course, all of the above is my own opinion, and you may have a different idea of boatbuilding entirely.

To be reassuring, I must say that the actual milling of the wood is a very simple operation. You should have a table saw and a router anyway for other uses. With them in your possession, the milling of sea-rails, berth-rails, corner posts, drawer faces, support poles, etc. should be neither difficult nor time consuming. For exact procedure, these things will be itemized in the construction section of this book.

Mast and Rigging

If you are happy with the sail plan, the rigging meets specifications for your size of boat, the swedging seems proper (see rigging installation chapter), and you have the money then factory purchase is advisable. If you have doubts on any aspect, then provide your own. You can buy an extrusion made to your specifications. Tapping holes in aluminum and installing machine screws is no great task. Here, as with all parts of the boat, the more you do yourself, the more you'll learn and the greater confidence you'll have in your craft and yourself.

The rigging will have to be made by a rigger. The turnbuckles you can buy anywhere yourself. If the factory has open-bodied, you could consider buying theirs. The open body is important (although partially a matter of taste) because you can see how much thread you have left inside the barrel.

Stainless on stainless makes by far the strongest turnbuckle, but it can and sometimes does gall, resulting in an almost unmovable bonding. A stainless and bronze combination is well proven. Seafast, Navtec, and Merriman have been functioning satisfactorily for years. For the strength they offer please consider tables.

ALL BRONZE: MERRIMAN

Turnbuckle Size (in.)	Wire Sizes (in.)	Turnbuckle Tensile Strength (lbs.)	Width of Jaws (in.)	Add for Toggle (in.)	Fig. 377 Length Between Centers		Length 2/3 Extended (in.)	Weight
					Extended (in.)	Closed (in.)		
1/4	1/8	2,750	1/4	1 1/2	11 1/4	7 1/2	9 1/2	5 oz.
5/16	5/32	4,300	5/16	1 1/2	11 1/2	7 3/4	10 3/4	9 oz.
3/8	3/16	6,500	3/8	1 1/2	12 1/2	8 3/8	11 1/2	13 oz.
7/16	7/32	9,000	7/16	1 7/8	13 1/2	9 1/8	12 1/4	1 lb. 2 oz.
1/2	1/4-9/32	10,300	1/2	1 7/8	15	10 1/8	13 1/2	1 lb. 12 oz.
5/8	5/16-3/8	17,000	5/8	2 5/8	18 1/2	12 3/4	16 3/4	3 lbs.
3/4	7/16	29,000	3/4	2 5/8	21 1/2	14 3/4	19 3/4	4 lbs.
7/8	1/2	43,500	7/8	2 7/8	25 1/4	18 5/8	23	8 lbs.
1	5/8	56,500	1	3 1/2	25 1/2	19 3/4	22	11 lbs.
1 1/4	3/4	81,000	1 1/4	4	36 3/4	25 1/4	32	18 lbs.

STAINLESS-BRONZE: SEAFAST

For Wire Dia. (in.)	Thread & Pin Dia. (in.)	Breaking Strength (lbs.)	Min. Lng. (in.)	Max. Lng. (in.)	Part No.
1/4-5/32	1/4	3,800	8	10 1/4	TT-8
5/32-3/16	5/16	5,600	8 1/4	11	TT-10
3/16-7/32	3/8	9,000	9 1/2	12 3/8	TT-12
1/4-9/32	1/2	13,000	13 1/4	17 1/4	TT-16
5/16	5/8	20,000	14 3/4	19 3/8	TT-20

Rope Dia. (in.)	Break Strength (lbs.)	Shank Dia. After Swaging (in.)	Ball Dia. After Swaging (in.)
1/16	480	.112	.190
3/32	920	.143	.253
1/8	2,000	.190	.315
5/32	2,800	.222	.379
3/16	4,200	.255	.442

Table 2.   Turnbuckle Specifications

Table 1.   Fitting Strengths

Tracks, tangs, spreader brackets, goosenecks, cleats, chicken heads, and sheaves you will find at good marine stores. Or you can have them made by most mast builders, many of whom will sell you the parts. Aluminum welding is no hobby to begin on your own mast. Leave it to someone who can do it very very well.

Of course if you love wood masts and the manufacturer offers only aluminum, your decision is made. If you do plan to buy the mast offered, however, check (besides the size of tangs, fittings, and turnbuckles) the following:

1. Mast shape and gauge. See table. The table is workable but it is dangerous to generalize, for a mast with thin walls and a great cross-section can be as strong or stronger than a mast with thick walls and a small cross-section. An aerospace engineer acquaintaince once worked out a formula for me in about two hours; it escapes me at the moment.
2. Welding. The beads should be clean and even.
3. Fittings should be bedded in good sealant

to prevent water from hanging between the fitting and the mast. Constant moisture can and will cause corrosion in the aluminum.

4. Track ends should be bolted if possible, although it is not vital.

5. Cleats for the halyards should be through-bolted. It is vital that you through-bolt them; it will be easy because machine screws are normally used and it's not an earth-shattering feat to reach into the base of a mast while it's down. Install a few lock washers and nuts on the machine screws just to be sure. It's a simple task, yet mast makers neglect it, saying that their method is strong and secure enough. I'd say exactly the same thing if I were bulding the mast for their boat.

Wiring, Plumbing, and Engine Hook-Up Kits

If the manufacturer's complete boats seem well thought out and well executed; if he supplies you with acceptable schematics; and if his reputation for building quality boats is un-marred and unquestioned, then buy whatever of these kits he suggests and has available. You may eventually end up changing a lot of the original system; but it's so difficult to obtain the exact parts you need when you need them, that it's advisable to buy whatever you can if ever you can so that you'll have it in an emergency

even though it won't fit worth a damn. The psychological reassurance its existence provides makes it well worth keeping in the back of some never-to-be-opened drawer.

Apart from the preceding itemizations, it may be well worth it to consider the purchase of hardware, portlights, latches, prop shaft, stuffing box, seacocks, etc. from the manufacturer. I would especially strongly recommend buying them from the manufacturer if you live in an isolated area. I have met a good number of people who have tried building various boats in places like Chico, California, in the depths of New Mexico or Arizona, which resulted in a tremendous amount of frustration. I can certainly feel sympathy for the people although I cannot empathize because I built my boat in Newport Beach, the heart of an area that is inundated with sailboat manufacturers, sailboat suppliers, and various sub-trades that supply the industry. Here, anything I could wish for was no more than an hour's drive away.

I can appreciate the frustrations of those in isolated or non-marine areas and to them I have one recommendation. Hoard everything you possibly can whether it is supplied by the builder, through catalogs, or through your local general store. Nothing is more frustrating than getting halfway into a job you enjoy or want to get done only to realize that you are short two No. 10 inch-and-a-half self-tapping pan heads, or you bought two T's instead of one T and an elbow and cannot complete the task.

6

Preparation for Arrival

Location

The greatest determinant of how long you will take to complete your boat is its location during construction. Minor variables like manual dexterity, common sense and other irreparable items aside.

Discussion on this subject may seem banal, but many people are at a loss for the best choice. The ideal situation would be to pack up the kids and dogs and move next to the plant where the boat is built. There you will be close to materials, parts, advice, and most important you will be able to run over and see just exactly how part A12 which looks like a kidney fits to B6 which resembles a limp artichoke. Construction manuals are fine (we had a 400 page one) but there is still nothing comparable to looking at the finished product in deducing how it was assembled.

We moved from the northwest to Newport Beach just to build our boat and were more than fortunate with our surroundings. We rented space in a boat storage yard for $16 a month (50¢ a foot). The lot was perfect. It was paved; it was just below a cliff that was usually covered with blooming desert flowers; it was fenced in with a high cedar fence; and the people who owned it, Bart and Sandy, were the most easy going

kindest people we have ever met.

Newport Bay was just across the street. From the deck of our land-locked fiberglass cave we could see the water and hundreds of sailboats. Apart from the romantic aspect this location was most practical; when we needed ideas, clarification, or just a visual change to a finished boat (after awhile one forgets that such a thing exists) we would just run across the street and feast our eyes. The rest of the surroundings were no less enviable. In the next block were two of the largest marine supply stores in Southern California. In between them was a huge hardware store, a marine radio shop, and a bank. Across the street was Minney's, a place that sells everything from antique barometers to nautical underwear. Also across the street were three shipyards, a boat brokerage, and a giant crane for launching. As a final topping, the Westsail plant was only six blocks away and the sun shone 320 days out of the year. Eat your heart out, America.

Other suppliers like mast makers, hardwood lumber yards, tool wholesalers, and stainless steel fabricators were within a radius of two miles. Our experience was one extreme. The other extreme is an enthusiast I've heard of who's building a 44 foot ketch in Nebraska in a gulch.

Even though everything seemed so perfect we still made one critical mistake. We wanted more hills and greenery than Newport Beach could offer, so we rented an old cottage 16 miles away in Laguna Beach – a fatal error. Our only occupation was that of building the boat and if our enthusiasm drooped during the day, we'd fold up and go home. By the time we'd get there we again felt like returning and working; but of course it was too far to drive, so we stayed at home and crossed the day off the calendar.

I do not think abundance of immediate supplies is as critical as having the boat near one's home; the nearer, the better. It is best if the thing is in your driveway with your garage or basement as a well-stacked tool shed and workshop next to it. That way if you have a regular job, the spare hours can be better spent working on the boat rather than driving, unpacking, and setting up, etc.

You will more than likely be some distance from suppliers if your boat is near your house, so you'll have to plan more carefully, purchasing everything in large quantities so you won't run out when you most need things.

Many people have done the contrary. Instead of bringing the boat to their home, they brought their home to the boat. In a boatyard nearby us was a couple from Virginia (and a gargantuan black labrador) living in a Volkswagen camper below their bowsprit. Not far away lived a man, his wife, and a five-week-old baby who came only to build the boat, from Ontario.

Others even out-extremed them like the one social-psych professor from Michigan whose boat was next to ours. He just pushed the sawdust out of the way in his half-finished boat and moved aboard. I would not recommend this action. There is nothing worse than attempting boat building on any kind of an organized system only to find yourself and your belongings constantly in the way. A boat is a small enough space where merely the tools and the materials you're using are interference enough. Anything like large pillows or chocolate pudding

will just be headaches that totally out-weigh the convenience of being near your boat. If you like to rough it, pitch a tent underneath the keel.

If you need criteria other than the above, here are a few basics to be considered:

1. Try to put the boat on pavement or concrete pads. It's likely to spend over a year there and it's good to level it once without danger of it shifting when the rains come. Leveling will facilitate construction by enabling you to use a level for installation of cabinetry and bulkheads instead of attempting to measure and square everything from reference points that are at best, arbitrary and at worst, non-existent. The absence of mud and dirt will make a significant contribution to speeding up construction.

2. Try to leave a space at least 3 feet wide around the boat so that you can put up a scaffold to work on the exterior items like caprails and decks. It's much easier to work from scaffolding looking up than to hang upside down over the bulwarks. And it's much easier to lay teak decks from a scaffold than to work backwards from a deck, constantly trying to keep out of your own way.

3. Try to stay as far away from neighbors as possible. It's very intimidating to run a drill motor at 11:30 at night when the neighbor's bedroom is only a few feet away.

4. Hide it. At first you will think it's great fun to be the hit of the block but soon you will be out with the molten lead and boiling water when you hear footsteps on the bottom of the scaffold. There is nothing (and I must emphasize *nothing*) more detrimental to boat construction than visitors, some of whom are interesting, but most of whom are embarrassingly boring and uninformed.

5. Build a roof of some sort over the boat if you can. Even if you are lucky enough to

build a boat in Southern California where you will not need to fear rain, it is advisable to have a roof over your head. Dew can keep everything wet until noon and if you're laying teak decks, gluing hatch boards, or spraying gelcoat, this moisture can be disturbing.

6. A tool shed is an almost must. To everything there are exceptions; but it is beautiful to have a shed near you where you can mill your wood, prefabricate things, and above all store the mountains of junk that you will accumulate. We had a small shed about 12 by 20 feet that we found adequate for band saw, table saw, and routing table. We managed to squeeze a lot of shelfage out of the areas above the tools.

A few prefabricated pieces of scaffolding can also be handy. Avoid building scaffolding at all costs. Wood is expensive and if you look around you'll find old scaffolds everywhere. It's nice to have your ladder removable so that you can chain it to the boat's cradle when you're not there. You'll be amazed at the number of inconsiderates wandering around in cowboy boots on your varnished hatches if you leave the ladder, and therefore the deck, accessible.

Prefabrication

Without being facetious one can safely say that almost every wood part of a fiberglass boat can be prefabricated. That statement really means that you need not initially invest $20,000 in a hull and deck, etc. and then finish it off. But you can actually start with a few dollars worth of tools and some comparatively inexpensive raw wood stock and begin construction. The only awkward possibility could be that by the time you finish the pre-fab, the company that manufactures the hull and deck would have gone out of business.

Apart from such an occurrence, you can put a deposit on a hull and begin work on the less expensive items while you save enough to pay for the boat. The degree of completion to which you carry this prefabrication will vary from item to item. But if the manufacturer supplies you with an exhaustive construction manual you can at least mill many of your wood parts and even completely finish and ready some for installation.

Items that you can completely finish including varnishing and oiling:

hatches; belaying pins; Samson posts; teak grates; bowsprit; masts, booms, spreaders; boomkin; ladders; tiller; grabrails; doors; compass boxes; drawers; dorade boxes; tables.

Things you can completely mill and cut to rough lengths:

searails; teak deck covering boards for cockpit trim; corner posts; grabrails; berth rails; bulkhead trim; hatch coamings; deck beams; table legs; cap rails.

Things you can mill to size but to random lengths:

cleat stock; plywood seating cleats; small trim slats; tongue and groove covering; teak deck and cabin sole stock.

Other items to keep you busy:

fuel and water tanks (metal); winch mounts; electrical panel; tangs and fittings.

The greatest help will be if you can get full-sized paper templates (available from most factories for about $150) and proceed to precut all your plywood cabinetry. If you are hesitant about finalizing your layout, you can ask the manufacturer to sell you a scale model of an empty hull, see photo. You can then mock up, out of balsa or foam, a perfectly to-scale interior. Only then will you actually know whether some of your planned changes can be practically applied or not.

If a scale model hull is not available, try to secure line drawings. They are more difficult to use than the scale model hull but they are better than nothing. If you are fairly certain that you will adopt the standard construction procedures, arrange to receive the construction manual ahead of time and study the thing from cover to cover. Familiarize yourself with pieces, parts, and assembly methods. Ascertain how they are fitted together; thus you won't have a great cold fear when your hull arrives and you're standing in an icy panic not knowing whether to scream or go blind.

All these trim pieces, slides etc. can be milled and cut to rough lengths before your boat arrives. You can actually have most of your interior cabinetry precut, trim pieces milled and doors and drawers all finished before you spend a penny for your hull and deck.

7

Tools

I accept that the finest boats were built with an axe and hand saw, but I have less time, and a few half decent improvements have been made in technology during the last century. Tools should not be scrimped on. Buy everything you may need (you won't need very much) and buy the best quality you can; otherwise, the cheapies will give you nothing but trouble and they'll fall apart before the boat is half done. You will find a checklist of recommended tools in the appendix. an analysis of the best ones is given below.

In general, I would say that the best hand tools like hammers, plyers, levels, and squares are made by Stanley. They are costly, but well worth the difference. If you go cruising, most of your hand tools should accompany you. So you may as well get the best, take care of them, and let them help you.

With power tools, you have two choices. You can get the very expensive Milwaukee or Rockwell saws, routers, and drill motors and hope they last forever. They probably will. Or you can buy, fairly reasonably, a good product from department or home-building stores. Most have every tool you can think of and some that you can't think of. Although the quality isn't the ultimate, they are worth the dollars spent. They also have one fabulous advantage. Most of them carry a year's guarantee which means that when

something breaks, burns out, etc. you can return the tool to the store and they will immediately replace it with a new one.

In a way, this guarantee is somewhat of an inconvenience because some tools pass away rather predictably. But there is one tremendous advantage to the system. You can burn out a $3/8$ inch drill motor three or four times during the construction of your boat. Every time you can go in and demand and receive a new one, except the last time when the boat is almost done and the tool dies. Take it back and tell them that you're sick and tired of replacing it and you want your money back. They will oblige. By this time (probably a year later) the price will have gone up and your investment will have paid dividends.

There are a few power tools every boat-owner will want to retain. These should be of the best quality. To play about with cheapo tools, which, although they don't completely die, spark and spit and scream and jerk, would show most improper judgement. If any long distance cruising is to be undertaken, carting decomposing carcasses of wretched junk about would show folly.

The minimal hand-power tool menagerie should include a reversible drill-motor, with variable speed and a $3/8$ inch chuck, an excellent sabre saw as small and as heavy duty as possible, and the small, indestructible vibrator sander discussed later.

Hand Tools

Give forethought before you buy and get the best.

1. Saws

Probably the only hand saw you will use for wood with great frequency in the boat's construction will be a dovetail, see photo. It has a reinforced very heavy blade that will not flex or bend and therefore gives perfectly straight cuts. It's ideal for use with a miter box during construction of drawers, doors, and trim. A good 12 inch dovetail is an ideal length and weight, although I have heard people exclaim that smaller ones can be used to a greater advantage in short cluttered spaces where a hand has difficulty manipulating.

Keep the saw very sharp, for if it becomes dull you may tend to force it through hard work, bend the blade, and render it useless. This tool should be kept for cruising; it may be the most important cutting tool you have.

A good hack saw is also a must. The one that can be adjusted to accommodate blades of different lengths, is convenient, even though it tends to be less accurate than the fixed-length ones because it does occasionally wobble about. Buying the most expensive blades is advisable. They last much longer and they are infinitely better than the cheapos which become dull, heat up, and become even duller after only a few uses.

I have seen people build a boat with only a hand cross-cut saw. Construction can of course be done by such means, but power tools can be used to much greater advantage.

2. Hammers

A good claw hammer is a must. Many people like the lightweight handled rubber equipped ones but I find that they tend to wear out faster because the rubber deteriorates, or the rubber to metal adhesion breaks in which case the hammer comes flying off, hitting you in the forehead. Wooden-handle ones also lose heads but at least they give warning and can be re-wedged.

The claw is necessary for prying and pulling nails. Get one with not too dramatic a curve or you will have difficulty using the pryer in corners. If the curve is too great the handle will be forced to angle off to one side drastically.

A small hammer with one end rounded is very good to have although I have not yet found everyday use for the bulby end of it. Take excellent care of hammers. Their heads get easily covered with glue, resin, etc. and any unevenness will cause the hammer to bend nails every which way. Beware of using any old hammer you find. If it was ever used for major construction the flat face may be rounded on the shoulders. The hammer is then prone to either bending nails or glancing off and marking the wood.

3. Mallet

A decent mallet with a coiled leather head is desirable. If you spend $15 for a good chisel with a leather-tipped handle you do not want to bash the leather tip to shreds for want of a $5 mallet.

4. Chisels

You can get by with two or three chisels. Again, get the best quality. The better ones have wood handles with leather tips. If these tips ever wear off, they can be replaced by using a thick cut of hide and making minor adjustment to the wood handle.

A 1 inch wide chisel will probably prove narrow enough for most jobs yet wide enough to guarantee a straight cut. The 1/4 inch chisel is good to have for fine detail work and also to cut radiussed curves like the recess for deck fills. Keep a low-quality 1 inch cheapo for brutal usage like scraping dry glue, cutting through fiberglass, and dropping onto the cement floor.

To keep the chisels good and sharp, avoid

You'll probably only need one hand saw for your building and that should be the dove-tail saw shown here. It has a very stiff well reinforced blade which can make first-class finishing cuts.

A hammer used aboard for most jobs should be fairly small and light for you'll often be working with fragile pieces in small spaces. When working with wood, use the kind of plyers shown. These have broad, flat jaws so that if you're pulling staples or nails there should be no damage to the wood, for the broad jaws distribute the pressure well and leave no mark. Use caution non-the-less.

A good hacksaw is a must for cutting metal. Get only the best blades for you'll be cutting mostly stainless steel and brass, and stainless steel is murder on cheap saw blades.

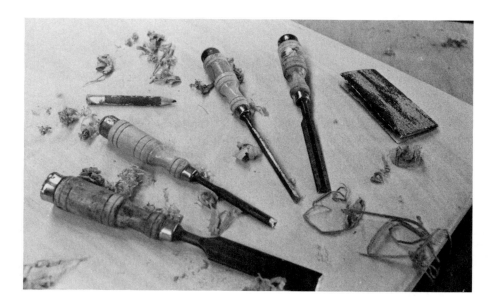

*Noah also had some very good chisels and so should you. A set of four – 1", ¾", ½" and ¼", will do you nicely. Always have them razor sharp and **never** use them as screwdrivers, glue-scrapers or crowbars. To store them, make a little sheath for each blade so it doesn't get nicked in the toolbox among the other tools. A piece of cardboard folded and taped is as first-class as you need.*

hitting anything hard like screws and keep the tips covered when not in use by a sheath arrangement of some sort. A piece of cardboard doubled over and taped is quite sufficient. When working with teak, always have a wetting stone handy and periodically run the chisel over the stone to renew the edge. If you ever suffer any nicks you should grind the edge until it's totally even, then re-sharpen it with a stone.

5. Planes

You should probably own and keep two hand planes. A small 6 inch one is a must, for with it you can shape anything effectively. I prefer this size to the large two hand variety because the little one always leaves the other hand free which is most desirable if you can't use a vise or blocks.

Planes seldom require sharpening, especially if you remember to never store them upright. If you do, the blade dulls a little every time you put it down. Avoid planing hardened glue or resins.

Another shaping tool which I dislike, but Candace and most other people that have used it swear by it, is the *idiot tool*. I christened it by that name feeling that it's mostly used by those afraid to use a small hand plane. The idiot tool is more commonly known as a "Sur-Form." It has many teeth, like a rasp, but unlike a rasp, they are flat blades like tiny planes.

The Sur-Form is excellent for minor shaping, especially where danger of chipping or over-planing exists. Both the Sur-Form and the hand plane are made by Stanley and Craftsmen; however, the one disadvantage the Stanley has is that it is manufactured in England and this makes replacement of the blades quite difficult for they are often unavailable. The teeth do get rapidly clogged with glue or paint, so take care. When the blades are in stock, get a goodly number of them to last you through the whole boat. Sur-Forms come in two sizes, one requiring two hands, the other only one. The small one seems more functional, because the real advantage of a Sur-Form over a common

plane is that the teeth extend clear to the tip of the blade, making work in tight corners possible, and for this type of work, the smaller the tool the better.

6. Levels

I found a 24 inch quite sufficient. Anything larger would be awkward to use inside a small boat. And a much smaller one would react violently to tiny irregularities, thereby give inaccurate readings. It's advisable to get one with vertical readouts at both ends so you won't have to make like a baton twirler 50 per cent of the time.

Making anything completely level is not merely a matter of esthetics. Both unlevel and unsquare assemblies lead to greater problems later when other parts are to be fitted to them. Take your time; level and square things; you'll save yourself cutting hundreds of trapezoids.

7. Squares

Three types of square prove very useful in boat building:

(a) Framing square. The large carpenter's steel square proved necessary on large assemblies of cabinetry, bulkheads, etc. where a smaller one would have given inaccurate lines. It also proves invaluable as a straight edge for marking out plywood and as a cutting edge along which a knife blade can be slid when cutting insulative foam.

(b) Small square. This square is used constantly for squaring off ends of smaller pieces like cleat stock, sea-rails, and door frames. The wood portion is much thicker than the metal, see photo, thus you will not have to worry about a part of the square *slipping* from the wood's side. Take very good care of this square and don't drop it. If you toss it about or hammer with it, the central bronze pin can work loose and the thing will then be useless.

(c) Bevel square. This square is probably the most important tool in boat building, see

An older type wood-body plane is an excellent finishing plane because its wood base is less likely to mark up your woodwork than a steel one. The tiny finger-plane beside it is excellent for final, delicate trimming.

A good medium-sized plane is a must for boat building. Keep the blade sharp and never put the plane down to rest onto its blade. Lay it on its side and the blade will remain un-nicked forever. And for God's sake don't try to plane fiberglass with the poor thing.

A small plane, a carpenter's pencil and a folding rule are excellent finishing tools.

A chisel is almost never too old to use. It can be ground down until there is almost nothing left. Some craftsmen intentionally cut their chisels short for then the cutting edge will be much closer to their hand, meaning they'll have better control over the movement of the tool. A good sharp scraper should be kept around as well. Never scrape with a chisel; use a cheap scraper. The small brush is for applying glue.

The world's narrowest plane.

The adjustable angle, bevel-square and the fixed finishing-square are basic tools without which one cannot build a boat. Even Noah had them. The finishing-square has its arm etched for measuring (usually up to 8 inches) and it's very accurate at that, because the handle can be pressed right up to the edge of your work.

photo. The joint is adjustable with the aid of a wing nut, enabling you to size and duplicate any angle. The steel arm is notched in the center so that it can slide back and forth allowing you to measure in tight corners as well as at open ends. Stanley makes the best of these squares, although many other fine ones exist. With the wing nut type, use caution when buying to make sure that in the locked position one wing does not protrude past the outside corner of the square as in figure. If it does, measuring inside corners accurately will be impossible. You will find that the handles are notched so that the blade can be recessed when not in use to prevent it from bending when being abused. Always store it in this position.

8. Rasps and Files
The best shaping tool for fine work is the shoe rasp, see photo. One side is rounded; the other side is flat and the two halves (longitudinally) have teeth of different coarseness. This tool is an absolute must. It can form, shape, and smooth any joint with great speed and accuracy. Keep it clean with a wire brush. If the teeth get clogged with glue throw it away and get a new one or you'll waste hours of your life.

Files of other shapes and grades come in handy. For woodwork a ³⁄₈ or ¼ inch diameter round file is sometimes helpful. And of course for metal work you'll want a good weight bastard file as well as one with some curvature.

Keep a rough square-edged metal file handy. Without a handle (so it fits better) you can do wonders in 90 degree corners working both pieces evenly. This process is the one thing the shoe rasp cannot do.

9. Brushes
Acid brush, see photo. This brush is excellent for gluing and throwing away at the end of the day. It only costs a nickle and it is definitely not worth your time and acetone required to clean it. If you

made 60¢ a hour you would probably break even.

Resining brushes, see photo. The most important consideration here is that the brushes be cheap and have no paint on the handle. They must be cheap because it's impossible to clean them after a full day's use. They can't have paint on the handles or the acetone will slowly eat it off and you'll find great chips of paint all over your masterful bonds. You should wash them between uses during the day, but you will find the base full of hardened resin by the day's end.

Paint brushes. It is best to get a good batch of different sizes from 1 inch to 3 inch if you find a deal. You will use them for the strangest things such as dusting, oiling, etc. For varnishing you are well advised to get expensive, well-made brushes. The good ones are about $16 for a 2 inch brush but they save the agony of picking out hairs from the varnish every 4 inches. Wash them diligently with paint thinner and warm soapy water until they squeak, unless you make $60 per hour.

10. Other hand tools
You almost cannot live without a matte knife, see photo. This tool comes with removable blades, most of them with two different points. The blades last for a very long time. They are also very sharp and their blades can be set at different depths depending on how thick the material is that you are cutting. They are excellent for whittling, for sharpening pencils, for cutting everything from insulation to cane, and if everything else seems totally gloomy, your wrists.

A new tape measure is good to have. A 12 foot long one is sufficient for most cases. I say 'new,' for once the tip becomes loose, the accuracy becomes unreliable. With this problem in mind one may be well advised to invest in a folding rule, see photo, which cannot lose its accuracy (especially for short pieces) unless you hack one end off with a saw.

As described in *Construction*, a good compass with a wing-nut tightener is a must for scribing,

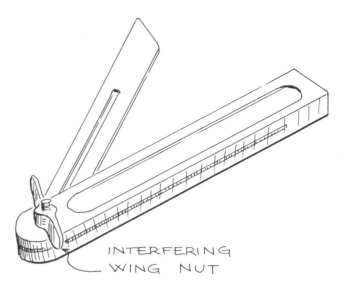

When buying a bevel-square check to make sure that the wing nut does not stick out past the edge of the handle or it will be impossible to accurately measure inside angles with it.

Cheap, throw-away brush for glue.

Cheap throw-away brush for resin. Make sure handle is unpainted or paint will flake off and mess up your work.

making circles, etc.

A hand drill is advisable to have but it will be of greatest use at sea because anything it can do a drill motor can do just as well and a little bit faster. The auger is too large and clumsy a tool for most interior work, but a small wheel type can be often useful, especially if one has an adjustable drill bit. It can make cutting odd sized holes a possibility although it is the worst possible cutter imaginable.

Two good pairs of plyers come in extremely handy. The adjustable jaw kind, see photo, is excellent for substituting as a wrench, while the heavier fixed jaws have a more accurate tip, perfect for digging out almost buried nails. This type also has cutting jaws which are very useful for shortening nails and cutting heavy wire. Speaking of wire, you will also need a combination stripper-crimper, see photo, as explained in the *wire connectors* section of *Electrical Installation.*

Another handy tool that isn't elaborated on in *Construction* is a pointed awl which is absolutely perfect for splitting plugs in half and pulling or digging them out. You will also have other needs for it.

11. Miscellaneous
   (a) Pencils – by the hundreds because they always get lost.
   (b) Center punch.
   (c) Screwdrivers (all kinds).
   (d) Countersink.
   (e) C-clamps, see photo. Two with 2 inch opening jaws, and one tiny one.
   (f) Bar clamps, see photo.
   (g) Rat-tail brush.
   (h) Wetting stone.
   (i) Broom.

Files are fairly inexpensive and an absolute must. A good coarse rasp is handy as is a fine metal or bastard file with a fine and a rough face. A small round file is very good for reaming holes while a triangle file with a 90 degree corner on it is the best for cleaning out corner cuts. Not shown here but very handy is a shoe-rasp, a 10 inch file-rasp combination that's divided into four sections (two per side), with each section having a different grain of coarseness. Get one.

These bar clamps are the fastest kind to use. When loose, the lower half of the jaw can be slid up and down the bar as quickly as your hands can move, whereas a threaded C-clamp requires endless turns of its handle to make the jaw crawl slowly along the threaded rod. Have a couple of the large ones around, and have three or four of the small 8 inch ones on hand. A couple of very small 2 inch C-clamps can come in handy for tight places. Try to buy all of them used.

A clever, homemade sanding block. The hard, smooth bottom guarantees that you will do an even job of sanding.

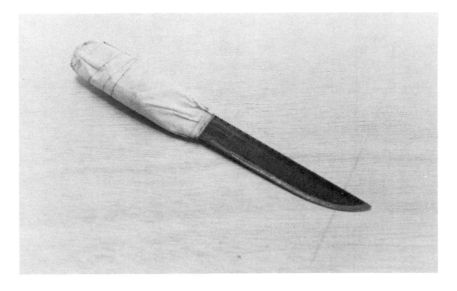

I found this on an old French craftsman's workbench. It's an old hacksaw blade with the saw teeth on one edge, while the other edge has been sharpened into a good cutting edge. Tape has been wrapped around one end to form a handle.

A good collection of screwdrivers is a must. Nothing will ruin a screw head faster than the wrong screwdriver.

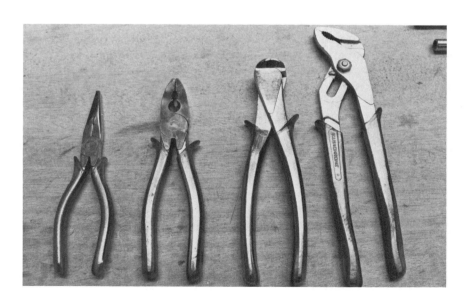

You'll need – from left to right – a pair of needlenose pliers, regular pliers, wire cutters and a channel-lock whose jaws are broadly adjustable so they can grip things, like nuts and bolts, as broad as 2 inch across the head.

Power Tools

It is true that you may have a lot of money tied up in tools if you buy the best or most expensive. But if you are near any kind of working community where other boat builders or builders of any kind live, passing the tools on with very little loss should be no problem. I bought all new tools such as a table saw, band saw, router, etc., and sold them for only 10 per cent less than I paid before I even finished the boat.

1. Table saw

Even if you plan to purchase every piece of wood milled and precut from factory, you will still need to fit everything together. Without a good table saw, you'll waste many precious hours. To say that a table saw can do almost any kind of cutting is over-simplification, but it can, with the occasional aid of attachments, rip to width, see photo, cut to length, miter, rabbet, tongue-and-groove as well as act as a table disc sander when used with a hard cored sanding disc in place of the blade. It can make the most accurate cuts on even the smallest pieces with the minimum amount of threat to your fingers. To get the very best, you need to spend no more than $500. Very good older saws of the heaviest construction can be bought used from woodworking shops, furniture factories, cabinet makers, or through want ads.

The older the tool, the more likely it will be that its construction will be heavy. Things like guides, miter arms, and other adjustments will have exceptionally heavy, positive locking settings which will provide the most accurate and safest cuts. The most dangerous thing about any table saw is poor construction, such as guides that shift, miter arms that twist, and blades and mounts that quiver and bend unduly.

Any of the above will cause the saw to *bind* and kick a piece of wood back very hard at you. Poor equipment will also cause you to take undue chances and resort to catastrophic maneuvers such as trying to twist a piece of wood so that the wobbly blade cuts straight. Any time you have to use force to push or pull wood through a table saw, you are begging for danger. The saw can bind and kick the wood out, either smashing your fingers or drawing them into the blades.

Good equipment will stand fast, requiring only mental energy to prevent accidents. Again, Rockwell is an excellent source for a good table saw if you are in the market for a new one. Construction is heavy and service dependable. Try to buy at least a 10 inch bladed saw. Anything less will not cut through wood thicker than 2½ inches.

For boat building you must secure a carbide-tipped blade, see photo. You will most likely be working with woods like teak, ash, oak, and mahogany, none of them very soft and all of them blade-culling. A carbide-tipped blade will pay for itself by saving sharpening fees, not to mention the number of trips required to visit the saw sharpener. The more teeth the blade has, the finer will be the cut and the longer it will hold the edge. Of course, the more teeth it has the more expensive it will be to purchase and later to sharpen. Check to be sure that the steel part of the blade is thick and heavy. I once spent $65 for a beautiful 12 inch carbide blade that bent like a cigarette paper upon the first contact with wood. The blade has to be thick and it has to be stiff.

Most good saws have a choice of motors you can use with them. At least a 1¼ horsepower motor is necessary or the thing will heat up and the coil burn out when you cut hardwood for any length of time. If you have 220 wiring available, by all means get a 220 motor. Most of them provide more power and will last longer than the smaller 110 ones, which seldom reach more than 1½ horsepower.

Avoid buying the fancy gadgets that some manufacturers install for 'safety and convenience.' They are usually a hindrance to accurate cutting and will give you false confidence about safety, resulting in mis-cuts and accidents. Get the best built, simplest tool and remember that

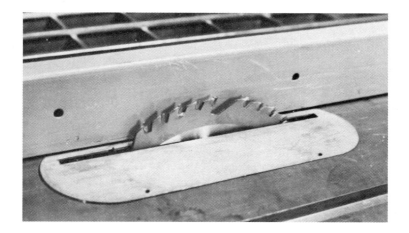

Carbide-tipped table saw blade holds edge well. You need one to cut hardwoods like teak, ash and oak.

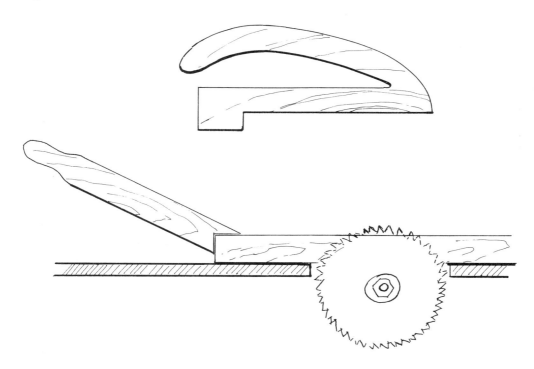

*When using a table saw **never** pass your fingers through between the guide and the blade. Use one of the two pushers shown. The top one is safer.*

you are not just a bystander. You have to do all of the cutting. The saw motor only turns the blade. Concentrate and you should never have any problems.

I will refrain from reviewing the multi uses of the table saw, because most handbooks that come with the tools are very elaborate and thorough. Basic things like dado blades are also well documented, so I'll avoid being redundant. A few items that are worth mentioning follow: Always use a 'pusher,' see figure. It can be cut from scrap plywood. Cut a goodly bunch. Always have one near the saw and always use it. Never pass your fingers between the blade and the guide; that's making it a little bit too close.

To avoid most accidents, set the blade only high enough to barely cut through the piece of wood. This way, binding is almost eliminated and the chance of drawing your hand through the exposed blade is minimized.

When your saw is not in use, either sink the blade below the table surface or pull the guard directly next to the blade and lock it there, see photo. This way, if you are sitting on the saw and somehow the thing is switched on by mistake the chances of your voice being raised three octaves will be eliminated.

Ripping. I found the ripping of random width planks into even-width strips (for decking, cabin sole) one of the most demanding tasks. Working with large planks is in itself awkward. Apart from that, use of the guide is not possible because the edge of the plank is usually too irregular to act as a true edge.

Therefore you have two choices to guide the plank. If it is horribly bowed or very irregular, use a chalk line to mark a straight edge. You will now have to hand-guide the plank along this line, but it is not impossible. After this cut you will have a good straight edge with which you can use your guide to rip the rest of the plank.

If the planks are long, over 6 or 7 feet, it's desirable that you set up rollers behind and in front of the saw. This way you can rest one end of the plank while concentrating on cutting. Be sure to set the rollers at exactly the table level. If you don't, you will find the plank teeter-tottering. As it does so it will make irregular and, in the case of teak, very costly nicks in the wood.

If the bow is not too severe, you can set the guide ¼ inch wider than the width you require of the final product as in figure. Most guides are 24 inches long so that any small irregularities in the wood will be nicely evened out into long curves. You will find that first cut usably even. You can now reset the guard to your exact desired width and, using your freshly cut edge against it, trim the raw, uneven ½ inch off. The rest of the plank can be cut, using the fresh cut edge as an even enough guide.

Mitering. Whether the piece of wood is large or small, the blade has a tendency to push the wood along the miter edge, resulting in more of a curve than a straight edge. To prevent this curve, clamp all the wood to be mitered to the miter arm, see figure. Your hand will then be free and distant from the blade. When you are doing 90 degree cuts, using the miter guide is still a must for accurate cuts. Clamping will be unnecessary. Your hand is quite adequate, as it will be for most angles, approaching 90 degrees. When you get close to 75 or less, you will need to use clamps.

Keep the table free of glue and dirt. Oil it regularly to avoid rust and to aid in smooth wood movement. Take good care of your table saw; you will find it to be your greatest aid.

2. Band saw

I do not consider this saw the second most important power tool, but it is the second most expensive one. I have many acquaintances who completely by-passed the band saw and managed to complete their boats by substituting saber and table saws. A good heavy-duty saber saw can indeed imitate a band saw in many cases. Problems arise only when one needs to cut small pieces. Clamping will then be necessary to keep the small piece from jumping about.

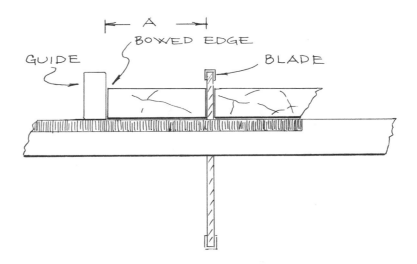

GUIDE

BOWED EDGE

BLADE

A = ½" WIDER THAN DESIRED FINAL WIDTH

If a piece of bowed lumber is to be used, it must first be trimmed as shown to create a straight edge.

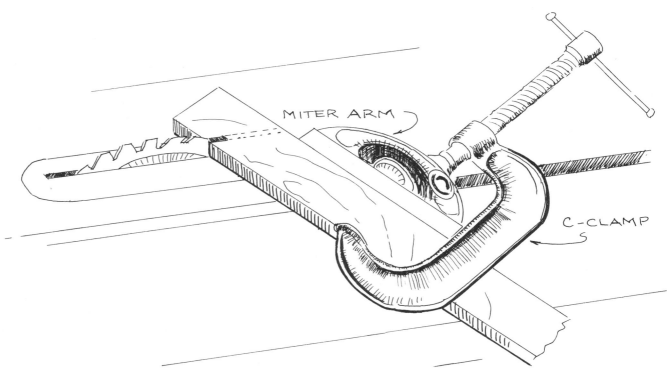

MITER ARM

C-CLAMP

When mitering (cutting a piece of wood on an angle) with a table saw, it's advisable to clamp the piece to the miter-arm, otherwise the force of the blade will tend to push the piece off to one side and you'll end up cutting a slight curve instead of a fair edge. If you have strong hands forget the clamp.

But the angles that the saber saw cuts can in no way be compared to the exactness of a band saw no matter how thick a saber saw blade is. Because it is attached only at one end, it has a tendency to bend and flex and therefore not cut an accurate angle. Band saw blades on the other hand are guided directly above and below the wood, guaranteeing exact results. If the wood is $1^1/_2$ inches or thicker, even the hardest working saber saw will not be able to do an acceptable finishing cut in less than five minutes.

I loved our band saw. Once we bought one we never use that nerve-wracking, jumping, sliding, bouncy little saber saw for finishing work again. Of course a saber saw is invaluable and irreplaceable for hole-cutting, trimming, or work where a small tool needs to be utilized in a small space. But for quick accurate work which needs little rasping or trimming to fit perfectly, the band saw is unsurpassable.

Again, Rockwell appears to excel in this field. They manufacture a very good 14 inch wheel band saw that is almost light enough to move. But it is heavily enough built to last through thousands of board feet of teak and ash. The 2 hp motor it usually comes with will have adequate power to cut through as much as 6 inches of teak, but do use prudence. It is not a steam roller.

Always maintain the correct blade tension. If it is too slack the blade will tend to bend and not only execute horribly inaccurate cuts, but also break. To help it somewhat, always set the upper bearings as tight above the piece you are cutting as possible, see photo. They will keep the blade from twisting.

The best blade I found was a medium-toothed $3/_8$ inch one. We tried $1/_4$ inch wide blades, believing that because of their narrowness they would bend more easily and have less tendency to bind, heat up, and snap. They didn't work out. The narrow blade was proportionately weaker, and the slight difference it offered in lack of surface friction was insignificant. In short, it broke.

Keeping the blades sharp was a great help. No other tool is more sensitive to force and pressure than a band saw. So guide the wood; don't force it through the blade. If you go off the scribe line don't try to twist your wood back onto the path. It is not possible for a blade to cut sideways, but it will break sideways.

Our saw cost $440 new. We used it for five months and sold it for $400. Even if I had to give it to an orphanage at the end of the five months it would have been well worth the cost.

3. Router

This tool *is* the second most important power tool in boat building. Used without a table it can shape cap rails, cut holes, bull-nose deck beams, cut patterns, and even decorate door frames, see figure. Used upside down and attached to a routing table it becomes a miracle worker bull-nozing pre-fab parts, rabbeting doors, and shaping even the smallest piece of wood with little danger to your fingers.

Stanley and Rockwell make fabulous routers, each available with a myriad of assorted bits. The most useful bits we found were the $3/_8$ inch bullnose, the straight bit, and the $3/_8$ inch rabbet bits. With that combination you can do anything. For a smaller radius or shallower rabbet you can just lower the bullnose and the rabbet respectively to get your required depth. To do detail, as in figure, simply raise the bullnose and you will have a sharply etched line to your liking above the curve of the bullnose. To do shallower work horizontally with any bit, use a guard to control depth. The guard is a piece of wood with the central area cut away to accommodate the router bit. The ends are clamped to the table.

It is an amazing tool, but care should be taken with it. Slip the wood in straight for initial contact, then always proceed with the rotation of the bits. If you go against the rotation you will find chips of your wood splintered out.

A note for your health. Routers turn at fantastic speeds and have very sharp bits (or at least they should have very sharp bits). Therefore when you are changing bits, please unplug the

To make the best cuts with a bandsaw, the roller guides that guide the blades should be kept as low to the piece being cut as possible, then the saw blade will not be able to twist. It could be a couple of inches lower in the photo for the cut that's being made.

A router built into a plywood table will be one of the most important tools you'll have.

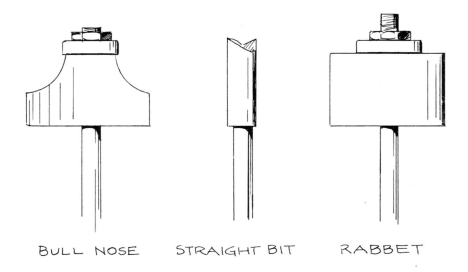

BULL NOSE   STRAIGHT BIT   RABBET

Various router bits for wood shaping. These three will probably be all you'll need.

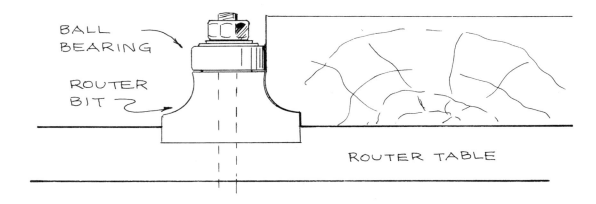

BALL BEARING

ROUTER BIT

ROUTER TABLE

Set upside down into a routing table (which is how you'll use your router 90 per cent of the time) detailing a piece of wood is child's play. It's probably best to make your own plywood table (a 30" × 30" surface is plenty) full table height and set it up outside the boat. You'll be milling a lot of stuff and the silly little metal tables that you buy in stores are too wobbly and usually much too low to be of any use at all.

machine. I know you've turned it off but just to be sure, unplug it. It wouldn't hurt. A fast turning router blade might.

4. Disc sander

For fine joiner work this tool is the best to have, see photo. You can get one with an adjustable table in order to arrive at exact angles. The sander can take off very small amounts extremely evenly. You will probably save by buying just the disc part with a take-off pulley, scrounging up an old washing machine motor, and building a plywood box. The whole investment should not run over $20. The sandpaper is self-adhesive and comes in all grits. Make the table good and firm so that even with the smallest piece of wood you'll have a perfectly good base.

If you cannot afford the time or the money for a separate disc sander, the next best solution is to set up a jig to hold a belt sander firmly without requiring any manual support, see photos. As you can see, the solution is simple and inexpensive. Make sure you have a clamp at the top of the sander holding it to the box, because when you apply firm pressure to the belt, the machine will have a definite tendency to *climb up* your piece of wood then along your arm, etc. Sixty grit sandpaper does much cleaner work than Nair.

The uses you can put the sander to are obvious. Its most important function arises when small pieces of wood that require two hands to hold need to be shaped and fitted.

5. Drill motors

I begin by mentioning these items in the plural for you do need two. The most rapid way of building a boat is to have two drill motors plugged in beside you, one holding a drill bit and countersink, see photo, the other a screw gun bit. The first one, for drilling, can be the least expensive 'cheapy' ¼ inch drill motor you can find. I bought mine brand new for $4.95 and it just now (after drilling about 10,000 holes) passed away. This motor needs no reverse or variable speed or anything. As long as it goes off and on almost when you want it, it's perfect.

A special note concerning the bit and countersink: the combination in the photograph is by far the best team. They are made by Fuller. The countersink is a separate tool with a set screw that can be released or tightened by an allen wrench. The set screw enables you to secure the countersink to any point on the drill bit depending on how deep a hole you want to drill.

One tends to use a ⅜ inch countersink for most occasions. This size will fit any drill bit between ⁵⁄₆₄ and ³⁄₁₆. A larger countersink is of course available for use with larger bits or even bits of ⅛ inch diameter. It is a wise idea to hoard as many drill bits and countersinks as you can. They do often break or get dull, or even more often they get lost. However, tool sharpening places can sharpen them so don't throw them away when they become frustratingly dull to use. The tapered drill bit has its advantages both with fiberglass and woodworking. Your drilled holes in the wood will seldom be too tight or too loose if you set the bit as shown in the illustration.

The drill motor you substitute for a screw gun has to be slightly more sophisticated than the 'cheapy.' a reverse gear and variable speed motor will be necessary if the most time is to be saved. Some people frown on a screw gun, calling it an overuse of power tools, but I don't particularly consider the hand-tightening of 10,000 screws either a romantic or emotionally rewarding endeavor.

Better tools and variable speed drill motors are available for this purpose, namely *screw guns*. They have a built-in clutch which is activated once the screw is tight. It is a very good tool, for not only does it protect the motor from straining and burning out, but it also keeps the screw heads from being snapped off by a motor whose torque cannot be immediately sensed and counteracted. Drill motors without clutches also have a tendency to keep spinning once the screw is tight, then jump out from the groove of the screw and chip or mark up the surrounding wood. After a

Small disc grinder is excellent for making adjustments to cuts. It can be made cheaply from an old washing-machine motor and store-bought disc.

The world's largest grind-stone (about 4 feet in diameter weighing 300 lbs.). The 4 inch wide edge is excellent for shaping and trimming pieces of wood. Every home workshop should have one, then when things go really badly, you can just take the sucker and tie it around your neck and heave yourself into the river. Bye.

Heavy duty, Milwaukee drill motor. Ours has built a boat and a four-story house and it's still as good as new.

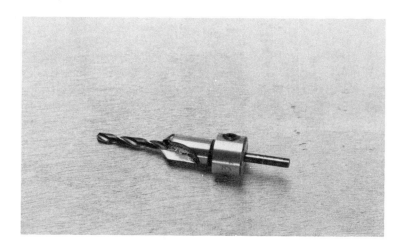

Drillbit with countersink. The countersink can slide up and down the bit and can be set at any point with the setscrew you see at its top. It will have to be sharpened from time to time like any cutting tool.

few chips and marks, you should, however, be able to feel when a screw is beginning to tighten, and back off slightly.

When you are setting screws, there's absolutely no need to pull the trigger back as far as it will go. Putting in screws at low speed with a variable speed drill motor is advisable. You will then run no risk of breaking the screw, breaking the wood, or breaking the screw gun bit.

Screw guns are much more expensive than drill motors. A good Milwaukee costs $90 to $100 and carries the added disadvantage of not being able to be substituted as a drill motor when needed. I do not think that a screw gun is an absolute necessity for building one boat only. If you intend to go on building boats or anything else, it may prove to be a valuable asset.

Another drawback to the cheapo drill motor/ expensive screw gun combination exists. The cheapy should be ¼ inch with little power. This size will, however, leave you in a dilemma if you need a tool requiring low rpm's for metal drilling, or considerable torque for use with a hole saw, see photo.

To this end a good ½ hp, ⅜ inch chuck variable speed drill motor is needed. If you don't have one, you will suffer because you will miss out on a great variety of uses.

Hole sawing. This occupation will recur during the building of your boat for installation of scuppers, conduit, seacocks, cockpit drains, instruments, deck-fills, and hand holes.

Good hole saws that can stand up to repeated use, especially on fiberglass, are expensive. A good one has two pins in the arbor to keep the saw from skipping under stress. The hole saw shaft is hollow and is equipped with a set screw so that a drill bit (with one side of the stem flattened off) can be set through the shaft and tightened, leaving whatever amount of protrusion you require. You can simply mark the center of the spot for your hole and proceed. By the time the hole saw hits the material to be cut, a positive, firm guide has been drilled.

This hole saw is made by Milwaukee and is very expensive. The arbor itself is about $15 and each hole saw costs between $7 and $13 depending on its diameter. Of course they are not adjustable, so for each different size hole you require a new $7 or $13 hole saw. But, their price does reflect their quality. The less expensive items put out by Black and Decker lose their sharpness with uneconomic rapidity, especially through fiberglass.

Some hole saws have solid shafts, leaving no potential for drill bit insertion. Attempting to start a hole with a saw of any diameter usually results in the saw dervishing about, gouging the life out of the surrounding wood.

Hole sawing should not be treated frivolously because it is dangerous, especially in confined spaces. If you apply too much pressure unevenly the saw will tend to bite and stall (particularly in fiberglass and thick wood). Most people have the frightening habit of pressing the drill motor trigger into a locked position when they are hole sawing, knowing that it will be some time before they penetrate. When they use undue pressure; the saw binds, stops, and immediately the motor begins to spin. If your hand is in an awkward position the torque of the motor can snap your wrist. A friend broke an arm hole sawing, so the above information is dripping with experience.

To recap:
- Do not force a hole saw (or for that matter any saw). Allow the blade to do the cutting.
- If you press, do so very evenly.
- Under no circumstances, lock the trigger in an 'ON' position.

For the cosmetically inclined, it is worth mentioning that drilling through wood from only one side is a mistake. Some pressure will always be present on the saw as it breaks through the other side, and this pressure is certain to cause the edge of the wood to chip away. It is advisable that you drill through only far enough for the drill bit to come out the other side. The center guide for your hole saw is now made. Then come around the other side and complete the cutting. The possibility of wood chipping will then be

Various size hole saws. Buy only the kind that go with the arbor in next photo. Do not use much force with your drill motor when using a hole saw, for a wide saw blade can bind and stop instantly and the motor will give a quick jerk that can easily break your wrist. Hold the drill motor very firmly but do not press down too hard.

This is the arbor you should use with your hole-saws. It's made for real hole cutting not for dollhouses like too many others that fall apart after a few cuts. The two little knobbies you see sticking out of the arbor toward the tip of the drillbit, actually fit into the hole saw taking a lot of the load off the threaded shank which, on a cheap tool, can be torn out.

eliminated.

A light lubrication oil (like WD40) may be applied to both the inside and outside of the hole saw to lessen friction.

Grinding and sanding. Probably the ugliest work that must be done on a fiberglass boat is grinding fiberglass. It's most unpleasant because the tiny glass shrapnel settles into your pores to itch and irritate. But sometimes this process must be done, and the quickest possible way of doing it is with a drill motor and one of the assorted shapes of stone or metal grinding bits.

For shaping wood in hard to reach areas, a drill motor again comes in handy. The same shapes you saw for grinders are available with sandpaper attachments. One or all will be necessary for some use during your boat's construction. The fitted sandpaper pieces are inexpensive so you are well-advised to stock up and have ready a good number for that awkward moment when an impossible piece in an impossible place must be ground.

To save on the cost of the grinding wheel for sharpening tools you can buy a $3 attachment for your drill motor. Set the drill motor in a vise and you will now have the potential of sharpening any knife, any plane blade, or any chisel.

For sanding jobs of major proportions the flat disc sander or the smaller mushroom sander attachments are ideal. Because of their size they can sand large surfaces fairly evenly and yet, because of their flexibility, they readily adapt to corners and awkward orifices.

Most disc sanders have the sandpaper changed by a set screw and washer system. On the smaller mushroom sanders, two systems are in practice. One uses an adhesive to secure the sandpaper to the rubber and the other has snap-in plastic cogs. The second is the quicker and cleaner of the two to use; of course it is slightly more expensive.

For the larger disc sanders a buffer is available. This instrument is at best a ring of sheepskin with a drawstring around the edge to tie beneath the disc. At worst, it's a nylon plush rag that will mat and clog upon the first application of rubbing compound.

Wire brushes of different coarseness and diameter can also be used with a drill motor. They are excellent for cleaning and polishing metals. Even more important, when used in conjunction with paint remover, they will take paint off fiberglass. I mention this function because all too frequently we found ourselves overanxious and began painting somewhat prematurely, only to find that we had neglected to bond something important to the hull. Polyester resin of course will not stick to paint, so the paint had to be removed before bonding.

On cloth or over resined mat, paint removal is an easy task because the surface is smooth. A judicious layer of paint remover followed by scraping with a putty knife will clean off all the unwanted paint. On a more textured roving, you will find paint remaining in the dimples. To remove it you will need a wire brush. The higher the rpm of the drill motor the better. Do beware of the erosive potential of wire. If you maintain rotation over one area, you may find you have quickly worn through numerous layers of fiberglass. Grind with a back and forth motion. When the paint is gone move to another spot.

Plug cutters. Plug cutting can be performed by the purchase of a $4 plug cutter, see photo, and a small drill press adapter for the drill motor, see photo. Plug cutting without aid of the drill press is not advisable, for most of your plugs will end up badly chewed or slightly eliptical or both. The adapter can be bought at Sears for about $20, well worth the price. Apart from being used for plugs, it will help with the cutting of holes that need precise accuracy in wood or in metal.

Paint or foam stirrer. A very inexpensive attachment is a paint stirrer. We used it not only to homogenize paint but also to mix, or rather *whip*, the two-part polyurethane foam we used for insulation of the icebox, engine pan, and dinghy flotation. You may find this attachment impossible to clean once the foam has catalyzed, so buy or beg a goodly number when available.

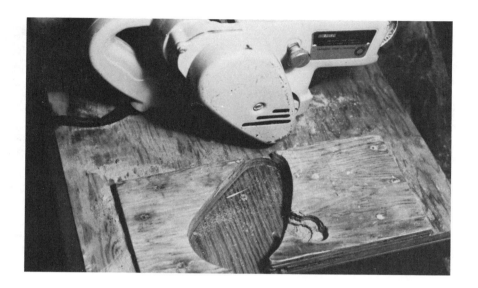

Quick and easy jig can be fabricated for belt sander, enabling it to double as grinder for shaping wood.

6. Belt sander

This devise is probably the most valuable *butcher* tool for boat building. It can remove enormous amounts of surface very rapidly and because of the size of the belts, very evenly. A great number of them are available, the most common being 3″ × 21″ and 4″ × 21″ or 24 inch belt users.

Consensus has it that the 3″ × 21″ is to be preferred not only for its lower price but because of its smaller size which makes it lighter and a more flexible tool. Apart from its previously discussed use as a small wood shaper, it is ideal for sanding large surfaces such as decks, cabin tops, counter tops, and cabin soles. It is very suitable for primary dressing of any wood.

Care must be used however, for like the wire brush it is a very potent eroder. If not moved about constantly and with even pressure, irreparable gouges may be inflicted in the wood, especially if one tends to press the forward or the aft rotating barrels tenaciously. One should hold the sander parallel to the surface and seldom press. The tool's weight is more than adequate to enforce the paper's friction. Stanley, Rockwell, and Sears all make very acceptable belt sanders at various prices. It is difficult to pick one over the other.

Two points of caution. A spring-like steel leaf is located on the underbody of the belt sander. One end is attached, the other free-floating to act as a spring. This leaf is a very thin piece to begin with. After a few hours of use its edge, particularly the free-standing trailing edge, becomes as sharp as a razor blade. Do take care when you are changing belts to avoid deep painful cuts.

The next point may seem obvious, but it happened to me on two separate occasions, therefore I feel its mention worthwhile. I used a belt-sander while building a floating house. The house was under construction on the water so power tools and materials were strewn everywhere. One impatient afternoon while belt sanding an outside patio area, the extension cord got hung up on something. When I jerked the sander to try and free the cord, I jerked out the sander's plug.

I laid the sander down on the deck, went back, freed the cord and plugged in the sander. With the power back on and the trigger in lock-on position, the sander scooted off across the deck like a little electric Sherman tank. I dove for it and barely managed to grab a piece of the extension cord just in time to hear the splash and get the salt spray in my face. I saw a few sparks and waved goodbye to $88.46 plus tax.

7. Vibrating sander

The customary vibrator which has fore and aft motion has proved to be a little less than useless. It adequately massages one's palm and nothing else.

The rotary vibrator on the other hand, is almost invaluable for finishing sanding. It is designed to be held in one hand and is built to last through hundreds of hours of non-stop sanding. It cannot, however, act as a shaper of any consequence unless it's being used to put a round of small radius onto the edge of a piece of wood. It is perfect for fine sanding and ideal for use with 60 grit or higher sandpaper, ideal for preparing gelcoat for respray or bottom paint, and irreplaceable for that refined touch between coats of varnish. Regular sheets of sandpaper cut into quarters fit exactly onto the sander and the change is accomplished rapidly with two spring clamps attached to either end. The process can even be speeded up by attaching five or six layers at one time and simply ripping off the layers one at a time as they wear out.

The rotation is even, therefore it will not gouge the wood and the only need for caution arises when one is sanding next to a perpendicular surface. If one comes too close (and it's very easily done) the vibrating clamps have a tendency to nick the vertical piece. Come only within 1/4-of-an-inch and finish the last bit by hand.

8. Saber saw

As violently frustrating as a saber saw can be, it does perform services without which a boat

A vibrating sander, a rat-tail brush and a few rolls of masking tape will keep you busy detailing (doing final readying) before painting and varnishing. Actually the rat-tail brush is a lifesaver right from the first day, for any small job in a boat creates a mess, and the cleaner you keep the boat the more pleasant will the work be and the quicker it will get done. Always clean up the whole boat at night and put everything in its place or you'll go berserk in the morning searching for tools under sawdust and wood piles. A poor way to start a day.

A good quality, heavy jigsaw is a must for good quality cuts. A cheap one will just squirm and twist and jump about and mess up your work. You might as well have used an axe.

could hardly be built. Whatever you do, you must get one. But, whatever you do, do get a good one. The cheapy smaller ones lack power and weight. The consequence is the blade chews instead of smoothly cutting and the body begins to madly vibrate, jerking the tool off a given line. Some cheap ones have bevel adjustments that are tightened with a set screw. The set screw holds reliably only until the saw begins to vibrate, which is the second the blade touches the wood or fiberglass.

Again, Rockwell makes very dependable ones that utilize heavy wide-bodied blades for wood, metal, or fiberglass cutting. The bevel adjustment is done by a hefty positive locking nut removing fear of loss of accuracy. The motor and body are heavy-duty and long lasting, but I did find one frustrating point. The part of the blade that receives any support from the mount is very small. The small set screw that holds the blade tight seems inadequate because it allows the blade to angle backwards when pressed. I realize that one is not supposed to *push* saws. But when one is cutting the first of twelve portlight holes in ³/₈ inch thick fiberglass and one has gone only an inch in a minute, one tends to get impatient and begins to *push*. When the blade slips and angles backwards, its cutting becomes less efficient; one pushes harder; and the blade heats up and breaks. If you find a good heavy tool with what looks like a more ideal blade securement method, by all means buy it.

Check the construction of the bevel plate carefully. It tends often to be flimsy and can bend if stressed or dropped. If it does bend, you will find it impossible to cut accurate angles.

One completely useless attachment that is on the market is a small lightweight metal table offered by some hobby tool manufacturers. Ideally this table is utilized to mount the saber saw onto it upside down. This assembly does eliminate some of the vibration from the saw but the blade is still unsupported at one end, making accuracy very dubious. Besides, what is the advantage of having to control a jumping

table instead of a jumping saw? Methods for using the saber saw are dwelled upon in more detail in the *Construction* section.

9. Other electrical tools

By far the most important unit is a good hard sucking vacuum cleaner. Painting, varnishing, and bonding become almost futile if you haven't previously gotten rid of dust and dirt.

Again, I don't know if you would consider it an electrical tool, but it's nice to have a small electric heater which can be safely set close to certain bonds that you require to catalyze rapidly. It also helps to dry paint, set caulking compound, etc.

A small soldering gun becomes useful during wiring. Soldering does make for a most corrosion resistant joint.

A portable tape recorder may prove invaluable at hand. It can be readily flipped on when you begin screaming at your wife and it can adequately record the sound of smashing objects and falling bodies. You can then go home at night and listen in amazement at what a fool you are and just exactly how much fun building your own boat really is.

I'm uncertain whether lights are commonly alluded to as tools, but they are vital. Even if you have portlights and the boat is in the open air under a merciless sun, some areas of the interior will still be underlit. To provide even light in all weather, six or eight 100 watt light bulbs should be constantly on. They can be attached to a bar of wood and screwed to the ceiling, cabin top, or wherever they'll be the most out of the way.

An additional work lamp, see photo, on an extension cord is most useful for hard to light areas, like interior cupboard corners. For this purpose, be sure to use only a lamp with a wire cage around it. The most dangerous thing you can do is to have bare bulbs lying about in unsupported sockets.

I once placed an unlit light bulb onto our beautifully finished teak decks and went below to work. Sometime during the day I mistakenly

Work lamp with clamp.

plugged in that lamp and kept working. Only an hour later did I come running from the cabin trying to locate where the smell of burning teak and burning polysulphide was coming from. I found it. On the aft deck was the light bulb lying on the wood and around it in a 4 inch radius was a piece of smoking charcoal that had once been our deck. It was the saddest, most depressing moment during the building of our boat.

We were fortunate, if one can call it that, in that the bulb was directly next to a deck fill. It is due to this mistake that you see such an elaborate little pad around our two fuel intakes. A good habit we got into was to use only well protected or well secured light bulbs. Even thus, we unplugged the main incoming wire and rolled up the extension cord before going home each night. You can only have so many deck fills with elaborate deck pads around them on a 32 foot boat.

10. Electric fan
A very vital accessory that's indispensable during bonding, sanding, and painting is an electric fan. A good-sized one that will completely cover a hatch will help tremendously. Keep a good safety screen over it so clothing and hair will remain safe.

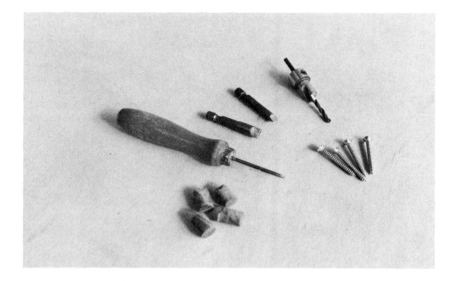

The tools for drilling, setting screws and plugging the holes after them. The drill and countersink cut the hole, the screws go into the hole, and the screwgun bits (with the help of a drill motor) drive the little mothers home. Then the plugs plug up the little holes. If you break a plug you can dig it out with the sharp-pointed awl.

A good cross-section of drillbits is handy to have, and a simple wood box like this one is a perfect thing for storage, saving you hours of searching for loose bits.

Drill motor made into drill press with attachment.

Plug cutter.

8

Hoarding and Scrounging

Once you have selected the layout you will build and are awaiting delivery of your boat, you can begin the most fun part of boat building: hoarding and scrounging. This effort will take a lot of time and a sizeable amount of money; but if you couple a little inventiveness with the former, the latter can be kept to a minimum.

Used Material

Nowhere is the saying, 'One man's garbage another man's jewel' truer than in boat building. I have known people who have, after buying a new hull, finished the entire boat from used and salvaged materials. One friend who finished off a Spencer 35 hull kept his final expense under $10,000 plus the hull. And I must admit his was one of the best equipped boats I have seen set to sea. I helped him gather some of his supplies and here's what I learned:

Plywood for deck and cabinets can be had at ½ the customary price if one goes to the factory and gets damaged sheets. They seldom have exactly what you want and it helps to have a friend who drives a forklift at the plant. He can arrange to slam his forklift (gently) into a designated bunch of plywood, nicking the edge of every sheet on the pile ever so slightly. You will have to cut around the nicks, but that's no prob-

lem. The pile of plywood is damaged and it will be cheap. If it's ⅝ inch instead of ½ inch, so what?

Teak was cheap at one time in the old days. It was customarily used in very great quantities on all yachts and old luxury liners. You can go to any large marine salvage place (San Diego, Long Beach, Seattle, New York, etc.) and find mountains of the greyed wood. All you have to do is pry it from its original bedding. Most doors on old boats are solid teak or solid mahogany. A 2 inch thick cabin door can yield an awful lot of trim. Berth rails, cabinets, etc. can also be salvaged and used either as is or cut up for lumber. If you don't mind tearing everything out yourself, you'll find prices like 10¢ per board foot very common.

For samson posts, bowsprits, and boomkins the best material to use is oak. Most of it checks badly, but if you go through a large enough pile you are bound to find some good stock. These large piles can be found in the backs of boatyards where abandoned boat cradles are stored. Most of the older cradles are, because of its great strength, built of oak and most of the older ones are free for the taking. You will have problems cutting the steel-hard wood, but free is a good enough price to warrant the extra labor.

Engines

One of the best engines for any use is a 4-cylinder Mercedes diesel, which can be found in newspaper ads and junk yards. You will have to put a marine conversion on it and perhaps rebuild it; but all in all you can come away with a total expenditure of $1,500 for an almost new engine. Mercedes are somewhat delicate engines because the aluminum head can warp when subjected to great heat, but if you are cautious and watch over your oil level you should have no problems.

If you have a boat over 40 feet you may consider the old Buda diesels the Navy used until recent years. They put out over 100 horsepower and are extremely reliable. They do weigh over 900 pounds and parts are sometimes scarce, but they can be bought for $400 to $800 each. If you can make one good one out of two bad ones, you will still be ahead and you will have learned a lot about diesels.

If you don't live near large cities you still have a chance. Old tractors use (a lot still do) fairly small 4-cylinder Ford diesels. If you write to Ford they will be happy to provide you with pamphlets on how to convert these engines to marine use. Any small Nissen diesel, which is commonly used world-wide in taxis and small trucks, can also be used as a starting base for marine diesels.

Ballast

SCOOP: Large hospitals receive radioactive materials in lead cases. These cases can be bought very cheaply, especially if you know the hospital's buyer (20¢ per pound instead of the customary 60¢). If you can't find lead, railroad track is second best; when it is surrounded snugly by steel machine punchings the results are very satisfactory. Be sure to pour in generous amounts of resin.

Spars

Used wood spars are the easiest things to buy. They come off salvaged boats or older racing boats whose new owners have decided to go to aluminum for less upkeep and added performance. If any bad spots of rot or knot or fastener holes have to be contended with, cutting out the problems with a chisel and then scarfing in a new piece using resorcinal glue is no problem.

Do beware of almost new spars from the Far East. I was offered a near new 50 foot mast with booms, spreaders, and hardware for $560. The offer was tempting but I had no money at the time so all I could do was sit back and hope no one else bought it. They didn't. I ran back three weeks later with the money and found the thing had delaminated in four spots and popped out three good sized knots. I was then told by the shipyard owner who was storing the mast that it was from a Taiwan boat. Many others he had seen were at least as bad. That was five months ago. No one has yet jumped up to grab the bargain.

Aluminum bargains are less frequent. An old aluminum mast is hard to convert to your specific needs, for its stainless screws can be very tightly corroded and their removal is almost impossible. Even if you could remove them, how could you plug up the holes in an aluminum mast?

Take care if you are buying new surplus aluminum extrusions. Some may have a small, almost undetectable dimple which will lead to a buckled mast upon the first opportunity.

Hardware

Bronze portlights are not extremely expensive. Only two major outlets exist for new ones: Perko and a small church bell manufacturer in Milford, Connecticut. Rostand, the church people, do beautiful work and will do almost any custom portlight you desire if you can wait long enough. They're never in a hurry and never on time. If you call on the phone in an expeditiary attempt they will tell you that, 'Al is not in right now but he knows what the score is and he will get in touch as soon as he gets back,' or that 'Al is out but he left a message that the portlights should arrive tomorrow, for they were shipped over a week ago.'

The portlights did of course arrive, but it wasn't tomorrow, as a matter of fact it was almost four-and-a-half months later. I'm now convinced that 'Al' is a myth and attempted communication with him is completely futile. So order your portlights in advance and if they still don't come on time, phone them up and tell them that 'Al' is standing beside *you* but he can't come to the phone because his mouth is full of pastrami sandwich, but he says to ship the portlights today or else. Punctual or not they are very kind people and do beautiful work but you should order ahead.

Used portlights are everywhere if you know where to look. Old boat salvage yards have all sizes hidden by coats of paint. If you don't mind the elbow grease and the smell of paint remover, you can usually buy them at less than half-price. The rubber sealer probably died years ago, but you can scrape it out and buy a new one in lengths, cut it to size, and put it in yourself.

I bought ten 6 inch opening portlights for $125, which is about 200 per cent under list price. Old ships and salvage yards also have huge collections of miscellaneous hardware like brass hinges, beautiful double jointed hooks, giant bronze Herreshoff cleats, ladder hardware, door handles, drawer handles, and incredible, unidentifiable but irresistible items. I found one in the long abandoned skeleton of an old freighter (along with a beautiful dove-tailed teak box) and used it for years as an incense burner. Only lately did I discover that it's a depth sounding device whose two holes in the sides scoop up bottom samples, thus an invaluable aid to anchoring. Therefore, if you find anything

interesting, keep it; you never know.

The best cowl vents I've ever seen were old ones of either soft brass or aluminum, only found in salvage places.

It seems that bronze deadlights are almost unheard of in modern new marine supply stores. Thus old ones have to be bought and usually repaired because the glass is either broken or pitted or both. I have no concept of how a deadlight gets pitted. But it does, so you will have to take out the old glass and replace it.

The glass is usually held in place with a brass ring which is most likely brittle from age and will snap if you try to force it out of place. To prevent its breaking, you will have to do something that at first glance seems most illogical, but I vouch that it does work. Take a small propane torch and heat the whole ring until it's almost red hot. If the glass breaks, no matter, for that's what you're trying to replace anyway. When the ring is very hot, drop it into a bucket of cold water. Believe it or not it will soften the brass. You will have no trouble removing the glass and spring the ring back into place. Recaulk all the new glass with silicone sealer or polysulphide for best results.

Beware

Many items are available that should not be bought used, because testing them is difficult. And even if they don't fail immediately they may fail the next time.

Turnbuckles and fittings could fatigue at any moment if they are old, especially if they are bronze. The same holds true for old seacocks and bronze chainplates. Old mechanical things like heads and bilge pumps should not even be brought close to a new boat because their reliability is almost nil. Even if you replace all the packing there is a good possibility that the cylinder walls are scarred, rendering the whole thing less than perfectly safe.

Apart from being a money-saver, scrounging is great fun and your total boat building bill could come out something like my friend's did back in 1975:

Hull $5,000
Plywood for deck and interior $600
Fiberglassing materials for deck and
 interior (scrap ends) $380
Portlights $139
Used teak $200
Tanks (integral) $140
Engine (Mercedes) rebuilt . . . . . .total $870
Prop, shaft and wheel $210
Used oak . . . . .free
Anchors (2 Navy, 1 Danforth) $140
 (plus a sack of avocadoes)
Interior hardware (liberated from old
 ship) for gas $2.85
Galley stove (alcohol) $85
Marine head . . . . .free for asking
Used wood mast $220
Galvanized rigging $120
Used chain . . . . .plus bicycle $25
 (3/8" × 200')
Re-galvanizing $30
Sails (from an old 6 meter,
 resewn himself) $200
Winches (used) (2 sheet, 2 halyard) . . .$150
Windlass (new, single action) $180
Line (halyards and sheets, new
 drum – 600' × 7/16") $95
Plumbing (new hose and fittings) $130
Bilge pumps (1 new, 1 rebuilt) $110
Wiring (surplus, new breakers
 and batteries) $180
Used compasses (4) $175
Scrap lead and steel ballast $500
 $9,881.85

A few more thousand dollars were spent on miscellaneous blocks, stanchions, kerosene lamps, lifebelts, spare engine parts, sinks, battery charger, chronometer, sail cover material, mainsheet traveler, etc.; but, all in all, not a bad new cruising boat for under $15,000.

New Materials

To save on new hardware, one needs first a piece of information and second some gall. The information is that a lot of marine hardware stores operate at 100 per cent mark-up. This margin is partially acceptable because they must have in inventory huge quantities of dissimilar and very costly items. I can sympathize with their position but I refuse to pay their prices.

Now the gall. You have to convince the owner-manager to sell you everything for less. First try honestly and tell him that you are building a boat and will be spending a few thousand dollars on hardware, fasteners, electronics, etc. within the next year. Tell him that you'll give him all of your business if he'll agree to open an account for you and constantly apply a healthy discount, say between 25 and 50 per cent. Tell him that if he won't do it you'll go somewhere else.

If he says no, connive to get a resale number. Get a license to operate a small marine supply store. You will then be able to buy everything wholesale. The license costs about $55 in most municipalities. If they want an address for your shop, give them the address of your aunt Muriel.

If you can't get a license then band together with other boat builders and start a co-op. You'll be able to buy things cheaply if you buy them in great quantities. The only inconvenience of this approach is that it forces you to plan ahead and order things like screws, line, wire, etc. when it's most convenient to everyone else.

If you are greedy you can actually start a small marine hardware outlet. Don't buy anything unless people order it and put a small deposit on it. You can then run around, pick up the materials, and pass them on with say a 10 per cent profit. And then of course buy all of your materials at wholesale for your own boat. This kind of business you can operate from your basement, or your attic with very little or no overhead. Whichever way you choose, do not pay retail unless you absolutely must.

SIX MODERN INTERIORS

BENETEAU FIRST – 30'

BALTIC 35

SWEDEN YACHTS 38

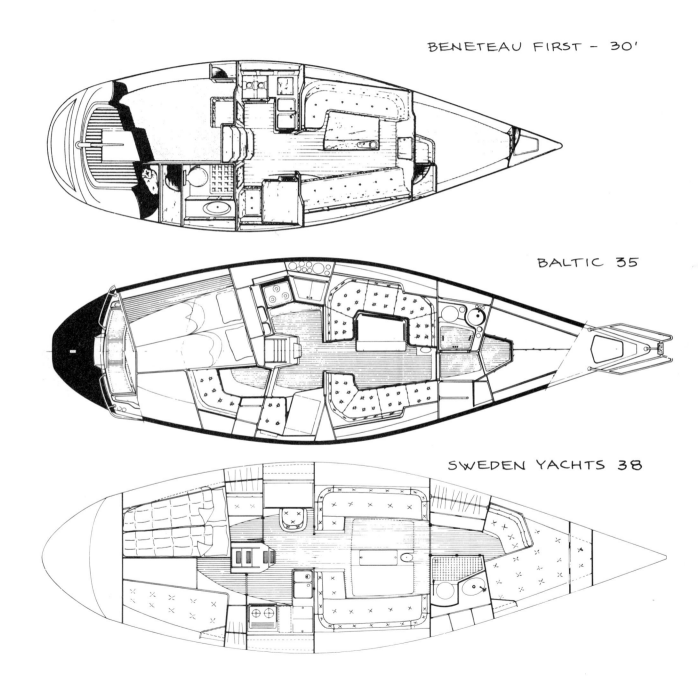

(BOATS NOT TO SAME SCALE)

SWAN 43

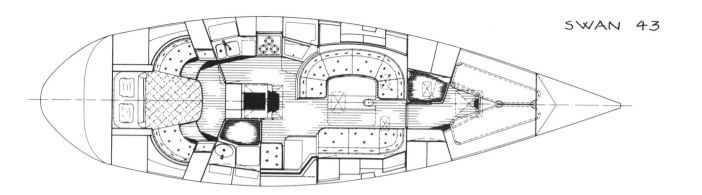

CAMBRIA 44

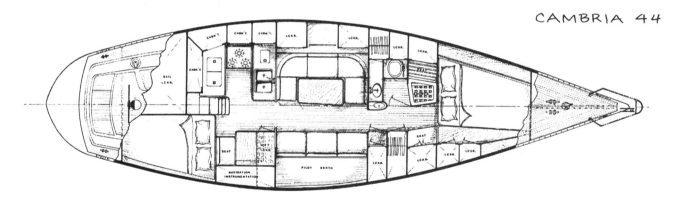

LITTLE HARBOR 53

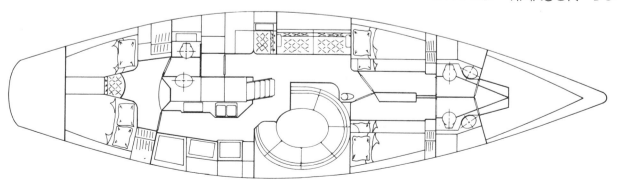

9

Ballasting

Abruptly one morning a painful realization will hit you in the face: You can't stall any longer. You've prepared until there's nothing left to prepare, you've set up a shop with all your tools in all their places. Now you've got to get your hands dirty and get glue all over that leather apron.

If you insist on ballasting the boat yourself, here are some hints on installing various kinds of ballast:

Steel Punchings or Lead Shot

Probably the least expensive ballast (except for cement) is steel boiler punchings. Perforated metal fabricators will be happy to ship punchings to you in discouragingly heavy 55-gallon drums. Upon receipt, immediately punch fifteen good-Christian-sized holes at the bottom of each barrel. You will find oil, usually a lot of oil, coming out through these holes. Machinists use oil on the tools that punch the punchings to keep them lubricated and cool. This oil, if not drained off, will eventually seep to the lowest part of the boat where it will build and build to the lower gudgeon holes, dissolve any bedding or sealing compound, and then seep out into the water. When the oil stops seeping out into the water, the water will start seeping into the ballast.

Whether this seepage is critical or not, I'm not entirely certain, but it is an unnerving thought so you may as well drain the punchings and perhaps pour in a gallon of acetone or other solvent to expedite matters.

Meanwhile, to keep the punchings away from the extreme stern of the hull and the gudgeon bolts, one should install a dam as shown in the figure. A piece of ¾ inch plywood loosely fitted and bonded over extremely cautiously should suffice. In most hulls this operation is difficult, for the keel in this area is probably no wider than 5 inches. But it can be done and should be done with great care, even if you must lie on your stomach on a piece of board and stretch your arm into the abyss a foot farther than you ever thought you could. You should use two layers of mat-cloth combination. To use roving here would be rather daring, for you may miss one row of heavy weaving and leave an air tunnel. The oil will find it. The overlaps onto the sides of the hull should be a generous 6 inches and similar at the base of the dam. This bonding point is critical. Because of the tightness of the hull and the two sharp corners, you will most likely make a mistake here and leave a void. Don't.

Wet out the paired layers as well, see *Bonding* (the section after *Rough Interior Installation*), and

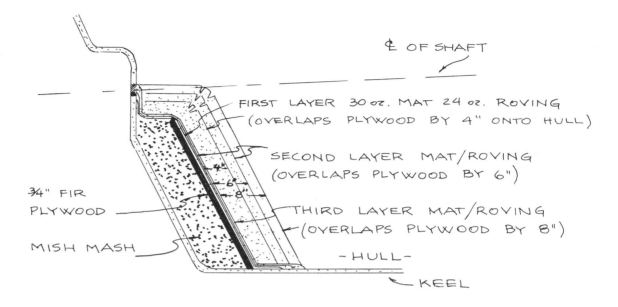

£ OF SHAFT

FIRST LAYER 30 oz. MAT 24 oz. ROVING
(OVERLAPS PLYWOOD BY 4" ONTO HULL)

SECOND LAYER MAT/ROVING
(OVERLAPS PLYWOOD BY 6")

¾" FIR
PLYWOOD

THIRD LAYER MAT/ROVING
(OVERLAPS PLYWOOD BY 8")

MISH MASH

-HULL-

KEEL

when you've laid them in place, punch every square centimeter with a coarse bristle-type paint brush well soaked in resin. You can attach a piece of wood as an extension to the brush to help you fabricate the bottom. The bonds against the sides of the hull are a problem, for you may not be able to hit them with the brush end-on. I found the best tool to use here is your hand. The idea of having sticky resin all over one's fingers can be rather frightening, so use a pair of rubber gloves. Once all the bonds have gone off you can proceed to fill the space aft of the dam. This procedure you should do with a mixture of resin thickened to a still-pourable pulp with some sort of fibers. Asbestos is satisfactory and inexpensive, but mill fiber (finely chopped glass strands) will provide a less brittle result.

If you are enterprising you can pick up mountains of mat, cloth, and roving scraps from a local boatyard, fiberglass shop or the like and stir the mixture into the resin, then pour the concoction behind the dam. Using a stick, much like the vibrator in cement work, to ascertain that all corners are well filled.

Do not over-catalyze, for a great amount of heat will be given off which may warm the hull which will expand the dam which will crack the bond that will sink the ship that Jack built. As long as you put in a goodly amount of catalyst, see appendix, the witch's brew will eventually go off. It may take a day or so, but it will go off. To ensure that catalyzation is homogenous, pour the catalyst into the clear resin first, stir well, and *then* mix the fibers.

If you do over-catalyze and the dam gets hot, put a wet cloth over it. Keep changing it. Once the dam has set, put a mat-cloth bond over the top of it so that stray oil or water can't seep down.

Draw in lines which will indicate where the ballast level should finalize. The boat builder or designer should be able to supply you with measurements.

Once the dam has been installed and the lines drawn, the rest is all up hill, literally; for a few thousand pounds of punchings have somehow to get from the ground up to the hull and into the keel. The simplest method is bucketing. The next simplest is to have a friend with a forklift put the barrels onto a very very strong scaffold.

If you want to build a simple A-frame like the one shown in the figure and if you have a friend to help you, you can save a lot of time. The person at the bottom fills the empty bucket and the one on the scaffold dumps it into a plywood chute. While the man at the bottom rests, 'Dumper' can level the mounds of punchings in the hull with a rake. Ideally, after a 3 inch layer of punchings (or lead shot) has been dumped in, the entire thing should be saturated with resin. Here it is all right to over-catalyze, for the metal will absorb a lot of the heat and the resin will be slow in going off.

Rent a cement vibrator for this occasion. Not only will it mix the resin and punchings better, but you will be able to get the punchings to settle densely, thus lower down, resulting in a stiffer boat by lowering the center of gravity. If you do use one, don't be shocked when, after installing the given weight of ballast, you end up 2 or 3 inches lower than the boat builder's ballast line. He doesn't vibrate, usually.

Even off the top of the ballast as much as possible, then top off with resin. When the resin has gone off, put two layers of mat and roving over the whole thing (overlapping onto the hull by a good 6 inches on either side). If everything else fails these two layers will keep the ballast from falling on you if you ever turn upside down.

I have heard of people substituting cement for resin with the punchings (or shot). This material would make mixing child's play, because you could use a small cement mixer, but I've also heard of cement cracking and the ballast beginning to move. Using punchings only,

without any bonding agent would be short-changing yourself. The loose shot would be able to move about and settle and then move more at the spacious top, all the while slowly grinding away the sides of the hull.

Cast Lead

The manufacturer usually offers lead in the form of cast fish. It will be expensive (lead costs 60¢ per pound) but if it is all-lead you want, a fish may be ideal. You may as well have them drop the fish into place, see photo. To assure that it won't move about or slip out of place, ram a thick mixture of fibers, scrap, and resin between the hull and the fish. If you have large voids to fill (one or two cubic feet in an open area), pouring in two-part urethane foam, which boils and bubbles and expands and hardens, is a fast and functional method. When the foam is all done, bond over it extra well. At least two layers of mat-roving should be used.

If you want to cast your own lead it can be done, and it might be economical if you have access to scrap lead. You may as well melt it down to get the most from its density. You can get a good idea of the shape it will take by using the above mentioned two-part urethane foam. Line the hull with heavy polyurethane sheets, then pour the foam over it. The plastic sheets will enable you to easily *pull the plug* once it is set. From the foam plug, you can make some inexpensive tin molds into which you can pour the molten lead. Use gas to melt it down. The location of such semi-roughly made ballast castings is critical. You may put the boat out of trim, so think it out first, consult the architect, and after you're absolutely certain as to its position, make sure you leave lots of room for trim ballast.

I could elaborate on how to build the tin mold but then I may as well tell you how to smelt the tin, then how to build the furnace to smelt the tin, and then how to make the bricks to make the furnace.

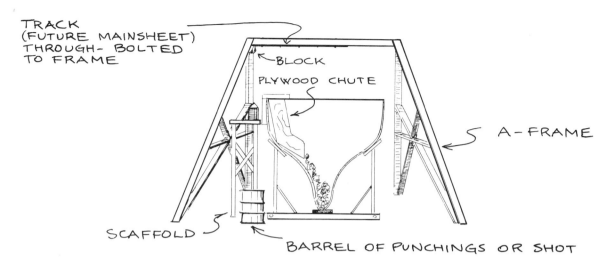

TRACK
(FUTURE MAINSHEET)
THROUGH- BOLTED
TO FRAME

BLOCK

PLYWOOD CHUTE

A – FRAME

SCAFFOLD

BARREL OF PUNCHINGS OR SHOT

Lead castings for internal ballast.

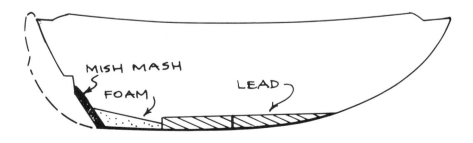

MISH MASH

FOAM

LEAD

INTERNAL LEAD BALLAST

10

Rudder Installation

There are no great mysteries clouding rudder installation. If you have the old-fashioned gudgeon-pintle set-up, see photo, then dry fit the factory supplied pintles onto the rudder. You should have the whole unit assembled at this point (gudgeons, pintles, washers, pins, etc.). If you have a rudder as heavy as ours, just struggle and strain and block it until you get it to align with the hull. It is wise practice to elevate the rudder's base about 2 inches above the keel so that if you ever ground the boat, the rudder will not be the one to take the punishment.

Once aligned, simply drill through the gudgeon holes. Using a pilot bit a good ¼ inch smaller than the final one may be advisable, for sometimes it's difficult to hit a hole through 3 or 4 inches of fiberglass. Once the gudgeon holes are drilled, remove all of the hardware, wash it and the hull with judicious amounts of acetone, then polysulphide everything in sight. Then re-assemble. The rudder installation is no place to save on caulking. If you are using stainless steel hardware, be sure to install some sacrificial zinc anodes to take the brunt of the electrolitic on-slaught set up with the bronze prop and bronze through-hulls.

If your boat has a single gudgeon arrangement into which the rudder shaft fits, see photo, you simply place a small worm-gear jack under the gudgeon with the rudder in it and jack it into place. When you can feel that the gudgeon is snug on the hull, yet the rudder swings freely, drill your pilot holes.

Single gudgeon at rudder base.

Old-fashioned gudgeon and pintle.

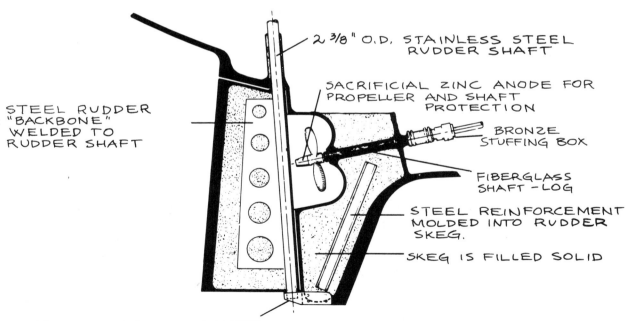

STEEL RUDDER
"BACKBONE"
WELDED TO
RUDDER SHAFT

2 3/8" O.D. STAINLESS STEEL
RUDDER SHAFT

SACRIFICIAL ZINC ANODE FOR
PROPELLER AND SHAFT
PROTECTION

BRONZE
STUFFING BOX

FIBERGLASS
SHAFT-LOG

STEEL REINFORCEMENT
MOLDED INTO RUDDER
SKEG.

SKEG IS FILLED SOLID

MANGANESE BRONZE LOWER
RUDDER GUDGEON THROUGH-BOLTED TO SKEG

GOOD RUDDER ASSEMBLY AND INSTALLATION

11

Leveling the Hull

Up to this point, eyeball leveling the hull upon setting it into the cradle was sufficient. Since the next operations such as cabin sole installation, bulkhead installation, etc. need to be precise to facilitate rapid completion, it is necessary at this point to level the hull fore, aft, and athwartships. Two common methods make leveling rapid; one is less expensive than the other.

String Level

For the less expensive of the two methods, leveling a bare hull athwartships requires a piece of slight string, pulled taut from bulwark to bulwark with a string-level set in center. Buy a cheap one because you'll probably never use one again. A small rented hydraulic jack will suffice for adjustment. If a trunk cabin is already installed, raise the bulwarks' height by attaching the string to the tops of two equal-length sticks. This procedure requires either two people or two C-clamps, so that you will have freedom to move into the center and read the level. Leveling fore and aft requires one more step since the bow of a boat is customarily higher than the stern. Therefore, you must compensate by setting the stern end of the string the desired measure higher than the bow and then begin the leveling. After fore and aft leveling is done,

recheck the athwartship level to make sure it has not been altered drastically.

Waterline and Tubing

Most fiberglass hulls have a scribe line etched into them to facilitate painting of waterline or boot stripe. By using (a) the knowledge that this line is level right around the hull and (b) about 70 feet of fairly costly transparent tubing, you can level the hull by a second method. Tape the tubing (garden hoses work as well although it's harder to see the bubbles through their walls) along the bottom of the keel, running it from a few inches above the waterline in the bow to a few inches above the waterline in the stern. Run another piece of hose from a similar height above the waterline amidships down under the keel and up past the line on the other side. Now fill the tubing with water until it is close to the waterline in both hoses; whether above or below is of little consequence because we're looking for equal distances and not exact fittings. Now you can jack and shim the cradle until the water level is equidistant from the waterline in both ends of each hose.

This method is preferred over the string and level, because it may be left on the hull indefinitely without getting in the way as the string-level system will. One danger here is that if the tape used to hold the tubing is left on for over a few weeks in a hot climate, it may be impossible to remove it without peeling off substantial swatches of gelcoat. It is advisable to retape in different locations at different times.

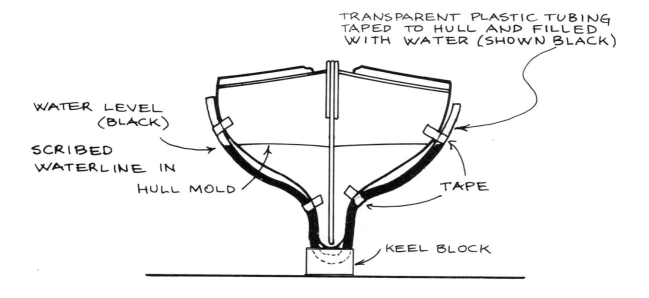

TRANSPARENT PLASTIC TUBING TAPED TO HULL AND FILLED WITH WATER (SHOWN BLACK)

WATER LEVEL (BLACK)

SCRIBED WATERLINE IN HULL MOLD

TAPE

KEEL BLOCK

NOTE: JACK, BLOCK AND ADJUST HULL UNTIL WATER LEVEL IN TUBING IS EQUIDISTANT FROM WATERLINE PORT AND STARBOARD. SET UP HOSE FORE AND AFT AS WELL, AND LEVEL SIMILARLY.

12

Installing the Cabin Sole

Fiberglass Cabin Sole

If you choose to install a molded fiberglass sole provided by the manufacturer, your task is relatively simple. Now that the hull is level, you can simply lower the sole into place, level it, then bond the usually un-gelcoated edge onto the hull. The ends of the sole will have to be screwed into the floor timbers mounted on your bulkheads.

Use a good bedding compound between the timber and the fiberglass so that moisture won't have a chance to come and stay. Again, make certain that you wash everything with acetone before bonding, then follow regular bonding procedures. Once the bonds have gone off, find a heavy friend or two and ask them aboard. Then ask them to walk about. You will spot areas, hopefully not too many, where the glass sole flexes under their weight. If the flexing is over ⅛ inch, mark the location, for here reinforcement will be required.

If this location is outboard of a hatch-opening in the sole, then a number of knees must be installed. They need not be elaborate; ¾ inch plywood is sufficient. Exact fitting can be by-passed because the strength will come from bonding the plywood to the hull. It is a good idea to dry fit the pieces of mat and cloth that

will be required, for working away loose ends smoothly in tight corners is a very difficult operation. It may be simpler to wet these pieces out in place. Be sure to bond the knees to both the hull and the bottom of the cabin sole. Here, double bonding two layers of mat and cloth is a good idea.

In accessible areas where you cannot double-joint your arms to bond both sides of the knees, a sole timber should be installed as in the figure. This timber can be fir, mahogany, or oak 2" × 4" with the edges tapered to fit the hull. I recommend a loose fit, about ¼ inch on either end, for if you sledgehammer it into place, you may have a sharp point adjoining the hull. Because a sharp edge puts great stress on a very small area, it can cause the glass to flex around it and graze the gelcoat, as well as prematurely graze the glass.

Once it has been loosely fitted, remove the timber and brush healthy amounts of Cuprinol or a similar wood preservative on all surfaces but the last 4 inches on either end. Then take some mat, about five times longer than the angled end of the timber, wet it out, fold it five times, then slip it onto the hull where the timber ends will be. Let the resin go off, only enough so that it won't move but is still soft and tacky, then slip

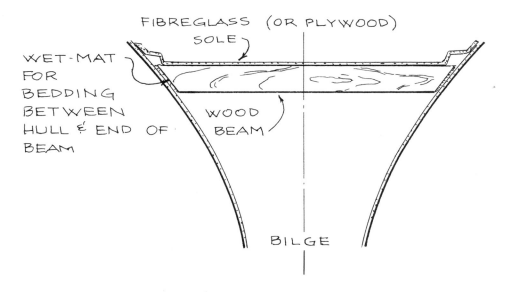

FIBREGLASS (OR PLYWOOD)
SOLE

WET-MAT
FOR
BEDDING
BETWEEN
HULL & END OF
BEAM

WOOD
BEAM

BILGE

Installing a floor timber to support the cabin sole.

the timber into place over the mat. After dry fitting some mat and cloth over both ends, bond the timber into place. Don't walk on the cabin sole above it for awhile. If you find after the bonds set that the timber has settled heavily, leaving a gap between it and the sole, slip a long preservative-treated slat of a wedge between them. Do not try to place a wedge between the timber and the hull. You will create hard spots.

Plywood Sole

This type of sole requires the laying of floor timbers similar to those mentioned above, about every 12 inches with a pair of longitudinal members, which must be let into the ones running athwartships, as shown in the figure.

The critical point here is that all timbers running athwartships, especially the ones that will adjoin bulkheads, must be absolutely square to the centerline. This alignment can be done by running a string fore and aft at sole level and using a large carpenter's square to adjust the timbers. The timber joints should be clamped

and glued (resorcinal glue may be advisable here), then bonded to the hull. Make sure that no bonding material comes any higher than the top of the timbers, for it will interfere with fitting the plywood sole over them. When the bonds have gone off, treat all exposed areas with the aforementioned Cuprinol or other wood preservative. Do not treat the tops against which the plywood sole will be laid, for the sole will have to be glued and glue does not adhere to the oily Cuprinol.

It may be necessary to make templates for the plywood, unless the manufacturer supplies you with patterns. For this purpose, one can use inexpensive ⅛ inch veneer and staples. The next step is to cut the veneer into narrow slats (2 inches wide is plenty), then cut them to about 1½ foot lengths and lay them on top of the floor timbers as close to the hull as possible. Overlap the pieces slightly, then staple the overlaps to each other. Staple some extra braces athwartships, so that you can handle the templates without changing their shape, then simply place the rigidified *or* reinforced template on a sheet of

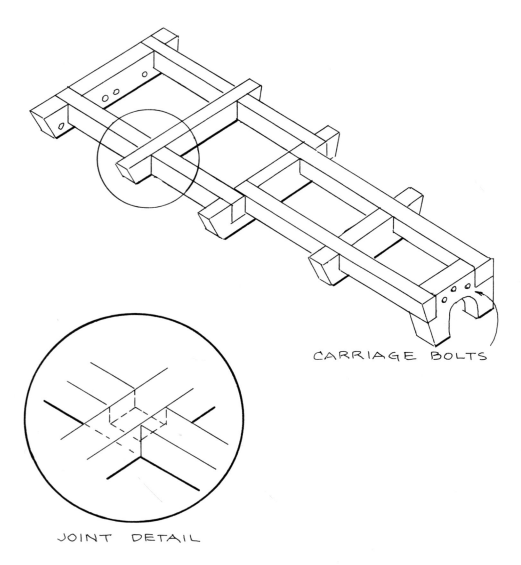

CARRIAGE BOLTS

JOINT DETAIL

If you build your own cabin sole, you'll have to build a set of floor timbers something like these to support it. If you want a simpler method, you could just make the transvers timbers, bond them into the hull individually, making sure they're perfectly level to each other as well as themselves, then lay a heavy plywood sole over it and bond it to the hull all around.

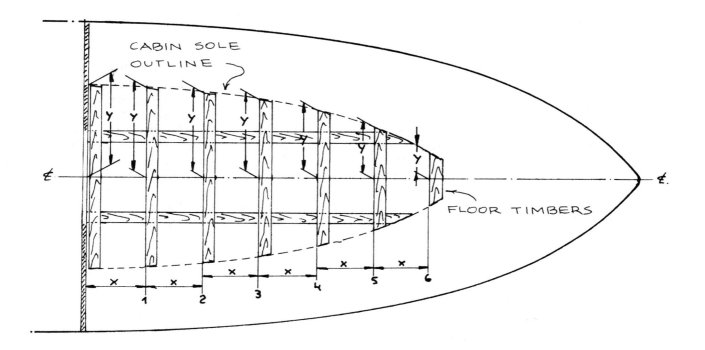

CABIN SOLE
OUTLINE

FLOOR TIMBERS

PROCEDURE :

A) MEASURE EACH TIMBER'S LENGTH (STATION 0 THROUGH 6)
B) MEASURE DISTANCE BETWEEN TIMBERS "X"
C) RECONSTRUCT EXACT POSITIONS OF ALL POINTS @ "X"
    AND "Y" ON PLYWOOD SHEET, THEN JOIN ALL POINTS
    AND CUT OUT OUTLINE.

plywood and trace.

It may be just as easy to substitute measuring for the templates. If one end of the sole timber is square, then you can simply measure points across each timber and place a mark at the opposite appropriate distance from the plywood square end, see figure. Then join the points and you will have your outline. If the resulting fit is within ½ inch of the hull (it can be left too small but not too big) do not worry, for you will glue and screw the plywood to the timbers, then bond the plywood to the hull. If the rest of your boat is built as solidly as this cabin sole, it will last forever.

If at all possible, crawl into the bilge and treat the underside of the plywood. You may have a demanding task, but it is well worth the effort because fresh water from sinks, glasses, or rains will easily find its way down here and cause dry rot.

It is also good practice to build the sole in sections, that is from bulkhead to bulkhead, then install the bulkhead, then go on with laying timbers for the next section. In this way you'll be able to have the bulkhead come down past the timbers enabling gluing and through-bolting, giving a very positive, lasting joint.

Mast Step Support

If you are stepping your mast on deck, you'll need to transfer the compression load from its base to the keel, or at least to the ballast. A support post should be wedged between the cabin top and the sole. This post in turn must be supported by a large block of wood at least 6 inches wide between the sole and the keel. If the block of wood is laminated from a number of pieces so much the better, for then it won't be as prone to crack or warp. The block should be fitted very snugly, as should the post above it. Then bond it into place, then treat it well or paint it. Working in these areas may be difficult because of the usually limited space but the extra effort will pay good dividends.

If design allows, the mast support post should be attached to the edge of a structural bulkhead to tie the structural posts tightly together.

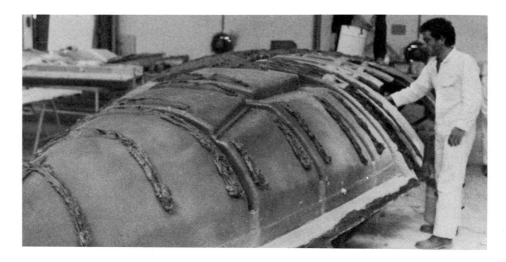

If a liner is used, its underside should be generously laden in the contact areas with great gobs of resin-putty, so when the liner is laid into the hull, good adhesion will be had and the liner will actually reinforce the hull instead of just hiding it.

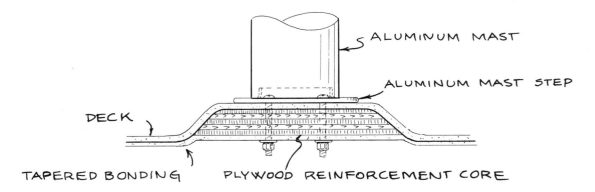

ALUMINUM MAST

ALUMINUM MAST STEP

DECK

TAPERED BONDING   PLYWOOD REINFORCEMENT CORE

The cabin top has to be generously reinforced if the mast is to be stepped on deck, usually built up about 2 inch out of layers of plywood with bonding over. From this point down the mast must be tightly shored.

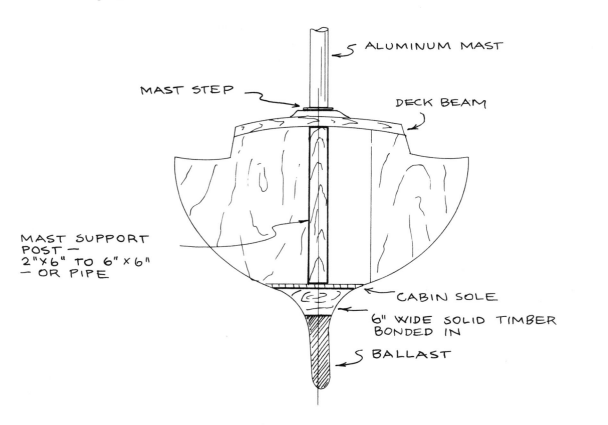

ALUMINUM MAST

MAST STEP

DECK BEAM

MAST SUPPORT
POST —
2"×6" TO 6"×6"
— OR PIPE

CABIN SOLE

6" WIDE SOLID TIMBER
BONDED IN

BALLAST

Deck-stepped mast and its support. Note: there must be continuous bracing (no spaces) from the top of the ballast right through to the mast. If the mast support can be attached to the main bulkhead, so much the better.

13

Bulkhead Installation

As mentioned before, this operation can and should go hand in hand with installing the floor timbers. You will get the most accurate results by installing them at the same time. If you choose, however, you may install either the entire cabin sole (leaving plywood spacers between timbers where the bulkheads are to go), or the bulkheads first.

Bare Hull Bulkheads

If the boat is not decked, your task will be easier, because you will have ample room to move larger pieces of plywood about, see photo.

First mark the distance your bulkhead will be from either stern or bow (whichever is closer), on your bulwarks. Make sure the points on each side are indeed equidistant from the bow or stern; i.e. square to the centerline, as shown in the figure. Temporarily attach, with either clamps or bolts, the least warped piece of $2'' \times 4''$ or even better $2'' \times 6''$ that you can find, from one bulwark to the other. This bolted or clamped attachment has to be a firm one, not only so that the piece of stiffener won't move fore and aft, but also to prevent the hull from losing its shape when you are standing in it.

If you have a prefab deck to be installed later, it is advisable to measure its width in the bulk-

head areas at this time and adjust the hull accordingly using the cross-piece as a stiffener. Later adjustment will be extremely difficult once the bulkheads are bonded in. If you have your floor timbers installed, your task will be simpler; for you can now install a true $2'' \times 4''$ vertically, attaching its bottom to the floor timber and its top to the temporary cross-member. This vertical $2'' \times 4''$ should be located at the point where the most inboard edge of your bulkhead will be. It, of course, must be perfectly level.

From this point on, you will have two choices: (a) make up the template for the bulkhead out of $^{1}/_{8}$ inch plywood strap or (b) measure across from the vertical member at given level points, see figure. The latter method is considerably more practicable because you won't have a giant template to move about. When using the measuring method, add an extra inch to your measurement and try to unite the outboard points with curves instead of straight lines. When cut, you will find the curve sitting fairly well to the hull with, of course, the bulkhead being 1 inch too wide.

Now, using an ordinary compass and a pencil set to a 1 inch gap, run the metal arm of the compass along the hull as shown in the figure. This procedure will leave a pencil line on your bulkhead which will be a true reproduction of

With most of the interior cabinetry finished and the deck completely equipped with hatches, hardware etc., the deck gets lowered into place.

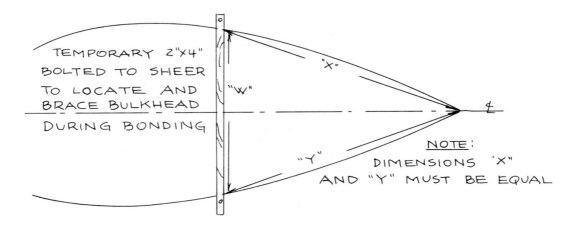

TEMPORARY 2"x4"
BOLTED TO SHEER
TO LOCATE AND
BRACE BULKHEAD
DURING BONDING

"X"

"W"

"Y"

℄

NOTE:
DIMENSIONS "X"
AND "Y" MUST BE EQUAL

Locating and setting up hull for installation of main bulkhead. Once installed, this bulkhead can be used to locate all others.

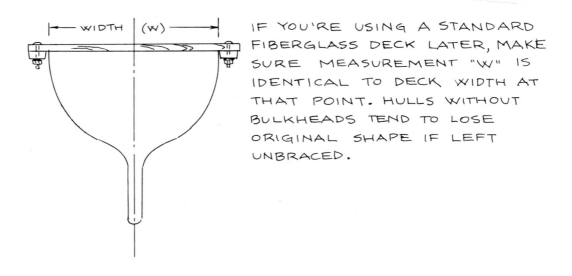

|← WIDTH   (W) →|

IF YOU'RE USING A STANDARD
FIBERGLASS DECK LATER, MAKE
SURE MEASUREMENT "W" IS
IDENTICAL TO DECK WIDTH AT
THAT POINT. HULLS WITHOUT
BULKHEADS TEND TO LOSE
ORIGINAL SHAPE IF LEFT
UNBRACED.

Bracing hull to proper width (measured beam) before setting in main bulkhead.

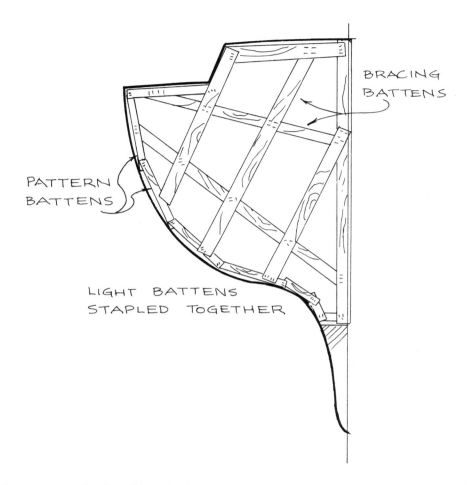

The more complex but ultimately the more accurate way of measuring for a bulkhead is by creating a pattern, made up of very light plywood battens.

the hull's curvature. In addition to trimming the bulkhead to fit snugly, you should somewhat overtrim, depending on what sort of spacer you intend to use between the bulkhead and the hull. One inch urethane foam (acetone or resin will not dissolve it) cut on 45 degree angles on either side of the plywood (see *To Find a Hull*) is commonly used.

We used urethane foam. It was simple and fast, but some argue that with constant work the bulkheads and hull undergo at sea, the foam will eventually wear away to dust. If so you will still have a very nicely curved bond over either side of the bulkhead. Therefore I don't think this argument is completely valid; but if you do dislike this method, you have the alternative of

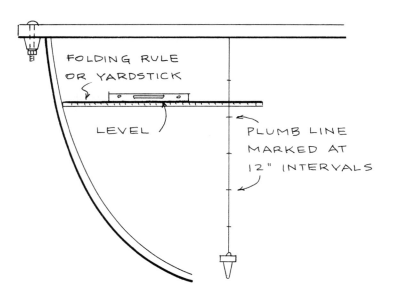

The quick and dirty method of rough measuring a bulkhead. If done by two people – one reading the level the other holding the ruler at the string and reading the lengths – it can be a good system. To make things easier tape the level solidly to the yardstick. To allow for mistakes, cut bulkhead 1 inch too large and trim later to size.

placing a run of fiberglass rope of generous diameter between the hull and the bulkhead. The rope is more expensive and will not give you as gentle a curve as the foam unless you get enormous line at enormous expense, but it will surely last forever and remain an ideal movement absorber.

You may think it a fatuous point, but make certain that you leave enough plywood on the upper end of the bulkhead to reach the top of the cabin and deck when it is installed. A good friend totally forgot that he *wasn't* building a flush-deck and chopped the upper end of his bulkheads off. Three-quarter inch ABX mahogany can run about $45.00 a sheet, and tearing out already bonded bulkheads is no fun.

Also, remember to cut off the lower end of the bulkhead that protrudes past the bottom edge of the sole timber. Water may be passing through here; this protrusion may catch flotsam and jetsum, absorb moisture, and rot. Therefore, cut it off and treat the bottom with a preservative.

Now that the bulkhead fits everywhere, temporarily clamp and screw it to the sole-timber, vertical member, and the horizontal member so that it is as immobilized as possible. Bond it into place. For smaller bulkheads such as the chain locker bulkhead, engine room, and lazarette bulkhead with no passageway through their centers and no floor timbers to meet them, clamp only the top horizontal members and use a plumb line or level. These bulkheads should be fairly small and easy to handle, so that making templates is advantageous over measuring for them.

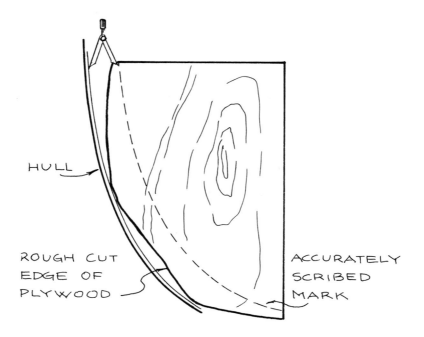

HULL

ROUGH CUT
EDGE OF
PLYWOOD

ACCURATELY
SCRIBED
MARK

Once you've got your bulkhead rough-cut to size (if it's as rough as Candace's bulkhead you may as well give up boatbuilding right now and start a career chopping firewood) you can scribe the final curve onto it with a pencil-and-compass, then trim it with the saber saw.

Deck and Cabin Top Installed

If you have bought a boat with deck installed, you will be more limited in your maneuvering, but you can do a good final job the first time you fit your bulkheads. Instead of attempting installation of a horizontal top member, screw some pads into the cabin top, making sure you don't come through the outside of the deck. Now measure the vertical distance from the cabin top to the lower edge of the floor timber at the spot where the most inboard edge of the plywood bulkhead will go. If the deck has a crown, make a small template for it, and scribe it onto the plywood. You can then add in the angle of the cabin side-slant, if any, with a bevel square as in the figure.

After you determine the distance from the cabin side's bottom to the hull, you may use either the template method or the level-measure method. Whichever you use, do it fairly accurately because it takes a lot of effort and patience to repeatedly trim and try-fit a bulky piece in a tight place. I guess that's why they call them bulkheads. Go ahead and bond the bulkhead to the hull and to the fiberglass deck or cabin top, especially if it's a main bulkhead adjoining the mast support.

14

Deck Installation

Fiberglass Deck

Leave on the temporary 2" × 4" cross members that you put atop the bulwarks and put the deck in place. Play around with the deck and make sure it fits everywhere; if not, this is the time to cut or modify. Then wipe off both hull and deck flange with acetone, cover the hull flange with great amounts of polysulphide, and fasten down the bow or stern then work amidships, pulling out the temporary cross-members as you go. This is not the time to through-bolt, for it's a slow two-man operation. Use hefty No. 14 sheet metal screws. They will be more than sufficient to hold the hull and deck together while all of the fitting is done. You can then pull them out and replace them with bolts. When so doing, don't be afraid to shoot a blob of polysulphide into each hole before you slip the bolt into place. It will be messy for the man putting on the nuts and the washers, but it will stop leaks.

If you have bulwarks, the fitting will be easier because you can cut plywood U-clamps, see photo. Using these plywood clamps in conjunction with a pair of bar clamps, you will get a perfect match throughout.

For through-bolting, use at least ¼ inch flat head stainless steel machine screws. You will have to countersink them so that you can cover the heads with filler or caprail or whatever. Be careful not to countersink too deep, for you'll go right through the glass and lose any grip of the bolt's head. On the inside, you will require a flat washer, a lock washer, and a nut. You can substitute a nylon insert lock nut for the lock washer and nut to save you handling an extra piece but they are expensive and harder to turn than the ordinary nut, which you can usually just spin on until it hits the washer. Pull the nuts tight. You may not have a chance to get at them again.

Wood Deck

I will not elaborate on wood deck and cabin construction. There are many excellent books (for example Chappelle) that are extremely thorough and their authors are much more knowledgeable than I on this topic. I will, however, mention those items which are relevant to fiberglass hulls only.

1. Hull to deck joint
The best hull-to-deck joint in this instance is achieved by usage of a sheer clamp. The clamp should be a clear (no knots) length, a full 5" × 3" mahogany or oak or fir. If your hull is as beamy as ours and a double-ender to boot, you may have to laminate the clamp from four pieces of

Plywood clamps for holding deck during installation.

stock, placing one on the hull after another, using resorcinal glue in between each. You should screw the pieces together, for if you use clamps you'll have to wait until the glue goes off on the first joint before you are able to proceed. As for choice of wood, oak holds screws the best but it also rots. Fir is easy to get and easy to work with, so perhaps it is the best wood to use. Mahogany is also relatively inexpensive and comes in long clear pieces.

Now bond (just tack, see hull reinforcement) the sheer clamp into place, then when you're sure it's where you want it, double bond it as shown. The location of the sheer clamp from the top of the hull is, of course, vital. Predetermine how thick your laminated deck beams will be; add to that number the thickness of the two layers of plywood or whatever you will use as decking. Using this total, measure down from your sheer. This total will give you the location of the top of your sheer clamp, see figure.

When you are laminating be sure to wipe the glue that squeezes out, immediately. If you don't, it will take you twenty times longer to chisel off the hard brittle little mounds later on. Through-bolt the sheer clamp every 6 inches, then place the deck beams atop it on 12 inch centers. Through-bolt and glue the deck beams to the sheer clamp, using one $5/16$ or $3/8$ inch bolt. Stainless would be nice here to use, but galvanized costs about one-eighth the amount, so I will let your own discretion and pocketbook determine the selection. Fill the space between the beams atop the sheer clamp with blocks.

2. Sheeting

Now comes the rapid, rewarding part – sheeting the deck. If you prefer a nautical interior you can use a layer of tongue-and-groove directly over the beams. The type of wood you use is not important, but I would advise against cedar. Pretty and rot-proof as it is, it does not glue well

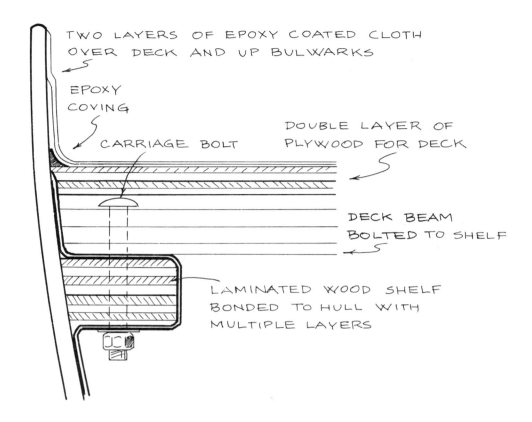

TWO LAYERS OF EPOXY COATED CLOTH
OVER DECK AND UP BULWARKS

EPOXY COVING

CARRIAGE BOLT

DOUBLE LAYER OF PLYWOOD FOR DECK

DECK BEAM BOLTED TO SHELF

LAMINATED WOOD SHELF BONDED TO HULL WITH MULTIPLE LAYERS

The proper way of building a wood deck onto a fiberglass hull. The laminated shelf is bonded to hull, then the deckbeams are bolted to shelf. Two staggered layers of ¼ inch or ⅜ inch plywood (¼ inch is enough if you're putting teak over it) follow, covered by two layers of epoxy coated fiberglass cloth or teak decking.

and soft as it is, it's not the finest nail holder in the world. Glue each tongue-and-groove onto each beam and nail it. Bronze ring nails are much less expensive than stainless steel screws. They hold almost as well and are fun to put in because they go fast.

The spacing of the tongue-and-groove is vital and must be planned for future changes in the wood. If you are certain that your wood is very dry, then don't squeeze the pieces perfectly tight. Once in the water, the wood will swell and the strips buckle. If you think your wood is at all green, hammer your tongue-and-groove as tightly as you can; otherwise as it dries it will shrink and open unsightly gaps between. It's advisable to lay the center piece of the tongue-and-groove in first, for then you will get a true line to work from. When pounding the tongue-and-groove into place, use a block of soft wood. Tongues and grooves as well are very delicate

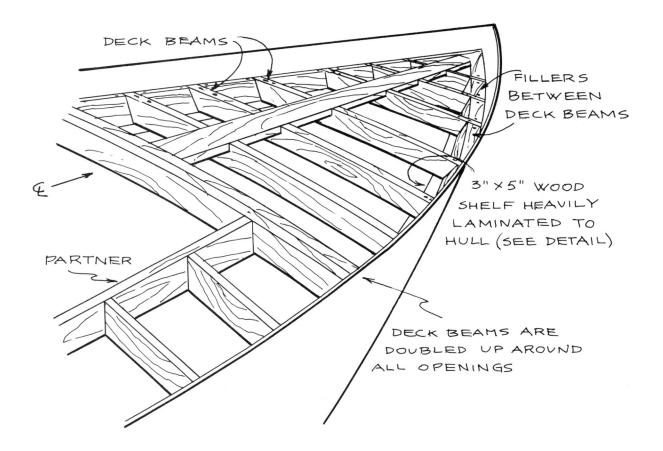

DECK BEAMS

FILLERS
BETWEEN
DECK BEAMS

3" X 5" WOOD
SHELF HEAVILY
LAMINATED TO
HULL (SEE DETAIL)

PARTNER

DECK BEAMS ARE
DOUBLED UP AROUND
ALL OPENINGS

The framing for a wood deck built into a fiberglass hull. The shelf is the actual piece that supports the deck structure. (See detail diagram.) The underneath part of the deckbeams are dressed and bullnosed and remain exposed belowdecks as the finished overhead. This may be the best way to build a traditional looking yacht.

beasts. It doesn't take much to break them off. Apart from looking bad because of chips or dents, they become almost impossible to fit together.

The laying of plywood is a somewhat similar procedure. It is cheaper, even though you may suffer more loss through scrap than with the narrow tongue-and-groove. It is a good idea to use plywood with tongue-and-groove edges, a material which is commonly used in decking for house construction. If you can't find a high enough grade manufactured thusly, then run your plywood through a table saw and rabbet the edges. It's not as firm a joint as the tongue-and-groove but it's infinitely better than butting the sheets together.

Two layers of ½ inch plywood laminated with the seams well staggered (or the second layer put on a diagonal as you would over tongue-and-groove strips) is preferred over a single sheet of

1 inch plywood. Where the first layer had to be nailed into the beams and the blocks above the sheer clamp, the second layer can be nailed anywhere into the first. When laying the second sheeting, mix only enough glue to see you through one sheet of plywood, for it may get tacky and be worthless. The best tool for spreading the glue evenly and not too thinly over a large surface is a serrated metal trowel that tile layers use. After the second layer is on, fill all of the cracks and flaws with a resin and mill-fiber combination (the nail heads should have been sunk just below the surface and filled as well), then sand the entire deck. After the deck-to-hull seam has been filled and sanded, you are ready to lay the fiberglass.

3. Laying the fiberglass
To get a well-sealed bond between hull and deck, the fiberglass layers covering the plywood deck sheeting should lap well over the seams and be bonded to the hull. The first layer of mat and cloth should overhang the second by 2 inches. In this way you will get a gradually even layer which will be easier to fill and feather than one obese seam.

4. Fairing out the bond
The filler to use for fairing out the bond is a mixture of resin and micro-balloons. Micro-balloons, a red foamish-looking powder, makes a very fine putty that, although it does not possess the inherent strength of mill-fiber or scrap fibers, is incomparably easier to sand and shape. Once the final shaping has been done, decrease the grit of sandpaper to 120 and finally 240, then do the gelcoating and painting, or lay your teak deck.

5. Gelcoating
For spraying gelcoat over fiberglass use a fine-tipped nozzle and do thin layers, constantly moving the gun to prevent runs. Be sure to tell the man at the place where you are renting the compressor (it costs only about $10.00 a day) what you will be doing and what kind of nozzle you will require. He will be happy to help you.

Catalyze the gelcoat only after it is in the sprayer; use it all up. If you have any left over, dump it and immediately half fill the gun with acetone. Spray it through to clean the nozzle. If you let the gelcoat go off, either in the can or in the nozzle, the job of cleaning will be monstrous. Spray a green APB over the gelcoat. APB seals it from air and helps in catalyzing.

6. Finishing the deck surface
For the deck, use something other than gelcoat. A good marine epoxy paint will do the job. After sanding the deck with 220, wipe it with acetone (I know this procedure is redundant, but you should never forget it). Then, using a roller apply the epoxy paint. While the paint is still wet, sprinkle on either silicone or ground walnut shells using a fine salt shaker. Either silicone or the walnut makes a perfect non-skid surface. When the first coat has dried, paint on a second one. Don't sprinkle it with anything.

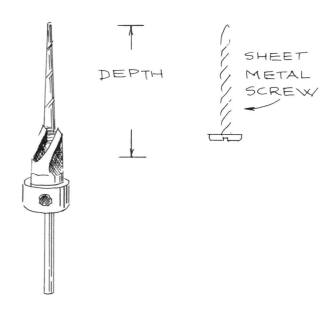

DEPTH

SHEET
METAL
SCREW

Set the depth of your drill-countersink as shown here. The extra ¼ inch or so is to allow room for the plug which will cover the screw head.

15

Rough Interior Installation

Whether you have bought the precut plywood interior or not, you will find installing the rough interior one of the quickest and visually most rewarding operations. The basic question is where to start or which piece to install first. Since the only immediate requirement is to have a flat place for assembly, I suggest you build a work bench. I don't mean to do extra work and fabricate a bench; I mean assemble that piece of cabinetry which will best substitute for one. A lower settee berth in the salon is ideal. It is wide enough, long enough and has a lot of elbow room around it.

Tools

If you are short on money, you can delay a large expenditure for a band saw, for it will not be of any great use here. A table saw would be of some help, but if you have access to one that could be enough. Then you will need a first-class saber saw to cut the plywood and cut out door holes, etc. You'll need a bevel square to measure angles, a small builder's square and perhaps a large one, a short one-handable level, two drill motors, three screw gun bits and three tapered drill bits with three No. 7 countersinks. For a 35 foot boat with a good amount of cabinetry you will need roughly: 10 pounds of Weldwood plastic glue

(resin glue that mixes with water); about 1,000 stainless steel No. 10 pan head self-tapping sheet metal screws 1 inch long and about 500 No. 10 screws ¾ inch long; 300 feet of ¾" × ¾" mahogany cleat stock (in 6 or 8 foot lengths): fifty acid brushes; fifty disposable cups; and a lot of rags. The above will enable you to permanently assemble the entire interior and set it temporarily in place, ready for bonding to the hull.

Since the construction of templates has been touched upon in the section of bulkhead installation, I will go on immediately to patterning and cutting.

Layout and Cutting

It is vital, whether you oil, varnish, or paint the plywood surface that the grain goes the same way on all of the pieces. If it does not, the boat will be an eye-disturbing frenzy of lines which may show through even four coats of paint. Therefore, make sure you have the grain either all horizontal or all vertical on each section of cabinetry.

When marking out door and drawer holes make certain that if a series exists in the same face, you cut the holes exactly the same size. It's well worth checking, for I've found it much easier to build and fit three identical drawers

Inserting saber saw blade into plywood.

than to plane, sand, and gouge three dissimilar ones to fit three dissimilar holes. This tip may seem trivial, but do try to make doors in different areas to an identical measurement if possible. I'm not advocating making twenty identical doors in a boat. But if one door is 9 inches and the other 8 inches why not compromise; it makes life a little bit easier.

For cutting, always use a sharp medium (7 teeth per inch) blade in your saber saw. Anything rougher than 7 teeth, or duller than very sharp, will have a disgusting tendency to chip irreplaceable chunks out of the plywood.

Cutting openings that will be filled with drop boards (tops of settees, berths, etc.) requires special attention, for the piece that you cut out should be used as the cover for the same hole. Therefore, you cannot use a drill to start a point of insert for the saber saw blade. You'll have to place the blade above the line, resting the frame of the saw on the wood for a pivot, see photo. Then start the motor, tilt it down slowly and gently so that the blade has time to penetrate evenly. At the Beneteau boatyards I have watched craftsmen cut *finished doors*, that is to say doors cut from a piece of teak plywood that will act as doors *in* the same piece and they do it freehand using only care.

For a lid, it's also good practice to mark the corners with a compass or a quarter so that you can execute its extraction with one uninterrupted cut. Not only will rounding the corner enable you to escape making four 'tilt penetration' cuts; it will also give you well rounded corners on the lid that will not break off nor penetrate your big toe when dropped.

The edges of the lids should be lightly bull-nosed (1/4 inch). Cut the finger holes to a 1 inch diameter, a dimension which seems to fit an average finger. Any hole smaller will not allow you to reach into it with sailing gloves on. The finger hole should be generously bull-nosed with a 3/8 inch bit for an easier fit of the finger and thus an easier lift. Once the lid has been cut off, seating cleats will have to be installed around the perimeter of the hole as shown in the figure, to keep the lid from disappearing in the abyss. Two inch or 1 1/2 inch stock cut from 1/2 inch plywood scraps is ideal here. A 3/8 inch lip is more than enough to support the lid. Make sure that you round and sand the corners of the seating cleat or slivers may befall you. Painting the bottoms of these surfaces before installation is a commendable idea, much easier at this time than trying to work around the corner hanging upside down in a dark hole later on.

Cabin sole cutouts should have seating cleats right around the hole, for much weight will be carried here; even a small hatch like this might carry the full load of a 200-pound sailor.

Cutouts in settees and cabinet tops can get away with just a pair of seating cleats along the long sides of the hole.

LID

½" × 1-½" OR 2" WIDE PLYWOOD STRIPS

A hole in a surface will have to have seating-cleats around it so when you put the lid back into place it doesn't fall through. Most lids will require just a piece on two facing sides of the hole, but cabin sole cutouts should be framed right around with seating cleats to support the load of a couple of people standing on it at a time.

A simple door of Bruynzeel plywood whose edge has been finished with a strip of veneer. But you have to make a nice cut with a good saber saw to do it. Take your time; it just takes a bit of care.

Cabinet side complete with cleatstock awaiting installation of adjoining plywood pieces.

Assembly

The assembly process falls into two major sections. One is plywood to plywood, the other is plywood to fiberglass (hull).

1. Wood to wood

The simplest way of attaching two pieces of plywood that come together at an angle is to use cleat stock made of mahogany or another wood that will hold screws well and will not split. To this cleat stock both pieces of plywood will be glued and screwed. A good size to use is ¾ inch square, for then you can rip it from ¾ inch by random width, random length stock, as shown in the figure. If an angle joint other than 90 degrees is to be made, simply rip your cleat at the required angle.

Once the pieces of plywood have been dry-fitted, wipe one piece where the cleat goes and the side of the cleat to be glued, with a wet cloth. Not only will the cloth clean both surfaces of dust and bits and pieces, but it will also wet them so that the glue won't be too rapidly absorbed. Measure and cut cleat stock to length, but make certain that you leave the last 4 inches of plywood which *adjoin* the hull uncleated. You will be able to make a much cleaner and better finished fiberglass bond if you leave the corners clean, see figure. Now:

- apply glue to ply and cleat with acid brush
- clamp cleat to plywood for steady drilling
- drill and countersink at 10 inch intervals going from plywood to cleat
- countersink should penetrate one-half way into wood
- insert screws
- remove clamps

It is important that you go from plywood to cleat with your screws because you prevent the possibility of the screw coming through the veneer or the cleat stock splitting if the screw is set too tightly.

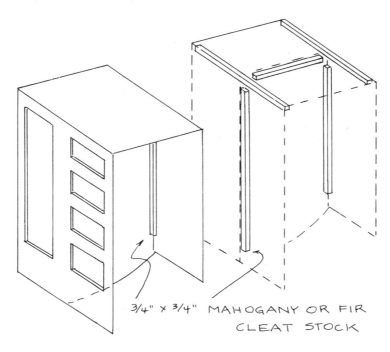

3/4" × 3/4" MAHOGANY OR FIR
CLEAT STOCK

Cabinet assembled using cleatstock that's glued and screwed to intersecting plywood pieces. As you can see from Candace's drawing, there is no need to make the cleatstock fit absolutely perfectly to each other for you won't be screwing that close to corners. Anyway, whoever crawls around inside your cabinets to check?

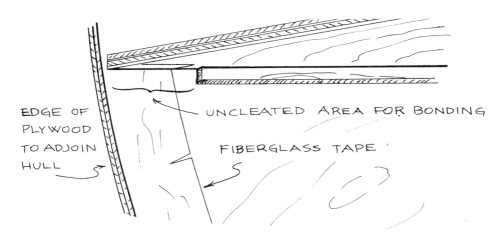

EDGE OF
PLYWOOD
TO ADJOIN
HULL

UNCLEATED AREA FOR BONDING

FIBERGLASS TAPE

When installing cleatstock into a cabinet that's to be bonded to the hull, stop the cleatstock about 3 inches short of the edge that'll touch the hull, otherwise you'll have one-hell-of-a-merry-time trying to finish off your bonding up and over and around the piece of cleatstock.

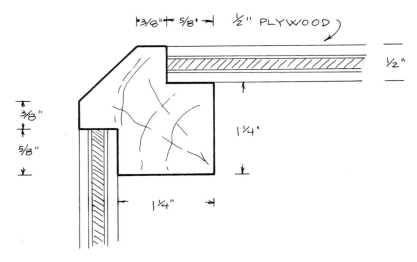

Cross-section of a milled teak cornerpost that acts as a structural as well as esthetic finishing piece where two pieces of plywood cabinetry join.

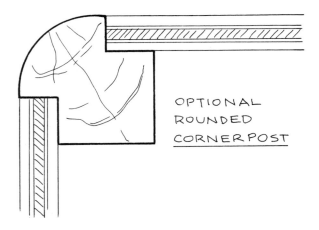

OPTIONAL
ROUNDED
CORNERPOST

A perhaps nicer cornerpost, but you'll have to do a lot of alert sanding with a belt-sander to create that nice curve.

Once the wood is assembled, all excess glue should be removed immediately and the wood wiped clean with a damp cloth. Nothing is more unsightly or harder to remove than a long brown dribble of hardened glue.

When joining two, what are to be finished surfaces at a corner, the simplest method is to use a corner post, as shown in the figure. The post should be milled out of hardwood, preferably of the kind to match the rest of your trim since it will remain exposed. Screws will be applied from the exterior faces of the plywood pieces, only slightly staggered so that they will not run into each other, forcing a new hole to be drilled. The diagram depicts standard corner posts for adjoining two ½ inch plywood pieces.

A milled corner piece coved to form an inside-corner cornerpost.

Milled corner piece so designed as to take sliding plexiglass doors.

2. Bonding to hull

The installation of cabinetry should be treated as seriously as the installation of bulkheads. In a fiberglass boat, every piece of plywood, whether longitudinal or lateral, will act as a structural component. The degree of importance of each cabinet will vary with its location and size but I don't believe any piece should be neglected.

Once the piece has been dry fitted to the hull (using a foam spacer may be time consuming, but it does isolate a potential hard edge from the glass) attach it temporarily into place by screwing into bulkheads or cabin sole or even temporary blocks. Make sure both horizontal and vertical surfaces are level; it will be much easier to fit adjoining pieces and trim. If something is out of square or level, now is your last chance to correct it. After you have bonded it into place, changes will be time consuming and very tiresome.

It is advisable to leave off the face or top from the piece of furniture to be installed to facilitate bonding. If you are using teak veneer surface plywood you should grind the teak veneer off the area where the bond will lay (3 inches adjoining the hull). Teak has great amounts of natural oil which will not allow it to bond with any reliability.

Grind all paint and rough burrs from the area to be bonded. Resin will not adhere to paint, and burrs will become an impossible nuisance to work around because they will act as a tent pole, creating a lofty air pocket between the surface and the bond. When grinding, cover eyes with goggles and wear long-sleeved shirts and gloves or you will suffer insufferable itching caused by glass specks lodging in your pores. It's advisable to tape the gloves to the shirt and tape the shirt sleeve shut tight to keep out the varmints. If you do get stuff on your skin, rinse it with soap and *cold* water. Warm water will open your pores and let the critters go deeper.

Once everything is sufficiently secured so that it won't move out of plumb even if knocked or leaned upon, and both surfaces to be bonded have been well washed with acetone, you are ready to bond.

Bonding

Bonding is a simple operation that is best left until the whole interior has been assembled and reasonably well secured.

1. Preparation

Since preparing for bonding is a rather complex proposition, I believe it to be much more practical to entirely clean the whole boat *once* of dust, scrap, dirt, and moisture; then all the cabinets can be bonded in with one or two full days of labor. If you try to do it over a number of days, at different stages of assembly, you'll waste tremendous time repeatedly cleaning up your boat, and much material for each bonding operation. You will have to use a new brush, new gloves, and a new container every time. Therefore, once the foregoing preparations have been done, gather up your bonding materials.

To bond cabinetry to the hull, it is common practice to use a layer of mat covered by an overlapping layer of cloth. You should use rolls of 6 inch wide mat and 8 inch wide cloth. They are both strong but the cloth gives a more pleasing and easily manageable finish. The average 35 foot boat will require about 100 yards of each.

2. Dry fitting

Cut and dry fit the pieces to their designated positions. If long areas are to be bonded, use lengths no greater than 2 feet at a time. Once the mat and cloth are wetted with resin they will hang, droop, and cling all over you like a coquettish cobra. Overlaps are not a moral crime, so cut the pieces shorter than 2 feet and save a lot of agony.

When bonding a curved surface to a hull it is stylish to cut V's into the mat every 10 or so inches, depending on the radius of the curve, so

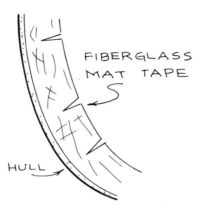

When taping (bonding) cabinetry to the hull, you'll have to notch the inside curve of the fiberglass tape or you'll end up with ugly little gathered lumps and that's a fate worse than death.

The outer edges of a teak bulkhead are routed down about $\frac{1}{16}$ to $\frac{1}{8}$ inch to make room for the bonds that will laminate the bulkhead to the hull. This will give a nicely finished edge to the bonds and will guarantee better adhesion to the plywood, for the top layer of oily teak is very difficult to bond to.

that the unstretchable mat will not bunch up and form a ghastly mound over which the cloth will not adhere acceptably. There is, however, no real need to cut V's into the cloth. It stretches and conforms and if you do get an unsmoothable bubble in a curve, just cut it in half with scissors and mat it down with a resin-wet brush. Clean your scissors with acetone as soon as possible or they will never shear again.

3. Wetting out
Once you have a few pieces dry fit (have a good batch done at one time so that you can wet out uninterruptedly for awhile) get a piece of cardboard that will be larger than your largest piece of cloth. You will use it to wet out the mat-cloth. 'Wetting out' means simply saturating the fiberglass with resin.

But first, have a good sized large-bladed fan over one of your hatches. The fan should be in operation at all times when bonding, because the resin emits highly intoxicating fumes which can result first in a good time, then, in brain damage. If you are working in very closed airless areas, place the fan as close to you as possible, blowing as much fresh air *towards* you as it can. It is important that the fan blow air into the boat rather than draw out the fumes. Blowing fresh air in prevents the possibility of the fumes and fan motor combining to start a fire.

Wear a disposable paper mask to keep floating bits of fiber out of your lungs. I suggest the disposable variety, for you will be incessantly touching the mask with your resin covered hands and an expensive mask would just become unusable after awhile.

Wear gloves. We found the cheap (10¢ each) surgical type rubber gloves the best kind. You might use up a dollar's worth a day but at least you are always working with clean supple gloves. If you try and use a good pair over and over, they will be covered with hardened resin and stray fibers which set like porcupine quills. They catch and gnarl every piece of fiberglass cloth at every opportunity. Don't try to wash

them with acetone. The thin rubber will break down and come apart like rotting onions.

Use disposable brushes with unpainted handles (the paint gets dissolved by acetone and flakes off in annoying little crusts). Cheap ones, about 50¢ each, can be had at surplus stores. To wash them when you take breaks during the day is fine, but by the day's end they will have a mountain of insoluably hardened resin at their base. Throw them away. The acetone you waste trying to clean them will cost you a lot more than the brush.

The best containers we found for mixing resin and catalyst were the plastic gallon or quart milk jugs. You can cut them away, see photo, leaving a large opening and a very useful handle. Drink lots of milk. It's good for you and it will save a lot of problems, because once the resin has set in the jug it is impossible to clean it completely. Hardened lumps will constantly turn up in the next batch, ruining your otherwise pristine work. If you must reuse a jug, allow the resin to harden, then jiggle, shake it, and smash it against a wall. The very pliable jug will flex and the rigid resin will gallantly fall away.

4. Catalyzing
MEK peroxide is the only commonly used catalyst. It must be thoroughly mixed with resin at a proportion of between 10 cc. and 70 cc. per gallon depending on the temperature and gel time required. At an ambient temperature of 77 degrees Fahrenheit, 1 per cent equals 10 cc. per US quart .

Accelerators such as DMA can be used if necessary, but only if mixed independently into the resin. If catalyst and accelerator are mixed together a nice explosion will likely occur.

I found it practical to use only a pint of resin at a time. This practice assured me of not wasting any resin through premature catalyzing in case uncalculated interruptions occurred. They always did too, because either the mat wouldn't fit or the power went off or something.

When all is ready, mix in the catalyst and stir

thoroughly. Lay the mat and the cloth on the cardboard; then pour resin over them. Spread it evenly with a brush soaking the mat-cloth with quick jabs, making certain that saturation is complete; that is, no white fibers remaining. Then peel the gooey mess from the cardboard (it will come away easily). After applying a good layer of resin on areas of the plywood and the hull that the bond is to cover, put it in place. Lay at least half the width of the tape onto the plywood, for resin won't adhere to plywood as well as it does to fiberglass. If a choice must be made on or near a curve, put the wider half onto the wood; then, while holding with one hand, punch the mat-cloth with short punches of the resin-wet brush.

Do every square centimeter and get every air bubble, see photo. Any loose strands or protruding edges can and must be worked completely smooth at this time. Letting them go, only to have to grind at a later time, is absolute lunacy. You'll have itchy, irritating glass in your eyes, your clothes, and your nose. Work fast or your expensive resin will gel in the jug. Work off all the excess resin with a brush and go onto the next piece.

It's very rewarding to have two people perform this operation. While one is wetting out on the cardboard, the other can be putting a piece in place. It is most difficult to have to do both operations yourself, especially if you have to crawl to the depths of some locker with each new piece. As mentioned, be sure to get the fan very close to you in these confined areas. You'll need every gasp of fresh air you can get. If you get to feel like you'd like to lie down and go to sleep; get out of there before you do for a long time. If the resin starts to gel badly before you finish the piece, tear it out and acetone what remains on the hull. It can become so bad that you'll end up with a hard irremovable clump. On the opposite end, if after a few hours the resin still hasn't gone off, then place a small electric heater close to the bond to help it set.

You will find the inside corners most difficult to bond. If you followed advice and did not put cleat stock on the last few inches, your task will be easier. The best bonding method is to run the two straight pieces as close to the corner as possible, leaving only a small crack. Then take a square piece of mat-cloth (about 8" × 8") and cut 1½ inch Vs in all four sides. Wet out and work into place. It should be easy.

If possible, double bond both sides of plywood. In spite of other advice I would bond each cabinet so as to isolate it from all others. Not only will this localize leaks to keep water from spoiling goods in other lockers, but it will also help you find the source of the water in much less time.

After the bonds have all gone off, check for flaws or missed corners and, worst of all, lumps and cowlicks. These protrusions must be ground or you will have dangerous weapons in your cabinetry that will tear not only clothes and wrappings but also skin. Nothing can penetrate quicker or more painfully than a hardened strand of needle sharp fiberglass.

Bonding fiberglass to fiberglass (hull to deck) requires the same procedure. Upside down bonding, however, does present problems that you will be able to solve only after a giant piece of goo has draped all over your head. Use as small pieces as practicable.

As you can see, bonding requires no great amount of practice. The steps are basic and the results predictable. If you miss cleaning or pre-resining a surface, don't go to the river. It's important that you do the ritual but exactly why I'm not certain. Once, while bonding, I threw a running shoe into a sawdust filled locker. When I retrieved it an hour later, only half of it was willing to come away from the hull. The whole upper body remained solidly bonded where some resin had been spilled . . . and I hadn't even carefully washed my sneakers with acetone for quite some time.

Milk jug with part of top cut away but with handle intact makes for good resin container.

For large bulkheads, two pieces of plywood will have to be butted. The joint shown in the photo is simple to make requiring only a couple of passes through the table saw for both pieces. If your pieces are so large that you can't use clamps to hold them while the glue sets, just lay the pieces on the floor and use weights.

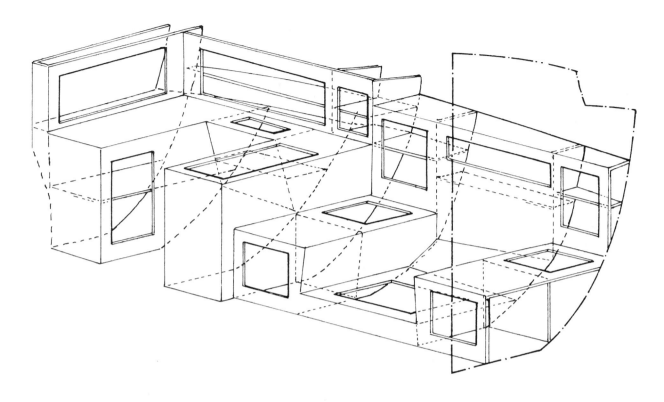

Recommended Sequence of Interior Assembly

1. Fit, install and bond all bulkheads.
2. Fit, install and bond cabin sole.
3. Fit and install (but don't bond yet) lower *vertical* cabinet parts, such as berth faces, iceboxes, galley cabinet faces and sides etc.
4. When all lower verticals are fitted, glued and screwed, *then* bond all pieces to hull.
5. Cut drop-board holes for top-loading lockers and install seating cleats. (See lower photo p. 246 and drawing p. 247)
6. Fit and install lower horizontal cabinet pieces, such as berth tops, seats, locker and counter tops.
7. Install upper cabinets.
8. Bond all lower cabinet horizontals and all upper cabinets to hull.

Note: To make life much easier, be sure all pieces are square to each other (whenever possible) and, if your boat is level, make sure all pieces are level *before* glueing and screwing together. If you don't, you might as well keep the axe handy; you'll need it for remodelling.

16

Insulation

One common complaint of all fiberglass boat owners is that their hulls 'sweat.' This condition is more aggravated in colder climates where condensation is more frequent, due to the great temperature difference between the heated interior and the very cold exterior.

Many excellent thermal insulators are available to boat builders and each has its own very valuable place in a boat.

Styrofoam

This material is a very good insulator. A ½ inch of styrofoam has the 'K Factor' (insulative quality) of 2 inches of common house insulating glass wool. It is easy to cut with a sharp knife and a metal straight edge. It's very light, quite inexpensive (about 30¢ a square foot), and very uncomplicated to attach. Any common tile cement applied to a few critical spots will hold it in place until a hard covering of wood liner is laid over. It is perfect to lay onto a hull, cabin side, or cabin top where tongue-and-groove or plywood can be used to cover and protect it. It is most impractical inside cabinets or in a place where no protection over it is planned, because even a paternal tap with a can of anchovies will cause a rivulet of cascading foam chips. Such an accident is messy and affects the life span of the foam quite adversely.

To cover over styrofoam with either plywood or strips, requires some ribbing to which one can fasten the covering wood. Two methods can be used for ribbing, one a little more expensive, the other quite dumb because it consumes a tremendous number of hours.

1. The dumb way
   - rip ¾ inch plywood into 1½ wide strips
   - cut to 24 inch lengths
   - run it through a table saw with the blade set so high that it will cut all but the last two layers of veneer
   - slit in this fashion at about 1 inch intervals, see figure
   - mix up a batch of mish-mash and using a putty knife squeeze it into the cracks, leave a judicious layer over the rest of it
   - acetone hull where rib is to fit, then fit it into place. It should bend easily. Now the only problem is holding it there. Brace it, however, with whatever you can until the mish-mash goes off

When using mish-mash the catalyst must be stirred into the resin first, then add the asbestos or whatever. It is advisable to practice on a small quantity until you ascertain the amounts of catalyst you require.

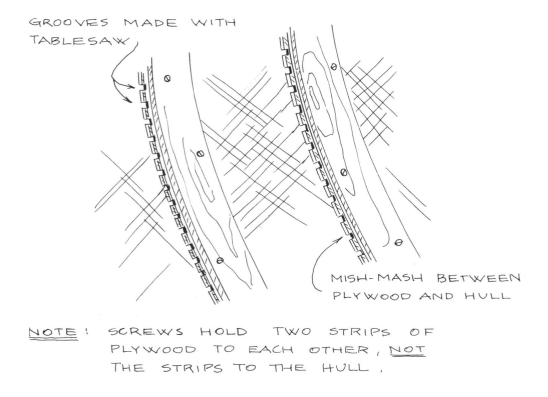

GROOVES MADE WITH
TABLE SAW

MISH-MASH BETWEEN
PLYWOOD AND HULL

NOTE : SCREWS HOLD TWO STRIPS OF
PLYWOOD TO EACH OTHER, NOT
THE STRIPS TO THE HULL .

This is the dumb way of making ribs that get bonded to hull. See text. The smart way is just to scribe in some cheap fir and cut it to shape.

Once the mish-mash has gone off, put at least a bond of mat tape over the rib just to be sure. You can nail or screw into the ribs, as well as slip ½ inch sheets of styrofoam in between them. The centers need not be more than 18 inches if you are using ⅜ inch plywood or tongue-and-groove to cover. If you are butting slats without any tongue-and-groove or other overlap, use 12 inch centers.

Decks and cabin tops usually have a core for stiffness; thus the ribs can be fastened with screws to the inner fiberglass skin while the mish-mash is going off so that awkward bracing won't be required.

2. The more expensive way

In the same fashion that you scribed plywood to fit the hull, scribe ribs out of 1¾ inch stock of fir, mahogany, or other easily workable woods. Ribs may have to be cut from as wide as 6 inch stock if the hull's curvature is drastic. Because once cut out these ribs have no tension forcing them straight, mish-mashing and bracing can be by-passed. A single layer of mat will bond them to the hull quite securely. You can fabricate your ribs to the thickness of styrofoam you wish to use.

Needless to say, I did our ceiling the dumb way, that's why I know it so well.

Rigid Urethane Foam

To insulate the rest of the hull, inside the cabinets, etc. is a grueling two day job but it may save mildewed clothes and soaked underwear. I at first thought it a simple matter, believing it feasible, economical, and rapid to simply spray the whole empty hull with urethane foam and then glass over it. You can rent a sprayer and the bonding should be easy in an open area.

This method has two giant failings: (a) if you insulate before you install the cabinetry you will have to bond the insulation to the thin covering of glass. Since the foam has no structural strength, the exercise would be similar to putting wallpaper over a layer of air, then trying to nail a picture hanger into it; (b) it's impossible to spray on a smooth even coat of urethane, even for the most experienced craftsman. The result, at best, would be wartish to the extent where a solid week would be required to bring the surface to a condition smooth enough for bonding over. The week would be spent at planing, curving, and grinding the foam, a dusty, itchy, miserably unrewarding task. Avoid it.

The remaining alternative is fitting and installing solid urethane foam sheets into cabinets after they have been bonded to the hull. This procedure is no dream job since you'll have to crawl into spaces you've previously considered too small for a dog, and work often in very dim light with very little air. The foam can be cut with a knife. If the surface is large and curved, the foam should be cut up to allow small straight pieces to form the required arch. A few spots of tile cement will suffice to hold the pieces in place until bonding.

Since bonding over the foam is necessary to protect it, one must use urethane. Like styrofoam, urethane comes in sheets of varying thickness and, although it is more expensive than styrofoam, it has two advantages. First, it is a 30 per cent better insulator. Second, it will not melt when used in conjunction with polyester resin. It is usually green or tan in color, is very

brittle, and is much itchier than styrene but you have to use it.

Because it is almost impossible to measure and cut large accurate pieces of mat to fit over the odd curves and angles of a cabinet's belly, I used 6 inch mat tape (the same that I used for bonding plywood to hull). A single layer of ounce and a half mat (with edges overlapped an inch) proved sufficient after numerous stress tests. The tests were quite basic, involving little more than dropping a quite ordinary hammer from assorted heights. If you can devise more profound testing, proceed.

One noteworthy point. When you are putting in the foam, leave a 2 inch gap between its upper edge and whatever plywood surface you have above it. When you bond over the foam, finish off the bond only onto the hull and not onto the plywood, see figure. We had made the mistake of doing the opposite. When water found its way onto the horizontal plywood surface, it ran behind the bond and into the sealed pocket formed by the lower bond. We didn't discover this mistake until installing a transducer. l was drilling from outside of the hull, waiting to see light, only to be showered by brown stale water. We ended up tearing a part of the insulation out and rebonding the whole cabinet. So beware.

Perhaps a few inconspicuous drain holes through the bottom of the bond would not be overcautious, but try to be sure that you don't drill through your hull. Again, as in bonding cabinetry, do as clean a job as possible, leaving no hard strands or upturned ends.

Once bonded, paint over all surfaces, first with a coat of undercoat (Z-Spar 105 or equivalent) then with one or two coats of easy-to-clean gloss or semigloss enamel. It's best to get mildew-proof paint. Although manufacturers of marine paints insist that their product exceeds all others in quality and wonderfulness, I have been reassured by those who know that paint is paint is paint. So use almost any exterior mildew-proof

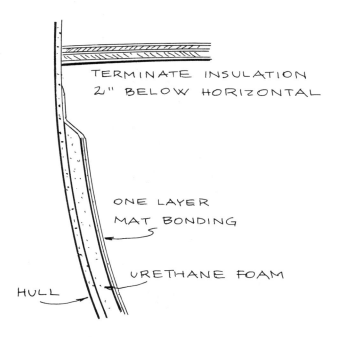

TERMINATE INSULATION
2" BELOW HORIZONTAL

ONE LAYER
MAT BONDING

URETHANE FOAM

HULL

When insulating the hull, it's best to end the insulation, and the bonding over it, a few inches short of the horizontal surface above it, then if water somehow seeps down from above, it won't end up being forever trapped in the insulation.

oil base. The cheaper the better.

Soft Urethane Foam

Some people advocate the use of soft urethane foam (like cushion) with a vinyl contact-cemented to the hull. I think that it is quite satisfactory under a wood cover, but I cannot see how a clean tidy fit can be achieved inside cabinets, for the shapes created by compound curves are almost unimaginable. Apart from esthetics, if heavy objects such as cans and tools

are to be stored, the soft foam will collapse to such an insignificant thickness that its insulative qualities will be measurably decimated.

I do, however, believe that neoprene foam (preferably the non-flammable type) is ideal for soundproofing the engine room. This material represents an expensive venture, but diesels are annoyingly noisy; therefore it may be worthwhile. Thickness of up to 1½ inch may be required to be effective. Applied to the engine room bulkheads and around the cockpit sides it should provide very comfortable passage.

17

Surface Covers

Once the rough interior is in, insulated, and painted the next item should be installation of cabinet surfaces.

Formica

This surface is inexpensive, easy to work with, and stands up fairly well to abuse; but it has its failings. If something hot is placed upon it by accident it will buckle and lift. To repair without tearing the whole thing off is impossible. If chipped or cracked or burnt, the same situation will exist. If you leave any kind of space, no matter how tiny, between the formica and the plywood, water may find its way in and rot the plywood beneath. If you still insist on using it, in spite of all these reasons, here are a few pointers I learned while applying it (not on our boat):

It can be rough cut to size with a skill saw. Overcut by at least $1/16$th of an inch. To rough cut, lay the formica onto a scrap sheet of plywood and set the saw blade so that only enough protrudes to barely cut through the formica. You'll have to flip up the guard and hold it, so you had better get a good two-handed grip on the saw. You'll need to grip well anyway because the formica is extremely slippery. Any little inattentiveness can result in wasting the whole $40

sheet. Once dry fit, cover the plywood top and the formica with contact cement. Don't miss any spots. I have heard of people using epoxy cement; I don't know how well it works, therefore I'll just mention the contact cement.

Once the glue has set sufficiently so that it is not tacky, cover the counter top with sheets of newspaper. Over the paper lay the formica in place as accurately as possible, then lift up one edge and pull out the piece of paper nearest the edge still resting on the plywood surface. Let the back few inches down and pound that area evenly but hard. Your fist will be the best tool to be used here. Now pull out the next piece of paper and repeat. In this way you'll be sure to get out all of the air bubbles. When adhered, rough grind the outer edge with a good metal file or trim with a small hand plane. If you chip the edge somewhat, don't worry, for a sea-rail will cover it.

Holes for drop boards will have to be treated differently. First of all, you have to cut them out with a saber saw. Begin by drilling to make room for the blade. To try the angle immersion method will only result in chipped formica or broken blades. Use a sharp hacksaw type blade with very fine teeth for a very smooth cut. Once the formica has adhered to the surface, file the overhangs into the hole with a good metal file (bastard file). When close to the plywood edge either apply a vertical formica edge or angle-file so that no sharp formica lip will stick out to crack and chip. If you use the vertical piece, file calmly and evenly until a 45 degree joint is achieved as shown in the figure. I have seen a lot of people cover both sides of their drop boards as well as the edges with formica to prevent warpage. This practice is probably very good, because a drop board of any size will in time absorb moisture unevenly, dry unevenly, and warp badly.

Wood Surfacing

A more preferable surfacing material is solid wood. It will not lift if heated; and if chipped, burnt, or scratched it can be sanded, filled, or just left. It will still look quite acceptable, and I think that teak or maple or oak looks an awful lot warmer and more emotionally stimulating than black formica with gold marble cracks and silver specs to boot. I admit that wood is more expensive and its fabrication is a lot more time demanding, but to me the results well justify the extra effort.

Wood selection is not critical. Teak is oily and will not rot, so that it can probably be used without any varnish or urethane protection. Oak and maple are very hard and stand beating well, but they are prone to rot, therefore they have to be coated with varnish or urethane. Oak is rather dark, offering little contrast to teak sea-rails.

To make a long story end, we used ash. It too is prone to rot and has to be sealed, but it has nice grain and an occasional beautiful knot. Even when it's varnished or oiled it remains sufficiently light to contrast ideally with teak or mahogany sea-rails. I must admit, it is an extremely hard wood, thus very difficult to work and fabricate. Ripping it requires patience and an exceptionally sharp carbide-tipped blade. Cutting to length on a band saw again demands an unhurried attitude or the blade will heat up and break. On the band saw you must not force the wood to cut curves. If your curves are of

drastically minute radius, get a very narrow blade (¼ inch) and feed your wood through with little, even force. Also, be familiar with your band saw; lower the blade-backing bearings as much as possible to offer maximum protection to the blade.

The width of planking used is a matter of personal preference. The narrower they are, the less loss in scraps. But of course the narrower they are the more labor required to fit and fasten them. At any rate, width can be left a choice. But thickness, I must emphasize, should not exceed ⅜ inch. I recommend this dimension because: (a) wood is expensive (about $1 a board foot for ash, at printing); (b) it adds substantial weight to the boat; and (c) a thinner piece is infinitely easier to sand or trim, when you are working with end grain. To this end I propose either having a mill rip some 1 inch stock in half for you or doing it yourself. I did ours myself without a joiner, ending up spending a considerable number of hours grinding the uneven thicknesses to some semblance of smoothness.

Once your stock is ready, clean off the plywood surface completely. Even the slightest sliver or drop of old glue (which should have been wiped up when still wet) can cause a most frustrating teeter-tottering. At this point the decision to use glue or bedding compound between the plywood and wood is to be made.

1. Bedding compound

This is not the cheap way to do it. Even the least expensive one like acrylic sealant bedding compound is expensive (about $1.00 per tube). It is also terribly messy to work with because to achieve proper sealing you must put a bead of caulking on the edge of each piece as well as the bottom of it to seal all cracks. Consequently, when two pieces are butted together, a great gush of caulking will surge upward onto your hands, screws, drill bits, and ears. In spite of all this, I think that bedding compound is preferable in areas where water may frequent such as the galley counters, cabin sole, and head sink counter.

The compound should be spread evenly, especially on the edges, to allow a tight fit. Clamps may be used in certain instances but I find them quite awkward. Therefore the most feasible although slow alternative is blocking and wedging each piece. This practice requires screwing a block (a piece of 1 inch by 2 or 3 inch ash is fine) into the plywood at whatever intervals you feel intense pressure will be necessary. The distance should be no more than 2 inches away from the piece to be wedged. If it is greater, the pressure may cause the wedge and the piece to tent up. Now, drive a wedge between the block and the piece to be fitted. Tap it only until the butt-fit is made. Any further wedging is superfluous and may even cause the screw in the block to bend. Should it bend, extraction is very tiresome and the screw will have to be discarded. Just think of throwing 5¢ into a lake each time you ruin a screw. Once butted, drill and countersink every 6 to 9 inches. A single screw per piece is sufficient up to 2½ inches in width. If your plank exceeds that dimension, I would use two screws side by side to make sure that the edges won't lift if any warping occurs.

If you are using the suggested ³/₈ inch stock, your countersinking skills will be put to the test, for you will have to penetrate deep enough to leave space for a secure plug (at least ³/₁₆ inch), yet shallow enough to allow the screw's shoulder to have a goodly thickness of wood to rest on (at least ³/₁₆ inch). So you can see your room for error is nil. To aid in this direction you should use flat head screws (No. 8's are heavy enough). Their heads are spacially less demanding than the pan heads. However, the heads also have a wedge-shaped bottom, as mentioned before, which may split the ash in half if not cautiously tightened. Therefore don't lean on your drill motor when screwing, but tighten it down so that all surfaces will be flush and all underbodies will be sealed.

When fitting the surfacing hardwood for drop boards, the most accurate method is to cut one piece to length at a time. Fasten down a piece leading to the edge of a hole; then using a continuation of the same piece to match the grain, cut a piece which will cover the drop board. Butt this piece tight to the first piece. Now, butt up the last section of the same piece and screw it into place. This way you'll have a tight fitting lid which will need trimming, for it's almost impossible to set each end up along the same line. The other alternative is to leave your hole cutting for last, but then installing the seating cleat will be a horrible job.

2. Glueing

On areas not likely to get wet often (I'm not sure such a thing exists on a boat), using resin glue instead of bedding compound is quite acceptable. It is also quicker and easier to wipe clean. You may save on screws here, because the screws act only as a clamp until the glue hardens. I think it quite safe to remove all screws once the glue is hard and use them elsewhere. If taken to extremes it may be possible to build a whole boat with twenty-seven reusable screws.

One last reassurance – complex as these operations may sound through my verbosity, I assure you that in practice they are not particularly mentally or manually taxing. Commonsense will see you through most of your problems. If you think things through thoroughly, you will discover your own procedure sequences, such as wiping all glue and bedding compound off immediately before it hardens or gets tacky. If you don't think such a thing through, and you leave it to set slightly, then try sanding it; you will find that most bedding compounds are soft enough to clog up every pore of an $1.00 belt in 23 seconds.

After sanding, seal the wood with varnish or urethane. It may be a good idea to use either of the two sealers to insert your plugs. If you use glue you will have great difficulty extracting them if the need ever arises.

Lining Fiberglass

As mentioned before, house-tops, sides, etc. may be lined with either tongue-and-groove solid wood, or plywood. The plywood is quicker if two people are doing the operation, because they will have no difficulty in shifting and holding large pieces into place. Plywood is also cheaper, yet it will result in considerably more waste. We used tongue-and-groove teak in our entire boat and I swear I lost only a little more than 20 lineal feet of 2¼ inch teak stock. Plywood may also be applied directly to fiberglass cabin sides or tops, whereas to tongue-and-groove here without ribs would be folly. No matter how cautious the tooling was on your deck mold, flaws and lumps still remain which your tongue-and-groove cannot follow or if it does follow it will only emphasize the problem through its harsh, seamed lines.

1. Installing plywood liner

Plywood can be applied to ribs (install ribs as per the section on ribbing for insulation). I would also put glue on each rib before screwing the plywood onto it.

If you choose not to use ribs, you will have a lesser task. After you have dry fitted your plywood pieces, simply apply a thick layer of mish-mash, stick the piece in place, and screw it tight. Before applying the mish-mash, set your countersink right at the top of the drill bit and drill a few ⅛ inch deep pot marks (about six to ten per square foot). The holes will give the mish-mash a better grip on the plywood. At Beneteau they use a serrated piece of metal to roughen the surface.

If you are installing the plywood liner where no plywood core is beneath it, for example on the cabin side, it may be a good idea to do so without using screws. Even the most skilled of us will have difficulty screwing and drilling into ¼ inch fiberglass just deep enough for the screw to hold and just shallow enough so that the thing doesn't stick out the other side.

The alternative is simple if the cabin sides are being lined, because portlights will be eventually fitted here (the sooner the better for they will provide ventilation and much needed light). Find the location of your portlights. Somewhere within the circle (or oval or whatever) they are to occupy, drill a ⅜ inch hole. When you dry fit the plywood piece that is to line this area, continue that hole through the plywood.

Now, after pot marking the underside of the plywood, cover it with mish-mash and stick it into place. Slip a bolt through the hole (using large plywood washers to distribute the pressure) and tighten the nut onto it. I hope that you decide to put in a lot of portlights because then you will have a lot of holes to slip a lot of bolts through for good adhesion. If, however, you have large areas where no holes can be drilled, use braces wherever you can. Try to leave braces and bolts overnight to make sure that the mish-mash has completely catalyzed.

In areas of great curvature, use as thin a plywood as possible (¼ inch is enough) or you will be attempting an impossible fit.

2. Tongue-and-groove

If you are having your wood milled, make sure that they put a ⅛ inch bull-nose on both edges. Then if the pieces shrink and open (ours did) the consequent gap won't look as out of place as it would on a theoretically unseamed surface. Tongue-and-groove is easy to apply over ribs. Once you tap the tongue into place, the piece will stay there in all but the worst curves until you stick a screw or nail into it. Don't forget to glue each piece. We used bronze ring nails to fasten our tongue-and-groove. They have very salty looking unevenly cast heads which I do not find offensive to look at. Obviously nailing is much easier and cheaper than screwing and plugging. Take your pick.

In areas of compound curvature (bow), it is advisable to have some friends present. It took three of us in some instances to force one 7 foot long piece into place. Here the tongue-and-groove is definitely a nuisance, for you're fighting compound curves which require a twist of the wood while bending. Then you have to fit the almost invisible tongue into an almost invisible groove. Good luck.

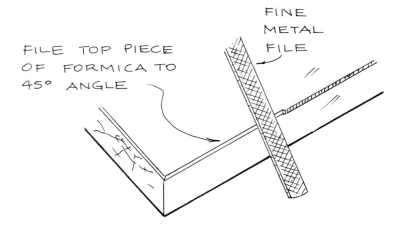

FILE TOP PIECE
OF FORMICA TO
45° ANGLE

FINE
METAL
FILE

If a formica surface is to take a vertical formica trim piece below it, run the surface piece past the trim piece then file the surface piece as shown for a nicely finished edge.

OPEN HINGE

Double flapped brass hinges that take the screw in their bottoms (that has an interesting ring to it) so the top is unbroken. Very Oriental looking.

18

Electrical Installation

This phase is most frightening if you haven't dealt with it before, but in actuality it is almost boringly undemanding. Most manufacturers will supply you with wiring diagrams which you can either follow or throw out. In most cases you can lead wire anywhere, place your lights anywhere, and put your switch panel almost anywhere. How to wire instruments is either self-explanatory or at least elaborately clarified on supplied instructions; however, I will touch upon a few generalities.

Primarily I feel obligated to press the aspect I consider most important: the best way to have a trouble-free electrical system is not to have one in the first place. If you must have one, keep it as basic and simple as possible so that it can't break down or, if it does, you can repair it with minimum effort and no parts. If you rely on parts, you're dead unless you never leave the US coast, because there is nothing more certain than as soon as you are out of sight of land, everything mechanical will cease to function as if on a given signal. The gravity of malfunction will increase geometrically the further you go and will reach its apex when you reach Tahiti, where, when you beg for a No. 10 butt-connector your cab driver will promptly locate for you a lady of the night.

That you will never find parts to fit your Acme

deep-freezer, your Sears Roebuck generator or your Warner-Brothers micro-wave oven is axiomatic, so think about it hard. If you can't do without, here are some points.

Batteries

Regardless of the size of your alternator you must have two batteries with a selector switch that enables you to draw off one or the other or both. One battery should be used strictly for starting the engine and nothing else. A blinding sign over this battery switch designating it as 'Engine' would not be a bad idea.

About 100 amp/hour heavy-duty recreational home or truck batteries will suffice. Place them in a plastic case, see photo, so spillage won't corrode everything in sight, but make sure the top of the box is ventilated so the very explosive hydrogen gas can dissipate. You can make your own battery cables. Since distances vary with each installation you may as well make your own. All you'll require is a given length of battery wire and four terminal couplings for the battery.

A Selector Switch

One four-position switch will be required. The

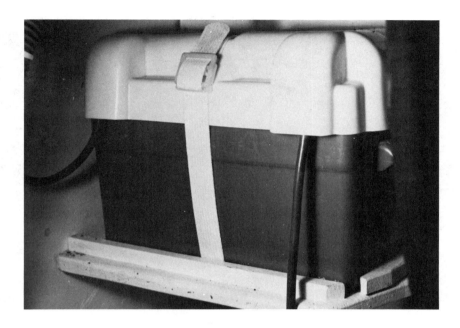

Plastic battery case.

positions are *Off, Battery 1, Battery 2,* and *All.* Buy a reliable switch for this purpose like a Perko or equivalent. Perko also makes an attachment for a large 60 amp fuse and it should be the only fuse on the boat. All other protection should be breaker type, because fuses are hard to replace in remote areas. Needless to say, the fuse should be installed as close to your switch panel as possible, both of them being placed well out of weather.

Breakers

To simplify matters, the best breaker system is the one which combines a toggle switch with a breaker in one unit, thereby halving the moving parts. It is quite true that you may wear out the breaker by constant use of it as an on/off switch. But practice has shown that these units last for very long periods without failure. Of course they are expensive, but I think well worth the cost. A

typical panel and system of fuses will have one common breaker for the navigation lights, servicing five breakerless toggle switches that control the mast head, anchor, red over green, and navigation and stern pulpit lights respectively. Their total draw does not exceed 20 amps, so the one breaker for all of them is sufficient.

Wire

Sixteen-gauge wire, color-coded for easy servicing will be sufficient for most 12 volt installations, including cabin lights and navigation lights. A 12-gauge wire should handle spreader lights, whereas 16-gauge will suffice for running lights. A No. 10 black can be used for a common ground to which all mast lights can be hooked.

I hear from experts that solid wire should be avoided in favor of the multi-strand cores. The multi-strand are more flexible and less prone to break in half if stressed or drastically bent.

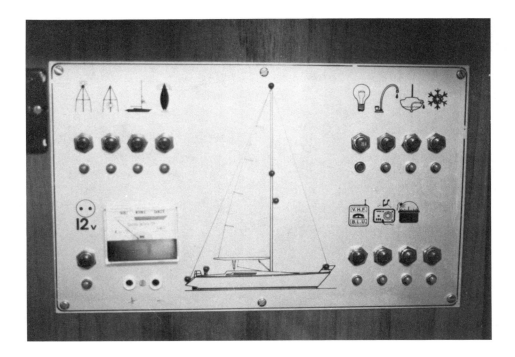

An electrical panel that even the most illiterate among us can comprehend.

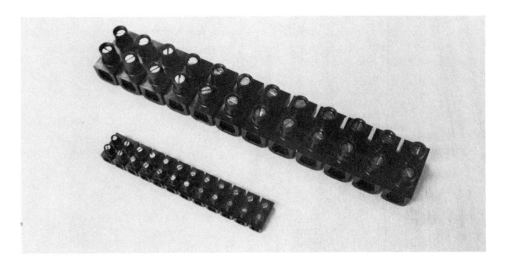

Bus-bar connectors should be used in a place where a large number of wires join.

Terminal Blocks

It is unwise to make inaccessible, unsealed splices in a boat. They will, in time, corrode. If the wire is hidden the corrosion may lead to problems. To make a group of wires more accessible all at once, a terminal block should be used where a number of wires are being spliced at one point (for example, at the mast base where the wires coming from the panel join the ones coming down the mast), see photo. The terminal block, in conjunction with end fittings, makes for a secure joint which can be inspected, cleaned, and serviced.

The same principal is applicable to the area around the chart table where wires from instruments meet the power supply lines. Blocks can be bought with different numbers of terminals on them. If the smallest block has too many terminals for you, cut it with a hack saw and use it wherever you can. On a multi-terminal block, save the fuss of connecting one return for each terminal by using a buss-bar, see photo. To the buss-bar you can connect one return wire and get a good job done inexpensively and accessibly. If you don't have the brass stock to make the buss-bar, a 10-gauge solid copper wire bent to interconnect the terminals will substitute nicely.

Conduit

All wires running through cabinetry or elsewhere in the boat should be run through a conduit. Here they will be out of harm's way instead of being cut or pinched or flying about madly chafing against each other. Inexpensive PVC of about 1 inch diameter will hold a lot of small gauge wires and it costs about 5¢ a foot. If wires turn sharp corners, it would be wise to use PVC elbows; the sharp edge of the pipe is prone to chafe through the wire casing.

To look slightly ahead and install two or three spare wires may be very advisable. Then should some uncorrectable failure befall a wire it could

simply be bypassed and one of the spares used in its place.

When terminating a conduit and running the wire on further, file the rough burrs off the end of the pipe. Then, as an added precaution, pull the wires out 3 extra inches, wrap a few generous layers of electrician's tape over the last protruding 6 inch length, and stick 3 inches back in the tube. The use of electrician's tape will help in potentially dangerous areas as well, for you will find places where the wires twist and turn over a short distance making conduiting impossible. In these areas, wrap all the wires over with electrician's tape and don't scrimp, see photo. To help with future servicing as well as initial connecting, use different colored wire and write down what is what.

Stripping

Be sure to use a good wire stripping tool with different gauges legibly indicated, see photo. There is nothing worse than having a beautifully laid out and executed system with wires that are half cut through because someone insisted on using cheapo adjustable strippers, or pliers, or an old bowie knife.

Tye Wraps

These items are very inexpensive and they can save a lot of chafing and unsightly wires, see photo. Tye wraps usually have an eye in which you can insert screws and fasten the mess out of harm's way. Make sure you put the wrap where you finally want it and make sure you don't have to run more wires through it later. Once it's pulled tight, the only way it can be removed is by cutting. This operation usually results in cut wires, or at least split wire casings.

Wire Connectors

Although inhumanly expensive for what they are, wire connectors are fast to use and they do

All wiring for the boat can be done in advance, made up into color-coded harnesses with fittings on both ends, ready to be put into the boat.

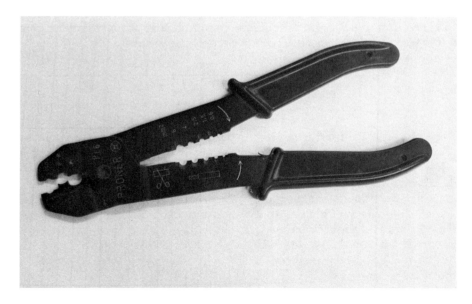

You'll have to have a good pair of wire strippers/crimps such as this one, if you are to do a good quality and relatively fast wiring job.

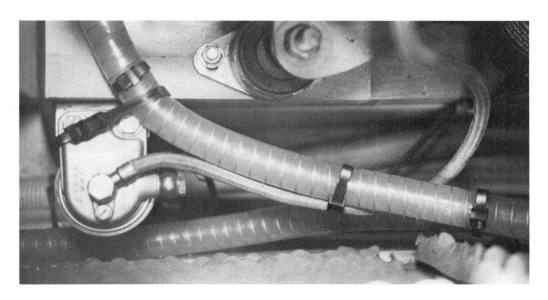

All hoses and wires should be tye-wrapped (plastic straps) to anything nearby as well as each other to keep them out of the way, and keep then from chafing.

Eye and fork connectors that can be readily crimped onto wire-ends with the black stripper-crimp in photo.

work. They come in different gauges and colors to fit all wires. When crimping, use only the appropriate tools (usually the same tool that you use for stripping will have a crimp on it) and press very firmly. Make sure you strip off only the amount of insulation necessary or you will have great lengths of unprotected wire dangling from the connector. Once crimped, you cannot hurt anything by applying a well spread dab of silicone sealer to either end of the connector to keep all the moisture possible out of there.

Lamps

Many will disagree, but I find the flat, diffused, relatively dim light given by dome lamps undramatic and boring. I much prefer a high intensity 12 volt light (same bulb as used in the powerful reading lamps) housed in a conical or cylindrical fixture. This type of lamp will give you wonderful amounts of light, see photo, for reading and working as well, lighting only specific areas, leaving others in the boat undisturbed, while adding depth, life, and mystery to your surroundings, through strong light/shade juxtaposition. (See Rembrandt.)

To connect these lights I began with the foolish surmise that I'll run one wire the length of the cabin, splice other wires into it at designated spots, and lead the branch wires to where the lights will be located. Very stupid. This method results in hours of extra work by creating the need for extra splices, which will probably be buried in some inaccessible pit. The logical solution is to run both wires to each lamp, terminate them in the fittings in the lamp, and begin the wiring for the next lamp on the same point (with, of course, the lamp switch in between). In this way you have uninterrupted wire from lamp to lamp, and connections only in the lamps where access is immediate.

One note. I have found, to my dismay, that only a pathetically meager selection of 12 volt boat lamps are available. All others are made for recreational vehicles; thus they are ordinarily steel which will last no time in salt air surroundings. A simple way to circumvent this problem is to buy critical parts of brass (swivel heads, switch buttons, etc.) and paint or shellac the other parts. If you are young and foolish like us you can have them brass plated, but that usually costs more than the lamps themselves.

Because we wanted the lamps in pieces (easier than taking them apart) for plating, we went directly to the manufacturer and were able to pick up many spare parts, like bayonet sprockets, switches, and springs and bolts, all of which would be most difficult to replace abroad. Stored in a well sealed plastic bag, they may be your best friends some day.

A good, all-brass directional reading light that uses high intensity 12v bulbs. Saves eyes.

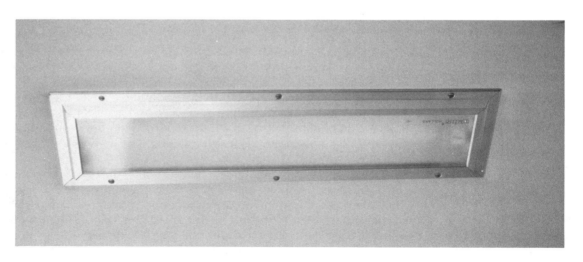

If you want fluorescent lights, don't get some monstrosity designed for mobile homes. This small, flush-fiitting unit is a Vetus, made in Holland.

19

Plumbing

Boat plumbing requires few specialized tools and no specific esoteric skills. The tools needed, you will probably have available. The only items you are likely to be missing are a pair of hole saws for the different sized seacocks you use, and a large channel lock which you must have to tighten the large inside nuts on the seacock through-hull fittings. A countersink to create holes into which the ¼ inch flat heads for the seacocks will be recessed, is also a must.

Seacocks

All underwater through-hull fittings should be fitted with seacocks of the levered manual shut-off variety. No gate valve should be substituted.

Wilcox-Crittendon and Groco make very good seacocks to choose from. If you're offered others, check to make sure that the T-bar shut-off holds, and that the T-bar shut-off locks and opens with a positive feel but with some facility. A most thorough engineer acquaintance has circumvented the problem of expensive seacocks by using all-bronze *ball-valves* which are common little doo-hickeys used in industrial plumbing. Now when I say *all-bronze* I mean *all-bronze* for the ball inside which does the shutting off is bronze as well, unlike most seacocks which use a neoprene drum for this purpose. Now whatever

you do, *do not* write or call me to inquire who sells these things for I haven't a single name, I promise. Try industrial plumbing suppliers.

Seacocks must, of course, be bronze, for plastic ones do harden after which levers and attachments can be snapped off with little force. Be sure the bolts, nuts, and washers you buy for them are also bronze and not red-brass, or you'll be inviting electrolysis.

1. Placement
Be absolutely sure that the location of each seacock will be such that ready access will not be hindered by cabinetry, wires, or hoses. Try shutting off and opening them in their final locale using both T-bar and the lever arm. Make sure you can do this in any circumstance. Make sure that if the necessity to dismantle arises you'll be able to get to all parts with tools without having to hack away through cabinets or dismantle half the boat.

Engine intake. It may be a very good idea to have two intakes, so if one gets clogged or covered by a floating plastic bag you'll have an alternative intake. Whether one or two are used, they should be guarded by exterior screens, see photo, which will limit the entry of most floating debris.

Head. Make sure that your head intake is

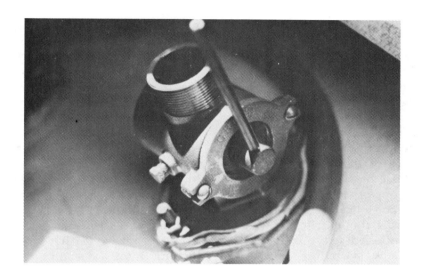

Barrel type seacock.

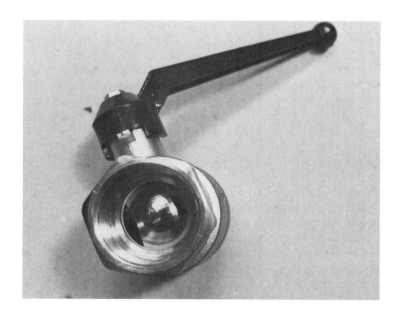

An all-bronze ball-type seacock with a 90 degree shut-off. It has much fewer moving parts than the drum-cored seacock, but it does have the disadvantage of not having a facility for being locked in the open or closed position, in other words it can relatively easily be opened or closed by mistake.

placed *forward* of your head outlet. Then if your boat is in motion (usually forward) or anchored in a current the refuse will not be immediately returned by the intake pump. An obvious point, you may say, but I've seen the most basic of mistakes made on a friend's boat by a supposedly professional marine plumber.

Place the head outlet below the head intake, as most water-logged refuse sinks or is forced downward because of the turn of the bilge. Pumping your refuse back into the boat is not only esthetically unpleasant, but it is most hazardous, as clumped toilet tissue can plug your intake solidly shut. I think it is also wise to install an aforementioned screen over this intake to minimize the possibility of such an occurrence.

2. Fittings and sealing

Dry fit all your seacocks. You may find, either because of hull irregularity or the drastic bilge curvature, that your seacock will not lie flush against the glass at all points. The remedy is simple. Grind the hull with a small disc sander until a perfect fit occurs; otherwise, you'll be inviting leaks.

Use a plywood donut in between the hull and the seacocks. The donut will take up some of the compression when you're trying to put the last half or quarter turn to get your seacocks aligned, see photo.

Be sure to use only polysulfide base sealers. Dolfinite drains out in hot weather and silicone sealer doesn't seem to stand up to salt water too well. Acrylic sealant is out of the question, because it is not waterproof. As redundant as this advice may be by now, I urge you to wipe all surfaces to be sealed with acetone to assure the best possible adhesion.

When tightening nuts, tighten only to the point where you can feel it begin to take hold. I did undergo the misfortune of stretching a soft bronze bolt over ¼ inch by relentlessly turning and tightening the nut.

If you install a seacock on the engine exhaust,

you can keep nasty following seas out of your engine, according to most experienced skippers. You don't need such an elaborate precaution on a yacht with blunt transom, as a simple flap made of leather or rubber and installed on the outside will work well. It should be top hinged so it will open only if the exhaust pressure forces it to.

The above is not a practical solution on double enders, however, where a following sea would hit the flap on an angle, forcing it open and rendering it useless. A more feasible idea would be installation of a seacock right at the through-hull. The seacock should, of course, be all bronze (some bronze ones have neoprene or plastic turning drums) to stand up to heat. And above all, it must be placed in a very accessible location where nothing will be stowed about it, possibly knocking the lever into shut position. It is an excellent idea to lock the seacock in the 'open' position; lock it shut only if drastic following seas occur. Opening and shutting the seacock constantly may result in the grave condition of forgetting that the thing is shut, starting up the engine, and drowning it.

You may reason that this seacock is a costly luxury, but you can actually use the spare seacock you save by not installing a drain for your head sink. I'm not sure that a head sink is a vital necessity; but if you do have one, arrange to drain it into the head. You then take double use of the head through-hull, instead of providing the seldom used sink with its own costly through-hull. Besides, the fewer holes in your hull, the better. Nor can one forget how appreciative any marine head would be if it were occasionally cleansed and flushed with nice soapy water.

Fuel

1. Tanks

Materials to be used for tanks were described in an earlier chapter, so they will be left out here. Refer to the figure for installation. Most discus-

A must on all engine intakes is this built-in screen which is part of the through-hull casting. It does a yeoman's job of keeping floating things like bits of plastic and such out of your engine's cooling system.

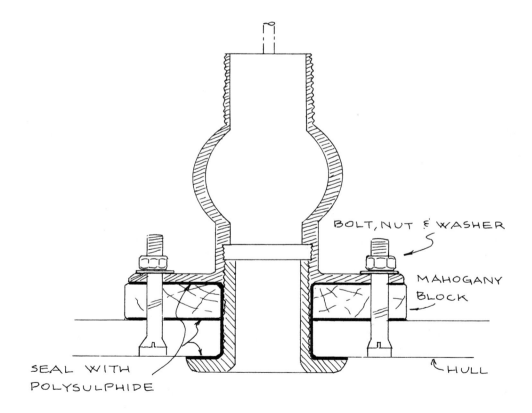

The proper installation for a seacock or through-hull. The bolt holes in the hull should be filled with epoxy putty and gelcoated over.

sion required was touched upon in the chapter on what to buy. Here are a few parts that were omitted.

2. Tank vents

These vents are required for all fuel and water tanks. Fuel tanks should vent overboard so diesel fumes or over filling will not foul the interior of the boat. Standard bronze vents exist for this purpose, available at most marine hardware stores. They should be installed as high up as possible to keep them as dry as possible. To prevent water entry, fill the vents with copper wool. And to help it even more, angle the vent hole about 45 degrees aft of vertical so your wake, or water thrown when heeled, will have a tendency to flow *by* instead of *in*. If you turn the hole higher than this angle you're inviting rain water.

As a further measure, it's good practice to put a loop into your venting hose. The hose itself can be clear plastic tubing, which is easy to work with. Be sure your loop isn't of such small radius that you overstrain or *break* the hose. Common hose clamps (all stainless) serve fine, and most plastic or rubber hosing will seal perfectly well onto plastic or bronze hose-barbs without requiring any additional putty or sealant.

The deck fills for diesel (should be bronze) should, if possible, be located directly over the tank's intake fitting. If so you will be able to use an ordinary piece of wood as a measuring stick to establish fuel level. Granted, other consideration should be given to fills (like not putting them where one may sit because they get awfully hot in the sun) to satisfy specific needs, but 'stick-check' potential should be a foremost consideration. The fills, of course, should be the screw down variety, see photo, of which keys are always lost, so have a few extras on hand. Some of the new generation genious caps are made to take a winch handle. Sometimes progress is just great. Bed the fills generously in bedding compound and cover the screw holes with a bead of it before installing the screws.

The best fill-to-tank connector is an accordion hose, see photo. These hoses are soft and pliable. They will guarantee an excellent seal even if the deck-fill and tank fitting are slightly out of ideal alignment. They come in different lengths, so get the best suited for you. See figure for fuel tank connections. Use these with diesel fuel only and make sure they are safety-rated.

A danger that is more likely to occur with gasoline engines is a spark of static electricity jumping from the fuel station's pump nozzle to the tank. If you are using a rubber accordion hose without a ground, this possibility is almost a certainty and it will mean a healthy explosion. To prevent such an occurrence run a piece of copper wire from the deck-fill to the tank. It is simple to solder one end onto the intake fitting and even simpler to attach the other to the screw that holds the small chain to the deck-fill. (The chain keeps the deck-fill from disappearing when unscrewed.)

Just a reminder; put some sort of cushioning beneath the tank, then strap or block or tie the tank down to something firm as heavily as you can. The cushioning should be very dense foam or better still rubber bedding. Not only will this material cushion the tank but it will also keep it from sliding about. I find this technique most critical on stainless steel tanks where the spot welds are usually covered by solder pads. These pads seem to be high spots on the tanks. They therefore are the initial supporters of the tanks, thus the first to be subjected to rubbing and wear. Rubber tape, at least under each seam, is strongly recommended. Do not place the tape in a closed pattern; be sure to leave openings in the pattern so that water will not be trapped below the tank but can flow out easily.

If you are using steel straps as hold downs for the tanks be sure to observe the following simple procedure: Wherever a strap touches the relatively sharp corner of a tank use a short piece of sliced rubber tubing laid over the corner of the tank. Not only will this tubing keep the straps from sliding about and becoming loose, it will

The new, intelligent fuel and water fills which are tightened and loosened by a common winch handle, instead of some bizarre looking tool which is always lost and even if found seldom works.

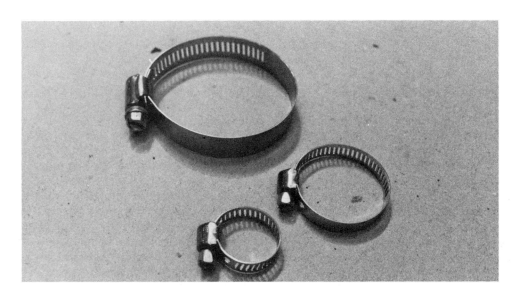

All hoses in a boat should be clamped with all stainless hose-clamps. Some cheap ones have galvanized bolt-shanks. Avoid them.

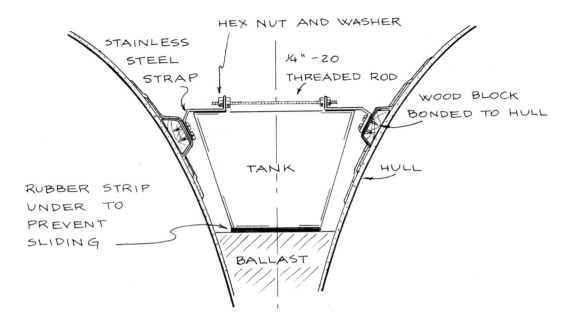

STAINLESS
STEEL
STRAP

HEX NUT AND WASHER

¼" -20
THREADED ROD

WOOD BLOCK
BONDED TO HULL

TANK

HULL

RUBBER STRIP
UNDER TO
PREVENT
SLIDING

BALLAST

Proper installation for a bilge-type tank. Rubber strips should be placed between the tanks and the straps as well as below the tank itself.

also act as a chafe preventer for the straps.

The type of hold down strap to be used is critical. I have heard of only two that have worked relentlessly without failure. One is stainless steel, the other heavy woven nylon (like the ones used for seat belts). The stainless steel ones can be adjusted by using a split strap system with a piece of all-thread (a stainless rod threaded from end to end) as a connector, see figure.

The nylon strap usually comes with buckles of some kind. I strongly advise against using the quick release type for this type may release the tank at the least desirable moment. The old-fashioned friction buckle system seems to work well. To pull them tight requires a great force so put them in such a way that you can *pull* toward you using the aid of your weight. *Pushing* on a strap is no easy task.

One point which has been brought up and

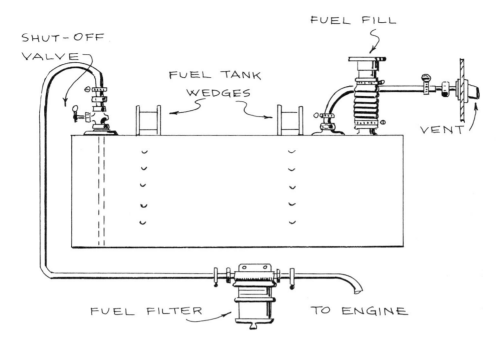

A pretty illustration showing the fittings and the plumbing of a fuel tank.

justifiably so, is that in case of fire, the nylon straps will melt very quickly and release the tanks to bang loosely about. Hence, if the tanks are anywhere near a fire-prone area the steel straps should be used.

Your fuel line should be copper or the best quality aviation hose. This hose is of thick walled rubber with mesh reinforcing that will stand great pressure. All bronze to bronze, or brass to brass fittings should be generously basted before threading together for the final time with liquid aviation gasket or equivalent. Don't tighten your brass fittings too hard; that is, don't brace your feet on the hull and yank with two hands. Brass is soft and can be easily stripped.

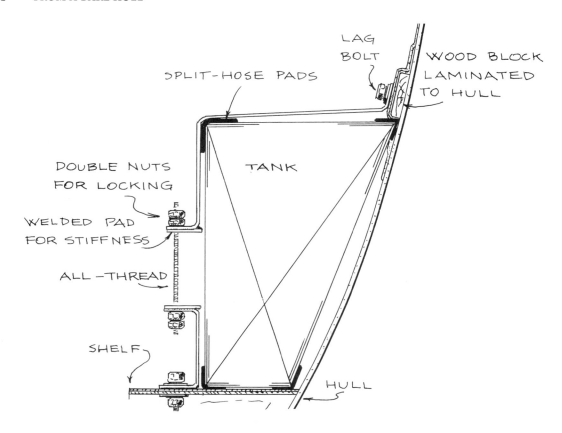

Proper installation of a saddle-tank placed on a shelf against the hull. Don't forget the split-hose pads.

Water Tanks

Water tanks require less attention. See figure for their construction. Their vents need not go overboard since water fumes aren't usually foul, so a length of hose run up inside a cabinet, well out of the way, and as high as possible will suffice. All fresh water plumbing in the boat can be taken care of by easy to buy, easy to bend, easy to use, and easy to mend ½ inch clear plastic FDA approved hose. For hot water under pressure, one should use reinforced spinnaker hose. It is not as expensive, nor as hard to use, nor as dangerous to solder as copper; and it is less prone to damage from banging, vibration, or kicking.

A friend tried solid PVC tubing and gave up after cursing for four solid days and wasting $100 worth of T's, elbows and pipe.

Water tank intakes should not be run from the deck. A simple accessible fitting right on the tank is preferable. Deck-fills are prone to be the same size as a hose end, thereby totally cutting off escaping air. If the water comes in, in great quantities, and under a lot of pressure it's extremely likely that the seams of one's tanks will open wide and let the water run out. A friend had just finished his whole cabin sole, all teak covered when he first thought of filling and trying his tanks. He stuck in a hose, went inside

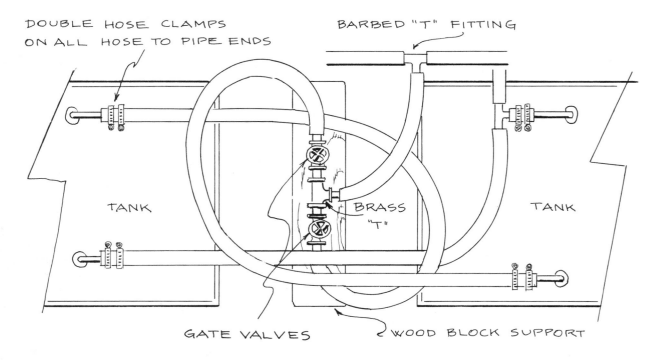

DOUBLE HOSE CLAMPS
ON ALL HOSE TO PIPE ENDS

BARBED "T" FITTING

TANK

BRASS "T"

TANK

GATE VALVES

WOOD BLOCK SUPPORT

NOTE! ALL HOSE ENDS SHOULD BE DOUBLE CLAMPED
BUT IF I DREW THEM ALL IN YOU COULDN'T
SEE THE DRAWING FOR THE HOSE CLAMPS.

Twin water tanks and the selecting valve system they require.

his house to answer a phone call, and was very surprised when he came back to find his cabin sole undulating with water coming up through the cracks. If you think it's more difficult to drag a water hose into your cabin than to tear out, resolder, and reinstall tanks; then go ahead and put in as large a deck-fill as your heart desires.

With water tanks, selective plumbing is a must; that is, you should be able to use one or other or both tanks at the same time; see figure for connections. For this purpose, accessible gate valves are sufficient, but make sure you grease them occasionally to stave off corrosion.

Hoses

1. Exhaust

Wire reinforced rubber hose is excellent for the purpose. Be sure you get the exact size for both exhaust fitting and through-hull fitting. Stretching or down-clamping a hose of this wall thickness can result only in eventual seepage problems, see photo.

2. Scupper drains, sink drain, engine and head intakes

Here again, the pressure resistant reinforced rubber hose is ideal. Again be certain that the diameter is exactly matching your fittings.

3. Fresh water plumbing

As mentioned before, the ½ inch clear plastic FDA approved hose is ideal, although others could be substituted here. Try to avoid rubber, for in a warm climate it adds a disgusting flavor to the water.

The rest of the installation is simple, requiring only hose clamps and the occasional adapter, see figure. Make sure all hoses fit onto tapered hose barbs; trying to fit a hose over a threaded fitting is very foolish and very difficult.

As with wiring, use tye-wraps to fasten hoses to interior of cabinetry to keep them out of harm's way and to make the job more sightly. But never bend a hose too drastically; as soon as you see folds on the inside of the curve you know you have gone too far, so ease off and your hose will have a longer life.

When attaching hoses to through-hulls, one should not be frugal. Go ahead and double clamp all hoses, see photo, just in case one clamp fails or breaks.

With hose clamps as with brass fittings, use brain and save the brawn. Tighten them only expediently. Once you see tiny particles of rubber or plastic drizzling through the cracks in the clamp, take the hose off, throw it away and begin over. You've destroyed the hose, dummy. Think and tighten only to seal, not to demolish. Once tightened and then removed, a hose end is not much good, so a few extra inches should be built into each hose to allow for initial foul-up as well as later repairs which might call for removal of the hose. Our engine water-filter gets fouled once a year or so, and each time I have to remove the rubber hose and cut an inch or so off. This is much handier than replacing 8 feet of expensive hosing.

Piece of rubber tye-wrapped onto copper plumber's tape guards rubber exhaust hose from chafe.

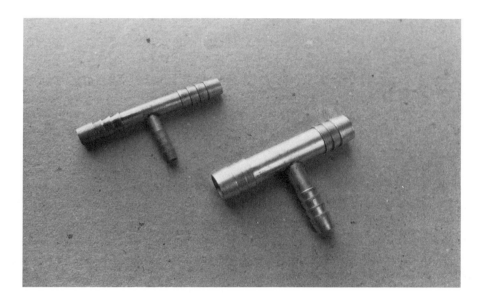

A pair of T fittings with barbed ends that provide a very good gripping surface for hoses.

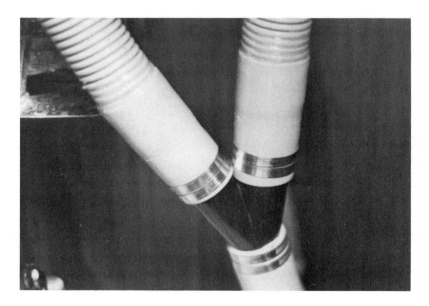

Accordion-type hoses should not be clamped directly to fittings, but should have solid tips glued to them first. Then they must *be double clamped.*

Brass compression fittings. You just slide in the copper tubing, tighten the nut and you have a secure pipe joint.

If you intend on doing any copper plumbing, you'll have to arm yourself with one of these pipe-cutters.

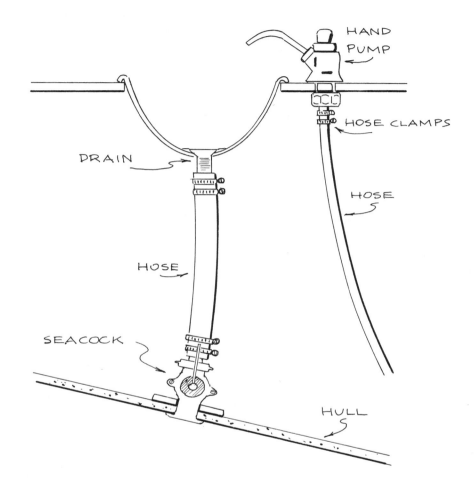

Head sink installation. Notice double hose-clamps everywhere.

20

Portlights

Portlights should be installed as soon as possible, that is, as soon as the cabin side liner is in place. Their location varies with each boat as does their size, but a mention of the type to use may be worthwhile.

If at all possible, use bronze. I have seen numerous boats in charter in the Caribbean whose black plastic rimmed portlights had all been broken by a combination of heat fatigue and winch handle or reaching pole bashing. The heavier the bronze casting, the better, for it is less likely to warp if over-tightened by the unthinker. The glass should be at least 1/4 inch thick even if the light is as small as 6 inch diameter. Double dogs are almost a necessity once 4 inch diameter is exceeded to guarantee an even seal. To help the dogs, the adjustable hinge rod offered by a few of the companies should be seriously considered. On this variety, two small set screws grace either end of the rod. These screws vary the tension that the hinge applies to the rubber sealer when rubber fatigue or ring warpage occurs.

To install portlights, I found it most rapid to trace the spigot onto the exterior of the fiberglass cabin side. After drilling but one hole to allow entry of the saw blade, I slightly over-cut the scribed line with a saber saw.

Use only very sharp blades. Heavy-duty hack saw blades are the best but even they dull rapidly, overheat, and break. I don't think I'm exaggerating when I say I annihilated at least one blade per one and a half portlights. By over-cutting slightly, you will save yourself the hideous task of trying to file or in some other miserable fashion trim, bits and chunks from 1/4 inch thick fiberglass.

When cutting these holes be sure to wear a mask and goggles (blessed are the near-sighted who wear glasses).

It is most unhealthy to inhale exiguous floating glass particles and even more painful to have one of the critters lodge in your eye.

I mention the following here in case it escapes my memory elsewhere. I think it quite intelligent to have a bottle of eyedrops aboard from commencement of construction. Since glass particles are angular and they cling tenaciously, it is most difficult to exhume them by other methods than flushing with eyedrops.

After the hole is cut to size, you have to dry fit your porthole and drill the bolt holes. But first a hint. Install your portlights so that the hinge is on top. True you won't be able to open it as one does a bathroom window. But it will be in a position where both dogs can be tightened most effectively. It is quite a simple matter then to open them wide by placing a hook in the cabin top above the light. Install an eye in a position so the hook can be set nto it tightly to prevent it from flapping noisily about when not in use.

Back to fitting. Do not go on the naïve assumption that the bolt holes in the portlight will match the bolt holes on your outside back-up ring. They may, but I have not yet encountered such a happy circumstance. I have, however, found a very simple remedy. Drill the topmost hole first by aligning the two holes by eye. If you don't hit the first time, bore about until you do. Put a bolt through the hole and tighten only to the point where the portlight and outer ring remain parallel.

You then drill through from the outside inward. The wood liner on the inside is easier to ream out than the fiberglass if you miss the hole. And there is no danger of leaks here from an oversized opening. Put all your bolts through to make sure they penetrate. It is easier to catch them now than after the whole thing is oozing polysulfide from every pore.

After the portlights have been dry fit, acetone well. Apply generous amounts of unbroken polysulfide beads on the inside of the exterior rings. I used two beads, one on the inside of the bolt holes and one on the outside. A bead of goo around the edge of the hole can't hurt. Now re-assemble the puzzle (hope you marked the top hole on the outside ring so you won't have alignment problems). Have a lot of rags handy and a large can of acetone to clean the mess.

When tightening, make sure that excess caulking squirts out all around the outside ring. Only then can you be certain that every water route is closed off. Don't try to wipe all of the goo off with rags. Use scrap pieces of wood (they don't scratch the gelcoat) to scrape off the bulk.

21

Interior Trim

This area requires a lot of preparation and its installation is time demanding. But you can limit the amount of time required, by doing as perfect a job as possible with the assembly of the rough interior. Except for searails, berth rails, and grab posts, trim is used primarily to cover mistakes. Keep them to a minimum; your finishing work will be less and your boat won't look like a gingerbread house with a little scrap here and another scrap there and a small chunk everywhere.

Searails

Height here is a primary consideration. The primary function of a searail is to keep things from flying off tables and counters when the boat is undergoing heavy motion. I think that a 2 inch height around the galley is not excessive; if it is less than that, things are prone to tip over a small rail.

The only other matter of importance is to keep the corners open. Open corners will make cleaning of the top child's play; otherwise, you will forever leave crumbs and other half-dead things squatting in sharp, hard-to-clean corners.

The shape can be whatever you like. We tapered the tops of ours to ease the bulky effect. Dimensions of the typical rail we used are in the figure. One can see from the drawing that milling out of ¾ inch teak stock is simple.

Please note the *pusher* used in the figure. A pusher should be permanently placed near the saw and used always when milling any piece of wood. It can be easily made of scrap plywood to the rough dimensions in the figure. Make a few at a time because the pushing lip will be cut off after a few tight cuts where the blade penetrates its lower edge.

The sloped face of the searail can be cut on a table saw at whatever angle you desire. It is best to figure out how much rail you'll need for the whole boat ahead of time. That way you'll have to set the saw only four times to mill all the rails for the boat. Once the rough stock is milled there remains only a simple job of running the rail through the router, using a ⅜ inch bull-nose to round off edges. Don't bother fine sanding until the rails are attached in place. You'll put a few nicks and dents in before you're through. Use a lot of glue when attaching searails, screw or clamp every 8 inches, and make sure that the glue seals the top seam everywhere.

Searail Corners

The figure should be self-explanatory. I can offer little assistance, as searail corners will require

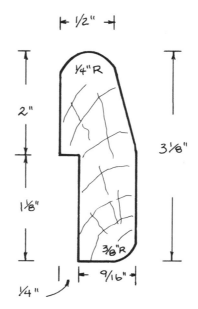

Cross-section of a simple searail requiring only three runs through the table saw (two for notch one for the bevel) and three runs through the router for the bullnose detail.

The simplest corner is to have the searails end short of the radiussed corner. You can finish the plywood with a thin veneer strip, or if the plywood is a very high grade marine plywood just sand its edge well and varnish it or oil it.

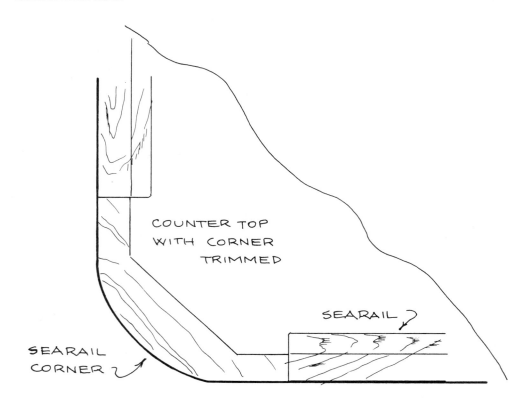

COUNTER TOP
WITH CORNER
TRIMMED

SEARAIL

SEARAIL
CORNER

Counter top or table top finished off with a corner trim piece that's flush with the surface to make cleaning of surface easier. If first-class marine plywood like Bruynzeel is used for the counter top, you could just round the corner and leave the finished plywood edge. See photo.

hand-filing or the occasional touch of the disk sander. One note. When attaching searail corners make sure that you have left at least 3/16 inch extra thickness on the outside radius. You will be able to shape it with a belt sander once it is in place.

Berth Rails

If the berth is to double as a settee, 4 inch cushions are advisable. To hold them in place, yet not cut off the circulation in your thighs, the same rails you used on the counters can be utilized. On berths used primarily for sleeping (pilot and forepeak), make the center portions as high as the cushions. I think it quite shippy and extremely reassuring in a rough sea to have at least the last 18 inches made about 4 inches higher. In light seas these rails will provide sufficient bracing without necessitating use of leeboards. Their milling and attachment should otherwise be the same as searails.

Deck Beams

Most fiberglass boats have a cabin structure strong enough to eliminate the need for deck beams in all areas except the support bulkheads. Beams do look romantic though; and since you'll probably have to make a few, you may as well make a few more. They are messy, but simple to make.

First measure the crown necessary for each beam. To measure, run a string from one side of the cabin top to the other at the location of each beam and measure at the points indicated in figure. On the edge of a bench, set up the required height blocks at the points using 2" × 8" stock. It is desirable if you have about three beams with almost the same crown, because then you can use 7 inch wide planks and rip them in three after laminating. Don't worry if the crowns aren't precisely identical. Something will give and bend enough to make up the slight divergence. The other method is to use the formula in the figure.

At any rate, cut from ¾ inch stock (gives you

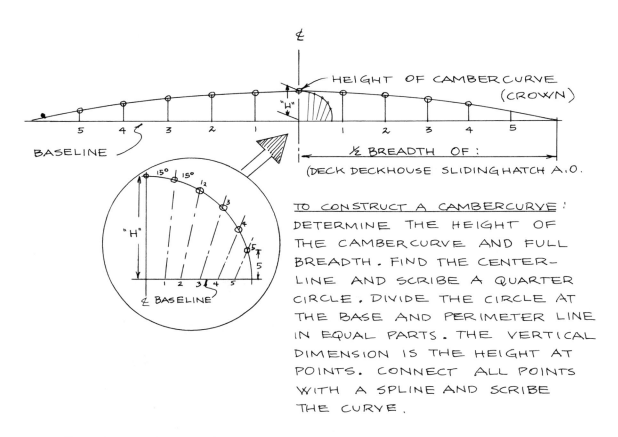

HEIGHT OF CAMBER CURVE (CROWN)

"H"

BASELINE

½ BREADTH OF :

(DECK DECKHOUSE SLIDING HATCH A.O.

15° 15°

"H"

₵ BASELINE

TO CONSTRUCT A CAMBER CURVE : DETERMINE THE HEIGHT OF THE CAMBER CURVE AND FULL BREADTH. FIND THE CENTER-LINE AND SCRIBE A QUARTER CIRCLE. DIVIDE THE CIRCLE AT THE BASE AND PERIMETER LINE IN EQUAL PARTS. THE VERTICAL DIMENSION IS THE HEIGHT AT POINTS. CONNECT ALL POINTS WITH A SPLINE AND SCRIBE THE CURVE.

How to measure the crown of a cabin top. If you think it's too complicated for you then just run a tight stringline from cabin-side to cabin-side and measure up to the coach-roof with a rule at 12 inch intervals. No big thing.

2¼ inch thick beams) three – 7 inch wide pieces of whatever wood you want to use. Try to avoid teak because it requires expensive resorcinal glue to laminate acceptably and even then the results can't be guaranteed. Be generous and cut each piece about 8 inches too long. It is much easier to trim the ends than to add on a piece. Spread glue on both sides that are to meet in the lamination, then place them over the jig. With big C-clamps, clamp tight at the two ends as well as at 1 foot intervals. Use blocks on top so that the clamp shoes don't mark your wood.

The crown is now defined. For even lamination, put as many clamps as you need to pull the three pieces together, see photo. When dried (leave at least 24 hours) you can rip the 7 inch wide stock into three 2¼ inch wide beams.

Fitting is quick. Since most cabin sides slope in at the top, just bring the beam up beneath the deck, mark in the angle on both ends, and cut. Don't try to fit it the first time. Overcut generously; then repeat the process and trim less and less off each end as you get toward the top. If you leave the beam snug at the ends, it can be a structural help. The best method of attachment is through-bolting as shown in the figure. If the beams are to strengthen bulkheads, it is advisable to use No. 14 self-tapping screws coming in through the bulkhead after through-bolting the first beam, see figure.

The shape and size of the rest of the trim will, of course, be determined by the size of the mistake they are assigned to cover. Use your imagination, but do it the simplest way possible. Whatever trim you install you'll have to plug the countersink holes made for the fasteners. Plugging is no mystery; it is simplified even more if sharp countersinks are used (see tool section) with a vertical unyawing pressure on the drill, for then you will not ream out the hole and make a perfect fit impossible.

If you have a drill press or at least an attachment into which a common drill motor fits, you can cut your own plugs from the mountains of scrap you'll have available. A plug cutter costs only $3.00 or $4.00 and it may come in handy in the corner of the world where they won't have heard of precut plugs. It is nice if your countersinks and your plugs are the same size. The fit of the plug upon insertion should be tight, but not so tight that the plugs split the wood when tapped in with a hammer. Plugging, as bonding,

Various size blocks act to give laminates for deck beam proper crown.

FWD. ⟶

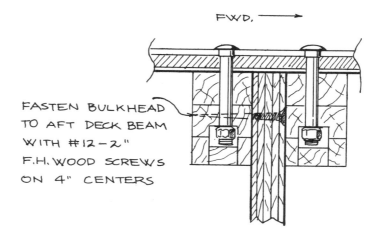

FASTEN BULKHEAD
TO AFT DECK BEAM
WITH #12-2"
F.H. WOOD SCREWS
ON 4" CENTERS

The first-class method for attaching deck beam, bulkhead and cabin-top.

3/8" CARRIAGE BOLT

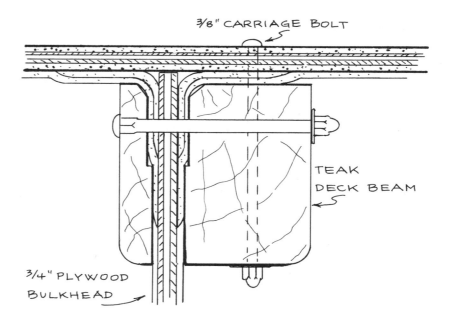

TEAK
DECK BEAM

3/4" PLYWOOD
BULKHEAD

Installing deck beams on either side of main bulkhead. If you want a really first-class job, then bond the bulkhead to the house top first then install the beams as shown.

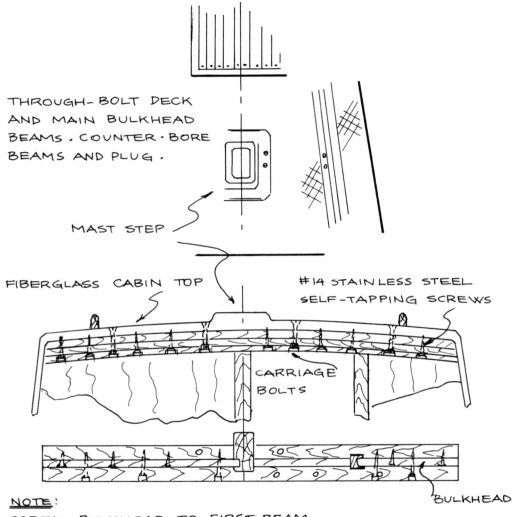

THROUGH-BOLT DECK
AND MAIN BULKHEAD
BEAMS. COUNTER-BORE
BEAMS AND PLUG.

MAST STEP

FIBERGLASS CABIN TOP

#14 STAINLESS STEEL
SELF-TAPPING SCREWS

CARRIAGE
BOLTS

BULKHEAD

NOTE:
SCREW BULKHEAD TO FIRST BEAM.
SCREW SECOND BEAM TO BULKHEAD.

More details of how to build a very strong main bulkhead/deckbeam combination, to stiffen boat where most of the torque of the rigging and mast will be applied.

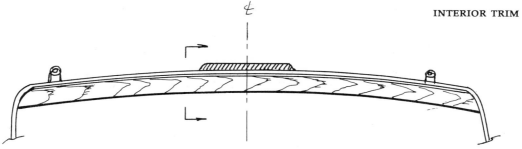

NOTE:
1. USE ¼" -20 X 3½ CARRIAGE BOLTS
2. USE WHITE ACRYLIC SEALER AROUND THE HEAD.
3. USE ¾" MAHOGANY PLUGS
4. CUT SQUARE IN FIBERGLASS DECK TO SEAT BOLT PROPERLY

is best left until all the pluggables are completed. Then with a few hundred plugs, a few cups of glue, a small mallet and a very sharp chisel you can be busy for a day or two.

The best glue pot for plugs we found was a paper cup cut down to about an inch and a half height with the bottom filled with ¼ inch of glue. You can then grip the plug in two fingers, align its grain with the grain of the wood it's going into, and dip it in the cup (if you have more than ¼ inch of glue in the bottom of the cup you will get glue all over your fingers and arms). Then insert the plug into the hole. When you have put in about ten plugs, go back and give each of them a firm tap with a mallet. Repeated bashings will either bury the plug too deep or cause it to crack and disintegrate; both very undesirable results.

It's preferable to have at least ⅛ inch of the plug sticking out after hammering. You can now take your chisel and with the beveled edge against the surface of the wood and going with the grain, trim a little of it off the top. You will then be able to see whether the grain is true to the chisel or whether the tool must be turned 180 degrees and chiseled the other way so that the plug will not chip out deeper than the surface of the wood. Once the grain has been established, you'll learn to clean off the head almost entirely with the chisel, necessitating very little following sanding.

It is most vital that all this chiseling be done before the glue has set. If you break a plug below the surface you can still easily dig it out without chipping the surrounding wood, and replace it. I heard from old shipwrights that they like to use shellac or varnish instead of glue to set plugs into. This idea may be excellent, making removal of the plugs possible at a later date without the danger of chipping out the surrounding wood.

I think it is advisable that all trim be oiled after plugging; then if drops of paint, or unwanted goo of other sorts fall upon it, it will be easier to wipe off without the risk of rapid penetration.

Doweling

You may find that you have to make a wide plank from two narrow ones for things like rudder cheekplates, icebox lids, etc. This can be accomplished by edge glueing and bar-clamping two pieces; but to have a long life, dowels should be used as a mechanical assistance. Without a jig, it's very difficult to perfectly align the holes you must drill in both pieces for the dowels. Therefore, it's advisable to attach the rough cut pieces to each other before you cut them to the final shape or size.

To guarantee a fairly close fit, clamp the two pieces side by side. Then with a thick ended square, draw lines across both of them at each location where the dowels are to be (every 8 inches should be fine), see figure. Now comes the tough part. Scribe in the centerline for the holes as close to the center of each plank as you can. If you don't, the pieces won't match and you'll spend hours trying to even off the surfaces.

Once the centers of the holes have been marked, use a center punch to set a starting point for the drill bit, then drill in. Be generous with the depth. There is nothing worse than with all holes perfectly matched and centered, dowels inserted, and pieces fitted together you come to find that the holes are too shallow. Drill deep, then apply a good coat of glue to the edges, the holes, and the dowels. Insert the dowels in the holes, then fit and clamp on the other piece. If you were very accurate with your measuring and your drilling, everything should fit like a glove; if not, hit it with a sledge hammer.

Good and very inexpensive doweling jigs are available, that eliminate all the guess-work and most of the foul-ups. If you are planning on joining more than one set of boards, get one.

Another simple way of joining two boards is by *letting-in* a common tongue into them, see figure. The grooves should be cut in both boards at the same time using the same setting on the table-saw, for it is almost impossible to reproduce the identical setting again.

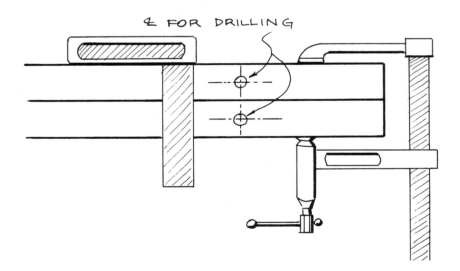

Homemade jig for dowels. This is handy for butting two planks together to make one wide one.

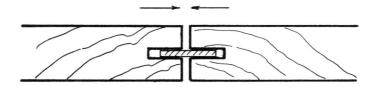

IT IS BEST TO RUN THE GRAIN AGAINST EACH OTHER IN THE BOARDS. THAT WAY IF THEY CUP THEY WILL COUNTERACT EACH OTHER'S FAULT.

Another method (other than doweling) used to butt two narrow planks together to make one wide one. It is a more foolproof method than the doweling, requiring only one run-through on the table saw for each board. A strip of wood milled to size, joins the boards together.

As you can see a high-quality marine plywood can be nicely finished by bullnosing and sanding its edge. A lower grade plywood would be showing a dozen voids.

22

Doors and Drawers

Almost every boat that I've ever seen had a different solution, different materials, different patterns for the doors and drawers. I hope that this situation continues, for I love going aboard strange new yachts and seeing new solutions to old problems. Therefore, I will tell you only what we have done and why.

Doors

For openings in the backs of settee berths where we will be leaning or falling against doors, we used solid teak pieces. The only detail put on them was a *deep bull-nose* which was achieved by setting the edge of the bull-nose a bit higher than the routing table. It then cuts deeper into the wood than normally. This solid door is costly in materials but extremely cheap in labor because it takes so little time to make one. For all other doors we used 2½ inch teak frames (with the same detail) with cane insert. The figure shows the door frame detail for inserts. Using

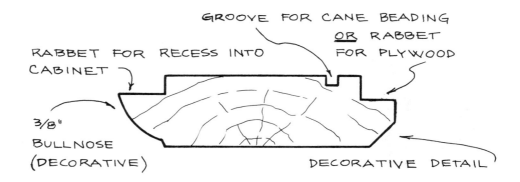

Cross-section of door frame piece. Only one of the top right-hand notches will be cut out depending on whether you want to use cane as in photo or solid plywood insert.

Double cane doors.

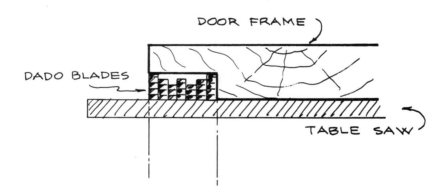

Rabbet being cut into doorframe with dado-blades which are actually a bunch of saw blade type things placed side by side.

cane is more expensive because it is time consuming and the woven caning, covered with dust in some junky furniture repair place, cost a usurious $3.20 per square foot. It would have been cheaper to use solid teak, but we wanted the ventilation. This reason is probably a lie; I just thought that cane looked good, so we used it. Ventilation was a nice excuse though.

Inserting thin plywood panels into teak frames is also common practice. I've seen very thin strips of woven teak that worked nicely. At any rate, we caned and here is how:

We cut a groove into the inside of the frames. We used dado blades to cut away the ends of each piece of door frame, see figure. Then we used resorcinal glue, a square, and clamps to clamp all of the corners. We were advised by the usurer to soak the cane in hot water for fitting. We did so, then rough cut the pieces (about 1 inch over required size) and laid them over the hole. Then we used cane-beading to wedge the tightly stretched cane into place.

While still wet and soft, we trimmed with scissors whatever excess we could off the overhanging cane, leaving only a very short stubble. We waited until the stubble had dried and hardened, then we used a belt sander to remove it. When the cane dried it became tight between the frames; nevertheless, I sprayed both sides with transparent, no-gloss sealer to be certain of keeping potential moisture out. If left unsealed, the cane absorbs moisture from the air and sags absurdly.

For handles, we used the world's greatest invention – the hole. It looks quite pleasant if cut to a 1 inch diameter and bull-nosed. Apart from providing some ventilation in solid doors, it gives access to what I consider the best lock for a sailing boat, the positive locking elbow catches, see photo.

A simple and effective drawer can be built by building a wood box of good plywood and then facing it with a piece of teak. A U should be cut into the box to accommodate a hole for the finger, plus a space for the finger lock above the finger-hole in the teak face.

Drawers

Our drawers are of very standard construction. The simplest way to learn how to do them is to have a close look at your home cabinetry (the older, probably the better the work). We did however replace the nails or staples ordinarily used, with stainless steel screws. The faces are solid teak with the aforementioned detail and handles. The simplest sliding system we found (although not necessarily the best) is the precut wood runners, see figure, and plastic slides available at most pedestrian hardware stores, see photo. They require only a square and a level for accurate installation. Drawers are kept from sliding out in rough seas by ½" × ¼" notches cut in the front ends of the sides.

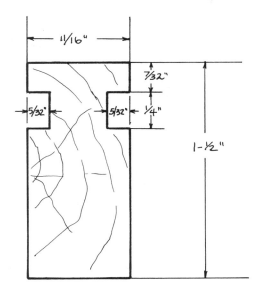

Cross-section of a drawer-track, easily milled from mahogany or fir (must be kiln dried of course or it'll warp). This kind of track is for use with the plastic slide shown in photo.

Plastic drawer guide.

The simplest way of making a drawer slide. An L-shaped molding is attached to a plywood base, and this holds the drawer in place. The bottom of the drawer has been left about ½ inch wider on either side of the drawer, and it is this lip that fits into the L.

Sliding Doors

Keeping doors shut at sea is quite a problem. Most snap-locks, bayonet grips, and magnets are inadequate. There is nothing more annoying in an already madly rolling boat than stupid doors slamming shut every 4 seconds. So if you don't like positive locks, the second best solution is sliding doors. They also have the indisputable advantage that they require no space when opened. I don't particularly like them for what reason I don't know, but I would encourage their use in galleys and other places where counter-tops may have to be cleared of pots, etc. before a conventional door can be opened. Their construction is simple, requiring pre-milled slides and little else as shown in the figure. The only other words I have on doors is a strong encouragement to put one on your engine room access. I didn't. I have drop boards and I'm sorry I do because they are a giant pain if they have to be pulled out at sea and set down somewhere only to fly up in the first sea and smash you in the Achille's tendon. A door with a hasp and an eye to keep it still, once opened, is an absolute dream in comparison.

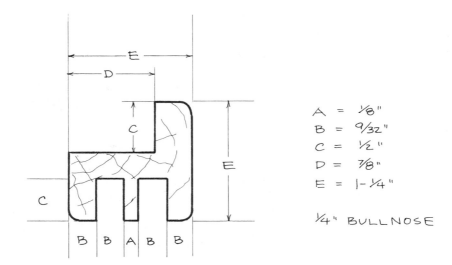

Cross-section of milled teak track for sliding doors. In this case the slots are cut to $9/32$ inch which means they'll take $1/4$ inch or $7/32$ inch plexiglass doors.

23

Cabin Sole Overlay

The simplest thing to use on cabin soles is the teak-and-holly plywood that was developed a few years ago and is used in all the finest yards including Beneteau, Baltic and Swan. The top layer of teak is about $1/16$ inch, which, if proper shoes are worn and all pebbles are kept off the sole, should last a very long time. If a piece does wear through in high traffic areas like the companionway, then the one piece can be removed and changed.

If you want a solid wood overlay, then most of the methods of construction discussed in countertop overlay apply here. I would not use stock thinner than $3/8$ inch because it would be difficult to plug and more likely to warp or wear or crack. I believe teak to be the best wood to use, even though we used ash. We wanted the contrast in a teak satiated boat. Of course bedding compound should be used instead of glue.

For access to the bilge be sure to undercut your hatches by at least $3/16$ inch or the thing will swell shut never to reopen. To keep these hatches (or large lids on the counter tops) from warping, use strong-backs of good dry hardwood. To lift hatches, the flush fitting pull rings are probably the most ideal solution.

I won't even mention how to lay carpeting into a boat, because any serious cruising boat will have its carpets constantly soaked. I think it's a great idea for mobile homes. You can, however, have non-absorbent carpet and a warm, non-slippery surface. A former mobile home owner used this material in his first boat to protect the teak cabin sole. Its well-known name is Astro-Turf and it was the most disgusting tasteless thing I have ever set eyes on. If you want me to hate you and your boat, use it.

I think we have come to the end of interior finishing. With the exception of the engine, there are many small points. But I think they have crept up periodically in other sections either on planning or scrounging or tools or what to buy. Many finer points were left out in order to keep the book a readable length. With what's absent, use your imagination and best of luck.

A kind of grate for a cabin sole, made by routing elongated holes into teak-and-holly marine plywood. Note that the holes are not lined up end to end, but are staggered, otherwise the first, hard stomping would break the thing in half.

24

Engine Installation

One tends to shake and tremble at the thought of installing one's own engine. I'm not sure whether fear is activated by the number of esoteric-looking parts or by the sheer bulk of the thing, but it appears universally accepted that engines and their handling are best left to the experts.

The work involved is truly no great mystery. The few hours of studying the engine, the manufacturer's brochure, and the parts such as stuffing boxes, cutlass bearings, shaft logs, engine pan, etc., will give you a more familiar, confident outlook on the whole situation.

As I mentioned before, I will be discussing only diesel engines, although admittedly most of the procedures described herein are applicable to diesel, gas, steam, or whatever your phobia.

Engine Pan

If at all possible, an engine pan should be utilized. Engine pans are usually made of fiberglass, with a combination of either wood or metal.

Construction of the engine pan is important. So if you want to make your own, be sure to use only hand laid up mat and roving or mat and cloth. A lot of vibration will have to be tolerated by the pan and with alternative methods of con-struction such as chopper gun or all-mat, pans have a tendency to crack and check more easily. For the horizontal surfaces of the pan (bottom and engine mount shoulders) use a plywood core. I have heard of one manufacturer who installs steel plates in the two shoulders; thus, instead of having the engine mounts held down by nuts and bolts, you can simply *tap and die* the steel plates, then thread the bolts into them. Otherwise, you will have to devise a method whereby the bolt heads under the pan will remain stationary while you twist and tighten the nuts above.

Shaft Hole

The drilling of the shaft hole will have to be your primary task. Its location can be detected by measurement on the exterior of the hull. I will be concerned primarily with boats that have dead-wood and propeller apertures in the rudder.

Free-standing spade rudders are not the most ideal for cruising; however, the task of locating their shaft holes is not too demanding. The engine can be placed on its mounts, then a shortened broomstick can be inserted into the coupling to detect the most comfortable place for the shaft to pass through. You will be governed by the angle at which you may set the engine,

Bronze casting supporting propeller shaft. Note also (if you have eyes like a hawk) piece of steel-held rubber flap that closes off cavity around rudder shaft.

Angled, fixed-socket wrenches are very useful aboard a boat where space around the engine is often limited. The snap-on sockets are good too but sometimes the sockets stick on the nuts and are a bit hard to remove.

If an engine is to be tolerable, this is the kind of insulation that should surround it. Note great fiberglass bedlogs that support engine. They are all part of the fiberglass engine pan. Note also handy fire extinguisher above engine.

but follow the manufacturer's recommendations; otherwise, the more level the shaft, the better the performance of the propeller is likely to be.

For boats with the aforementioned aperture in the rudder, you must locate and drill the shaft hole first, then align the engine to it. You have to hit the shaft hole in the center of the aperture, both athwartships and vertically. Otherwise, at best, you will get a disturbed flow of water and plentiful cavitation from the propeller passing too close to either the top or bottom of the aperture. At worst, if the shaft hole is placed drastically low or high, the propeller will have a tendency to slice the rudder or the hull in half like a salami cutter.

So locate the center, mark it, and use a hole saw that will very snugly accommodate the shaft log, be it bronze or fiberglass tubing. If your engine is to be level and your shaft likewise, drill the hole as horizontal as possible. In a respectable fiberglass boat, you'll be drilling through an inch of fiberglass. Thus any deviation may cause misalignment which can cause the cutlass bearing to be prematurely worn. Once the hole is cut, you'll be ready to install the engine pan.

Engine Pan Installation

It is most advisable to have the engine at hand in order to take accurate and lucid measurements from it while installing an engine pan. You will need to make up a jig locating engine mount and coupling levels. Although most engines come with extremely accurate graphic renderings of all elevations, there is nothing quite like having the real item at hand to get a more accurate *feel*.

Once you have located the mounts on the pan, mark their places. Or better still, screw down temporary pads which you can use as a base for the jig to set up a temporary shaft to assist you in pan alignment, see figure. Care should be taken with mount locations, because some boat builders design a pan for a certain engine but choose to use adapters or at least modifications of the mounts so that they become unrecognizable to the uninitiated. These modifications are done in order to accommodate hull narrowness or bilge curvature. If you are thoroughly confused, get in touch with the manufacturer and have him clarify.

Once you have screwed blocks in place of the mounts, you'll have to make a jig for the mock shaft. First, find the distance between the aft edge of the pan and the center point of the coupling. Fabricate a wood crutch to accommodate a broomstick or whatever you will substitute for the shaft. Make sure that its center will be at the exact center of the coupling when it's eventually fitted.

Next, from the specifications of the boat builder, determine the angle in degrees at which the shaft will sit in relation to the engine pan. Now fabricate a crutch in the forward part of the pan to enable the broom handle to maintain this alignment. Once the jig is perfectly aligned and secured in the pan, lower the pan into the space where it is to go. It's advisable to predetermine the centerline of the boat just before you begin so that the pan can be aligned on center. If the boat is level, the measurement along the engine room bulkhead will give you a good location in combination with the center of the shaft hole. Position the pan with jig as close to the centerline as possible. Then insert the 'broomstick' through the shaft hole, set it, and secure it onto the jig. You can now maneuver the pan-jig until the desired shaft angle is achieved. Use a protractor and level for this exercise.

Fore and aft location of the engine is important, although not critical. Ascertain that your fly wheel will not mascerate your engine room bulkhead or other items, yet keep the engine as far forward as possible in order to carry the bulk of the weight toward the middle of the boat. To this end, it may be quite advisable to refrain from ordering your engine shaft until the final fore and aft location of the engine has been determined. Then measure for the length of shaft required and specify at the machine shop.

Be sure that you bring the broom-shaft through the very center of the shaft hole. You may require blocks and wedges to hold the pan in position, for very few fit perfectly snugly against the hull. Once it's perfectly located, put some temporary bonds onto either side of it to hold it in place. While you're bonding, be certain you don't hit or jiggle the pan or you can push it out of alignment.

Once the bonds have set, mix up a goodly batch of mill fibers and resin, then fill in all the voids between the pan and the hull. Mix the concoction very thick so it won't run out. Try not to miss any spots. Remember, this fill-in will be the foundation of your engine pan.

Some manufacturers neglect to tape off the edges of the pans to allow for bonding. Under no circumstance should you bond over the gelcoat. You must grind it all off down to the bare fiberglass, then acetone it, and then bond.

If you have a plywood core in your engine pan, you will have to take your engine mounts to a welding shop and have them weld the mounting hold-down bolts onto a stainless steel plate. This plate will act as a large washer. More important, it will hold the bolts so that you can adjust the nuts without fear of the bolt falling into the bilge. It will also allow you to adjust the nuts without holding the bolt heads below the engine pan with a wrench.

If your engine pan maker has bonded pieces of steel into the pan instead of plywood, you will need only *to tap and die*, then insert the bolts from the top. Otherwise, locate the mount positions and tighten them loosely in place.

A note here on engine vibration. Whatever can be done to minimize engine vibration should be done, for not only is it completely annoying to have everything in the boat quiver to the tune of C sharp, but all this vibration will eventually loosen bolts and couplings and wear out cutlass bearings and shake expensive fillings from your teeth. So, three things can be done to cut down the vibration of the engine, and any one will help but all three would of course be best.

1. Be sure the engine-pan you make or buy is of the heaviest construction, otherwise it will quiver like a nervous toad and amplify any movement the engine makes. Now here we need real stiffness, and here it wouldn't hurt to have very heavy solid fiberglass to make the pan as un-undulatable as possible.

2. Once the pan is bonded into place, it would be a good idea to fill up the entire cavity below the engine-pan with a two part, expanding urethane foam, described in the section on iceboxes. This will not only help to reduce the pan's tiny movements but it will aid substantially in reducing the drum effect of the pan, which in fact echoes and multiplies all sounds emitted by the engine.

3. To further cut vibration transmission, a set of wood *bed-logs* can be used between the engine and the pan. The Beneteau yard does this with excellent results and one can understand why; try tapping on a fiberglass pan then try tapping on the trunk of an oak tree. The bedlogs should be about 4" × 4" to be of much help and they should be massive oak and they should be treated with wood preservative against rot.

Now, if after all this you insulate your engine-room as in the photo, your boat will be so quiet you'll think it's propelled by a rubber band . . . Now *there's* a thought!

Your next step is to haul your engine up to your boat and lower it into the pan. The least troublesome method is to rent a small crane or a high forklift. They usually cost $40 an hour. If you're prepared for their arrival the whole operation should not take more than 10 to 15 minutes. You will have to pay travel time for the crane, so it's better to have one come from close by even if his hourly rate is a bit higher.

Once your engine is sitting on the mounts, put on the mount-nuts, but don't tighten them. Insert your proper propeller shaft and attach it to the coupling. Tighten the coupling bolts so that the shaft is as close to its permanent location as possible. Now, with all your weight off the engine, check to see how well the shaft is centered in the shaft hole. It has to be exactly in the center before you can install the shaft log. If it is not, get ready for a couple of hours of shimming and trimming.

A note of advice concerning engine shafts may be appropriate here. When ordering the length of your engine shaft, take into consideration the fact that you do not want too much nor too little shaft sticking out of the hull. It's ideal to be able to remove your propeller without removing your rudder. Therefore the shaft cannot be too long or this task will be impossible to perform. On the other hand, you must not make the outhang of your shaft too short. It's advisable to have a zinc sacrificial anode on the shaft for which you will have to allow. In addition, if your deadwood is of any width, you should get your propeller as far aft of it as possible or the turbulent flow of water will cause serious cavitations, annoying with its sound and lack of performance.

Back to shimming and trimming. You will need a come-along, for this operation. The cheapest way to secure one is to rent it, but I suggest buying one (about $25) for you can never tell in what dark corner of the world you may have to remove your engine without any other hands than your own to help. So, shift and shim your engine both horizontally and vertically until the shaft passes through the hole, dead center.

One has a great temptation to use open-sided washers to eliminate the need of pulling the engine from the mounts each time another spacer is to be added. I'm not sure if the use of these washers is the right approach. Granted it is easier to slip them in by raising the engine only slightly, but it is also easier for them to slip out after a few years of vibration. At any rate, align your engine, then tighten every nut until they scream.

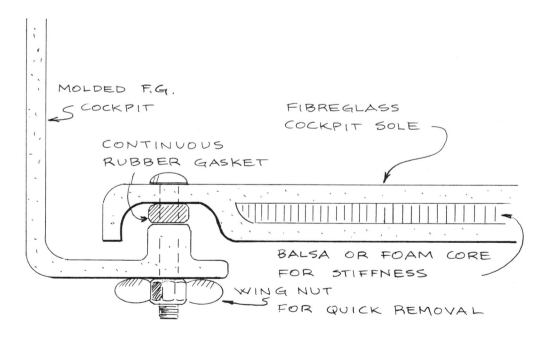

It's nice to have a removable cockpit sole if the engine is located below the cockpit for you will have much air and light in the engineroom. Wonderful when you feel like tinkering with the diesel.

Shaft Log

Two different shaft logs are in common use. One is the bronze log with a flange, see photo, and the other a flangeless fiberglass tube. Both methods work well. The first uses mechanical aids (two bronze bolts); the other is bonded into place. Both are equally simple to install and both have functioned admirably in the past.

Bronze with flange. Thoroughly clean the shaft hole and surrounding hull area for about a 6 inch radius on the inside. Remove all paint, grease, scrap, and dust. Cover the outside of the bronze log thoroughly with mold-release wax. With the cutlass bearing inside, set the log in place over the shaft with the flange on the inside of the hull. Mix a thick but very even batch of mish-mash. Cautiously fill in all the area around the shaft log on the inside of the hull. You are trying to make a supportive housing for the shaft log, so be thorough and build a strong well rounded dam. If the hull is close on either side, fill in the space completely, little by little, and be sure to leave no voids. If you can squeeze a little between the log and the shaft hole walls, so much the better. But don't force or nudge the shaft or the log, or you might put the whole thing out of alignment.

To avoid having to taper the forward shoulders of the mish-mash dam to a fragile point, a plywood donut cut to the shape of the shaft log flange can be used as a forward supporting wall of the dam. Smooth out the dam and leave it to go off. Use only a mild amount of catalyst in this mixture; for, as you know, the slower the curing the better the adhesion.

Once you're done, get out of the engine room and stay out. On your way, don't even breathe on the shaft or engine, or you'll put it out of alignment. Allow it to set at least overnight, then gently tap out the shaft log and pull it right out of the hole. If you have applied the mold-release wax judiciously, you'll have no problem.

Now check the sides of the mish-mash tunnel to ascertain that you have left no flaws or voids.

If you find some, you have to chisel out the whole dam and start again because if you leave a dam in with a large void, the log may be allowed to wallow and vibrate, causing the ocean to come in little by big.

If you find no voids, slip the log back in and drill two holes for the flange bolts. Drill as horizontally as you possibly can, as you will then get maximum support from your bolts. If you drill straight, you should come out at top and bottom of the cutlass bearing. A pair of hex nuts locked against each other with a flat washer will then forever keep your dam from moving, but don't tighten them yet.

Pull out the shaft log and wash off the mold-release wax until you can see your face in the bronze. Now wash the tunnel out with acetone also. Coat the log and the tunnel walls with polysulphide, then slide the log back in. You will have goo all over you again, but it's a small price to pay. Put some polysulphide in the flange hole, slip in the bolts, tighten the nuts, and you're almost secure. Wash off the excess polysulphide on the inside. Then on the outside lay large beads all over the heads of the bolts and right around the entire shaft log to cover the joint between it and the hull. Work the beads into swirls with a stick to be sure no voids exist inside the polysulphide scarf.

Fiberglass shaft log. The installation of this type of log is measurably simpler since, as mentioned before, it requires no bolting. The engine must be aligned in the same manner. Once aligned the log should be pulled and cleaned. Here it is unnecessary to apply any caulking. Simply shove the log back into its place. Then proceed to build on the inboard end, a plywood crutch of at least 3/4 inch thickness, made to conform to the hull. The usual length of the inward piece of the shaft log in the case of fiberglass tubing is about 1 foot. Placement of the plywood crutch can be about 2 inches from the end. This crutch should then be bonded to the hull. Over the top half of

Close-up of cutlass-bearing through which the prop passes. The slots in the black neoprene are for water which keeps the friction down and cools the rubber. The serrated bronze tube holds the fiberglass bonds well.

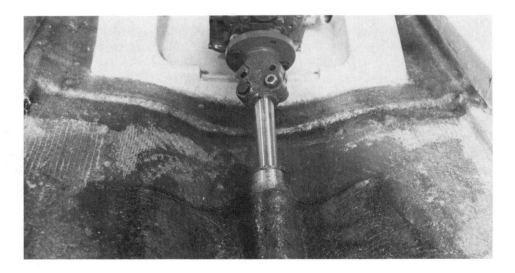

A bronze cutlass bearing housing, heavily bonded into place after the engine has been accurately set onto its mounts.

the fiberglass tube, a similar crutch can be made to keep the tube from moving upward. This crutch should also be bonded to the hull. Heavily!

Once the bonds have gone off and the tube is securely in place, fill the empty cavity between the plywood dam and aft end of the hull with a semi-runny solution of mish-mash. Again, be sure to avoid leaving any sort of voids as well as to avoid knocking the shaft or the shaft log. And again, let the mish-mash harden overnight before going back to do any other work inside the engine room.

Stuffing Box

If you have not yet put your stuffing box over the shaft, pull the shaft out now and do so. Do not bang on the crown nut that holds the propeller nor the propeller itself, to try to get the shaft out of the coupling. Rather, try to find a shaft puller, and tap it gently. If you hammer the shaft or the prop, you may bend the shaft or alter the prop's pitch. Neither result is too desirable.

Once your stuffing box is on the shaft, put four separate rings of 3/16 inch diameter flax packing against the inside end of the cutlass bearing. Stagger the joints of the four rings so that water won't have a nice clean path. When cutting the flax, slightly overlap a complete loop, then cut both pieces with a razor. This way, your loops will be exactly the correct length, with no gaps in between. Now, gently push the stuffing box over the flax and tighten with your hands only.

When you can tighten no more, put a half turn on it with a wrench. Then tighten it no more. If you do, you will crush the flax resulting in no possibility of future tightening when the packing wears and develops a leak at a later time. The entire idea behind this technique is that you can, at a later time, tighten down the packing instead of having to re-do it every time a tiny leak develops. More important, if you think you have over-tightened, don't back the nut off now. If you do, you can be sure of a leak at the moment of launching, for you have crushed the packing

then backed off, creating a nice viaduct.

Believe it or not, your engine is now installed, aligned, and sealed. All that is left is hooking in your exhaust, clamping on your fuel lines, and securing your battery cables.

Exhaust Installation

Two basic types of marine exhaust silencers are commonly used the 'Aqualift,' and the 'stand pipe' or 'riser.' The installation of the riser is documented with engine installations by most manufacturers such as Westerbeke and Perkins. The only item they do not point out is that the manifold undergoes tremendous vibration. They usually provide a single additional support arm that goes back onto the engine. But if you can fabricate a second one, you may be able to prevent premature failure of fittings.

Under no circumstances should you try to brace the riser by attaching it to a support arm whose other end is attached to a shelf or fixed bulkhead or anything but the engine. If you do, you will cause even earlier breakage of couplings or fittings. It can be compared to a piece of paper being flapped in the air by one hand. It flutters and shakes and it is undamaged; however, if a motionless hand holds the other end, the paper will tear as soon as the first hand starts to move violently.

The Aqualift variety requires no such precautions because it is solidly mounted on the engine. And because of its bulk and hefty attachments, it will not experience exaggerated flexing.

But another sort of precaution is necessary with the Aqualift. Unless well guarded against, following seas can come in through the exhaust and flood the engine. To this end an installation such as is illustrated in the figure should be used. Notice that the hose is run as high as the deck will allow.

Use of the gate valve exhaust through-hull fitting is highly recommended. This valve should be closed only in broken following seas where

A transom mounted exhaust is bound to get flooded by overtaking seas. A simple hinged, rubber flap can be hose-clamped to the through-hull neck to solve the problem.

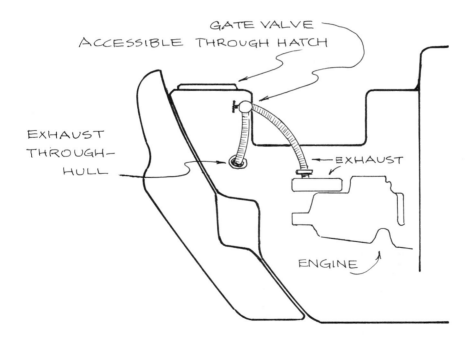

If a flap cannot be used on an engine exhaust outlet (a flap is useless on a double-ender because the seas will open it up instead of forcing it shut) then a loop should be run in the exhaust hose running as high as possible from the engine back down to the outlet. For very heavy seas, a gate valve should be installed and closed once the seas start getting mean.

An exhaust fitting through-hull should be constructed as in photo. The short stub and the flange sit outside the hull so the dirty water, which inevitably drips from exhausts, will fall away from the hull instead of dribbling down it and staining it.

Wherever a potential for a wire being chafed exists, the wire (or better still a bunch of neighboring wires together) should be wrapped heavily with tape.

danger of flooding is accentuated. A safeguard system should be devised to prevent the possibility of the gate valve being left closed as the engine is started up. Storing the ignition key beside the valve at all times might be a solution.

One note: avoid any drastic bends in the exhaust hose. Most hoses are wire-reinforced and tape-fortified rubber, thus very strong. But a violent bend can cause the wire to cut right through the casing and ruin the hose. It is best to use bronze U's to avoid this. All fittings should be exactly the correct size. If the hose is of too great an ID it can and will slip off and leak. If it's too small you can ruin the hose by forcing it over an over-sized fitting.

Hooking in Fuel Lines

This procedure was discussed to some degree in plumbing; therefore I will only touch upon it. Fuel hoses should be the high pressure aircraft variety just to be sure, and all hose clamps should be stainless. Be certain that you look for the engraved words 'all stainless,' because some stainless bands have galvanized screws which will rust once the galvanized has been scraped off.

Tanks should have their inlets and outlets on the top to avoid the possibility of leakage through a bottom fitting, which could empty the tank's entire contents before discovered and checked.

At least a double fuel filter, see photo, for every tank should be used, apart from the filter on the engine. CAV filters with a settling bowl for water have stood the test of time well, although I have heard of a newer type with a coalescer. This device separates water from the fuel by taking tiny droplets out in suspension, then causing them to bead and settle to the bottom of the bowl. The double filter per tank system illustrated in Don Street's *Ocean Sailing Yacht* is a fine concept, for it allows continuous running even though one filter may get clogged.

Once your fuel lines are hooked up, fill your tank with a couple of gallons of fuel (just in case they leak diesel). Bleed the system starting from the top most filter and working your way down to the injectors. The operation is simple. Loosen the bleeding screw until fuel starts flowing instead of air, then tighten it and go on to the next one. But be sure you tighten one before you ascend to the other, or you'll be wasting time, for the bottom one will be letting in air.

Fuel filters set up in series.

Controls

Engine controls are of two types: the monoshift single lever which acts as a throttle and gear shifter at the same time, and the dual shift which has a separate lever for each purpose. The monoshift has a tendency to fall out of adjustment somewhat more readily, but you will never have to worry about anyone going from forward to reverse at very high rpm's as you do with the double levers.

When you are installing your control cables, use as much caution as you do with your hoses. Don't force them or bend them too sharply or they will snag and bind; such a situation may stop you from shifting when you most need to . . . like when coming into a concrete dock. Also, be sure that they are out of the way of feet desperately looking for a foothold on the engine room sole in rough seas. This practice also holds true for other items such as fuel lines and battery cables. Keep them out of the way of traffic or you will have nothing but unexpected problems.

Now hook up a garden hose to your engine intake seacock. You may need an adapter for a good fit. Check your engine oil level, hook up your batteries, be sure the engine intake seacock and your exhaust gate valve are open; then turn the battery selector switch to 'All,' turn the breaker switch marked 'Engine' to 'on,' put the gear shift lever into neutral, give her a bit of throttle, turn on the water in the hose; then turn the ignition key, and listen to it start on the first attempt . . . That's why I say, get a diesel.

Check for fuel, water, and exhaust leaks. Correct them now. Check to see if water is coming out of your exhaust through-hull; if not, shut off the engine and check your connections and water pump.

I must say that having the engine hooked up and running properly makes one think that completion cannot be too far distant.

No reason why the space in the standing part of the center table shouldn't be used for a cutlery drawer.

How is this for a nice touch: you flip an insert in the center table and voilà a secure place for glasses or mugs.

25

Hardware

Outboard Chainplates

Since you will most likely be using the standard rigging or at least the plans for it, you should pay strict attention to chainplate and tang installation. I have seen far too many production boats of all types where the chainplates were misaligned or the angles on them were wrongly bent. When installing chainplates, the rigging plans will usually give measurements from the bow to the centerline of the center chainplate. From this point, they'll give distances to the lower *and* upper ends of the two lower shroud plates. These measurements are critical for they determine whether your chainplates will line up correctly with the shrouds or not. If they don't line up, undue strain will be put on one or two bolts, see figure. If you're not satisfied with the plan, consult the architect and ask him to verify.

If your hull is thinner than ½ inch at the sheer line, it would be an excellent idea to beef up the laminates by at least two layers of cloth and mat in the areas where the chainplates will be placed. You can then use either ⅛″ × 3″ diameter stainless steel back-up plates for each bolt. Or here's a very bright idea which I once saw executed. A man made up a replica of his chainplates and installed them without the top bent portions on the inside of the hull. Be sure that the bolt holes will match perfectly and this solution should be very strong.

Once the angles and measurements have been computed for the chainplates, drill the holes cautiously. Be absolutely certain that the drill bit size matches the bolt size exactly. If the bit is smaller, fine, it can be filed out. But if the holes are too large, you've wasted all of your alignments because the bolts will work around in the loose holes, become looser, and leak. Then clean and caulk and use nylon collared lock nuts on the inside.

When placing a liner over the hull, make sure that you leave access holes to each nut on your chainplates. You will have to tighten or recaulk someday. The same practice must be followed with tangs. The one-piece back-up plate mentioned on the previous page has one failing. If a liner is placed over the chainplate bolts and a leak does develop, it would be almost impossible to remove the one-piece back-up plate without tearing the ceiling apart.

Inboard Plates

Inboard shroud bases were discussed in the *To Find a Boat* section; consult it for construction.

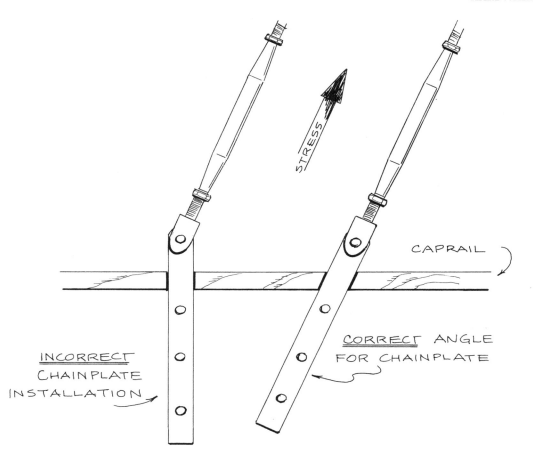

Traditional chainplate installation. If you install your chainplates as shown in the first diagram with the bolts running at an angle to the stress loading (angle of shroud), you can be sure you'll torque the bolts right out of the hull at the onset of the first good wind.

Tangs

If your boat is of traditional rig like ours, you'll have to suffer a bowsprit and perhaps a boomkin. In both cases, you'll need tangs for whisker stays, which continue the work of the forestay and backstay, see figure. To be of optimum value, installation of these tangs should be left until both the bowsprit and boomkin are permanently in place. Since each tang has two bolts holes in it, its alignment and installation at this point will be simple. If you already have your rigging, hook it up to the eye-band or boomkin tangs, turnbuckles and all, then dangle the tangs from their ends. Set your turnbuckles at a point where a little less than half the threaded rods are inside the barrel (the wire may stretch one day and you will need to tighten the turnbuckle; wire very seldom shrinks).

Now find the approximate location; then mark, drill, and bolt the bottom hole of the tang.

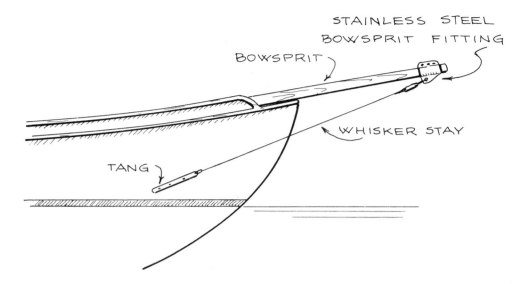

The best way to install whiskerstay tangs is to locate the tang position per the plans, drill the lowest hole only in the hull, and insert the bolt. Now tighten your whiskerstay to get a perfect alignment, then drill the other two holes.

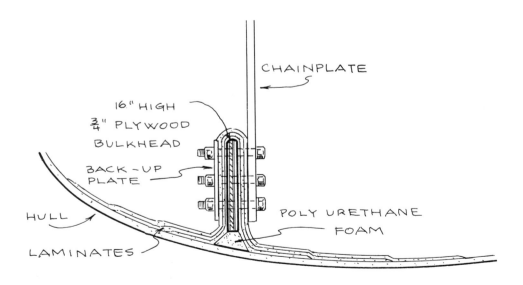

Low fore-and-aft bulkhead acts as base for inboard shrouds. The laminates over the bulkhead are as thick as the hull itself, and run well past the point of bulkhead–hull contact. The laminates are run over the bulkhead over its entire length, which should be from one athwartship bulkhead to another.

Put a hand turn on the turnbuckle to tighten the stay. The whole system now will be perfectly aligned. Drill the second hole.

If you don't have your rigging, use a piece of string tied to the eyebad. Be sure that it's approximately the right length to fit the rigging plans. It doesn't have to be exact, because your rigger can cut the whisker stays to whatever length you like. If you plan to change the length of these stays by relocating the tangs, think sufficiently ahead. You don't want to end up trying to drill through a 4 foot wide bulkhead end on. Use polysulphide to caulk.

Stanchions

It is rather difficult to be specific on this topic because there are so many different varieties of stanchions. Generally, optimum triangulation of fasteners should be attempted. Of course, the fasteners should be through-bolted only with judicious size back-up plates. The only valuable advice here is to caulk everything with poly-sulphide sealer and tighten the bolts well or the stanchions will work and areas around the fastenings will leak. One valuable note perhaps: if you have high bulwarks as we do, with no structural bracing in between where the stanchions are to be mounted, blocks of wood well treated with Cuprinol or zinc chromate should be wedged between the hull and deck. You can then put your bolts through these blocks and end up with an attachment that won't have as much play nor as great a potential for leaks.

Other Hardware

Other deck ware such as blocks, travelers, tracks, pad-eyes, leads, fairleads, anchor rollers, etc., should be through-bolted, back-up plated, and mercilessly caulked inside and out. All the nuts used in these installations should be the locking type; or at least lock-washers should accompany a common hex-nut. Also, pay particular attention everywhere to drill bit size, to assure that you don't over-bore.

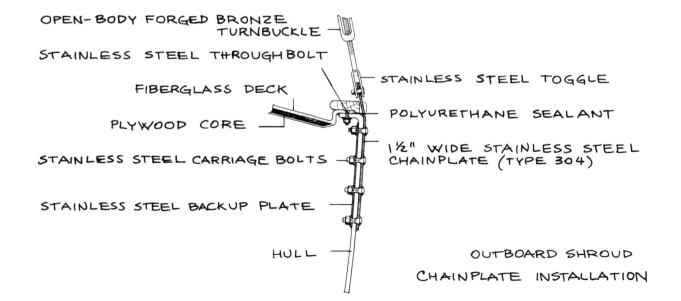

OPEN-BODY FORGED BRONZE TURNBUCKLE

STAINLESS STEEL THROUGH BOLT

FIBERGLASS DECK

PLYWOOD CORE

STAINLESS STEEL CARRIAGE BOLTS

STAINLESS STEEL BACKUP PLATE

HULL

STAINLESS STEEL TOGGLE

POLYURETHANE SEALANT

1½" WIDE STAINLESS STEEL CHAINPLATE (TYPE 304)

OUTBOARD SHROUD CHAINPLATE INSTALLATION

A well engineered foredeck-well that stores anchor, anchor chain and even the windlass.

A good solid installation for a steering mechanism. Note that the upper end of the steering shaft comes through a hefty beam which gives it much support. The solid fiberglassed pipe in the foreground is the duct for draining the cockpit. A very secure system without hoses that can be cut or burnt or worn, and without hose-clamps that can fail or loosen.

A simple, handy little piece added to the bow-pulpit makes a good storage place for reaching pole.

A clever back-stay tensioner that takes the winch handle obviating an extra piece of hardware to buy and to lose.

26

Hatches

You only need to consider two main types of hatches: the sliding and the coaming (lift up) varieties. I prefer calling the lift ups 'coaming hatches' because coamings are the most vital aspect of them if they are to be made leak-proof. I firmly believe that only the double coaming variety is worth building.

Whether this hatch will be hinged or lift up, the coamings make it absolutely watertight, see figure. This feature requires the lower bedlog to be of 1¾ inch stock. Then ¾ inch high lips on it should be high enough to stop all the water and low enough to remain not too fragile. The inner coaming should be 1 inch higher than the bedlog. Then if any water makes it past the first one, the inner will surely stop it. Half-inch drain holes in the four corners of the bedlog will easily let brave water drops drain away. If you are not varnishing the hatch and coaming, make the hatch a loose fit over the bedlogs; otherwise, the first moisture will seal it shut, never to reopen.

Sliding hatch coamings are no more complex to fabricate. The slides themselves will prevent water from entering. They can be fabricated as shown in figures. We used all teak on the exterior; but less expensive woods, such as mahogany, will suffice if kept well varnished. Whichever you use, bed it well in either Dolphinite or polysulphide. And whichever you

use, make sure you have learned to drill and screw into fiberglass before you attempt building a hatch. I am emphatic on this point, because I had problems of all varieties before the method was taught to me by a shipwright who has been working with fiberglass for years.

As I mentioned before, the hole cannot be either too large or too small. In the first case, the screw will spin freely and in the second, the head will snap off when the threads can turn no more even though the screw may be only halfway in.

Therefore, use only the tapered drill bits shown in the tool section. Set the bit at the right depth as shown in the figure. Plug the holes immediately, so that no rain water or dew can seep down into the plywood deck core and rot it. To make the forward end of the hatch waterpoof presents a larger problem. This area is critical, likely to take on head seas; so take care. We used a dual purpose baffle system on ours as shown in the figure. Here the baffle not only keeps water out, but also interacts with the coaming to stop the hatch from sliding backwards and out of the groove. We screwed our baffle onto the hatch from the inside. Then we used bedding compound instead of glue so if we ever have to remove the hatch from its track, we can unscrew the baffle and slide the hatch off.

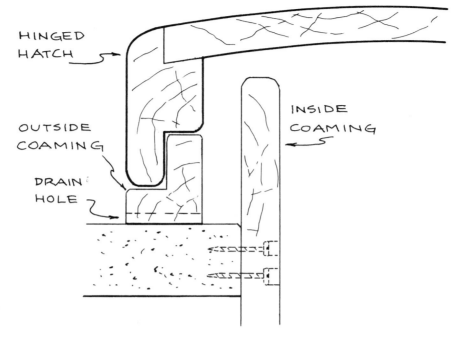

A fine double coaming hatch of the lift-up, hinged variety. If the water makes it through the little S-maze of the outside coaming it'll have to hurdle the inside coaming to get into the cabin. If conditions are so bad that somehow the water is going to get past the inside coaming it's no problem really, because by that time your boat will be sinking anyway.

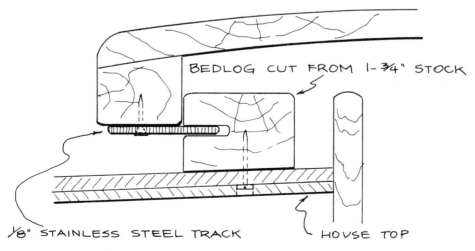

The first of a seemingly endless series of hatch drawings. Here we go. This is a piece of a sliding main hatch. The stainless steel track is just a piece of flatbar. Keep it waxed and it will work like a charm.

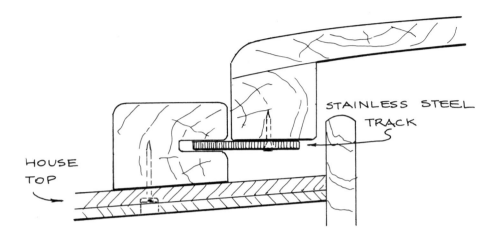

HOUSE
TOP

STAINLESS STEEL
TRACK

This is exactly the same as the last drawing but with the bedlog now outboard of the hatch itself. This method should be used if a wood hatch-cover is to be built in front of the hatch (a highly recommended idea for any boat) for then the bedlog can continue right under the turtle hatch and serve as its foundations. This creates a strong continuous line that ties the hatch and the hatch-cover together.

I must admit, we did something else as an extra precaution. We built a solid teak hatch cover over our hatch, see photo. It does double duty by acting as a base for dinghy chocks as well as helping to keep water out of the cabin. The hatch cover is fastened permanently to the deck. One vital point if you are installing a hatch cover: before final installation of your hatch put a generous coating of some sort of preservative onto the underside of the hatch cover. It will keep all moisture away from the wood, thereby avoiding problem-causing swelling. Preservative of any color is fine here for it will never be seen.

Although hatch coamings are the critical part, the construction of the hatches themselves is also vital if they are to remain strong, unwarped, and leak-proof. I would hesitate to build hatch frames smaller than 1¾ inch stock. Not only will ¾ inch stock warp without a doubt, but rabbet-ting or dove-tailing the corners results in not much more than slivers at the joints. Such areas are much too prone to warp or crack or both when exposed to the weather.

The corner joints can be dove-tailed if you have a jig, or lapped, see figure. Lapping can be assisted by screws and resorcinal glue for a very satisfactory joint. Dove-tails are admittedly more

Teak hatch with teak hatch-cover is about as leakproof as you can get.

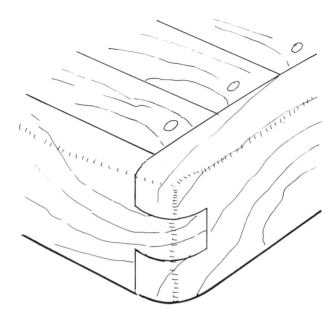

The joint of a hatch corner. A simple let-in such as this is easy to do and gives you lots of good glueing surface inside the joints. A single screw can be run through from the bottom for an even more positive coupling. An alternate of course is dove-tailing but it's much more difficult and the dovetails will be a little more fragile, maybe too fragile exposed to the elements as they would be here.

traditional, but they tend to crack and split more easily than lapped joints because of their fragile size.

Hatch tops, if made of wood, can be laid into rabbetted shelves cut into the inside of the frames as shown in the figure. Whether painted or teaked or mahoganied, the procedure is comparable.

Since most hatches are at least 22 inches wide, a 1 inch thick shell is necessary to provide long lasting resilience to jumping and falling bodies. This requirement is no problem, as 1 inch could be built up of any combination of plywood, or plywood plus teak or other solid wood thicknesses. If teaked, ½ inch plywood with ½ inch overlay of solid wood works well. As mentioned before, anything less than ½ inch is difficult to plug with any dependability.

Since all our hatches have a crown, we had to curve our plywood. To curve ½ inch ply presents tension problems during work as well as after construction. Not only will it be difficult to bend the plywood into place, but even after it's bedded and screwed to the frames it will have a tendency to flatten out and, as in the case of our hatch cover, cause the originally free-sliding hatch to be incessantly trapped.

To avoid this problem, use two layers of ¼ inch ply laminated together. Fit and attach the first layer to the frames; then place the second ¼ inch on top of it. Gluing and screwing ½" × 1½" teak slats atop this base will provide a nice effect. Screws should be no farther than 8 inches apart and well countersunk or the plugs will be very shallow and will pop out after only a few months of contraction and expansion.

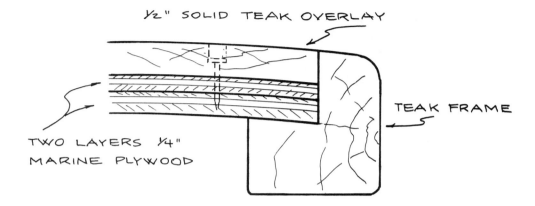

½" SOLID TEAK OVERLAY

TEAK FRAME

TWO LAYERS ¼" MARINE PLYWOOD

Construction of a wood hatch. Two thin layers of plywood should be used if the hatch is to have any crown, for a piece of thick plywood will simply not bend. Glue everything to everything.

Solid teak hatch.

Here, as with the countertop liner, you may want to use wider than 2 inch slats. If so, you'll have to put two screws side by side in each spot or the unfastened edges will rapidly curl up, see photo. Surfacing can be done either with tight butt joints or caulked open seams. The first is recommended for varnishing, the second for oiling, where the wood will undergo much work through moisture absorption and drying. On companionway hatches, a central rib should be installed to add sufficient rigidity. A 2" × 2" is adequate.

If additional light below is desired, dead-lights can be cut into wood hatches, or the plywood-teak central surface can be replaced by plexiglass. Large unprotected surfaces of this material scratch easily and warp in the heat. Three-quarter inch thick laminate or solid plexiglass is needed on companionway hatches and 1/2 inch on smaller ones.

To alleviate the worry of scratching transparent plexiglass, it can be purchased opaque to start with, or regular plexiglass may be made opaque by sanding the surface lightly with 400 grit sandpaper. The second method may be cheaper, as you will be able to purchase second hand or salvaged plexiglass which has undesirable scratches in it. If exterior visibility is desired, it's advisable to use teak slats, to prevent major scratches and to provide a non-skid surface when wet.

If possible, hinge the forward hatch both fore and aft. Equip the hinges with quick release pins. The combination hatch will assist the ship's ventilation whether anchored from the stern or the bow.

Lazarette hatches, which cannot be made fast from below, need a method of dogging tight from the outside. A well-fitted hasp and eye on either side will enable you to lock it as well as close it tight. A chain attached to the hatch and the coaming will keep it from floating away if left unattended.

The question repeatedly arises whether to use drop boards or doors on a companionway hatch. I believe that when all has been considered, it is simply a matter of taste unless you have to mount your compass on the aft face of the trunk cabin like we did. In that case, doors, if ever left open would completely hide the compass card. Drop boards are usually fairly large, so it's best to use at least 13/16 inch stock to avoid drastic warpage which can render the critters immobile. Adjoining boards must be rabbetted, as in the figure, to keep out driving rain and nasty following seas. A good compromise is a pair of removable doors. This is made possible by a set of pin-type hinges which work exactly like a dinghy rudder.

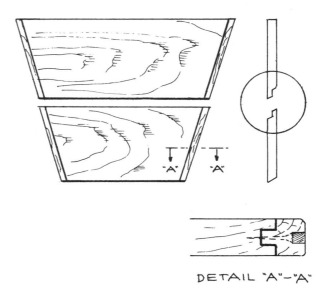

DETAIL "A"–"A"

INSIDE

Hatch drop-boards. The more sloped the sides the quicker they are to remove but also the quicker they'll fall out and be washed overboard. Ideally the sides should be parallel.

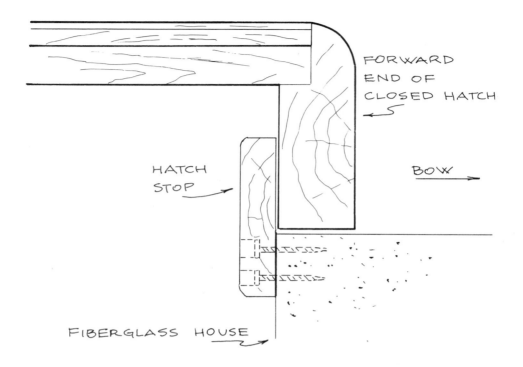

When you pull your hatch shut, it's preferable that it will not keep sliding continually until you stagger backward and fall into the sea. To help you stay aboard, you should install a hatch-stop as shown. But I think it's best to just surface screw it instead of countersinking and plugging it, because then if you ever need to remove the hatch for varnishing or whatever, all you'll have to do is remove the screws.

Grabrails

These handy handholds should be abundant topsides and belowdecks. The minimum requirement is a pair atop the cabin running fore and aft. If available, they are best bought premilled, for unless you have a jig, their fabrication can consume tremendous amounts of time. If you must make them, be sure to cut them from clear stock (no knots) and make them good and heavy. You might do well to use 1 inch stock. Be sure to leave plenty of wood between the handholds for screws. Make sure you leave the handholds deep enough that one can move a hand quickly if need be.

Installation is quite simple from here on, especially if your cabin top is at least ¼ inch thick fiberglass with a plywood core. In such a base, No. 14 self-tapping stainless steel flatheads will hold very well even if a 400 pound behemoth comes for a visit, see figure. If your cabin top is of plywood with only a thin covering of glass, screwing would be folly, because the chances of it holding under any conditions would be marginal. You have to through-bolt.

This procedure is more complex because it will require a person below with nuts, washers, a socket wrench, as well as some previous provisions for a reinforcing base under the headliner. The best solution here may be to install the grabrails before any interior insulation or liner has been begun. You may have to build around nuts, but it will still provide the strongest method of fastening. On the other hand, replacement of this hand rail, if it were broken, would be impossible without ripping off the headliner so that the nuts can be pulled.

Whichever system you use, fit and drill your grabrails dry (without bedding compound). If you are doing it yourself, it's ideal to put in the screws temporarily. Then the thing won't flip-flop about in the wind while you're drilling the other holes. When all holes have been drilled, remove screws and grabrail. You will see between the wood and the glass a tighly packed little mound of glass powder that the drill bit pushed out. This powder has to be cleaned off from both wood and glass. If you pre-caulk everything, then drill the holes and insert screws without any dry fitting first, these hard little mounds will remain under the rail. As well as preventing a tight fit and good seal, they'll cause a teeter-totter effect which will cause the grabrail to work loose and leak prematurely. So clean it well, caulk it well, and screw it down tight. But remember, you're using flat heads with a wedge shoulder and if you force the screws you'll split the teak. I know; I did it twice in one afternoon.

If you do split one, don't panic; spread the opening, fill it with resorcinal glue, clamp it and leave it for at least 24 hours. It will be better than new. I still wouldn't splinter them on purpose though.

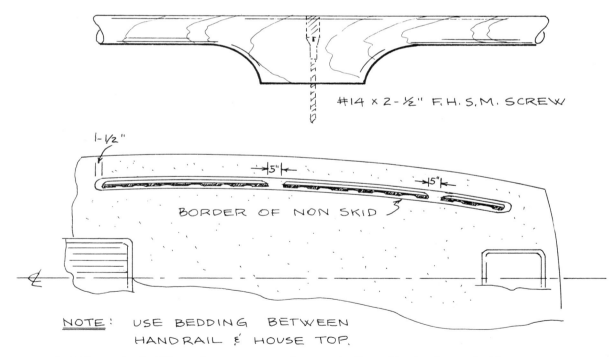

Installing grabrails. When using a screwgun to fasten grabrails to a fiberglass house, don't lean on the thing as if you were headed straight for China, for the relatively narrow piece of handrail will split like kindling. Once the bottom of the rail is flush with the fiberglass, STOP. You can't displace one piece of matter with another.

Boom Gallows

I cannot recommend too much the installation of a boom gallows. Not only will it enable you to set the boom off to one side so you won't open your skull every time you climb the companionway steps, but it also provides a marvelous place for an awning. Most of all, however, it makes a beautiful stern pulpit to which you can cling in desperate night storms when you're lucky enough to draw watch. It's the most comforting companion you can have.

All require some expert welding for either stainless or bronze. The gallows itself should be cut from 1¾ inch stock (preferably teak for it won't rot or check as easily as others). The best tool to use is a large 4 inch hole saw to cut out the area where the boom sets. If you don't have one, a saber saw will do. Whatever your design, make sure the gallows gets through-bolted and be certain that you triangulate the base, see photo, to help it withstand the force of your body against it.

Make the gallows solid and permanent. Removable ones are complicated, require a place to be stored, and begin to work loose in the first seven seconds of use. Avoid them.

Boom gallows make for a nice resting place as well as keeping the boom off your head.

Scuppers and Hawse Pipes

If your boat has bulwarks (as it should), you'll need some apparatus by which water will drain from the decks. If your bulwarks are of solid wood, the solution is simple; cut a few 1½ inch holes or build double caprails to start with.

If your decks are the double-walled fiberglass bulwark type like ours, the ideal solution for scuppers is a fitted set of sleeved bronze scupper pipes as shown in the figure. Larger ones can be used for hawse pipes to lead mooring lines (fair-leads on top of the caprails can be substituted for this purpose). Perko and a number of other companies make hawse pipes of cast bronze. The problem with cast pipes is that they do not overlap thus they have to be filled or fiber-glassed. The best sealant – if you can get at the pipe from the inside – is a large rubber hose, clamped to both pieces. They are each screwed into the fiberglass. It is ideal to use stainless steel sheet metal screws even though they contrast visually, for they are threaded all the way to the base of the head, thus providing a superior grip. If the space between your bulwarks is accessible, caulk the inside seams also. It can't hurt.

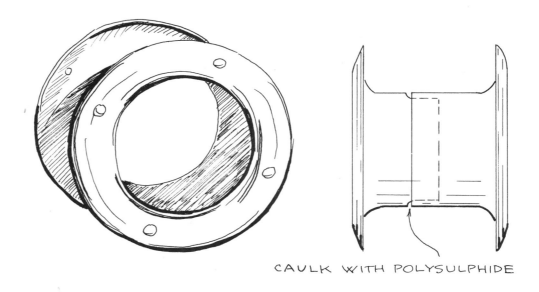

CAULK WITH POLYSULPHIDE

A hawsepipe that'll act as a lead for docklines should be of heavy cast bronze or aluminum. We had spun-brass ones for a few years but they were very thin walled (had to be for spinning) and they all cracked. For best sealing, it's nice to have the over-lapping kind.

27

Detailing

At the joyous moment when the completion of your boat flutters just past your fingertips, you will be faced with the grandpop of all icebergs. Somehow, somewhere, someone christened this horribly fidgety, monstrously time-consuming, and usuriously unrewarding task, 'detailing.' This cultured term refers to resanding, repainting, regelcoating, recleaning, and generally rebuilding the entire boat. Nowhere but here do things seem quite so futile because each job seems to mess up the ones you just finished.

At any rate, there are a few short cuts and precautions which can be pursued to achieve a completely satisfactory job in minimum time. The greatest time saver, of course, is sufficient preparation and careful rough assembly. If you did the job well, the task now facing you will be minimal.

Painting

It seems, through practice, that straight grain woods like mahogany make for a better surface than wide grained ones like fir. Though you may be considering covering your plywood cabinetry with paint, it may well be worth the extra few dollars per $4' \times 8'$ sheet to use mahogany plywood instead of fir. You may argue that with dedicated sanding the fir can be brought to just as fine a finish. Quite the contrary. The more you sand, the deeper will be the softer grains and the more highlighted the more pitchy, harder ones.

One solution that does improve fir, is painting the wood while still unsanded with a coat of undercoat, then sanding, then painting, then sanding, etc. By this process the softer grained areas will be protected by a semi-hard covering. I had to use this method on one piece of fir plywood that I recklessly substituted for mahogany. Not only did sanding take an unimaginably long time, but it possessed the added featurette of covering the minutest surface with a thorough coating of white dust that lifted and thickened the air every time I blinked. So try to use mahogany; if you can't, suffer.

Your painting chores will be much easier if you mask unpainted adjoining areas with tape. This practice is admittedly time-devouring, but not nearly as bad as scraping blobs of paint from wood. Since the paint will penetrate into most woods (the drier the deeper) overslop could lead to major problems. To get out all the unwanted paint, you will need to carve irrepairable gulleys with sandpaper. In solid wood, such repairs are less noticeable than on plywood. On plywood, very slight over-zealousness can result in your penetrating the thin (with teak plywood only one mil thick) top layer of veneer. I have not yet heard of a satisfactory method of veneer repair.

So tape off the perimeter of your areas and you will save hours of frustration. To help even further, seal off the area under the masking tape with a clear wood sealer. This procedure should prevent any paint from seeping under the tape. If it does not, at least the paint will not penetrate the sealed wood and it will be easy to remove.

On the painted surface, use a quick drying undercoat. Z-Spar 105 is very satisfactory, although I'm not convinced that other oil-based undercoats perform any less commendably. Even if you use mahogany ply, it is a good idea to sand well between coats. The first undercoat will be almost completely removed if you want a good job. Brush strokes are left by the finest brushes; if left unsanded, they will become more accentuated with each following coat. I'm not advocating a formica-like finish, but a soft smooth finish will bring hours of pleasure in silent dawning light.

Although Z-Spar 105 is a wonderful undercoat, I cannot recommend Z-Spar products for subsequent layers. Their finishing paint is very thick (I'm told that a good finish paint should be no thicker than fresh milk) resulting in a multitude of runs and brush marks. Apart from this problem, it has the irritating habit of never drying, thus clogging up a piece of sandpaper on the first stroke.

Interlux makes excellent finishing paints in many beautiful quick-drying shades. It also is difficult to sand, not because it fills the sandpaper, but for quite the opposite reason. It's a very hard protective finish.

A good rule is to use two undercoats (as mentioned, the first is all but sanded off completely) and two finishing coats. Some people advocate four or five finishing coats, but then some people mow their front lawn five times a week. After the last coat of paint has dried, don't leap to tear off the masking tape. If you do, you'll tear half the paint with it. Some paint will have overflown on to the tape and you will find a tendency for this overflow to pull the other paint with it instead of breaking conscientiously where the tape ends. To avoid pulling off paint take a sharp razor knife and literally cut the paint around the tape's edge. You can then pull the tape off cleanly and admire your masterpiece.

Masking tape will come in handy during procedures other than painting. If you are sanding a surface which is at right angles to another, you will be endlessly either hand sanding grooves into the other surface, or gouging it repeatedly while you use a vibrator or belt sander. To avoid the unnecessary repairs that will have to follow, tape the edge of the surface you won't be sanding, the wider the tape the better. This tape will allow some protection against sandpaper.

As exceptionally beneficial as masking tape is, it does have one villainous quality. If left on over a long period in a place where direct sunlight hits it, the glue will penetrate the surface it's on and cling tenaciously while the paper backing will crumble in your hands. We once left a strip of tape all around the fiberglass bulwarks when we caulked our teak decks. Absurd as it may seem, Candace and I spent eight tearful hours scraping off 64 feet of 1 inch wide tape. It was about as much fun as practice bleeding.

Sanding

If you are sanding wood, no matter how solid and thick it is, use sandpaper of no rougher grit than 60. You can still shape wood rapidly with 60 grit, if necessary. Any rougher grit will leave a deep gouge in your wood (especially if you are going cross-grain) which will be very difficult to remove. Cross-grain sanding should be avoided if at all possible. On exterior surfaces, I can see no need to go finer than 150 at the most. If you are oiling exterior teak, to go finer than 100 is almost a waste, because the grain of the wood will raise drastically within two or three days no matter who you know. If you are varnishing, you may consider going to 220 on your last run on the wood, but then varnish immediately because the grain will rise as soon as the dew falls. 220 is acceptable to use between coats, although some say to use 400 before your last coat.

If you can afford to (and you almost can't afford not to), buy sandpaper by the sleeve. A sleeve usually contains 50 or 100 sheets. It is cheaper and you will end up using it all, especially common grits like 60, 80, 100, and 150.

On interiors, you may consider using 220 on all your woods. If you are varnishing, you will need to; and if you are oiling, you may as well, for then you can oil the wood and immediately run over it with 220 to achieve a nearly hand-rubbed finish.

Oiling

The only important point here is to wash down the wood with acetone before oiling. Keep turning the rag you use to get all of the sawdust out of the grain. If you don't, it will have a tendency to darken once the oil is applied, rendering the wood lifeless and dark.

The first coat of oil you apply should be of a resin type, like Watco interior Danish teak oil. It does have a pungent odor, but it seals and protects wood better than wood sealers. Later coats can be of resinless variety, like lemon oil.

Be sure to wipe off all excess oil (that which has not absorbed) no more than twenty minutes after application. If you don't, it will become tacky and attract every speck of dust and fluff as well as make the surface unsightly with patches of unequal sheen.

For the exterior, use oil recommended for that purpose only. Watco makes one that has a tendency to turn grey and unappealingly black within a very few weeks. Others, like Tip-Top Teak Oil, blacken to a lesser extent. Light sanding is highly recommended before a new coat of exterior oil is applied. A very fine product called Te-Ka cleans the wood better than sandpaper because it penetrates deeper. A very good idea

after sanding a coat of varnish or a coat of oil, instead of using acetone which may be spilled and cause patches, would be to use a product by the name of Tac-Cloth. It is a messy, toadish feeling cloth that is treated with a substance which absorbs fantastic quantities of dust from even the grainiest woods.

Varnishing

As mentioned, you may want to prepare the surface with 220 grit sandpaper. Then, a thinned-down sealing layer (about 20 to 25 per cent paint thinner) should be applied followed by light sanding, then a full strength varnish coat. It is a fallacy that each coat has to be sanded to the point where no hairline is left untouched. Unless you want a glasslike finish, light sanding will do nicely. Apply the varnish in thin coats. Five thin coats are better than three thick ones which may run and curdle when touched, even four days after application. After sanding, wipe with a Tac-Cloth or similar product.

Be sure your varnish is applied at least three hours before the dew falls, if you are doing exterior wood. In climates where the day may have been cooler than 60 degrees, try to have your varnishing finished by mid-morning or the dew will ruin your precious work. For the eccentrics it might be a great matter of pride to use refrigerated varnish. Varnish, thus cooled, will have a tendency to dry *from the inside out* and consequently have a better hold. I was told this by an eccentric and I never did quite figure out what he meant, but it might be worth a try.

Do not be frugal. Buy a good quality brush and clean it meticulously after using. There's nothing worse than picking molting hairs or kernels of hardened varnish from your otherwise perfect surface.

Filling

Small marks which are deep or irrepairable can be drilled and plugged. A teak or mahogany plug out of place does not look as bad as a worm hole or a blob of white paint or a deep gouge. If the spot is large, patching could be considered. Patching is nothing more than the old art of inlaying wood. If you have a bad area, chisel it out very carefully and fill it with a piece of wood. If the grains match perfectly, that's wonderful. If they don't match at all, it looks good, and if you use entirely different kinds of wood, it looks even more intentional. Whichever you use, cut your filler piece to size first, then use it as a pattern on the damaged wood to scribe in the perimeter, then chisel out the damaged piece. Use a very sharp cutting tool or you will cause more damage through chipping than what you set out to repair to begin with. Keep a wetting stone handy.

If you suffer long splits in wood like we did with our hatches, the repair is simple. Many people use just glue or glue mixed with sawdust.

I find either solution most unsatisfactory. You will end up with very dark colored seams or cracks which probably look worse than the crack itself. The best way to fill cracks in wood is to use wood. Cut long wedges, cover the sides with glue and drive them into the cracks with a mallet. Then chisel and sand off the remaining bulk.

If you pick your wood color to match, the inserted wedges will be unnoticeable.

Gelcoat Touch-up

The gelcoat will be chipped during construction in many places on your boat. The best solution is to leave all repairs until the end. To prevent the problem of chipping and minimize necessary final cleaning, a coat of latex base protector can be applied before any work has begun, see photo. It will peel off easily even if left for a few months.

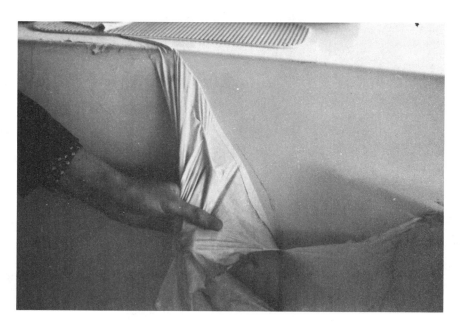

A coat of latex can be painted onto fiberglass surfaces to protect them during construction. Saves a lot of cleaning and touch-up afterwards. Peels away easily and cleanly.

If, however, chips in the gelcoat do occur, follow this procedure:

1. Clean the area with acetone.
2. Fill the crack with body putty.
3. Sand with 400 grit sandpaper.
4. Spray on gelcoat.
5. Spray on sealer.
6. Peel off the tape before the gelcoat hardens.
7. Wash off sealer with water.
8. After it has gone off, sand the whole area with 600 grit. If you don't do your final sanding immediately following the catalyzation of the gelcoat, you may run into another problem, especially if you had taped off the area around which you sprayed. Very likely you will have a sharp edge of fresh gelcoat protruding which, if not feathered in immediately, may result in chipping. So sand with 600 grit and feather in.

Other Problems

If you do have stubborn problems with overcooked masking tape or polyethylene which the sun baked onto your mast, deck, or caprail, only one economical remedy seems possible. People have attempted to use acetone, thinners, heat guns, and fingernails to no avail. The only thing that seems to work is steam cleaning. You can rent portable units or find companies who will come out to your aid. If your mistake is portable (like a boom) take it to the nearest do-it-yourself car wash and do-it-yourself.

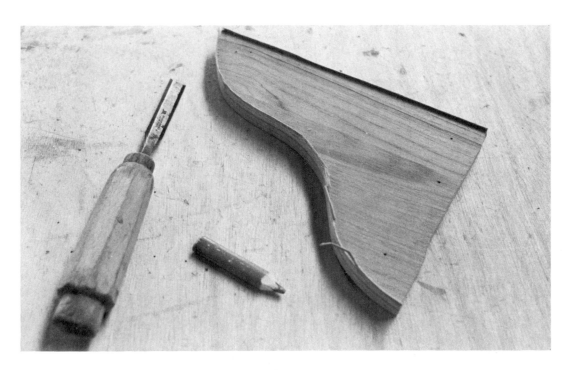

Thin veneer edging which you can buy in rolls, is a good thing to use for finishing off the edge of a piece of plywood. Always use edging a little wider than you need, then trim off with a very sharp chisel.

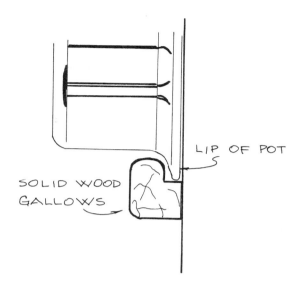

LIP OF POT

SOLID WOOD
GALLOWS

Bulkhead-hung pots can be kept from becoming The Bells of St. Mary's *by putting the bottom edge of their lips into little wood gallows.*

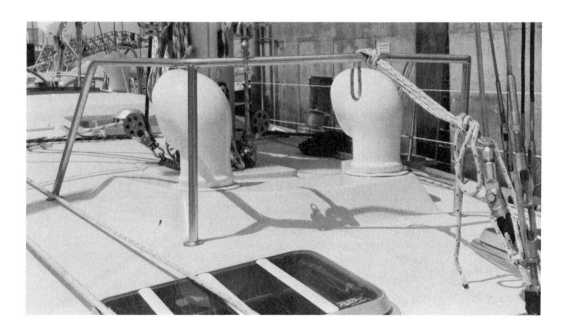

Pipes around mast keep lines from fouling on cowl-vents, are a good place to tie and shackle lines to, and add a bit of safety when one is working around mast.

28

Teak Decks

I have intentionally left this section as the final item in construction for I believe it to be a non-functional item, application or exclusion of which can be decided only after lengthy deliberation between you and your ego. I have always thought it would require a babbling moron to take a perfectly solid, non-skid, water-proof and rot-proof fiberglass deck, spend $2,000 on teak and fasteners, then drill a thousand holes to hold the wood down, then spend $300 on caulking and bedding compounds to seal and waterproof the thousand holes he has just drilled.

Needless to say, we put teak decks on our boat at great expense, and almost 200 hours of screamingly frustrating labor. But they are beautiful and they are non-skid and we do love them and I wouldn't trade them for a brand new Porsche . . . well, maybe a silver one. Here's how it's done.

Type of Deck and Wood Selection

Try to pick the straightest, least knotty pieces you can find. The longer, the better. If need be, shop around for long clean pieces. One of the worst jobs in doing the decks is butting ends together, so try to avoid too many joints. Knots look beautiful down below if oiled or varnished, but topsides they'll just weather and pop out, or if you are bending your planks they'll surely snap in two at the knot.

If you do have to have joints in your deck, be sure to place them in the area of least curvature, even if your planking is milled to as narrow as 1¾ inch each. It will be almost impossible to bend the last foot of a piece of teak, so try to get your joints to stagger, as shown in the photo and try to put them amidships where the curvature of the deck is at its least.

Try to predetermine the width of the planking you intend to use. If you are running your deck-ing straight fore and aft without bending as in the photo, the width of your planks is unlimited. Running them in this fashion is a traditional procedure and it is very simple to do, but only if your cabin sides themselves are uncurved or only slightly curved. If their curve is drastic, an attempt at straight decking can only result in a myriad of short, unsightly, slivery pieces. If you intend to have a curved deck with either a king plank, see photo, or herringbone foredeck, see photo, using planking wider than 2 inches will lead to grave problems during bending unless the boat is very long on deck and of a very slight beam. If it is of this design, perhaps you could push the width of the decking to 2⅜ or to 2½ inches. I mention this tradeoff here because it's

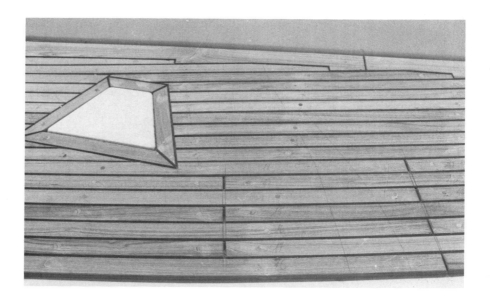

Where planks are joined, the joints should be staggered to provide some strength to neighbouring pieces. Notice nibbing at top of photo where the ends of the teak planks are blended into the covering boards along the cabin-sides.

Straight fore and aft decking.

Traditional king plank.

Herringboned foredeck.

good to know your intended plank width before you buy your teak stock so that you will select only those widths which will lend themselves economically to your purpose.

The thickness of the stock should not fall below ½ inch. Anything thinner will be very difficult to plug as well as more inclined to warp and crack with constant weathering. If the plug thickness ends up being less than ⅛ inch, the plug is guaranteed to crack and pop out before the year is over.

Milling

Whether you use straight decks or curved ones, you should mill a caulk groove into the edge of each plank. You will need this groove into which to pour polysulphide sealant after your deck is laid. The caulking not only seals the deck and keeps water from entering into the plywood core through the screw holes, but it also remains flexible to allow the decks to shrink and swell without causing the wood to buckle or crack. The caulking groove need not exceed ¼" × ¼". I have seen some teak decks without grooves but I have never known how they survive. The grooves can be milled into the planks with either a dado or two cuts of a table saw.

Covering Boards

Making covering boards will probably be the single most time-consuming task in your decking. They should be cut with a band saw (if one is not available a table saw will do) out of wide planking. I managed to cut ours on a table saw; if you set your blade at a height barely sufficient to cut through your wood and no more, you will be able to do it too if you concentrate.

To determine the shape of the covering boards, you will have to scribe them to fit the cabin and/or your bulwarks. To be sure that you don't waste expensive teak, cut templates for each board out of ⅛ inch thick veneer. The length and width of each board will be dictated by economy. The wider and longer you make your covering boards, the more scrap you will have. Boards 3½ inches wide look wide enough to seem intentionally different from the 2 inch planking and yet are narrow enough to be fairly economical. The length of each board will depend on how drastically curved your cabin sides or your bulwarks are. If they are curved as much as ours, the boards cannot economically exceed 5 feet.

A side note: if you want teak decks, I think it practical to mill and lay them before you trim out the interior. The amount of large scraps from milling the decks is phenomenal, and all this scrap can be utilized inside for corner trim, shelf sea-rails, etc.

If you have an extremely small radius at your cabin-side-to-deck or deck-to-bulwark turns, fitting the boards flush against the cabin or bulwark will be simple. If, however, you have a substantial radius, you must choose one of two alternatives. You can (a) begin your decking at a distance from the vertical side where the curve will have no consequence, or (b) hand plane the bottom edge of the covering board to a curve large enough to accommodate the radius in the fiberglass. The butt end joints for the covering boards can be made using any number of traditional scarfs.

Do *not* mill caulk grooves into the covering boards. For the long sides you can use the groove in the first plank; as for the scarfs, it is preferred that you bed and screw the boards down in their final position first, then belatedly chisel in the grooves. This way, if your butting or alignment is not perfect (and they never will be even though the screw holes have been dry fitted), you will be able to cheat a little and chisel in a nice parallel sided caulk groove.

The King Plank

I am not sure that a single logical argument exists in favor of a king plank except that it is pretty. To do one is time consuming and painstaking. If you can get the pattern for it from someone, you will be far ahead; but if not, you will spend many hours drawing in the lines and routing them out.

The fastest procedure involves laying the planks with roughly hacked off ends. The angle at the ends is irrelevant and the fit unimportant for the ends will be later overlapped by the king plank. Once the planks are all down, make a pattern out of veneer or cardboard for the king plank. The width of the plank and the angles you use will be of your own choosing. Cut out the plank from a solid piece of teak, lay it over the deck, and draw its shape onto the over-long planks. Now take the router and set it exactly the depth of your teak decking. If anything, leave it $1/16$ inch shallower, because then you can easily penetrate the last bit of wood with an old chisel and remove the excess. This way you won't have your expensive router bit dulled by the fiberglass.

Now you can drop in your king plank and see how it fits. Don't worry about it being in perfect alignment. As long as your mistake is no greater than $1/16$ inch you will be able to correct it when you rout in the caulking groove between the king plank and the other planks.

Herringboning

This method is less demanding. It is quicker than a king plank, because it involves only the first stage in laying the deck. You must use more caution, however, in scribing your angles on the end of each plank to make certain you don't wander too far off the centerline. But again, remember that a $1/16$ inch mistake is allowable. You will then only have to rout in a centerline caulking groove to notch out the mistakes and complete the job.

An absolutely vital note, whichever method you employ, is to have the straight bit for your router sharpened just before you start working on your teak decks. Use a carbide-tip bit; whatever else you may have heard, teak is a brittle wood and prone to chipping, if anything but the sharpest of tools is used.

Deck Laying

The first step in laying a deck should be shaping and fitting the covering boards. Dry fitting should include the placement of each board into its final position and putting at least a few screws into their final places.

When it seems you have done everything you can to make the covering boards fit perfectly, take out those screws you have just put in and lift up the covering boards. You will find little mounds of white fiberglass powder surrounding the mouth of every hole. Some of the powder will have stuck around the screw hole on the wood too. This powder must be wiped off completely or the board won't set evenly and even teeter over the little mound, which can cause it to perhaps crack. This procedure of dry fitting and cleaning off the dust mounds should be observed with every teak-to-glass joining to guarantee better joints. Once the dust has cleared you can permanently install the boards.

The first step in installation is to lay two unbroken beads of black polysulphide about 1 inch from either end of the plank onto the fiberglass. Many people have used Dolphinite as the bedding compound, but Dolphinite has the tendency to expand and ooze oil in very hot climates even a few months after laying. I've heard of some decks buckling because of the expansion. And even if buckling doesn't occur, the seam-caulking may be pushed away from the wood, allowing water to penetrate.

At any rate, lay down two beads of polysulphide, and just for safety pop a drop into each screw hole. If you think that's being over anxious, just try not doing it and see how you sleep at night.

Once the covering boards are in their final place, the fun begins. Use your table saw to cut about ten pieces of $3/4$ inch thick by $4'' \times 4''$ plywood blocks. Now gather up all the oak, ash,

Teak deck being laid. The pieces have all been fit and the holes all drilled and cleaned and now great amounts of bedding compound is being spread all over the pre-drilled deck before the teak pieces are finally screwed into place.

and teak scraps you have and cut them into wedges ranging from 4″ × 10″ to ½″ × 5″.

The harder the wood you use, the better because you will be smashing these blocks with a hammer and you will want the wedges to last as long as possible under this onslaught.

Next, establish the athwartship points where you will be putting screws into the planks. The screws should be no more than 12 inches apart; if the bends are radical, use closer centers. At these 12 or whatever inch points, draw a straight pencil line athwartships on the fiberglass. Nothing looks prettier than perfectly lined up plugs, and the pencil lines will help you prettify.

Now get your first plank, cut it to length, then take the ¾ inch ply blocks you have just cut and screw them into the deck 4 or 5 inches from the covering boards and about 12 inches apart. Use one screw only and use it in the center of the block so that the block can swivel when you insert different shaped wedges. Drive in this

one screw deep, or the force of the wedges will cause the screw to bend, and it is almost impossible to pull a crippled screw out of fiberglass.

Now lay double seams of caulking down the length of the deck where the first plank will go. Spread it evenly and thickly. Be sure to put a bead right next to the covering board to seal the edges. Don't scrimp. It's easier to wipe off the mess that squeezes out than to try to fill the voids under a screwed down deck. Also have a couple of rolls of paper towels ready along with a can of acetone to wipe the goo from your hands, tools, and your left ear lobe. Rags are passable, but too frequently you'll end up wiping old goo onto your hands, instead of wiping the new goo off; so, use paper towels and throw them away. It's only money.

Now, summon the bulkiest friend you have and secure his loyalty for the next four days. You will need every ounce he carries. The longer his reach, the better.

With a screwgun and drill motor, some 1 inch pan-head sheet metal screws (remember flat heads split wood) and a couple of hammers, you will be set. You will also need about thirty tubes of polysulphide. Have them handy, for it's very ulcerizing to run out when you're raring to keep going on your job.

Now, with the goo spread evenly, and with the large friend hanging onto the other end of your plank, bend the plank and place it behind the blocks. Once it's down behind the blocks, don't ever take your weight off it. Be sure to hold down both ends and both centers, and tell Chubby not to lose his balance or the plank will spring up like a steel coil and smash his face in.

Now comes the critical point. Insert wedges between each block and the plank; begin to tap each wedge gently and evenly, one tap each at a time. Give your helper a hammer too, but tell him to be gentle and never to take his weight off the plank. As the plank is stressed more and more, the more vital this constant pressure becomes, because the greater the tension the greater the tendency of the plank to spring up and smash in the aforementioned face.

Be certain, also, that all wedges advance evenly. If one proceeds or lags behind the others by too much, the plank will crack and literally explode. Teak shatters in the most frightening fashion, taking its toll of skin and blood as it does. Try to keep the leading edge of the plank somewhat off the fiberglass. If the plank is squeezed down completely tight, you will be scraping off all of the preciously spread polysulphide; so, keep hammering gently until the plank is butted tight against the covering board.

Once in place, screw it down and screw it down tight immediately. Drill your countersink holes about halfway through the plank. If you drill any less you will not have a deep hole for your plug; as mentioned before, if the plug is less than 1/8 inch it is guaranteed to crack and

pop out very shortly.

If by some chance you hear a nasty cracking sound before you wedge the plank into place, don't start bashing in the nearest portlight in anguish. As a matter of fact don't even move. Take a bit of epoxy glue (which you should have sitting around ready mixed) and pour generously into the obviously cracked wood. Now hammer the wedges home and, as if nothing has happened, screw the plank into place. You may have to disturb the straight line of the plugs and put a couple of screws out of sequence to make sure the crack won't open up. Wipe off the excess epoxy glue and try to forget about it. You may now get off the plank.

Move your blocks back about 2 inches, screw them down, and start the whole process over again. Some people advocate not cutting the planks to length until they are laid in their final place. This idea is probably very good, for then you won't have to worry about getting the planks in exactly the right location. While you are attempting to bend them it's almost an impossibility anyway.

On the other hand, it's simple to set in a board and screw it, then just wack the end off with a good sharp chisel. Use only the sharpest chisel or you will split the teak. Don't try to hack the whole end off in one oafish blow. Penetrate no more than 1/8 inch per blow; then chisel out the groove and do the next vertical penetration. Don't use this chisel to go right to the fiberglass. Nothing can ruin a good chisel quicker than a few blows at a steel-hard deck. Have a duller chisel at hand to cut through the last 1/16 inch.

Other Things

There are a few problem items with teak decks, like nibbing, see photo, which I prefer to making wedges where the hull no longer parallels the cabin sides. Nibs can be angled and lengthened to taste. Other problems, like corners, deck fills, cockpit trim, etc, are shown in the photographs.

Depending on the complexity of your deck design, some of your covering boards may just require a lot of finesse.

The best craftsmen will put a lovely covering board around his hatches and have his planks fit as prettily as this.

Caulking

Once you have finished laying the deck, the fun is just beginning. Your next job is to plug the 1,000 screw holes. Make sure you align grains of the plugs and tap them in good and deep. It is preferable to use a clear epoxy glue on the plugs instead of resorcinal, for resorcinal is a very dark red color which leaves a very dark brown ring around the plug, no matter how great your care.

Now go back, and with a chisel wack off the tops of the plugs. Don't bother to get them flush at this time. Just get rid of the bulk, so that if someone kicks one, it won't break off and require replacement.

Now get the most powerful vacuum cleaner you can find and clean all the scrap and dust from the caulking grooves. Make sure you unlodge every piece of junk you find.

Now go shopping and take a lot of money. You will need about three gallons of "Grove" two-part polysulphide. About ½ pint of hardener comes with each gallon kit, and each gallon kit costs about $50. You will also need to buy about 40 empty caulking cartridges, a quart of Grove teak primer, a gallon of acetone, and a lot of paper towels.

I mention the trade name of the two-part polysulphide here because I have not heard of anyone else manufacturing this. The only other name I've heard it called has been "Black Death." After you've half finished filling the first empty cartridge you will be completely empathetic to the etymology.

The one item you may have difficulty finding is the empty cartridges. I did, and when I found them I was so happy that the atrocious price of 50¢ each (for an empty cartridge??!!) gave me heart failure for no more than 49 seconds. You will get used to highway robbery like this throughout your boat building career. It seems that in boat building, the boat builder is fair game, so by no means hesitate to lie, cheat, and rob all you can (see chapter on scrounging). At any rate, secure about 40 of these tubes early and have them ready.

Now, using a small acid brush, primer all the immaculate caulking grooves thoroughly. Don't worry about getting primer on top of the teak deck itself. It will be sanded.

Caulk right away. To be economical time-wise, you will have to mix a gallon of caulking at a time. Mix in the catalyst thoroughly. This procedure is a demanding task, because the polysulphide is as thick as tar. Fortunately the catalyst is a light brown color so its path is easily traceable.

Stir the catalyst in completely but slowly, or you will trap a jillion air bubbles which will stay in the thick caulking compound. They will be transferred and trapped in the caulking grooves only to pop when you are sanding the hardened caulking. Once you sand off the top of the bubble, you will be left with gaping holes which you will have to open, clean out, and fill with more "Black Death." To this end save a quarter of a gallon of polysulphide and a bit of hardener. You will need almost that much for repair work.

Don't be afraid to let the polysulphide fill the grooves to overflowing, see photos. When it hardens it will shrink and settle. It is a lot easier to cut off the excess than to fill the voids. Once the poly has gone off, trim off the overflow rubber with a sharp chisel. Then get a belt sander and about four 50 grit sanding belts (anything finer will have its pores filled in no time) and grind the caulking right down to the wood, see photo. If you find any air holes in the seams, fill them now.

You will find if you curve your decks that the edges of some drastically curved planks will have a tendency to turn slightly upward, necessitating very extensive belt sanding to bring it to an even level. After you have leveled the deck with the 50, use 80 grit paper to get out the cross-grain gouges, and finish off with 100. Then oil or let bleach or whatever you like. Watco makes an exterior teak oil with a very high resin content that has a tendency to turn black a few months after application. I have heard of Te-Ka oil used on the exterior with very good results.

You can see from the foregoing that laying a teak deck is not something you can leave for a dull Sunday afternoon. It does take time (as mentioned, approximately 200 hours) and quite a bit of money to do a satisfactory, lasting job. If you can afford it, by all means don't hesitate for there are very few sights to a sailor quite as heartwarming and satisfying as the sight of a freshly scrubbed, bright teak deck. . . . Anyway, it's probably the best non-skid you can find.

After you plug your decks this is what they will look like. Then you come along with a chisel and take most of the top off, making sure you don't take too much or you might chip deeper than the deck. You'll be grinding it all with a beltsander anyway, so don't be afraid of leaving a bit extra.

Filling in grooves with two part polysulfide. Fill them to overflowing. The access rubber is easy to slice off with a chisel after it has set up.

Belt sander removes what chisel leaves.

The same 38 with a beautiful hatch over the recessed anchor-well that also houses the windlass. All this keeps the foredeck clear for sails, feet and lines. Note recessed trough in which anchor chain feeds overboard.

29

Rigging

Mast

I waded for four months through people's opinions, prejudices, and whims, trying desperately to decide between a wood and an aluminum mast. My final decision came; not from conviction, but by default. And although I am overjoyed about my aluminum mast, I may have rationalized myself into this emotion.

I always felt slightly ill at ease about the vulnerability of a wood mast; the susceptibility to rot, the weakening it suffers from fastener holes, the potential delamination of the pieces, and the tremendous amount of upkeep it intransigently demands. Apart from the preceding, wood masts are difficult to find at a reasonable price. I finally did find a man who would build my 43 foot mast, spreaders, and booms (main and staysail) of knotless Sitka spruce. The price was $600 plus freight. I would have had to install the hardware. However, he was in the process of moving his shop and the new place wouldn't have sufficient heat for glueing for two and a half months. I decided to rush and get the readily available aluminum mast.

Aluminum, of course, has its own disadvantages. Although it won't rot, it will oxidize to a point where after a year or two one may find the removal of stainless steel fasteners impossible. It

is advisable to use some sort of lubricating compound like graphite to ensure future removal. The mast section selection was a problem. I wanted whatever would be the heaviest and strongest, but I was assured that it would be rather folly to get something beyond *overbuilt*. The mast size would create extra windage and weight aloft (see chart for IXX and IYY measurements).

The wall thickness should be considered if two similar extrusions are being evaluated. The thicker the wall, the greater the number of threads that can be tapped into it. The more the threads, the greater the fastener's holding power. And the thicker the wall the smaller the cross-section can be and still achieve the same IXX and IYY measurements, therefore the same strength.

You can, of course, argue and rightly so that most modern masts have grooves for sail-slides and spinnaker cars so they don't need tracks, and that winch pads are welded on or not used at all if the halyards are lead aft to the cockpit, and if they are lead aft you won't need to bolt on cleats either, and I would have to say you're right. But for those considering offshore cruising, a storm trysail track should be had and very

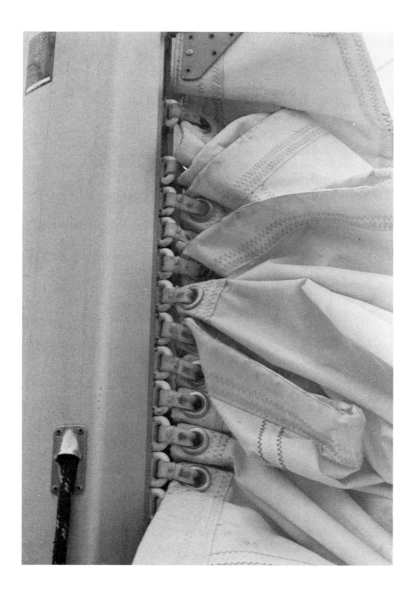

Plastic sail-slides fit into slot extruded in mast itself. No more rivets to re-set or tracks that tear loose.

few extrusions have this incorporated. Anyway just to be on the safe side, one might be wise to choose a mast which has opted for thicker walls instead of greater girth. While we're talking about masts let us consider a few points:

Self-furling mains

As wonderfully handy as they may seem, great caution should be used before investing in one for: (a) they have hidden mechanical parts that could jam at the most awkward of times like when you're trying to furl them in a storm, and (b) the deep slot in the mast creates such a heinous howl when the wind blows across it that even in a light wind you'd swear you're in a gale. This is nerve-wracking not just for you but for anyone else who has the singular misfortune of being tied up within a quarter mile of you. So get what you want, just keep that howling banshee away from me.

Mast Heads

Welded aluminum mast heads are the lightest and most practical if well-welded. Look for smooth even beading on the welds. This level of quality is the sign of an artist. Installation of an extra sheave is desirable in case a halyard breaks, a sheave cracks or fouls, or if you intend to utilize twin running sails. The sheaves can be of either aluminum or phenolic. Both last and perform equally well.

In a mast of greater head-girth than 5 inches a double set of sheaves should be installed to keep the halyards from chafing on the mast. This mast head setup nicely distributes all forces over two pins.

I do not much like tapered aluminum masts. A one-piece taper is much too expensive and the standard two-piece method (the bottom part unshaped, the top tapered, and the joints riveted) leaves me somewhat uneasy. If I wanted to feel uneasy I could have bought a wood mast.

Wiring must be run to the masthead for at least an anchor light and perhaps a strobe light.

It is also advisable to install a radio coax for an eventual VHF or single side band antenna as well as wire for an anemometer. If you are uncertain whether or not you will want this equipment, at least have a spare line installed to enable future wiring to be pulled through.

Regular 12 volt wires should be run through a PVC tube that's rivetted to the inside of the mast. The tube will keep the wires from flapping madly, chafing themselves to death.

Mast Steps

Most small and medium-sized aluminum masts are stepped on deck requiring a footing or mast step. The rims of the step should be quite high (³/₄ inch is not too drastic) to keep the mast *in step* if it has a tendency to jump about in its place, see figure. If the cabin top is well reinforced with the compression taken care of (see *Mast Step Support*) this motion should never occur. Through the rim should be drilled at least two drain holes to allow any water that has found its way into the mast through the sheaves, rivet holes, etc. to drain off. Salty water will corrode anodized aluminum if the metal is closed off so that it cannot air.

A tabernacle mast step, see figure, is a very nice idea. Not only will it enable you to have greater freedom in roaming below low bridges through the canals of Europe and Asia, but it will also enable the mast to drain completely and easily, and to air at all times. To prevent interior corrosion whether your mast is a tabernacle or not, it is a good idea to coat the lower 3 feet of the extrusion's interior with either primer paint or a thin layer of heavy grease. Either material will protect the mast and extend its life.

The tabernacle mast has one great advantage over its unhinged counterpart. You can rake the mast at whatever degree you desire, while a standard mast has to sit evenly on the mast step. If you rake a standard mast too far forward or aft you will cause one end of it to lift from the step, putting all the compression strain caused by the stays on the other end. This strain can cause premature metal fatigue and potential buckling.

A modern extrusion that sports even internal tracks in which slide the plastic tubings that house all the wires. This keeps a mast silent because the wires do not incessantly bang against the mast walls. If you shrug your shoulders and say, 'What's a little banging?', then you obviously haven't tried sleeping in a gently rolling anchorage with eight mast wires banging out When Irish Eyes Are Smiling, *on the walls of the mast. Try it.*

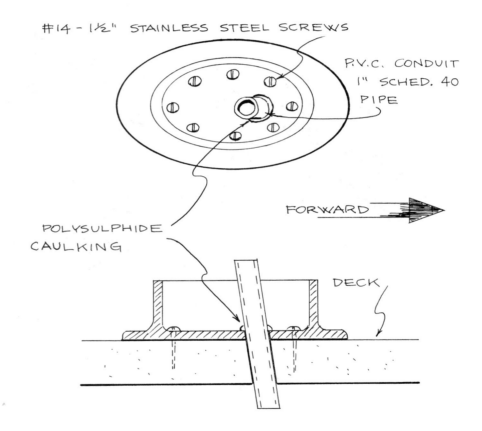

#14 - 1½" STAINLESS STEEL SCREWS

P.V.C. CONDUIT 1" SCHED. 40 PIPE

FORWARD

POLYSULPHIDE CAULKING

DECK

Aluminum mast-step for deck stepped mast with a pvc pipe to lead the mast light wires belowdecks.

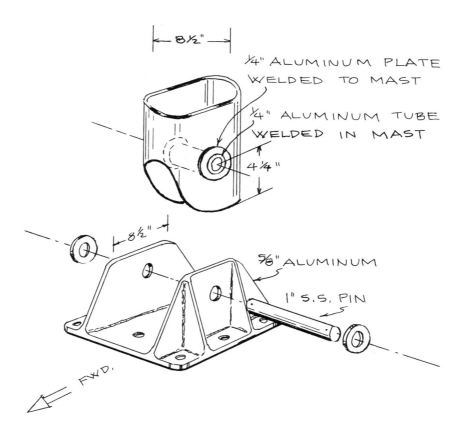

8½"

¼" ALUMINUM PLATE
WELDED TO MAST

¼" ALUMINUM TUBE
WELDED IN MAST

4 ¼ "

8½"

⅝" ALUMINUM

1" S.S. PIN

FWD.

A tabernacle mast step which allows the mast to be lowered forward onto the pulpit. It's handy to have for canal cruising or to enable mast repair without the use of a crane.

Sail Tracks and Slides (for wood masts)

Another decision that should be made is whether to use internal or external slide track, see figure. The external type is made of stainless steel, looks less cumbersome, and will not corrode. The way the rivets are recessed in the center will allow for some rivets working loose and eventually protruding into the track groove. Since the slides are contoured in the opposite direction, a small protrusion will not interfere with their movement. On the internal track, however, the slides pass directly next to the track's face. In this case, a small rivet sticking out even $\frac{1}{32}$ inch can snag a slide and necessitate a trip aloft to free it.

But, on the other hand, stainless steel track comes in short lengths requiring the use of a number of pieces to cover the mast length. Aluminum (most internal tracks are made of this material) comes in unbroken lengths, thus reducing the possibility of a foul at the joints. The aluminum track has, I think, another great advantage. Since it has its outside extremities resting on the mast, the central rivet has the support of these points, whereas the stainless track tends to pivot around the rivet thereby greatly increasing the potential of it being worked loose with the constant and tremendous forces applied by the sails. I think this factor outweighs the advantages of the stainless steel track.

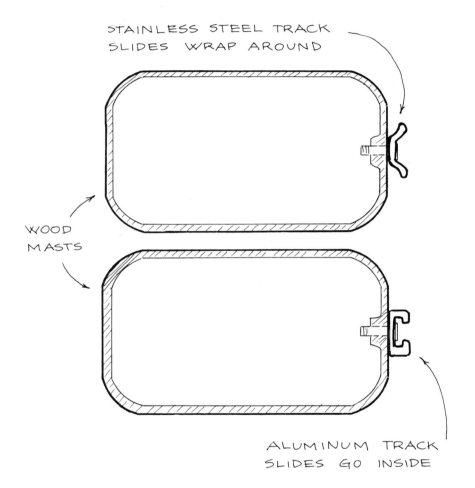

STAINLESS STEEL TRACK
SLIDES WRAP AROUND

WOOD
MASTS

ALUMINUM TRACK
SLIDES GO INSIDE

Two types of track for wood masts (assuming that most aluminum masts will have a slot in the extrusion, see photo). The aluminum track seems the better to use for its flat base makes a more solid contact with the mast.

Booms

The new double slotted booms seem to be a godsend. The top slot has all the advantages of the slotted mast and the bottom slot eliminates all the potential hassles one has with all the bails one had to install – up to three for the main-sheet and another for the vang – with no fewer than six holes per. All these can now be replaced by large metal slides (something like the plastic sail slides) which can have spacers in between them to hold their position with only a few rivets in the whole mess to keep everything in place.

Slotted booms are infinitely more desirable than ones with tracks. There are fewer parts so that their potential for failure is reduced. Sails with rope along the foot that slide directly into the slot seem to have an esthetic advantage over the common slugs. Slugs tend to rattle menacingly in confused airs and disturb the occupants. On the other hand (as usual) the slugs allow for use of a rubber snubber or preventer by merely passing either of them through between the slugs.

Bye bye boom-bails. A slot is engineered into the aluminium extrusion into which large stainless slides are fitted and the blocks for mainsheet, vangs etc are shackled onto these. Flatbar spacers are rivetted in between the slides, and the slides themselves are rivetted to the boom to hold their place.

If you don't recognize this instantly don't feel bad, because I didn't recognize it at first either and I took the bloody picture. Anyway, it's a series of stops *built into the boom for the reeflines and clew-outhaul line, obviating the need for nasty little cleats all over the boom. The lines run inside the boom so you don't have drooping lines hanging all over everywhere. The lines are color-coded for easy recognition.*

Rivetting

If you, for some reason, do have tracks, take care, for the spacing of the rivets in the track is essential. I think that 3 inch centers are maximum, and the bottom and top 4 feet of the track should be double riveted (1½ inch centers). If you have reef points (and hopefully not roller reefing) it is advisable to double rivet the main track in the areas where the head of the sail will set when reefed and when double reefed.

Eighteen inches above and below these points should be sufficient. The storm trysail track should be riveted every 2 inches with the top and bottom ends riveted at 1½ inches. The lower end of this track should come within a foot of the base of the mast so that the sail can be permanently bent on for quick use in any emergency, see figure.

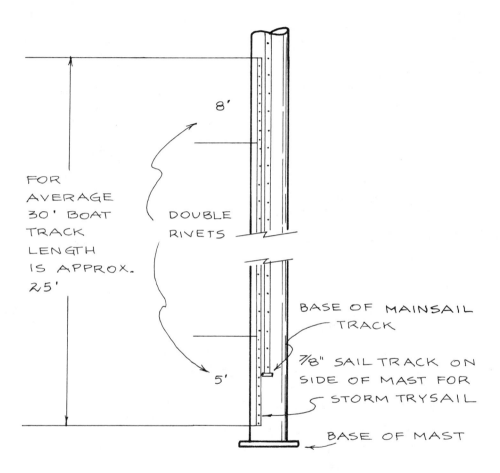

FOR
AVERAGE
30' BOAT
TRACK
LENGTH
IS APPROX.
25'

8'

DOUBLE
RIVETS

5'

BASE OF MAINSAIL
TRACK

7/8" SAIL TRACK ON
SIDE OF MAST FOR
STORM TRYSAIL

BASE OF MAST

Installation of storm-trisail track (left-hand side of drawing). The track need not start as low as dear old Candace drew it, but can safely begin about 18 inches from the cabin top.

Reaching Poles

If you intend to use any large head sails you will need to have a reaching pole to help your sail set. The length of this pole should be derived from a discussion with your rigger and naval architect. The fitting to be used on the inboard end, however, should be of only the bayonet type with no compromise, as shown in the figure. The snap hook fitting is the more commonly used on small boats and it is indeed fine for weekend cruising where longevity can be bypassed. The hook fitting with a ring stationary on the mast has no ability to swivel, or give, or twist, as the shape of the sail demands. The torque may be so much here that eventually the cast aluminum fitting can snap from excessive stress.

The inboard end should be as shown in the figure. It is an open-ended arrangement that slips over a pin which in turn is attached to a car. This arrangement is infinitely better, for the pole can swivel without obstruction to whatever degree the sails demand. The mast fitting itself is usually recommended only for boats over 50 feet, so I think it should be adequate for a 40 foot cruising boat.

If you will be using a number of head sails with varying clews, you may be well advised to install a track of about 8 feet in length on your mast. This track in conjunction with a slide fitting will allow numerous positions for the inboard end, guaranteeing a better fitting sail.

This method will of course lead to more paraphernalia, for you will need a topping lift and a down haul to adjust the slide's position on the track. An endless line is best used for this purpose to prevent the possibility of it coming loose. The line will have to be secured with a pair of clam cleats or equivalent to prevent the pole from riding either up or down. The two cleats must work in opposite directions, and a generous space should be left between them to allow some slack to the line so that the extraction and insertion into the cleat can be accomplished with ease. Putting the cleats at least 2 feet apart should give you enough slack to enable easy maneuvering.

All-cast aluminium car for reaching pole. Note good broad track in the extrusion itself. Car is teflon lined for easy sliding, and no-chafe and wear. The make is Barbarosa.

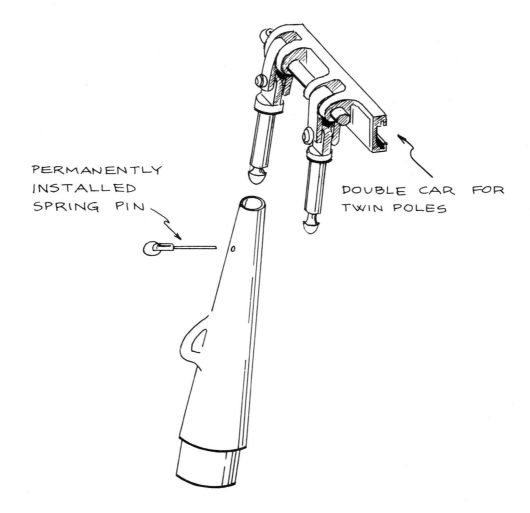

PERMANENTLY
INSTALLED
SPRING PIN

DOUBLE CAR FOR
TWIN POLES

The world's best and also most expensive reaching or spinnaker pole system. The fittings on the car are double-jointed so they can swivel in any direction plus the pole can turn freely around the car stubs. The spring-pin just sits in the groove of the stub to keep the pole from sliding off the stub.

Goosenecks

In recent years the trend has been toward a mechanical down haul for the main boom, see photo. The trend came because it was reasonable to assume that in time the main sail would stretch necessitating adjustment of the foot. This down haul created additional moving parts, and many failures in even the best built boats occurred because the down haul track worked loose on the mast. A recent resurrection of the fixed gooseneck is underway. This concept is more solid and it is one that can still allow for stretching of the sail by inserting a cunningham hole a few feet from the foot. Through the cunningham hole a line can be fed which can be made tight if stretching of the luff is necessary. I have the fixed version, as shown in photo; because of its simplicity and positive attachment, I do prefer it.

Rivetting

Attaching sail tracks with rivets is not a great task; a pop-rivet gun is inexpensive, and no great magic is involved in its use. It works on the principle of drawing a large ball through a small tube, thereby enlarging the circumference of the tube which then becomes a structural shoulder or flange around the drilled hole.

The only thing to watch for is the drilling of the hole. It should be a good fit, but not a tight one around the rivet stem. The drilled hole will have to be perfectly straight. I heard from a veteran mast maker that he likes to put a dab of bedding compound around the rivet's base to seal the narrow space between the flange and the mast wall. This way moisture cannot settle in and oxidize the aluminum.

The question of whether or not a bedding compound should be used under the track keeps emerging. If you are willing to do a thorough job, I feel that it is an excellent idea. But a thorough job you must do or you will only create sporadic pockets in which moisture can settle. It will be an extremely messy operation working with bedding compound but well worth the effort if well done.

Tapping

Using stainless steel machine screws requires more time than rivetting, but it becomes necessary for cleats, winches, and large fittings. Tapping the threads is a basic operation requiring only a $15 tool. Drill a hole through the diameter of the machine screw's shank not taking into account the threads, then place a drop of oil or A-1 aluminum cutter fluid on the tapping tool. Hold it perfectly vertical and start to tap. Do not allow the tool to oscillate, for your result will be pitiable and worthless. Tap straight and true. For tapping each hole, apply a drop of oil to the tapping tool to keep its grooves clear and make it work more effectively by enabling the cut aluminum to slide out easier.

If you have your halyard cleats near the base of the mast as you should, you may consider putting nuts on your machine screws for extra strength. If you use lock washers you should be safe; if you don't, the nuts can work loose and can fall off. You will then have the most infernal rolling and clanging in the base of the mast. Your only remedy lies in removing the mast and gathering the nuts. If you want to change cleat positions you will find removal of the machine screw impossible unless you send a very small and very slim person inside to hold the nut; so think twice before you indulge.

Rigging

For a boat with a 40 foot mast I would not use less than $1/4$ inch 1×19 wire. This wire has a strength of 8,200 lbs., see table, more than enough to guarantee that something other than it will fail before it does. Heavier than $9/32$ inch wire will add tremendous weight aloft unnecessarily. This wire used with $1/2$ inch turnbuckles (thread and pin size) compares similarly in breaking strength with the turnbuckles. Over-rigging beyond this point shows a lack of thought, for you must remember that rigging is a chain, and if any link is weak (like a tiny tang somewhere aloft) the whole thing will find its way overboard in little time. Swedging the marine ends (eyes, forks, etc.) onto wires should be left to a good shop using a multiple roller swedger to give an even thorough press. Cruisers should consider Norseman fittings, for these can be attached to the wire without specialty tools; a great advantage in the Amazon river

Turnbuckles

Turnbuckles of the toggle variety, as shown in the photo, are recommended. With toggles at two ends, an extra joint is put in to relieve torque on the fittings. In ordering rigging, every attempt should be made to give a clear picture of the wire including all fittings. A simple sketch is recommended. Measure every shroud length between the centers of clevis pin holes and fittings or from center clevis pin to end of the threaded terminal.

If a turnbuckle is included, measure the length from center of clevis to center of clevis and turnbuckle with the turnbuckle two-thirds open. Ascertain if your choice of turnbuckle has the body threaded at least as deep as the circumference of the threaded rod. This qualification is most important in turnbuckles where the body and the rod are both stainless, because this combination tends to gall as most similar metals do. The more threads used, the less the pressure on each thread, so the less likely this eventuality will be.

Turnbuckles with naval bronze bodies and stainless steel rods will not be subject to this occurrence because one metal is softer than the other and thus it will always give sufficiently to guarantee movement. I do like the open-body turnbuckle, see photo, for one can readily see the amount of thread left inside the body.

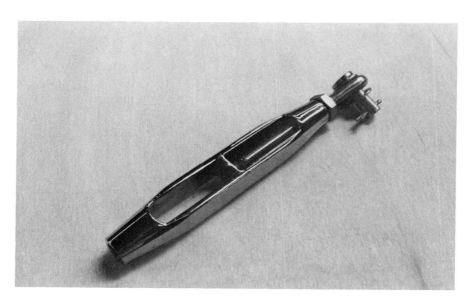

An open-bodied turnbuckle. You can always see just exactly how much thread is left inside the barrel.

Genoa Tracks and Deck Blocks

Genoa tracks and deck blocks should all be through-bolted with at least flat washers, better still back-up plates, on the underside. Use nylon-insert lock nuts to guarantee a good long-lasting hold. Wise planning would be reflected by allowing access to these nuts in case a leak develops or modifications need to be made. Cap or acorn nuts can be used if the ends of machine screws are to be left exposed.

If you dislike tracks you can use pad-eyes at two or three positions where your head sail sets best during beating, reaching, and running. A snatch block can easily be moved from one position to another depending on sailing conditions. This solution is not the ultimate, but it is a solution.

A first-class genoa block. It fits onto a track and has the two rollers in front of the pulley to prevent chafe no matter how un-fair the lead.

Running Rigging

Braid, sized $7/16$ inch or $1/2$ inch is very good for sheets and halyards. Some people prefer $1/2$ inch for this generous diameter makes for easier handling. All-rope halyards are recommended by many cruising people who feel totally opposed to wire halyards or even wire halyards with rope tails. The latter requires a splice to the rope tail. This splice may become a weak point in the halyard. Wire chafes noisily on aluminum masts and removes the paint. It can also fray and develop fish-hooks which cut fingers deeply.

If you use heavy line, look for a widely mortised block. This solution will alleviate the need for unsightly oversized blocks. Blocks with plastic sheaves are sufficient for all-rope running rigging. If you choose to use wire at some point, then sheaves of 'radically wound phenolic or scored aluminum' should be used. Be sure that your sheave is large enough; too small a sheave can cause undue friction with rope halyards and can cause wire halyards to fray. Colour-coded braid is a first-class idea and will save a lot of guessing and cursing.

The following pointers are taken from a Schaefer catalog on hardware and I think paraphrasing would do them injustice.

Lever-stops allow use of a single winch for two lines. One line is winched tight, stop closed, then the other line is winched tight and stop closed. Faster than cleating and cheaper than using a winch per line with a cleat beyond each.

Block Strength

We determine the ultimate strength of any block by a series of tests that stress it to the point of failure. Fifty per cent of the figure we then advertise as its safe working load, allowing the remaining 50 per cent as a safety factor. This is 'insurance' against breakage. When selecting hardware be sure the advertised strength of the block is at its safe working load and not its ultimate strength.

Fairleads

Every block must be free to align itself with the rope that leads into and away from it. The rope should not chafe or the block bind in the performance of its function. In cases where the alignment does not vary appreciably (such as main and mizzen sheets and forestay-sail sheets), there is a common tendency to use swivel shackle blocks which usually only tangle the sheet. A *front/side shackle block* should be used. On a spinnaker halyard, pole lift or mainsheet lead block on deck, where the lead changes constantly, *swivel blocks* should be used. Upset shackle blocks are the answer for tangs that will only accept a shackle pin, boom down hauls, or where a shackle bail won't fit through the point of attachment, or where slight universal action is required.

Sheave Diameter, Score and Material

Many boat owners prefer to use heavier lines because they are easier to handle and to haul. If this is your preference, look for a wide mortised block that will accept the heavier line. This eliminates the necessity for a yachtsman to outfit his craft with blocks that are too big for the job.

Understand the job that you want done and choose a block designed to do it. As any block will break if misaligned or overloaded, respect their limitations. If you have any misgivings about the right piece of equipment for the job, see your nearest dealer.

Aluminum

Although aluminum is well known for its lightness and resistance to corrosion, certain of its alloys are stronger than structural steel. Aluminum is also exceptionally workable. It can be easily stamped; cast or welded and accepts a wide variety of finishes. The alloy most widely used is 6061-T6, which has a tensile strength of 45,000 psi and a yield strength of 40,000 psi.

Anodizing

This process coats the surface of aluminum with a corrosion resistant protective film by subjecting the metal to electrolytic action. A hardcoat anodizing process adds about 1 to 1.5 thousandths of an inch of tough aluminum oxide to the aluminum. Hard coat anodized finishes have withstood corrosion for more than 1,000 hours in salt spray tests.

Bronze

Bronze and bronze alloys are used in turnbuckles, and in bushing for larger blocks. It is a copper alloy which contains manganese, zinc, nickel, tin and aluminum. Bronze bushings (a detachable metal lining used as a friction reducing bearing on shafts and axles) are impregnated with oil, which provides a strong and well lubricated bearing surface.

Electropolishing

Manufacturing processes such as machining, welding, grinding and sanding add impurities to the surface of stainless steel which can encourage corrosion. Electropolishing is an electrochemical process subjecting the stainless steel to a light electric charge while immersed in a sulphuric acid solution. This removes a thin layer from the stainless steel surface, giving it a hard brilliant finish as it removes most of the impurities.

Epoxy Coating

For applications where extreme abrasion is a consideration, such as on cleats, a black epoxy coating can be used. Epoxy coating is chip resistant, highly abrasion resistant and corrosion tests have been very successful.

Forging

The forging process forms metal to a desired shape through the use of pressure or impact, while maintaining a strong grain structure.

High Impact Plastic

Generally used are either Delrin or Lexan plastic. Both are extremely tough plastics with properties of high tensile, impact and shear strength. Lexan, in particular, possesses toughness and rigidity exceeding any plastic known.

Investment Casting

The first step in this process involves making a wax part from a master, or permanent die. The wax part is then used in making one, or a series of temporary molds, which have a high degree of accuracy. The actual parts are then cast from the temporary molds without any wear on the permanent die.

Passivation

Conducted with a nitric acid solution, this surface cleaning operation helps eliminate contamination which may cause corrosion or discoloration and permits the steel to generate its own protective oxide.

Phenolic

Phenolics are laminates thermoset under high pressure which have an extremely high resistance to frictional heat. Most synthetic line will burn before the phenolic begins to distort.

Stainless Steel

A steel alloy containing iron, carbon, silicon, manganese, nickel and at least 12 per cent chromium (which makes the iron passive in air at normal temperatures). Generally used is type 304 stainless steel, whose combined properties of corrosion resistance, strength and elasticity make it ideal for marine use.

Contrary to the implication of its name, stainless steel is not totally rustproof. All stainless steel will rust to a certain degree, due to natural chemical reaction to air and salt water (particularly in areas of abrasion, friction and welding where a chemical imbalance in the metal might occur). The problem though is mainly a cosmetic one and is solved with metal polish and frequent fresh water rinsing.

Knowing Your Hardware

The hull of a sailboat has often been described as the platform upon which the process of sailing is performed. Gear and hardware are the tools used in this performance. Selecting these tools with care and intelligence not only keeps the process smooth, simple, and efficient, but adds greater enjoyment and safety to the sport of sailing.

To keep pace with the variety of jobs that must be performed on sailboats of all sizes, shapes and makes, producers of yacht hardware are developing and producing an ever increasing variety of equipment from which choices can be made. Helpful in the choice of proper hardware is a basic knowledge of its anatomy, terminology, and function.

The basic piece of marine hardware is the block. The following information should help you determine whether the block of your choice is strong enough, assumes a fair lead, has the right sheave and is made of the proper material.

Snap Shackle
Can be easily moved from place to place. Instant disengagement.

Quick-release snap shackles make for easy and efficient sail changes.

Upset Shackle
Used where the tang will only accept a shackle pin. Slight universal movement.

Swivel Shackle
Used where the rope angle varies. Allows block· to pivot.

Front/Side Shackle
Used where the rope angle is reasonably constant.

Spring Mounting
SS spring keeps block upright while allowing block to swivel and tilt.

Becket
Used to dead end a line on the block in multi-part systems.

Slide
Used where block is mounted on track for rapid fore and aft or athwartship adjustment.

Exit Block
Leads internal halyards or other lines out of mast, boom or spinnaker pole. Specify a plastic sheave for use with rope.For use with rope and wire combinations, specify a scored aluminum sheave.

Fairlead Block

For use with genoa sheets and halyards. Block is shown in use with genoa sheet and is mounted on a slide (block should be used in conjunction with a turning block in genoa sheet applications). When used for leading external halyards aft from the base of the mast, no slide is used.

Turning Block

Used for turning spinnaker sheets and jib sheets. When turning jib sheets the turning block should be used in conjunction with a fairlead block. Usually mounted near aft end of boat, along the rail.

Cheek Block

Used for turning sheets and halyards. Mounts on spar itself (mast or boom) or on deck, deckhouse or coaming. Specify a plastic sheave for use with rope. For use with rope and wire combinations, specify a scored aluminum sheave.

Fiddle Block

For use in multi-part systems such as mainsheets and boom vangs. Has two or more sheaves. Can be ordered with or without snap shackle or with an adapter for use on traveller systems.

Winches

A discussion of winches could be an endless topic, consequently I'll barely touch upon them. Barlow and Barient print beautiful catalogs with intricate explanations and recommendations. Secure one of each and memorize them if you like.

Meanwhile glance over the enclosed winch guide, see table, for comparisons of the *name* winches.

I have found through longish research that a 30 to 45 foot cruising boat can usually utilize single-speed Barlow #16 or equivalent for all halyards including the main if it does not exceed 450 square feet. If you like for a 400 square foot main the use of Barlow #20 or equivalent is almost warranted.

Winches for *jiffy reefing* need not be larger than Barlow #15.

Sheet winches on a boat over 30 feet should be at least Barlow #24, etc. if head sails of any size, like a genoa or drifter-reacher, are to be used. Any smaller winch will only suffer under the great strain if head sails over 400 square feet. Overall stainless steel winches are the strongest. Bronze winches are only slightly less strong and do look more traditional. Shop around, the mark-up is sizeable.

Stepping the Mast

Before the mast is stepped, a few items should be checked. After you have outfitted everything to your liking on deck, attach all your turnbuckles to chainplates and tangs. Be sure to put them all *right side up*. Most things tighten clockwise and untighten anti-clockwise. This order is fairly common and it is a universal expectation. Problems in times of crises can be avoided if your turnbuckles are installed conformingly. Have all of your clevis pins in place and ring-a-dings dangling. Now attend to your mast. With a battery and a light, check all mast lights and all wires. Repair and adjustment is made much more easily standing on unmoving pavement than dangling from a bo'sun's chair.

Check all your fittings and tangs, and tighten your bolts. Make sure that nothing has wedged its way into and around your sail tracks. Use a stiff paint brush with the bristles cut down to ¾ inch lengths to clean out everything. Spin your masthead sheaves and listen for a grinding sound which could indicate sand or other impediments present.

Now feed through your halyards, attach your shrouds, and tie the whole thing to the mast with line. Do be sure that everything is secured and will not wobble, chafe, or destroy while the truck is taking the boat down for launching. A loose stainless steel shroud can easily crack mast lights, chafe paint, or even, in extreme cases (like a trip from Arizona to San Diego) chafe away a part of the aluminum mast.

When the boat is launched and the crane is dangling the mast over the deck, take all your neatly packed wires and feed them through a protruding and well sealed PVC tube into the cabin down below or into the bilge. Don't miss any wires.

Once the mast is on the step, take your fore and aft lower shrouds and anchor them fast to their appropriate turnbuckles to moderate adjustment only, just to be sure that all four are providing support. The crane is now free to leave; the lowers will hold sufficiently while you attend to the rest of your stays. After everything is attached, tune your rig. Loosen all the shrouds, but do not make them slack. Now set your forward and aft lower turnbuckles a few turns at a time. Shake each shroud heavily from time to time to see if they have equal amounts of *give*.

If you have a bowsprit and/or boomkin, tighten your whisker stays first. These stays should be taut but not over-tightened to the point where they destroy the column of either boomkin or bowsprit. They must remain unbent. You can now adjust your forestay and backstay. The foremost point of reference for any adjustment is the mast step itself. Be sure that the mast sits squarely upon it. Gauge it all the way around to be sure that it is not squatting on its toe or heel or one side.

Tighten turnbuckles a little at a time, walking back and forth from one side to the other laying your face against the mast wall, looking up along it to make certain you're not *warping* the mast. It, as with the boomkin and bowsprit, must remain in column, unbent, and evenly supported. Do the same thing for your forestay and backstay and keep checking your mast. Once your shrouds are tight, calm yourself and don't tighten your turnbuckles any more. With a large crescent wrench as an accomplice, you can easily overtighten the rigging and crack your deck with the tremendous compression of the shrouds.

Now walk about and check each turnbuckle extremely closely. You must have at least one-third of your threaded rod inside the barrel, but you should also have about one-half of the threaded rod on the outside. You will need, eventually, some space to tighten them. If any turnbuckle is closed tightly, call your rigger; your shroud is too long and it must be re-cut and re-swedged. If only the last few threads of your rod are inside the barrel, the shroud is much too short. Have it redone.

Make fast your halyards so that they won't fly away and tangle somewhere high in your rigging. Now step off the boat and back away. . . . God what a beautiful sight. . . . Mothers must feel ecstatic when they see their newborn. . . . Don't back too far . . . beware of the short wharf.

A bowsprit platform and pulpit make changing headsails safe and fun.

Two good manual bilgepumps are the minimum for an offshore cruiser. One should be below in case it's too dangerous or vile to be in the cockpit, and the other should be in the cockpit in a place where the helmsman can operate it without leaving the helm. The one in the photo is a 35-gallon-per-minute Whale diaphragm pump.

After the bottom of the grate has been dadoed out, the planks are cut into narrow strips and spread out with spacers, then . . .

. . . the shallow strips are glued and tapped into place.

The underneath of a finished grate shows that water can easily drain off through the channels.

A very small woodburning stove will keep an insulated 30 foot cruising boat warm in the coldest weather.

30

Diesel Engines

Well, things have certainly changed in the last eight years. There were only a handful of diesels available for sailboats eight years ago, and what there were, were mostly on the large, heavy side since most of them were built up from four-cylinder auto engines. But now we have a great number of one- and two-cylinder models from Volvo, Yanmar, and Farymann of the old school, plus new ones from MWM of Spain, Renault of France, and perhaps best of all the beautiful little diesels from Germany's BMW, made especially for sailboats and very small power boats. Among larger new motors is the very long list of well proven Mercedes Benz diesels, and the amazing little VW diesel which puts out 47 horsepower and weighs but 360 pounds (164 kilograms). Of course it has to turn at 4,000 rpm to achieve this, whereas most diesels reach their rated horsepower around 2,500 rpm, but then you can't have everything. This lightness of engines is an important point in small sailboats, and when you're looking for engines it's best to look for a medium weight one (unless you want to go very light); medium weight meaning an engine that gives you 1 horsepower per about 15 pounds of engine weight. To give you an idea of the range of horsepower-per-pound engines that is around, it's enough to tell you that an older Bota two-cylinder gave you 1 horsepower for each 23 pounds of engine, while the new VW will give you 1 horsepower for every 7.6 pounds.

An even more important question than *how heavy* should the engine be, is how many horsepower should an engine have for a given boat. All sorts of numbers have been tossed around over the years, and all sorts of boats have been moved by all sorts of engines (one well-known world sailor, who has since been lost at sea, used to have his 22 ton yawl pushed around by a 7 horsepower engine) but generally speaking, if an engine is to last and perform well in tides and currents, it should have about 3 horsepower per ton of boat. Some very reputable engine manufacturers call this an absolute minimum and I guess they ought to know how much torment their engines can stand.

The following pages carry the most interesting diesel engines I could find, ranging from the little 6 horsepower BMW, to the mighty Mercedes Benz turbo which unabashedly roars at 168 horsepower. Now I know most of our boats won't need one this big unless we want to do multiple backflips, but I thought the thing might be fun to look at.

This is by no means a complete list of all available engines, but it should give you a good idea of what you can expect.

Other good engines available are:

Farymann diesel – 7, 12, 24 and 32 hp.
Lehman (Ford and Peugot blocks) – 46 to 150
  hp.
Lister – 7 to 155 hp.

Universal – 11, 16, 21, 24, 32 and 44 hp.
Pisces (Peugot block) – 40 and 60 hp.
Renault – 8 to 150 hp.

Checklist Before Starting Engine

1. DO NOT HOOK UP BATTERIES BEFORE SPARK TESTING ELECTRICAL SYSTEM!
   A. Hook up negative cable to negative (–) battery terminal.
   B. Turn main switch (red) to 'ALL' and engine switch (switch panel) to 'ON.'
   C. Carefully tap positive terminal (+) with positive cable; if spark occurs there is *trouble!* In the circuitry, recheck wiring and spark test again — do not permanently attach cables until there are *no* sparks when testing.

2. BATTERY CABLES *MUST NOT* BE HOOKED UP WHEN WORKING ON THE WIRING!!

3. BLEED FUEL SYSTEM WITH HAND PUMP.
   A. Volvo – First at fine filter; second at injection pump.
   B. Perkins – First at filter on engine; second at injection pump.

4. CHECK LUBRICANTS (fill before installation of engine).
   A. Volvo usually filled – check level of engine and gearbox – top up with diesel lube oil (30) MS grade only. Both engine and gearbox use same oil.
   B. Perkins – Fill engine with diesel lube oil (30) MS grade only – gearbox with automatic transmission fluid.

5. CHECK KILL CONTROL: BE SURE IT WORKS *BEFORE* STARTING.
   A. Volvo must pull back against spring-loaded Stop and must not interfere with throttle opening. Be sure cable routing does *not* contact starter terminals – insulate if necessary.
   B. Perkins – Check out kill control solenoid – *does it work???!*

6. SET UP WATER INTAKE
   A. Close all drain cocks.
   B. Perkins – Fill fresh water tank and hook up hose to salt water inlet.
   C. Volvo – Hook up hose to salt water inlet.

7. START ENGINE
   A. Disengage gearbox button.
   B. Move throttle to half-open.
   C. Volvo – Push cold start button (if button does not remain depressed, open throttle more).
   D. Start engine – Quickly *reduce* throttle opening to fast idle: 800-1,000 rpms. Check exhaust outlet for water flow. Check oil pressure (gauge should read minimum 60 lbs. and alarm should be silent within a few seconds). Volvo warning light should go out; if not, kill engine, check alternator light on Volvo. On Perkins, meter should return to center within a few seconds.

8. STOP ENGINE
   A. Recheck lubricant levels.
   B. Recheck fresh water tank on Perkins.
   C. Recheck shaft alignment.
   D. Winterize if necessary.

BMW D-7 (Germany)

Power rating . . . . .6 hp
Number of cylinders 1
Strokes . . . . .4 cycle
Volume . . . . .280 c.c.
Weight . . . . .68 kg.
Compression ratio 22:1
Injection . . . . .Bosch w/automatic purge
Engine cooling .Raw water

Transmission – Standard reduction 2.8:1
– Optional reduction 2.3:1
– Rotation Right (looking fwd)

Electrical – 14 volts   25 amps per hr

Power ratings and consumption
rpm   3,600
hp   6
cons litres/hr   1.5
    gals./hr

Available fittings
Bilge pump – No
Forward power take-off – Yes
Flexible coupling – Yes
Engine controls – Yes
Extra drive pulley – Yes

Maximum installation angle: 20°

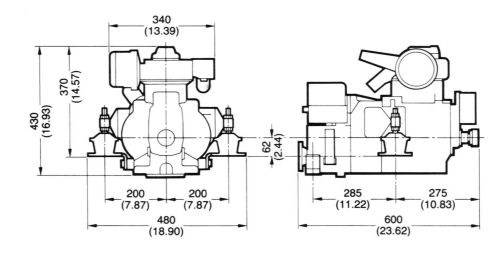

BMW D-12 (Germany)

Power rating . . . . .10 hp
Number of cylinders 1
Strokes . . . . .4 cycle
Volume . . . . .528 c.c.
Weight . . . . .108 kg.
Compression ratio 22:1
Injection . . . . .Bosch w/automatic purge
Engine cooling .Raw water

Transmission – Standard reduction 2.8:1
 – Optional reduction —
 – Rotation —

Electrical – 14 volts   25 amps per hr

Power ratings and consumption
 rpm   3,000
 hp   10
 cons litres/hr   2.2
   gals./hr

Available fittings
 Bilge pump – No
 Forward power take-off – Yes
 Flexible coupling – Yes
 Engine controls – Yes
 Extra drive pulley – Yes

Maximum installation angle: 25°

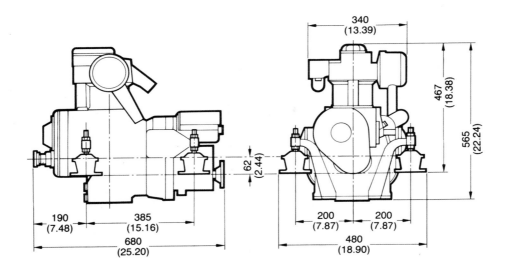

BMW D-35 (Germany)

Power rating . . . . .30 hp
Number of cylinders 2
Strokes . . . . .4 cycle
Volume . . . . .1,416 c.c.
Weight . . . . . . .234 kg. raw cooling/258 kg. fresh
Compression ratio 19:1
Injection . . . . .Bosch automatic purge
Engine cooling . . . . .Raw, or fresh with
heat exchanger

Transmission – Standard reduction 2.5:1
– Optional reduction 2:1, or
2.1:1 V drive

Electrical – 14 volts   75 amps per hr

Power ratings and consumption
rpm   3,000
hp   30
cons litres/hr   6.8
gals./hr

Available fittings
Bilge pump – Yes
Forward power take-off – Yes
Flexible coupling – Yes
Engine controls – Yes
Extra drive pulley – Yes

Maximum installation angle: 30° all directions

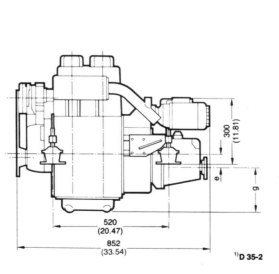

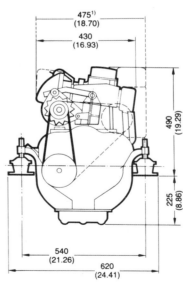

1)D 35-2

BMW D-50 (Germany)

Power rating .... 45 hp
Number of cylinders 3
Strokes .... 4 cycle
Volume .... 2,124 c.c.
Weight .... 292 kg. raw cooling/313 kg. fresh
Compression ratio 19:1
Injection .... Bosch automatic purge
Engine cooling .... Raw, or fresh with
heat exchanger

Transmission – Standard reduction 1.9:1
– Optional reduction 2.6:1, or
1.9:1 (both hydraulic) or
2.1:1 V drive

Electrical – 14 volts   75 amps per hr

Power ratings and consumption
  rpm   3,200
  hp   44
  cons litres/hr 9.5
    gals./hr

Available fittings
  Bilge pump – Yes
  Forward power take-off – Yes
  Flexible coupling – Yes
  Engine controls – Yes
  Extra drive pulley – Yes

Maximum installation angle: 30° all directions

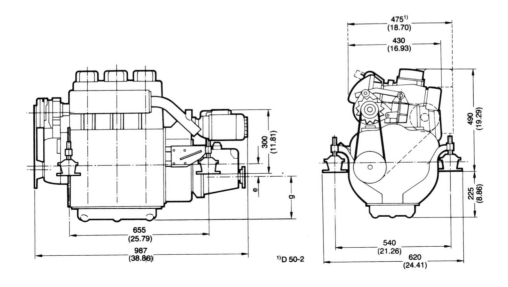

Detroit Diesel – GM – 3-53 (USA)

Power rating . . . . .92 hp
Number of cylinders 3
Strokes . . . . .2 cycle
Volume . . . . .2,610 c.c./159 cu. in.
Weight . . . . .494 kg./1,180 lbs.
Compression ratio 21:1
Injection N:40
Engine cooling . . . . .Fresh water

Transmission – Standard reduction Warner 1:1
           – Optional reduction N.A.
           – Rotation N.A.

Electrical – 12 volts   42 amps per hr

Power ratings and consumption

rpm	1,500	2,000	2,500	3,000
hp	50	60	70	90
cons litres/hr				
gals./hr	1.2	2.5	4	6

Available fittings
  Bilge pump – N.A.
  Forward power take-off – Yes
  Flexible coupling – No
  Engine controls – Yes
  Extra drive pulley – Yes

Maximum installation angle: 17°

GM – 4-53 (USA)

Power rating ....128 hp
Number of cylinders 4
Strokes ....2 cycle
Volume ....3,480 c.c./212 cu. in.
Weight.....................612 kg./1,350 lbs.
Compression ratio 21:1
Injection N:40
Engine cooling ....Fresh water

Transmission
  – Standard reduction Warner hydraulic 1:1
  – Optional reduction Warner direct 1:1
  – Rotation N.A.

Electrical – 12 volts   42 amps per hr

Power ratings and consumption

rpm	1,500	2,000	2,500	3,000
hp	50	70	100	128
cons litres/hr gals./hr	1.6	3.8	6	8

Available fittings
  Bilge pump – N.A.
  Forward power take-off – Yes
  Flexible coupling – Yes
  Engine controls – Yes
  Extra drive pulley – Yes

Maximum installation angle: 17°

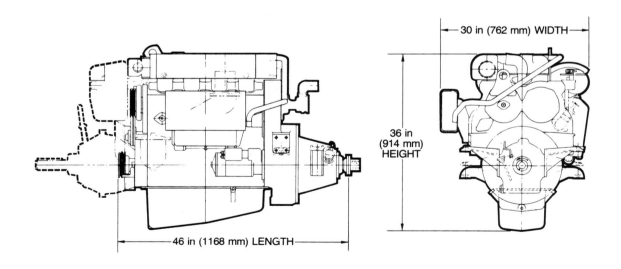

FORD (USA)
BSD 329, 332, 333, 333H
(Note: these are four different engines using the same block)

Power rating	40 hp	47 hp	54 hp	60 hp
Number of cylinders	3	3	3	3
Strokes	4	4	4	4
Volume	2,870 c.c.	3,150 c.c.	3,290 c.c.	3,290 c.c.
Weight	315 kg	319 kg	323 kg	323 kg
Compression ratio	17.3:1	16.3:1	16.3:1	16.3:1
Injection	N.A.	N.A.	N.A.	N.A.
Engine cooling	Fresh	Fresh	Fresh	Fresh

Transmission – Standard reduction Various
– Optional reduction Various
– Rotation N.A.

Electrical 12 volts   28 amps per hr

Power ratings and consumption
Note: All engines top hp at 2,100

rpm (1,600)	BSD329	BSD332	BSD333	BSD333H
hp	33	42	45	50
cons litres/hr gals./hr	N.A.	N.A.	N.A.	N.A.

Available fittings
  Bilge pump – No
  Forward power take-off – No
  Flexible coupling – No
  Engine controls – Yes
  Extra drive pulley – Yes

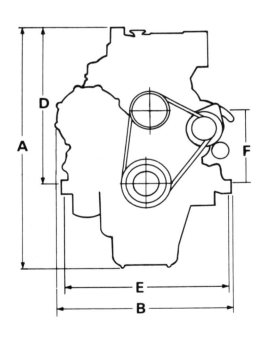

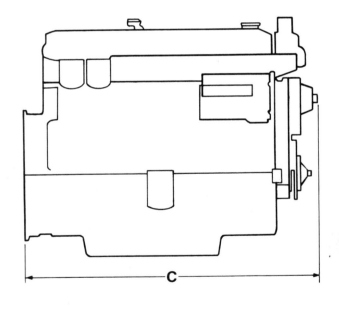

	A	B	C	D	E	F
2722	862 mm	623 mm	785 mm	569 mm	585 mm	268 mm
2723	870 mm	615 mm	1039 mm	570 mm	585 mm	268 mm
2725	870 mm	615 mm	1039 mm	570 mm	585 mm	268 mm
2726T	870 mm	758 mm	1103 mm	570 mm	585 mm	268 mm

FORD (USA)
Same block for BSD 442, 444, 444 Turbo

	BSD442	444	444 Turbo
Power rating	71 hp	81 hp	97 hp
Number of cylinders	4	4	4
Strokes	4	4	4
Volume	4,200 c.c.	4,400 c.c.	4,400 c.c.
Weight	402 kg	402 kg	408 kg
Compression ratio	15:1	16:1	15:1
Injection	N.A.	N.A.	N.A.
Engine cooling	Fresh	Fresh	Fresh

Transmission – Standard reduction Various
　　　　　　 – Optional reduction Various
　　　　　　 – Rotation N.A.

Electrical 12 volts　　　　28 amps per hr

Power ratings and consumption

rpm (1,600)	442	444	444T
hp	59	67	85
cons litres/hr	N.A.	N.A.	N.A.
gals./hr			

Available fittings
　　Bilge pump – No
　　Forward power take-off – No
　　Flexible coupling – No
　　Engine controls – Yes
　　Extra drive pulley – Yes

Also available 182 hp 6 cyl. Turbo

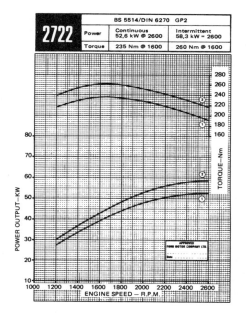

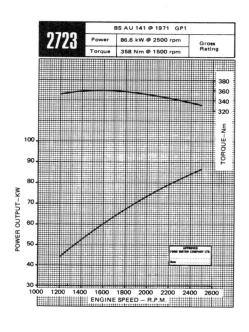

MERCEDES-BENZ (Germany)
WM36

Power rating . . . . .42 hp
Number of cylinders .4
                        (engine of MB 180 D car)
Strokes 4
Volume . . . . .1,767 c.c.
Weight . . . . .220 kg.
Compression ratio . . . . .N.A.
Injection . . . . .Bosch, direct
Engine cooling . . . . .Fresh water

Transmission – Standard reduction 2:1
                    – Optional reduction N.A.
                    – Rotation N.A.

Electrical – 14 volts   28 amps per hr

Power ratings and consumption

rpm	1,600	2,000	2,600	3,200
hp	15	25	33	42
cons litres/hr	4	6	7.3	9
gals./hr				

Available fittings
  Bilge pump – No
  Forward power take-off – No
  Flexible coupling – No
  Engine controls – Yes
  Extra drive pulley – Yes

Maximum installation angle 15°

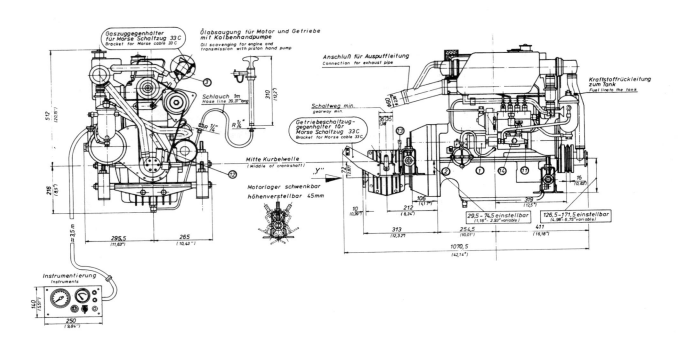

MERCEDES-BENZ (Germany) WM56

Power rating ....60 hp
Number of cylinders 4
(engine of MB 240 D car)
Strokes 4
Volume ....2,404 c.c.
Weight ....234 kg.
Compression ratio ....................N.A.
Injection ....Bosch, direct
Engine cooling ....Fresh water

Transmission – Standard reduction N.A.
– Optional reduction N.A.
– Rotation Anticlockwise facing flywheel

Electrical – 28 volts   27 amps per hr

Power ratings and consumption

rpm	1,500	2,000	3,000	4,000
hp	28	37	52	60
cons litres/hr gals./hr	6	9.5	12	16

Available fittings
Bilge pump – No
Forward power take-off – No
Flexible coupling – Yes
Engine controls – Yes
Extra drive pulley – Yes

Maximum installation angle – standard pan 9°, optional 15°

MERCEDES-BENZ (Germany) WM80

Power rating ....80 hp
Number of cylinders 4
Strokes 4
Volume ....3,784 c.c.
Weight ....378 kg. without gearbox
Compression ratio ....................N.A.
Injection ....Bosch, direct
Engine cooling ....Fresh water

Transmission – Standard reduction 2:1
– Optional reduction N.A.
– Rotation Anticlockwise facing flywheel

Electrical – 28 volts   27 amps per hr

Power ratings and consumption

rpm	1,400	1,800	2,200	2,800
hp	40	55	65	80
cons litres/hr gals./hr	7	11	14	18

Available fittings
Bilge pump – No
Forward power take-off – No
Flexible coupling – Yes
Engine controls – Yes
Extra drive pulley – Yes

Maximum installation angle 14°

MERCEDES-BENZ (Germany)
WM130 TURBO

Power rating ....168 hp
Number of cylinders 6
Strokes 4
Volume ....5,675 c.c.
Weight ....500 kg. without gearbox
Compression ratio .....................N.A.
Injection ....Bosch, direct
Engine cooling ....Fresh water

Transmission – Standard reduction N.A.
           – Optional reduction N.A.
           – Rotation Anticlockwise facing
             flywheel

Electrical – 28 volts   27 amps per hr

Power ratings and consumption

rpm	1,400	1,800	2,200	2,800
hp	90	115	138	168
cons litres/hr	16	23	28	35
gals./hr				

Available fittings
   Bilge pump – No
   Forward power take-off – No
   Flexible coupling – Yes
   Engine controls – Yes
   Extra drive pulley – Yes

Maximum installation angle 15°
Also available V-6 to V-12 diesels

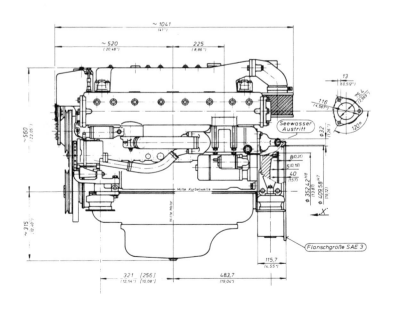

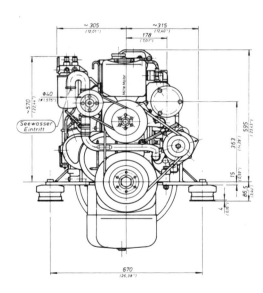

MWM – D892 DELFIN (Spain)

Power rating . . . . .15.8 hp
Number of cylinders .1
Strokes 4
Volume . . . . .754 c.c.
Weight . . . . .195 kg.
Compression ratio 1:17
Injection . . . . .220 kg./cm.²
Engine cooling . . . . .Direct

Transmission – Standard reduction 2:1
                – Optional reduction N.A.
                – Rotation N.A.

Electrical – 12 volts   N.A. amps per hr

Power ratings and consumption

rpm	1,500	2,000	2,500	3,000
hp	7.9	11.4	14.9	15.8
cons litres/hr gals./hr	1.54	2.16	2.75	3.12

Available fittings
  Bilge pump – No
  Forward power take-off – No
  Flexible coupling – No
  Engine controls – Yes
  Extra drive pulley – No

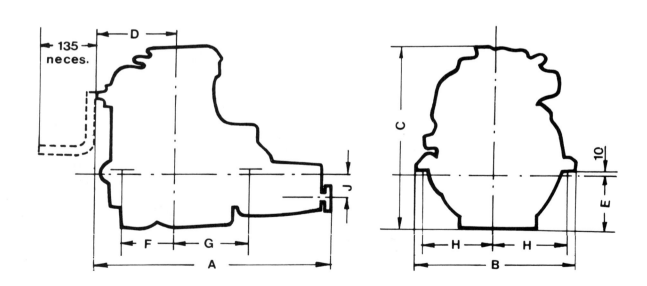

A	B	C	D	E	F	G	H	J
733,3	516	639,5	276	196	174	235,5	238	62

MWM – D202-2 (Spain)

Power rating . . . . .34 hp
Number of cylinders 2
Strokes 4
Volume . . . . .1,490 c.c.
Weight . . . . .240 kg.
Compression ratio 1:17.5
Injection . . . . . .Multiple openings 180 kg./cm.^{2}
Engine cooling . . . . .Raw or fresh water

Transmission – Standard reduction 2:1
                    – Optional reduction N.A.
                    – Rotation N.A.

Electrical – 12 volts   24 amps per hr

Power ratings and consumption

rpm	1,500	2,000	2,500	3,000
hp	18.5	25	31	34
cons litres/hr	2.97	4.22	5.35	6.14
gals./hr				

Available fittings
    Bilge pump – No
    Forward power take-off – No
    Flexible coupling – No
    Engine controls – Yes
    Extra drive pulley – No

Maximum installation angle: 15°

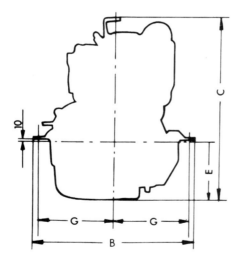

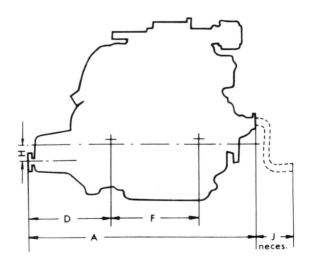

A	B	C	D	E	F	G	H	J
877	630	726	377	230	346	290	62	318

MWM – D202-3 (Spain)

Power rating ....52 hp
Number of cylinders 3
Strokes 4
Volume ....2,240 c.c.
Weight ....324 kg.
Compression ratio 1:17.5
Injection ....Direct
Engine cooling ....Raw or fresh water

Transmission – Standard reduction 2:1
                – Optional reduction N.A.
                – Rotation N.A.

Electrical – 12 volts   20 amps per hr

Power ratings and consumption

rpm	1,500	2,000	2,500	3,000
hp	27.3	38	46	52
cons litres/hr gals./hr	4.4	6.2	7.9	9.1

Available fittings
  Bilge pump – No
  Forward power take-off – No
  Flexible coupling – No
  Engine controls – Yes
  Extra drive pulley – No

Maximum installation angle: 15°

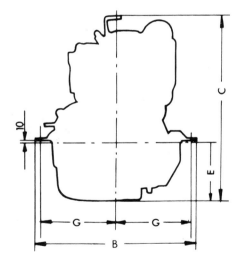
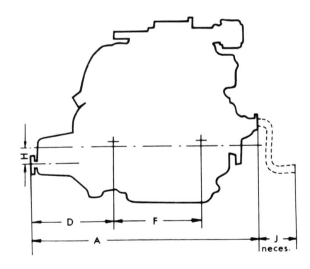

A	B	C	D	E	F	G	H	J
1.031	630	753	377	262	474	290	62	318

THORNYCROFT – (British Leyland) 230 (UK)

Power rating . . . . .63 hp continuous/
                                        74 hp intermittent
Number of cylinders 4
Strokes 4
Volume . . . . .3.5 litres/230 cu. in.
Weight . . . . .507 kg./1,116 lbs.
Compression ratio 16.8:1
Injection . . . . .N.A.
Engine cooling . . . . .Fresh water

Transmission – Standard reduction Borg
                 Warner 71 CR
               – Optional reduction All kinds
               – Rotation Either

Electrical – 12 volts   30 amps per hr

Power ratings and consumption

rpm	1,250	2,000	2,400
hp	36	56	63
cons litres/hr	7.6	12.2	14.8
gals./hr	1.7	2.7	3.25

Available fittings
  Bilge pump – Yes
  Forward power take-off – Yes
  Flexible coupling – Yes
  Engine controls – Yes
  Extra drive pulley – Yes

Maximum installation angle 12°

Type 230 Engine with PRM 310S Gearbox: Weight 507 kg (1116 lbs)

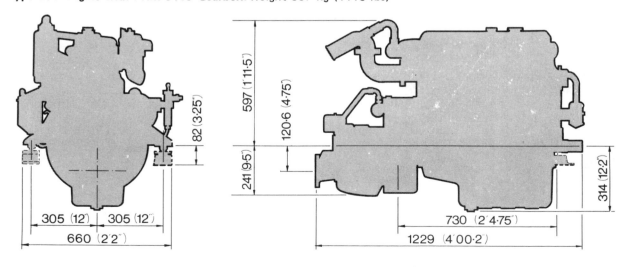

THORNYCROFT – (British Leyland) 760 (UK)

Power rating . . . . .164 hp continuous/
190 hp intermittent
Number of cylinders 6
Strokes . . . . .4 cycle
Volume . . . . .12.5 litres/761 cu. in.
Weight . . . . .1,371 kg./3,023 lbs.
Compression ratio 16:1
Injection . . . . .N.A.
Engine cooling . . . . .Fresh water

Transmission – Standard reduction 1.5:1, up to
4:1
– Optional reduction All kinds
– Rotation Either

Electrical – 24 volts   30 amps per hr

Power ratings and consumption

rpm	800	1,500	1,900
hp	68	138	164
cons litres/hr	15.3	27	33
gals./hr	3.4	6	7

Available fittings
Bilge pump – Yes
Forward power take-off – Yes
Flexible coupling – Yes
Engine controls – Yes
Extra drive pulley – Yes

Maximum installation angle 11°

Type 760 Engine with S.C.G. MRF 350 HD MK III Gearbox: Weight 1371 kg (3023 lbs)

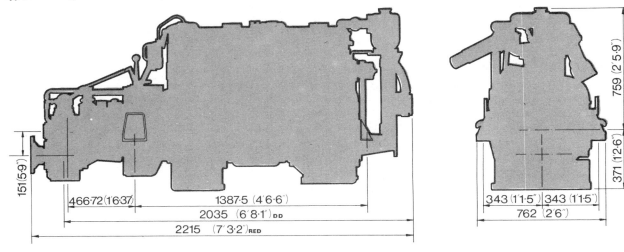

151 (5·9")
466·72 (16·37)
1387·5 (4′6·6")
2035 (6′8·1")DD
2215 (7′3·2")RED

759 (2′5·9")
371 (12·6")
343 (11·5") 343 (11·5")
762 (2′6")

THORNYCROFT – (British Leyland) 90 (UK)

Power rating . . . . .30 hp continuous/
36 hp intermittent
Number of cylinders 4
Strokes 4
Volume . . . . .1,489 c.c.
Weight . . . . .270 kg.
Compression ratio 23:1
Injection . . . . .N.A.
Engine cooling . . . . .Fresh water

Transmission – Standard reduction Various
– Optional reduction Mechanical
or hydraulic
– Rotation Either

Electrical – 12 volts   35 amps per hr

Power ratings and consumption

rpm	1,500	2,000	2,500	3,000
hp	13.5	20	25.5	30
cons litres/hr gals./hr	3	4.1	5.5	6.5

Available fittings
Bilge pump – Yes
Forward power take-off – Yes
Flexible coupling – Yes
Engine controls – Yes
Extra drive pulley – Yes

Maximum installation angle 10°

THORNYCROFT – (British Leyland) 108 (UK)

Power rating . . . . .38 hp continuous/
47 hp intermittent
Number of cylinders 4
Strokes 4
Volume . . . . .1,800 c.c.
Weight . . . . .270 kg.
Compression ratio 21.5:1
Injection . . . . .N.A.
Engine cooling . . . . .Fresh water

Transmission – Standard reduction Multiple
choice
– Optional reduction Mechanical
or hydraulic
– Rotation Either

Electrical – 12 volts   35 amps per hr

Power ratings and consumption

rpm	1,500	2,000	2,500	3,000
hp	21	27	33	38
cons litres/hr gals./hr	5.2	6.3	7.6	9

Available fittings
Bilge pump – Yes
Forward power take-off – Yes
Flexible coupling – Yes
Engine controls – Yes
Extra drive pulley – Yes

Maximum installation angle 15°

THORNYCROFT – (British Leyland) 154 (UK)

Power rating . . . . .50 hp continuous/
60 hp intermittent
Number of cylinders 4
Strokes 4
Volume . . . . .2,520 c.c.
Weight . . . . .370 kg.
Compression ratio 19.5:1
Injection . . . . .N.A.
Engine cooling . . . . .Fresh water

Transmission – Standard reduction Various
– Optional reduction Mechanical
or hydraulic
– Rotation Either

Electrical – 12 volts   45 amps per hr

Power ratings and consumption

rpm	1,500	2,000	2,500	3,000
hp	28	37	45	60
cons litres/hr	7.3	9	11	12.6
gals./hr				

Available Fittings
Bilge pump – Yes
Forward power take-off – Yes
Flexible coupling – Yes
Engine controls – Yes
Extra drive pulley – Yes

Maximum installation angle 12°

THORNYCROFT – (British Leyland) 402 (UK)

Power rating . . . . .118 hp continuous/
130 hp intermittent
Number of cylinders 6
Strokes . . . . .4 cycle
Volume . . . . .6.5 litres/399 cu. in.
Weight . . . . .801 kg.
Compression ratio .16:1
Injection . . . . .N.A.
Engine cooling . . . . .Fresh closed circuit or
w/keel cooler

Transmission – Standard reduction Mechanical
or hydraulic
– Optional reduction All kinds
– Rotation Left or right

Electrical – 24 volts   30 amps per hr

Power ratings and consumption

rpm	1,000	1,500	2,000	2,400
hp	49	77	103	118
cons litres/hr	10.6	15.9	21	25
gals./hr	2.3	3.5	4.6	5.5

Available fittings
Bilge pump – Yes
Forward power take-off – Yes
Flexible coupling – Yes
Engine controls – Yes
Extra drive pulley – Yes

Maximum installation angle 12°

VW – FENWICK 50 (Germany – France)

Power rating . . . . .47 hp
Number of cylinders 4
Strokes 4
Volume . . . . .1,588 c.c.
Weight . . . . .164 kg.
Compression ratio . . . . .N.A.
Injection . . . . .Bosch automatic purge
Engine cooling . . . . .N.A.

Transmission – Standard reduction 1.9:1
                – Optional reduction N.A.
                – Rotation N.A.

Electrical – 12 volts   65 amps per hr

Power ratings and consumption

rpm	1,000	2,000	3,000	4,000
hp	10	25	38	47
cons litres/hr	3	6.2	9.5	12.5
gals./hr				

Available fittings
    Bilge pump – No
    Forward power take-off – Yes
    Flexible coupling – No
    Engine controls – Yes
    Extra drive pulley – Yes

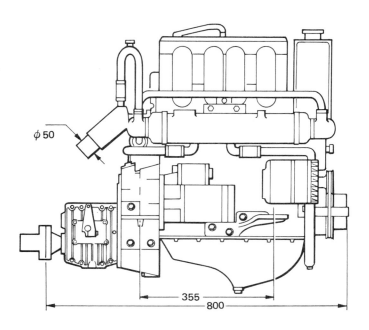

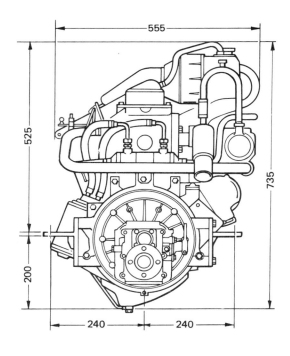

YANMAR 1GM (Japan)

Power rating . . . . .7.5 hp
Number of cylinders 1
Strokes 4
Volume . . . . .293 c.c.
Weight . . . . .70 kg.
Compression ratio . . . . .N.A.
Injection . . . . .Yanmar
Engine cooling . . . . .Raw water

Transmission – Standard reduction 2.2:1
             – Optional reduction N.A.
             – Rotation N.A.

Electrical – 12 volts   35 amps per hr

Power ratings and consumption

rpm	2,000	2,800	3,600
hp	3.2	5.1	7.5
cons litres/hr	1	1.5	2
gals./hr			

Available fittings
    Bilge pump – No
    Forward power take-off – No
    Flexible coupling – No
    Engine controls – Yes
    Extra drive pulley – Yes

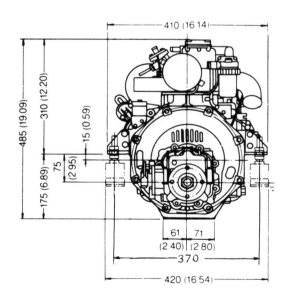

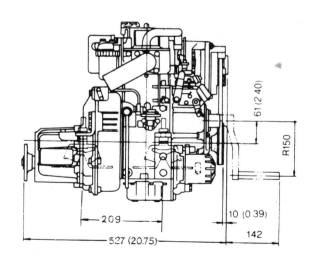

YANMAR 2GM (Japan)

Power rating . . . . .15 hp
Number of cylinders 2
Strokes 4
Volume . . . . .586 c.c.
Weight . . . . .100 kg.
Compression ratio .N.A.
Injection . . . . .Yanmar
Engine cooling . . . . .Raw water

Transmission – Standard reduction 2.2:1
                       – Optional reduction N.A.
                       – Rotation N.A.

Electrical – 12 volts   35 amps per hr

Power ratings and consumption

rpm	2,000	2,800	3,600
hp	7.5	11.5	15
cons litres/hr	2	3	4
gals./hr			

Available fittings
    Bilge pump – No
    Forward power take-off – No
    Flexible coupling – No
    Engine controls – Yes
    Extra drive pulley – Yes

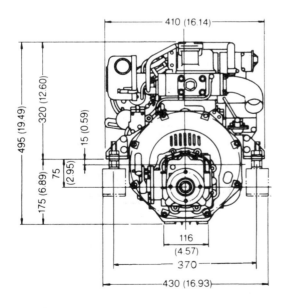

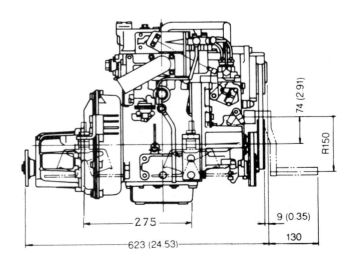

YANMAR 3GM (Japan)

Power rating . . . . .22.5 hp
Number of cylinders 3
Strokes 4
Volume . . . . .879 c.c.
Weight . . . . .130 kg.
Compression ratio . . . . .N.A.
Injection . . . . .Yanmar
Engine cooling . . . . .Raw water

Transmission – Standard reduction 2.36:1
              – Optional reduction N.A.
              – Rotation N.A.

Electrical – 12 volts   35 amps per hr

Power ratings and consumption

rpm	1,200	2,000	2,800	3,600
hp	5	12	17	22.5
cons litres/hr	2	3	4.2	5.7
gals./hr				

Available fittings
  Bilge pump – No
  Forward power take-off – No
  Flexible coupling – No
  Engine controls – Yes
  Extra drive pulley – Yes

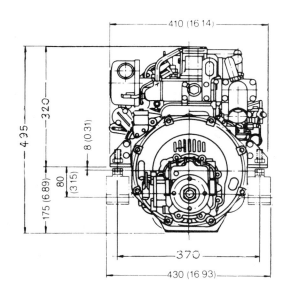

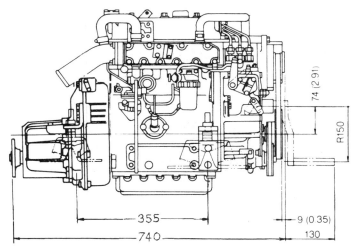

YANMAR 3HM (Japan)

Power rating ....30 hp
Number of cylinders 3
Strokes 4
Volume ....1,126 c.c.
Weight ....158 kg.
Compression ratio ....................N.A.
Injection ....Indirect, Yanmar
Engine cooling ....Raw water

Transmission – Standard reduction Mechanical
2.14:1
– Optional reduction N.A.
– Rotation Right (looking forward)

Electrical – 12 volts   35 amps per hr

Power ratings and consumption

rpm	1,600	2,400	3,300
hp	12	21	30
cons litres/hr	N.A.	N.A.	N.A.
gals./hr			

Available fittings
Bilge pump – No
Forward power take-off – Yes
Flexible coupling – Yes
Engine controls – Yes
Extra drive pulley – Yes

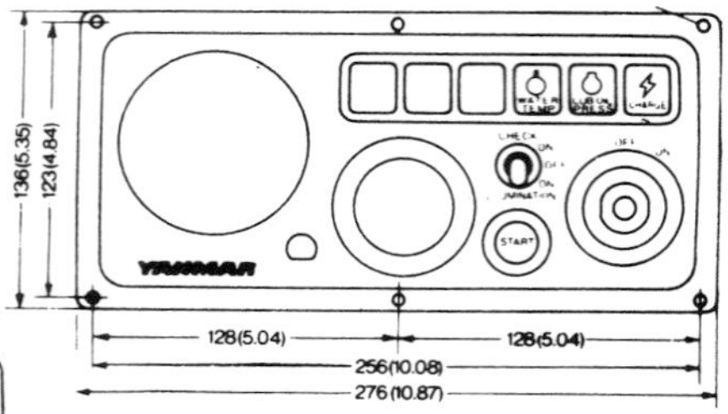

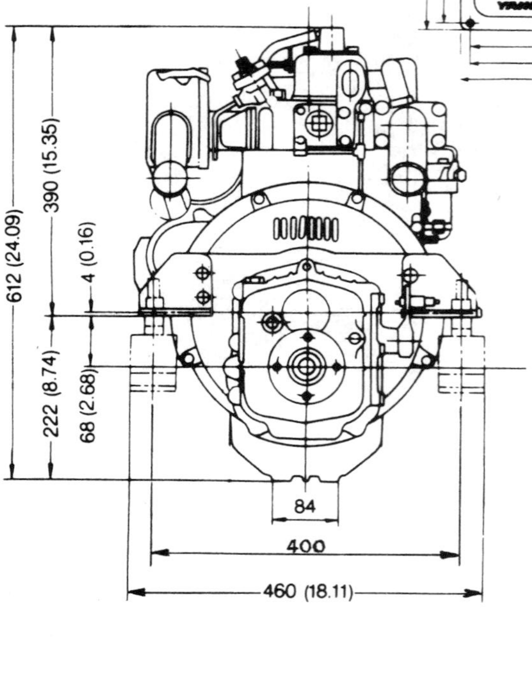

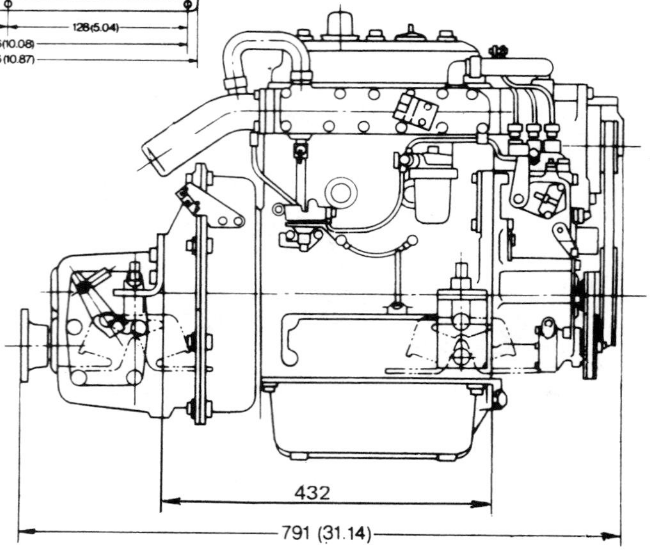

YANMAR 4JMT TURBO (Japan)

Power rating ....50 hp
Number of cylinders 4
Strokes 4
Volume ....1,490 c.c.
Weight ....245 kg.
Compression ratio ....................N.A.
Injection ....Yanmar
Engine cooling ....Fresh water

Transmission – Standard reduction 2.1:1
              – Optional reduction N.A.
              – Rotation Right (looking forward)

Electrical – 12 volts   55 amps per hr

Power ratings and consumption

rpm	1,600	2,400	3,200	3,600
hp	20	35	45	50
cons litres/hr gals./hr	5	8	11	12.5

Available fittings
   Bilge pump – No
   Forward power take-off – Yes
   Flexible coupling – Yes
   Engine controls – Yes
   Extra drive pulley – Yes

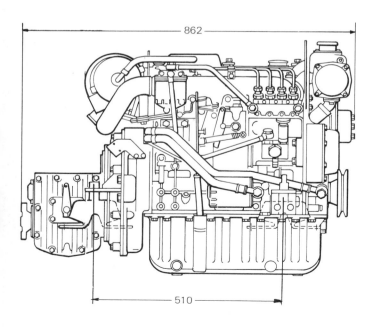

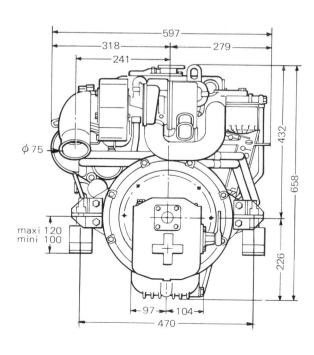

31

Materials and Equipment

Fiberglass

1. Resins – Polyester

(a) Laminating – basic resin for laminating hulls, decks, small parts and for bonding. Catalyze with MEK peroxide at ambient temperature of 77°F. 1.0 per cent MEK will gel in 26 minutes (1.0 per cent = 38 c.c. per 1 gallon). A #10 can almost full is approximately ¾ gallon and needs about 30 c.c. of catalyst.

(b) Surfacing – used for finish which can be sanded easily. Laminating resin cannot be sanded to give smooth surface. Surfacing agent added to laminating resin achieves same result.

2. Gelcoat

(a) Mold – gelcoat sprayed 12-15 mils. thick on hull, deck, parts. Thinned with 1:1 styrene/acetone for spraying consistency used for touchup of center line and imperfections. When used on exterior surfaces, must be sprayed with PVA.

(b) Ramanel – air curing gelcoat used for boot stripe and sheer stripe.

3. Mold Releases

(a) Mold release wax – applied to mold surfaces to prevent adhesion of gelcoat to mold. Can be applied to any surface where easy removal of excess resin is required.

(b) PVA – a liquid sprayed on mold surfaces to facilitate easy removal of molded part from mold. Must be sprayed over exterior gelcoat applications to obtain proper care.

4. Catalysts

MEK peroxide is the only commonly used catalyst. Must be thoroughly mixed with resin or gelcoat 5 c.c. to 70 or 80 c.c. per gallon of resin, depending on temperature and gel time required. Can be used with accelerators, such as DMA, if necessary only if mixed independently into resin. If catalyst and accelerator mixed together, a nice explosion will likely result.

5. Solvents

(a) Styrene – used to reduce viscosity of resin and gelcoat. Gelcoat may be thinned with a 1:1 styrene acetone mix at no more than 10 per cent by weight.

(b) Acetone – commonly used to clean brushes and other utensils and hands of resin. CAUTION: Acetone is highly flammable.

6. Asbestos Mish-mash

(a) A mixture of powdered asbestos and resin. Powdered asbestos is mixed with resin to the required consistency, either very thick, syrupy, or anywhere in between, depending on use. Thick mixtures are easier to use on vertical or near vertical surfaces. It is used to bond F/G to F/G or wood to F/G.

(b) If very thick buildup is anticipated, chopped strand should be added to reduce cracking.

7. Cabosil

A white powder mixed with resin to substantially thicken it to putty-like consistency. It can be mixed with a little gelcoat to fill hull or deck imperfections. As its main use is repair, surfacing agents should be added.

8. Microballoons

A lightweight red powder mixed with resin and used to fill voids in wood or fiberglass prior to laminating or bonding. Very easy to sand.

9. Glues

(a) Weldwood contact cement – or similar product – for cementing formica to table and counter tops. Strict adherence to container instructions is necessary.

(b) Weldwood plastic resin glue – mixed according to container instructions. Used on all interior wood to wood joints. Should not be used on teak exterior joints. Wiping completed joints well with damp rag before glue sets minimizes clean up.

(c) Weldwood resorcinal plastic resin glue – must be mixed according to container instructions. Used on teak to teak exterior joints, and on submerged or continually wet wood joints. Care must be taken to avoid staining adjoining wood.

10. Bedding and Caulking Compounds

(a) Dolfinite – all purpose bedding compound used on all fittings and wood parts fitted to deck or hull, such as teak decking to fiberglass, under cap rails and rub rails, under pintles and gudgeons, under deck hardware, etc. H2005 is the most common compound, 3905-TX is a fungicide compound for use where maximum resistance to rot and mildew is desired.

(b) Boat Life – life caulk – available in three colors, black, white and mahogany. Black is used to caulk decks, seal bolts on gudgeons, bed shaft log and thru hull fittings. White Boat Life can be used where white color is desired. Both colors available in liquid form which is excellent for fixing leaks as it flows easily. When used on oily woods such as teak, Boat Life primer *must* be used to maximise adhesion. Boat Life needs about one week to cure.

(c) Grove Specialties – Flo-Caulk – a two-part caulking compound used on decking. It cures in much shorter time (hours) than Boat Life. It also requires a primer on oily woods.

(d) G.E. Silicone Seal – a white sealant with excellent bonding properties. Its quick curing time makes it useful for sealing cabinet to formica joints in galley where water seepage is a problem.

Wood

(a) Teak – deck – 200 B.F.
    Cabinsole (solid) – 60 B.F.
    Searails – (interior trim) – 150 B.F.
    Caprails – 60 B.F.
    Rubrails – 20 B.F.
    Doors (solid; frames) – 180 B.F.
    Drawers – 180 B.F.
    Trim – 180 B.F.
    Hatch Coamings – 100 B.F.
    Hatches – 100 B.F.
    Plugs – mahogany – 2,000
    Plugs – teak – 1,400

(b) Plywood
    3/4 inch – 12 sheets
    1/2 inch – 25 sheets

(c) Adhesives
    Resorcinal glue – 4 quarts

Plastic resin glue – 25 lbs.
White glue – 1 bottle
Acrylic compound – 30 tubes
(d) Caulking Compounds
    Polysulphide – seacocks – 25
                other
    Dolphinite – caprails
                portlights
                other
    Silicone seal – above water – 10
    DECK – Polysulphide – 40 tubes
           two-part polysulphide – 3
           gallons
           40 empty cartridges
(e) Paint
    Undercoat – Z-Spar 105 – 2 coats – 3 gallons
    Inside cupboards only
    Gloss – 2 gallons
(f) Oil
    Interior – 2 gallons
    Exterior – 1 gallon
(g) Varnish – 2 gallons
(h) Acetone – 15 gallons
(i) Paint thinner – 3 gallons
(j) Resin – 25 gallons
    Mat tape, 6 inch – 50 yards
    Cloth tape, 8 inch – 50 yards
(k) Catalyst – 1 quart
(l) Resin brushes – 15
(m) Plastic gloves – 20
(n) Sandpaper
    60 grit – 4 sleeves
    100 grit – 2 sleeves
    220 grit – 2 sleeves
    400 grit – $\frac{1}{2}$ sleeve
(o) Paint remover – 1 can
    Paint thinner – 3 gallons

Fasteners

#10 × 1 inch ss pan head sheet metal screws – 2,000
#10 × ¾ inch ss pan head sheet metal screws – 1,000

#16 × 1¼ inch ss pan head sheet metal screws – 500
#10 × 1½ inch ss pan head sheet metal screws – 250
#10 × 2 inch ss pan head sheet metal screws – 50
#6 × ¾ inch brass flat head metal screws – 300
#8 × ¾ inch oval head wood screws – 200
#8 × 1 inch oval head wood screws – 100
#10 × 1 inch ss flat head sheet metal screws – 150
#10 × ¾ inch ss flat head sheet metal screws – 150
#8 × ¾ inch ss flat head sheet metal screws – 100
#8 × ½ inch ss flat head sheet metal screws – 100
#14 × 2 inch ss pan head sheet metal screws – 150
#14 × 1½ inch ss pan head sheet metal screws – 100
¼" × 1½" ss flat head machine screws – 150
⅜" × 1" ss flat head machine screws – 100
¼ inch ss flat washers, lock washers hex nuts
⅜ inch ss flat washers, lock washers hex nuts

Electrical

Battery level indicator
Battery charger
Battery switch – Perko 85 amps
Buss bars
Cable straps – Perko
Cable outlet – Perko – 42Y watertight
Circuit breakers – 10 amps, 15 amps, 20 amps, 25 amps
Circuit breaker panel
Conduit 1 inch i.d.
Connector – Butt – 80
             Spade – 80
Duplex receptacles and cover
Fuse – one time buss fuse 60 amps
Lugs
Radio coaxial
Shore power cord and adapter
Terminal junction block – 4, 6, 8, 10 post.
Toggle switches
Wire ties – 'Tywrap' with and without crew eyes

WIRE
    4ga battery cable
    10ga black
    10ga red
    14ga black, yellow, white, blue, green, violet

Plumbing

Bilge pump – 1 whole #10, 1 whole #25, 1 electric
Bilge pump – strainer – Wilcox
Bilge pump – switch
Bilge pump – through-hull
Head – Mansfield, Groco, Wilcox
Pump – fresh and salt
Sinks and fittings
Tape – Mylar and copper
Seacocks – 1½″ × ¾″
Seacocks tail pieces puc. (1 per seacock)
Through-hull fitting (bronze, plastic for cockpit)
Through-hull vents (fuel)
Through-hull deck fittings
Hose clamps #7, 8, 12, 16, 24, 28, 32, 36, 48
HOSE
    ½ inch white spinnaker hose – water – 100 feet
    ⅜ inch clear vinyl tubing – vents – 35 feet
    ¼ inch i.d. red fuel line hose – fuel – 25 feet
    1½ inch i.d. wire ins. rubber hose – exhaust – 10 feet
    1¼ inch wire ins. hose – Carlisle – bilge pump – 25 feet
1½ inch bronze gate valves – 1
¾ inch bronze gate valves – 3
Hose barbs – bronze and nylon – 10 approx.
Elbows – bronze and nylon – 15 approx.
T's – bronze and nylon – 15 approx.
1½ inch bronze anti-siphon loop – 1
¾ inch bronze anti-siphon loop – 2
Hose ties (tywrap)

Tools

Milling tools (power)
Table saw
Band saw
Planer
Router
Table sander

Milling tools (hand)
Chalk line
Scribe
Tape measure
Square
Bevel square
Pusher

Bonding tools and apparatus
Resin brushes
Milk jugs
Cardboard slabs
Squeegie
Rubber gloves

Construction (power)
¼ inch drill motor
⅜ inch variable speed drill motor
Saber saw
Belt sander
Disc sander
Vibrator sander

Construction (hand tools)
Level
Bevel square
Framing square
Scribe
Rasps (shoe, round bastard file)
Chisels (¼ inch to 1 inch)
Hole saws (for drill motor)
Hand saw
Dovetail saw
Hack saw
Drill bits (tapered)
Countersinks (Fuller)
Hand drill
Hammer (claw)
Hammer (machine)
Mallet
Center punch
Countersink (for rail heads)
Acid brushes

Glue cups
Caulking gun
Screw gun bit
Screwdrivers
Pliers
Crescent wrench
Vice grip
Wire strippers and crimp
Hand plane

Sur-Form
Pencils

Finishing
Vibrator sander
Sandpapers
Matte knife
RAGS

Glossary of Terms

A

ABX – A grading system for plywood indicating that one side is flawless (A) and one side is good, but perhaps seamed or patched (B) and the laminating glue is resorcinal (exterior grade) (X).

Acetone – A very combustible, fast evaporating cleaning fluid for cleaning surfaces. The only thing that will dissolve and clean polyester resin.

Acid Brush – A small inexpensive brush of about ½ inch bristle width with a tin handle; ideal for gluing or cleaning.

Accordion Hose – A flexible rubber hose used to act as a flex unit between a deck fill and tank.

ACX – Same as ABX except the second side holes and flaws are *not* repaired (C).

Aft – Toward the rear or stern of a boat.

Aloft – Upon the mast or rigging.

Ammeter – An indicating gauge that reflects the amount of amps being drawn.

Amp/Hrs. – A rating which reflects the number of amps per hour a device draws or charges.

Anchor Light – An electric or kerosene 'white' light placed in the rigging during overnight anchoring to advise other boats.

Anchor Roller – A stainless steel or bronze roller over which anchor-chain commutes.

Anchor Windlass – A mechanical winch, manual or electric, which aids in hauling anchors and chain.

Anemometer – An instrument used to measure wind speed.

Aqualift – An exhaust system, usually a small cast iron unit attached directly to the engine.

Arbor – An attachment used with a drill motor; supports hole saws of different sizes. Usually has a drill bit inserted throughout its center. center.

B

Backstay – The wire rope giving aft support to the mast.

Back-up Plates – Reinforcing plates, usually steel or brass, used when bolting through vulnerable material such as wood or fiberglass.

Baffles – Structural partitions in fuel and water tanks that restrain liquids from gaining momentum during violent boat movement.

Baggywrinkle – Fluffed, short rope ends fabricated to prevent sails from chafing on shrouds.

Ballast – High density weight (lead, steel, or cement) carried in the lower part of a vessel to give her stability and enable her to right herself.

Band Saw – A large saw with a flexible, thin loop of a blade, used to cut curves or fine finishing angles.

Bar Clamp – A very long adjustable clamp of 24 inches or more used to clamp large pieces.

Barograph – A barometer equipped with a moving graph that records barometric changes.

Battens – Flexible plastic fiberglass or wood strips utilized in a reinforced pocket in the leech of a sail, used as an aid to properly set a sail with a roach.

Battens Pockets – Reinforced sheath on the leech of the sail that houses battens.

Battery Box – A protective box, usually plastic, which protects the battery from external damage and also accumulates battery spillage.

Battery Cables – High output cables (usually #4 or lower gauge) that connect the battery with the alternator or generator.

Battery Straps – Strong non-corrosive straps used to lash a battery to its shelf or support to keep it from damage.

Beam – The widest dimension of a vessel.

Bedlog – A set of raised tracks upon which the main hatch slides.

Berth – A bunk or any sleeping accommodations of a vessel.

Berth Rail – A trim piece that keeps berth cushions in place.

Bevel – The act of cutting to a taper.

Bevel Square – An adjustable tool which with two arms and a wingnut can be used to duplicate or record angles.

Bilge – Area of the boat below the cabin sole utilized for tanks, storage, etc.

Bilge Pump – A high capacity manual or electric pump used to pump out bilge water.

Bilge Pump Strainer – A strainer or sieve (hopefully brass) attached to the lower end of a bilge pump hose needed to keep flotsam and jetsam from clogging the pump.

Binnacle – A housing for compasses.

Bobstay – The stay from the tip of the bowsprit to a fitting at the waterline, counteracting the pull of the forestay.

Boiler Punchings – Steel punchings, usually scrap, which because of their small size (thus high density) are commonly used as ballast.

Bolt Rope – Roping around the edge of a sail needed to take the strain off the sailcloth.

Boom Bail – A 'U'-shaped bracket screwed to booms through which blocks and lines can be led.

Boomgallows – A standard support upon which the boom rests when the sails are stored.

Boomkin – A horizontal extension off the stern of the boat used to accommodate a backstay if the main or mizzen boom length demands.

Boomvang – A rope and block mechanism which controls the upward movement of booms.

Bowsprit – A horizontal extension off the bow of the boat used to accommodate the headstay if the size of the headsails demand.

Bos'ns Chair – A canvas sling used for hoisting one up the mast.

Boot Stripe – A painted stripe above the yacht's waterline to catch oil or dirt; or just for esthetics.

Bridge Deck – A narrow part of the deck between the cockpit and the companionway or cabin.

Bulkheads – Usually structural partitions of a boat. Solid dividers, e.g. lazarette bulkhead, chain locker bulkhead, engine room bulkhead.

Bull-Nose – (a) to round off a sharp edge; (b) a concave bladed router bit used to round off a sharp edge; (c) the rounded edge itself.

Bullseye – A high strength plastic eyelet that can be secured to the deck to aid in fairleading lines.

Bulwarks – Raised portion of deck that follows the sheer line, usually used for protection of crew and equipment.

Butt Connector – A metal press fitting that unites two wires end to end without complex splicing.

C

California Reefing – Same as slab and jiffy reefing.

Cam Cleat – A piece of deck hardware consisting of two cogs between which line will pass in only one direction.

Cap Nut – A finishing nut with one side sealed off.

Car – A moving fitting attached to a traveler to which a block may be attached.

Carriage Bolt – A smooth-headed bolt with square shoulders to keep it from turning.

Catalyst – A chemical activator for an otherwise inactive substance.

Caulk – To drive cotton line into the seam of a wood planked vessel.

Ceiling – The lining which keeps things from touching the inside skin of the hull.

Center Bond – The laminations uniting two halves of a twin molded hull.

Center Punch - A pointed tool for making marks on wood or metal.

Charley Noble – A through deck fitting (usually with cap) for a stove pipe.

Cheek Block – A fixed pulley which is attached to a boom, etc. on its side.

Chicken Head –A metal fitting at the top of a mast to which are secured the shrouds, stays and sheaves.

Chocks – Blocks of wood or metal on the deck which act as pads for deck equipment such as a dinghy, spinnaker pole, etc.

Chronometer – A very accurate clock used for navigation.

Circular Saw – Also known as skill saw; a small electric saw with a rotating circular blade.

Clam Cleat – Similar to a cam cleat, but without moving parts.

Clamping – Mechanically holding two parts together.

Cleat – A T-shaped piece of hardware, usually of wood or aluminum attached to the mast deck or caprail for securing items.

Cleat Stock – Square cross-sectioned strips of wood used to join perpendicularly uniting pieces of plywood.

Clevis Pin – A stiff piece of metal rod which secures a joint (e.g. toggel and turnbuckle).

Clew – Lower aft corner of sail.

Clipper Bow – A bow that has a forward curve.

Club Footed Jib – A self-tending jib whose foot is attached to a boom at the clew rather than being free flying.

Coaming – Side of cabin, cockpit, etc.

Cockpit – The sunken area of a deck in which the helmsman and passengers sit.

Cockpit Sole – The floor of the cockpit.

Cold Chisel – A very hard chisel for cutting metal.

Companionway – The entrance by which you pass through when going below from topsides.

Companionway Ladder – The steps in the companionway leading below.

Compression Tube – A reinforcing tubing welded into aluminum mast, through which a bolt passes. It prevents the walls from collapsing.

Countersink – To set the head of a screw or bolt below the surface; tool used for this purpose.

Cunningham Hole – A hole and cringle in a sail used to tighten or stretch the luff.

Cutter – A single mast vessel with two head-sails.

D

Davit – An overhanging fixture from which a dinghy is supported.

Deadeye – Old-fashioned method of rigging adjustment used in combination with lanyards. Replaced by modern turnbuckles.

Dead Light – A non-opening piece of glass in deck, cabin atop, etc. for light.

Deck Beams – Athwartship beams that support the deck.

Deck Bridge – The piece of decking between the cockpit and companionway entrance.

Deck Cap – A metal cap that fits over a deck-pipe to prevent water from entering boat.

Deck Fill – A metal deck fitting with screwdriver top through which water and fuel can be administered to tanks below decks.

Deck Pipe – A metal deck fitting through which chain is fed below.

Displacement – Very close estimate of the vessel's weight.

Dolfinite – A very oily bedding compound best used on fiberglass to wood or wood to wood joints.

Dove-tailing – A very positive method of corner joints for wood, using intermeshing wedge shapes of each wood as fasteners.

Dove-tail Saw – A very stiff-bladed hand saw with well reinforced blade for very accurate cutting.

Dowels – Wood turnings used as a common attachment, usually to join boards on end.

Downhaul – Line used to pull down sails. Commonly used in reference to a moveable gooseneck on tracks.

Draft – The vertical distance from waterline to lowest point of keel.

Drop Boards – Removable boards that slide into gallows, usually to shut off companionway opening.

Drops – Wood 'doors' usually below cushions that cover access holes to stowage below.

D-Shackle – A 'D'-shaped shackle with threaded pin.

E

Echo Sounder – A fathometer.

Elbow Catch – A spring-loaded catch for cabinet doors, usually hidden and accessible through a finger hole.

Engine Pan – Usually a fiberglass molding bonded to the hull. The engine mounts fitted onto its shoulders. Below the pan catches oil drippings.

Epoxy Glue and Resin – A high strength synthetic adhesive that will stick anything to anything.

Eye – A closed loop in wire-rope or line.

Eyeband – A fitting on the tip of the bowsprit to which the forestay, bobstay and whiskerstays are attached.

Eyebolt – A bolt with an open loop for a head.

Eyelets – Brass loops sewn into sails for reef points, etc.

F

Fairlead – A fitting which alters the direction of a line to keep it from fouling.

Fathom – 6 feet of measure.

Feather – To even two levels into each other.

Feeler Gauge – Small metal sheets of given thickness used to measure fine spacings; e.g. coupling to engine alignment.

Fender – A bumper or rubber guard hung from the boat's sides.

Fiddles – Wood or metal guardrails along the perimeter of counters, tables, etc. that keep items from falling.

Flare – Outward curve of a vessel's side. To widen or ream the end of a pipe for coupling purposes.

Flathead – A bevel-shouldered screw.

Flex Coupling – A rubber fitted unit uniting the engine with propeller shaft. The rubber acts as an absorber of engine vibration.

Flex Mounts – Rubber fitted engine mounts that prevent transmission of engine vibration to the hull.

Flux – A cleaning paste used on surface just before soldering.

Foot – The bottom edge of a sail.

Footpump – A water pump operated by foot.

Fore and Aft – In direction of centerline. Stern to bow.

Forecastle – The forward-most accommodations.

Forefoot – The underwater part of the bow from the forward part of the keel to the foremost part of the waterline.

Forepeak – Generally same as forecastle.

Forestay – The forward-most mast supporting rigging.

Fork Wrench – Open ended wrench.

Freeboard – Vertical distance from waterline to sheer.

Fresh Water Cooling – A closed water system which circulates through the engine block to cool it. The fresh water is in turn cooled through a heat exchanger by circulating exterior water.

G

Galley – A boat's kitchen.

Gallows – Boom gallows.

Galvanize – A zinc coating put on steel to protect it from corrosion.

Gate Valve – A conventional shut-off mechanism for water and fuel flow.

Gelcoat – A very hard outer coating (usually color pigmented) of a fiberglass boat.

Genoa – A headsail filling the entire fore triangle and more.

Gimbals – A swivel arrangement by which stoves, tables, compasses, etc. are allowed to remain level in spite of the boat movements.

Gooseneck – A swivel fitting that holds the boom onto the mast.

Grabrail – Holed handrail on deck or inside a boat.

Graphite – A mineral base lubricant.

Grinder – A term used sometimes for a belt sander.

Grommet – A brass eye sewn into a sail.

Guard – An adjustable metal fence on a table saw, running parallel with the blade.

Gudgeon – A hull fitting into which the pintle of the rudder fits.

Gypsey – A wheel on the windlass notched for rope.

H

Hack Saw – A very fine tooth bladed saw (the blade is removable) made for metal cutting.

Halyard – Lines used for hoisting sails.

Halyard Winches - Winches with a drum for wire or rope used to aid in hoisting the sails.

Hank – The attaching clip of a sail that holds it to the stay but allows it to slide up and down

Hasp – The hinged part of a fitting that combined with an eye and padlock completes a locking unit for hatches, doors, etc.

Hatch – An access hole in the ship's deck; also the cover for this hole.

Hatch Coaming – Built up buffer around a hatch opening to keep out water intruding under the hatch.

Hatch Cover – A fixed housing under which a hatch slides.

Head – The toilet of a boat.

Headsail – Sails such as jib, genoa, staysail, set forward of the mast.

Heat-Exchanger – A cooling unit of an engine which allows circulating raw water to cool captive fresh water.

Helm – Tiller or steering wheel.

Hex (Head or Nut) – A six-sided nut, or six-sided bolt-head.

Hobby Horse – The pitching of the bow and stern of a boat about its athwartship axis.

Hold Downs – Straps of steel or nylon used to fasten tanks to shelves, floor timbers, etc.

Hole Saws – Circular heavy walled saw blades of infinite diameters used in conjunction with a drill motor to cut holes.

Hose Barb – A tapered fitting with terraced ridges that allow a hose to slip on but not off.

Hose Clamp – An adjustable stainless steel ring used to fasten hoses to fittings.

Hose Ties – Plastic ties with a barbed tongue and eye used to fasten hoses to bulkheads, sole, etc.

House Pipe – A fitting in the bulwarks through which mooring lines or anchor lines are led.

I

Inboard – Toward the centerline.

Injectors – The device on a diesel engine which turns the fuel from liquid to vapor.

Intermediates – Stays that support the mast at a point between the spreaders and masthead.

J

Jack Stays – Spreader lifts.

Jam Cleats – A small cleat with general shape of a mooring cleat but one end is tapered so the line can be wedged with a single run; used for sheets where quick release and quick making-fast is necessary.

Jib – The foremost headsail.

Jiffy Reefing – A method which quickly hauls the luff and leech of the mainsail down to the boom by means of lines and blocks.

Joiner – A mechanical table plane for dressing wood surfaces.

K

Keel – The fore and aft underwater members which stabilizes the boat's direction and prevents leeway.

Ketch – Twin masted sailboat with the main forward of the mizzen and the mizzen forward of the stern post.

Key Hole Saw – A very narrow bladed hand saw with one end of the blade unsupported, used for hole or curve cutting.

Kill Switch – A control mechanism on a diesel engine that shuts it off by cutting off fuel supply.

King Plank – The central plank of a deck.

Knot – A vertical speed rating – 1 nautical mile = 6,080 ft./hr.

Knotmeter – A boat's speedometer.

L

Lag Bolt – Square headed wood screw.

Lay Up – The laminations of fiberglass.

Lazarette – A stowage compartment in the aft-most section of a vessel.

Lead-Fish – Large lead castings used for ballast.

Lead-Pig – Small (1016-10016) lead castings used for ballast.

Lead-Shot – Very small lead chunks used for ballast.

Leeboard – Canvas or plywood slabs used to keep a berth's occupant in the berth in spite of the vessel's roll.

Leech – Aft edge of the sail.

Leeway – Sideways movement of a vessel.

Lifelines – The lines attached to the stanchions providing a 'railing.'

Limber Holes – Holes in bulkheads that allow drainage from one compartment to another.

LOA – Length Over All (not including bowsprit or boomkin or aft hung rudder).

Locker – A stowage compartment.

Log – A mechanical device that records the distance the ship has moved relative to water.

Lowers – The lower shrouds.

Lubber Line – Mark on a compass corresponding to the boat's center line.

Luff – Forward edge of sail.

LWL – Load Water Line – length of hull at marked waterline.

M

Machine Screw – A fine threaded, slot headed fastener made to be used with a tapped hole.

Mainsail – Fore and aft sail attached to aft part of main mast.

Make Fast – To attach or secure a line.

Marine Eyes – The looped fitting over a shroud.

Mast Head – Top of the mast.

Mast Step – A fitting on deck or below onto which the foot of the mast is fitted.

Mat – An unwoven fiberglass material made up of randomly layered short fibers.

Miter – To cut on an angle.

Miter Box – A wood or metal frame which is used with a hand saw to cut material at a given angle.

Miter Gauge – The sliding fitting on a table or band saw against which the piece of wood is laid to assure a straight cut. The gauge itself is adjustable to any angle required.

Mish-Mash – A mixture of polyester resin and fibers of asbestos or fiberglass combined to make a thicker putty-like adhesive.

Mizzen – Fore and aft sail attached to aft part of mizzen mast.

Mizzen Mast – The aft mast of a yawl or ketch.

Molding – Trimming pieces of wood or plastic that hide joints or mistakes or both.

Mooring Cleat – A large deck cleat to which mooring lines are attached.

N

Negative Roach – A battenless, hollow-cut cruising mainsail.

Non-Skid – A high friction surface for deck and cabin top.

O

Open End – A type of mechanic's wrench.

Outboard – Away from center line.

Outhaul – The gear used to stretch the foot of sail along the boom.

Oval Head – A screw with a head of that shape.

Overhang – Stern or bow of hull extending past the LWL.

Overhead – Inside cabin top.

P

Pad Eye – A through bolted deck fitting to accommodate blocks, lines, etc.

Pan Head – A type of screw with a head shaped like the bottom of a cooking pan.

Pennant – Short length of wire to which headsails are attached.

Pet Cock – A small 90 degree turn off-on valve ideal for fuel switch off.

Pilot Berth – An elevated single berth.

Pinrail – A rack that houses belaying pins.

Pintle – Rudder fitting that fits into gudgeons to form hinge.

Pitch – Sticky wood rosin.

Plastic Resin Glue – A powder base mixed with water that forms a very strong water resistant glue.

Plug – A tight fitting wood dowel used to fill screw head holes.

Plug Cutter – An attachment for a drill motor that cuts plugs.

Plug Remover – Any sharp tool to split an inserted plug and take it out.

Polysulfide – An unbelievably effective totally waterproof sealing-bedding compound.

Polyurethane Foam – A tight-celled polyester resin resistant insulation.

Poop – An overtaking sea swamping the aft deck and/or cockpit of vessel.

Port – Left side of vessel facing forward.

Portlight – A small cabin side window.

Preventer – Another name for a boomvang.

Pull Rings – Flush fitting swivel rings used to lift hatches.

Purchase – The lines and blocks used to gain mechanical advantage.

Q

Quarter Berth – Usually an excellent sea berth located in the aft quarters of the ship.

Quarters – The sections of the vessel from amidships to bow or amidships to stern.

R

Rabbet – A groove cut in a plank.

Radio Coax – Radio antenna wire.

Railstripe – A color line along the sheer.

Rake – Fore and aft inclination of mast, sternpost, etc.

Ratlines – Horizontal ropes or strips of wood between shrouds forming a ladder.

Rat Tail – Faired or feathered rope end.

Raw Water Cooling – An engine cooling system that circulates exterior water directly through the block.

Reaching Pole – A light boom for keeping light wind sails full.

Reef – To shorten sails.

Reef Points – Grommets or ties for shortening the sail.

Resorcinal Glue A two-part completely water-proof glue.

Roach – The outward curve added to a sail to increase its belly.

Rope Tail – A nylon end on a wire halyard.

Roving – A very heavy woven fiberglass material.

Rubrail – Bumper strip of wood or metal on the beams.

Rudder Preventer – A strip between hull and aft-hung rudder that keeps lines from catching on rudder.

Run – To sail before the wind.

Running Rigging – Sheets, halyards, etc., i.e. moveable rigging.

S

Sail Track – A track on the mast or boom into or onto which the sail slides are fitted.

Salon – Main living area in vessel.

Samson Post – Strong post in foredeck used as a hitch post for anchor line and mooring line.

Schooner – A rig that sports a smaller mast ahead of the main mast.

Scupper – An opening in the bulwarks allowing deck-drainage.

Scribe – To reproduce the curve of a surface onto another surface by using a compass with pencil.

Seacock – A 90 degree shut-off valve used on through-hull fittings.

Seakindly – having characteristics which respond well to any sea condition.

Searail – Fencing along table, cabinetry, etc. to guard items from falling.

Seating Cleat – Shelving upon which drop boards sit.

Section – Lines of a vessel as if cut in half looking fore and aft.

Set – To hoist sail.

Shaft-Log – A bearing supporting fitting guiding the propeller-shaft through the hull.

Shank – The shaft of the anchor.

Sheer – Curve of a gunwale.

Sheet – A rope used to trim sails.

Sheet Metal Screw – Heavy threaded self-tapping screw.

Shrink Tubes – Plastic tubing slipped over wire splices then shrunk by heat to seal the splice.

Shroud – Wire rigging giving the most athwartship support.

Silicone Seal – A quick drying non-hardening sealing compound.

Slab Reefing – Jiffy reefing.

Slides – Metal fittings that hold a sail onto the sail track.

Sloop – Single masted rig with single headsail.

Snap Shackle – Hinge bar shackle.

Sole – Cabin floor,

Sole Timber – Floor supporting beams.

Spinnaker Car – A moveable fitting that attaches the spinnaker pole to the spinnaker track.

Spinnaker Pole – A light spar that keeps the clew of the spinnaker well out helping fill the sail.

Spinnaker Track – A track attached to the mast over which the spinnaker car slides.

Spreader – A strut on a mast giving rigidity to rigging.

Spreader Lifts – Wires that keep spreaders in position.

Stanchions – Steel poles attached to deck or bulwarks to support lifelines.

Standing Rigging – Permanently attached wire stays and turnbuckles supporting the mast.

Starboard – The right side of a vessel facing forward.

Stay – A wire rope supporting the mast fore and aft.

Staysail – A triangular hanked sail.

Staysail Pedestal – A deck mounted base footing the staysail boom.

Stops – Moveable fittings on a track that keep a block in place.

Storm Jib – A very small, heavy clothed heavy-weather headsail.

Storm Trysail – Very small heavy clothed heavy-weather sail to replace mainsail.

Stuffing Box – A fitting at the shaft-log preventing the entry of water.

Sump – The lowest point in the keel where water collects.

Swedge – Method of attaching, by pressure, fittings onto a wire rope.

T

Tabernacle – A large deck bracket that houses the foot of the mast and the pin which allows it to be lowered.

Tack – The lower forward corner of a sail.

Taffrail – A rail around the stern – usually decorative if you like that sort of thing.

Tang – A metal fitting on mast or hull to which rigging is attached.

Tender – Given to heeling, antonym of 'Stiff.'

Terminal Blocks – An electrical, insulated block with fittings to unite wires.

Thimble – A round or heart-shaped metal eye chafe protector around which rope can be seized.

Tiller – A bar attached to top of rudder used for steering.

Toggle – A swivel fork uniting the turnbuckle to the chainplate.

Topping Lift – A line supporting aft end of a boom.

Transducer – A fathometer through-hull fitting.

Transom – A chopped stern, opposite of double-ender.

Traveller – A moveable attachment that allows control over movement of the boom.

Tumble-Home – Inward curve along the sheer line of some vessels.

Turnbuckle – Adjustable attachment uniting rigging to hull fittings.

U

Upper Shroud – That part of the rigging going to the mast head which provides athwartships support.

V

Vang – A rope controlling upward movement of a boom.

Vented Loop – A bronze fitting with a valve that prevents siphoning of water into appliances below the waterline.

W

Waterline – A horizontal line at the point of designed displacement.

Water Separator – A filter that takes water from diesel fuel by gravity.

Water Strainer – A filter for incoming raw water.

Whiskerstay – Standing rigging which prevents athwartships movement of bowsprit or boomkin.

Winch – A mechanical aid made up of a drum and pin and gears to aid in hoisting and trimming sails.

Winch Bracket – A fabricated mount for sheet winches.

Winch Pad – A welded pad on a mast serving as a base for a halyard winch.

Windlass – A winch to haul up anchor and anchor chain.

Y

Yankee Jib – Large foresail, its size between a working jib and genoa.

Yaw – To change bearing from side to side – unable to maintain course.

Yawl – A twin-masted rig, the mizzen being stepped abaft the sternpost.

Appendix

Type Wire	Breaking Strength in pounds									
Size Wire (in.)	$1/16$	$3/32$	$1/8$	$5/32$	$3/16$	$7/32$	$1/4$	$9/32$	$5/16$	$3/8$
1×19	500	1,200	2,100	3,300	4,700	6,300	8,200	10,300	12,500	17,500
7×7	500	1,200	2,100	3,300	4,700	6,300	8,200	10,300	12,500	17,500
7×19	—	—	1,760	2,400	3,700	5,000	6,400	7,800	9,000	12,000

VINYL COATED WIRE

Type	Size (in.)	
	Wire	Outside
7×7	$3/32$	$5/32$
7×19	$1/8$	$3/16$
7×19	$5/32$	$7/32$
7×19	$3/16$	$1/4$
7×19	$1/4$	$3/8$

Table 4.   Wire Strength

Speed Selection	Barient	Barlow	Gibb	Lewmar	Merriman
Single speed	—	—	—	#5	#8
	#9	#15	#571	—	—
	#10H	—	—	—	—
	#10	#16	#573	#8	#10
	#16	#20	—	—	#16
Geared singlespeed	#20	—	#847	—	—
Two speed	—	—	—	#10	—
	—	#18	#848	#16	—
	#21	#22	—	#25	#20
	—	#24	—	—	—
	#22	—	#809	#40	#22
	—	#26	—	—	#25
	#26	—	#1049	#43	—
	#28	#28	—	—	#28
	#30	#30	#810	—	—
	#32	#32	#1043	—	#32
	#35	#34	#808	—	—
	#35 special	#36	—	—	—
Three speed	#28	—	—	#45	—
	#30	—	—	—	—
	#32	—	—	#55	—
	#34	—	—	—	—
	#35	—	—	—	—
	#35 special	—	—	#65	—
Halyard winches	#1	#8	—	#3	—
	#2-A	#6	—	#3	—
	#2	—	—	—	—
	#3-A	#5	—	#2	—
	#3	#4	—	#1	—

Table 5. Winch Size Comparison

SERIES S-200 MAST SECTIONS

DEPTH		WIDTH	THICKNESS	LBS/FT	IXX	IYY	
6.50	x	3.50	.088	1.72	6.48 in.	2.92 in.	S-201
7.00	x	3.75	.094	2.01	8.96 in.	3.93 in.	S-202
7.50	x	4.00	.140	3.214	16.672	6.818	S-203
8.00	x	4.25	.140	3.43	21.04 in.	7.50 in.	S-204
8.50	x	4.50	.156	4.103	25.20 in.	9.80 in.	S-205
9.00	x	4.75	.156	4.207	32.111	12.945	S-206
9.50	x	5.00	.156	4.459	33.87 in.	17.38 in.	S-207

ALLOYS 6061-T6 OR EQUIVALENT

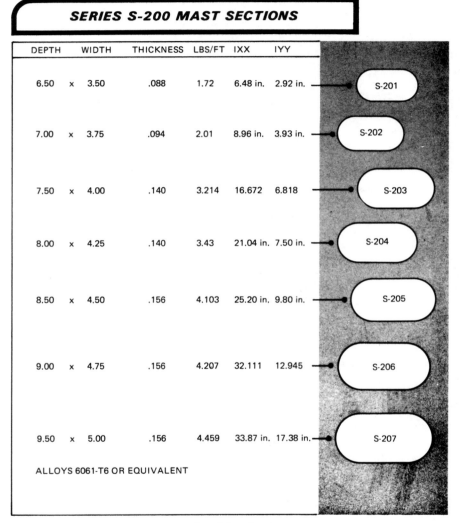

Table 3 — Mast Sections.

SERIES S-300 MAST SECTIONS

DEPTH		WIDTH	THICKNESS	LBS/FT	IXX	IYY	
5.62	x	3.50	.110	1.808	5.144	2.474	S-301
5.75	x	4.00	.135	2.364	7.196	4.104	S-302
7.00	x	4.25	.140	2.837	12.419	5.738	S-303
7.00	x	5.25	.150	3.311	15.314	9.832	S-304
8.50	x	4.50	.200	4.655	28.699	10.618	S-305
9.00	x	5.50	.200	5.209	37.582	17.503	S-306
10.00	x	6.50	.220	6.0	55.3 in.	28.2 in.	S-307
10.50	x	7.50	.190-.310	7.05	80.95 in.	40.08 in.	S-308
11.43	x	6.43	.220	7.35	80.0 in.	34.5 in.	S-309
13.60	x	8.50	.220	9.05	147.30 in.	72.0 in.	S-310
13.60	x	8.30	.250	10.26	163 in.	77 in.	S-311
14.70	x	10.20	.250	11.268	227.110	129.581	S-312

ALLOYS 6061-T6 OR EQUIVALENT

Table 3 — Mast Sections.

Boatbuilders

Pacific Seacraft Corp. 3301 South Susan St. Santa Ana, Calif. 92704	Flicka Crealock 37 Orion	C.E. Ryder Corporation 47 Gooding Ave., Bristol, R.I. 02809 (Ryder Custom Yachts)	Quickstep 24 Alberg 23 Luders 27, 34 Gillmer 28, 31, 35, 39
Morris Yachts Custom Boat Builders Clark Point Rd. Southwest Harbour, ME 04679	Frances Annie Leigh	Sam L. Morse Co. 1626 Placentia Ave. Costa Mesa, CA 92627	Falmouth Cutter Bristol Channel Cutter
Duck Trap Woodworking R.F.D. 2, Cannon Road Lincolnville Beach Maine 04849	Assorted wooden rowing boats	Bill Lee Yachts Inc. 3700 B Hilltop Rd. Soquel, CA 95073	Santa Cruz 40 Santa Cruz 50
Rawson, Inc. 9001 151st Ave. S.E. P.O. Box 83 Redmond, WA 98052	Rawson 30	Nordic Tugs P.O. Box 314 Woodinville, WA 98072	The Nordic Tug
Seamaster Yachts 3381 S.W. 11th Ave. Fort Lauderdale, Fla 33315	Seamaster 45	Marshall Marine Corp. Box P-266 Shipyard Lane South Dartmouth, MASS. 02748	Sandpiper Sanderling Marshall 22 Marshall 26
Yacht Constructors, Inc. 7030 N.E. 42nd Ave. Portland, Ore. 97218	Cascade 23, 27, 29 36 and 42	Apprenticeshop Maine Maritime Museum 375 Front Street Bath, Maine 04530	Assorted wooden rowing and sailing boats

Vashon Boat Works P.O. Box Q Vashon, WA 98070	Quartermaster 8 Quartermaster 10	P. & M. Wordwide Yacht Builders P.O. Box 10281 Costa Mesa, CA 92627	Westsail 32 Aleutka 25
Raider Yachts Box 365 - A1. RD1 Medford, N.J. 08055	Raider 33	Jarvis Newman Inc. Southwest Harbour Maine 04679	Pemaquid 25 Dictator 31
Martin Yachts 8091 Capstan Way Richmond, B.C. Canada	Peterson 35 Martin 32	Cherubini Boat Co. 222 Wood St. Burlington, NJ 08016	Cherubini 44 Cherubini 48
Miller Marine 7659 N.E. Day Rd. Bainbridge Island, WA 98110	Jason	Able Marine Southwest Harbour· Maine 04679	Whistler
A. & T. Marine P.O. Box 1423 Tacoma, WA 98401	Naja	Spencer Boats Ltd. 12391 Twigg Road Richmond, B. C. Canada V6V 1M5	Spencer 31 Spencer 34 Spencer 35 Spencer 1330
Cecil M. Lange & Son Rt. 3, Box 202 Port Townsend, WA 98368	Cape George 31 Cape George 36 Cape George 40	Sceptre Yachts Ltd. 1720 Cowley Cres. Richmond, B.C.	Sceptre 36 Sceptre 41
Bristol Channel Cutter P.O. Box 91387 West Vancouver, B.C. V7V 3P1, Canada	Bristol Channel Cutter	Headway Woodworks & Marine Services No. 5 - 8100 River Rd. Richmond, B.C. V6X 3A3	Buzzards Bay 14
New Orleans Marine, Inc. 3027 Tchoupitoulas St. New Orleans, LA 70115	Frers 40	Blue Water Boats P.O. Box 625 Woodinville, WA 98072	Ingrid
Tyler Boats 730 Poke St. San Francisco, CA 94109	Corsair 44	Whisstocks Woodbridge, Suffolk 1912 IBW, England	Naja
Alvis Marine No. 5 - 12331 Bridgeport Rd. Richmond, B.C. V6V 1J4 Canada	Evetts 31	Alajuela Yacht Corp. 5181 Argosy Dr. Huntington Beach, CA 92649	Alajuela 33 Alajuela 38

Hidden Harbour Boat Works 2029 Whitfield Park Ave. Sarasota, Fla 33580	Vancouver 36	Worldcruiser Yacht Co. 1300 Logan St. Costa Mesa, CA 92626	Worldcruiser 50
Jomarco 322 E. Dyer Rd. Santa Ana, CA 92707	Jomar 55 Westsail 28 Westsail 42	Coast Yacht Design Inc. No. 7 - 1285 Harwood St. Vancouver, B.C. V6E 1S5 Canada	Passage 34
Liberty Yacht Corp. Rt. 2, Box 548 Leland, N.C. 28451	Pied Piper 28	Menger Enterprises 77 Cedar St. P.O. Box 141 Babylon, N.Y. 11702	Oysterman 23
The Old Boathouse 2770 Westlake N. Seattle, WA. 98109	14' Whitebear Skiff	Seair Ltd. 20 Bewicke Ave. North Vancouver, B.C. V7M 3B5	vancouver 27
Clark Custom Boats 3665 Hancock St. San Diego, CA 92110	Clark 31		
Loomis Yachts Box 575 South Dartmouth, MA 02748	Sarah 31	Reliance Yacht Corp. P.O. Box 46527, Stn. G. Vancouver, B.C. V6R 4G8 Canada	Reliance 37
Soverel Marine 2225 Idlewilde Rd. North Palm Beach, Fla 33410	Soverel 30 Soverel 36	C & B Marine 1053 Seventeenth Ave. Santa Cruz, CA 95062	Tiffany Jayne

Suppliers

Adler-Barbour
Refrigerator systems
511 Fifth Avenue, Pelham, N.Y. 10803.

Air Cushion
Flexible tanks
15/35 Randolph Street,
Shirley, Southampton, England.

Allcraft Corp.
Stainless steel h/w heaters
55 Border Street, West Newton,
MA.02165.

Amfridge
P.O. Box 2267,
Elkhart, Ind. 46515.

Ampair
Wind generators
76 Meadrow, Godalming,
Surrey, GU7 3HT, England.

Aries
Self steering
Nick Franklin, Marine Vanes,
Northwood, Cowes,
Isle of Wight.

Atkins & Hoyle
Ports and hatches
69 Portland Street,
Toronto, Ont. M5V 2M9.

Avon
Inflatable liferafts
Dafen, Llanelli, Dyfed,
South Wales SA14 8NA.

Berco Fasteners
S.s. and bronze screws, bolts
Box 343, Randallston, M.D. 21133.

Bliss
Catalogue sales
100 Allied Drive,
Dedham, MA. 02026.

Bluewater Foods
Storeable prepared meals
P.O. Box 87421,
San Diego, CA. 92138.

Bomar
Hatches and portlights
Box W, Charlston, N.H. 03603.

British Seagull
First-class outboard motors
418 Ringwood Road, Parkstone,
Poole, Dorset BH12 3LJ, England.

Brooks & Gatehouse
Electronics
Bath Road, Lymington,
Hampshire, England.

Bruynzeel
First-class marine plywood
P.O. Box 59,
Zaandam, Holland.

Calvert School
Correspondence school courses
3 Tuscany Road,
Baltimore, M.D. 21210.

Clark Hardware
Traditional bronze hardware
3665 Hancock Street,
San Diego, CA. 92110.

Contech Mfg.
Ultrasonic pest control
P.O. Box 774, Fleet National,
Providence, R.I. 02901.

Corp Brothers
Compressed natural gas systems
1 Brook Street,
Providence, R.I. 02903.

Datsun Diesels
P.O. Box 161404,
Memphis, T.N. 38116.

Digital Marine Electronics
P.O. Box 287,
Acton, M.A. 01720.

Edson
Steering, pumps, etc.
494 Industrial Park Road,
New Bedford, MA. 02745.

E. G. Van De Stadt
Yacht designs book
Box 193, 1520 A.D.,
Wormerveer, Holland.

Famet Hardware Catalog
745 2nd Avenue,
Redwood City, CA. 94063.

Fancraft
Folding bicycles
Freepost, Hampton,
Middx TW12 1BR, England.

Fred Mitchell
Copper foil anti-fouling
East Street, Sydling St. Nicholas,
Dorchester, Dorset, England.

Frost Refrigerators
1326 S. Killian Drive,
Lake Park, Fl. 33403.

Gibb
Yacht hardware
c/o Barlow Marine,
26 Burnside Street, Bristol, R.I. 02809.

Goiot
Hatches, toerails, etc.
3899 Ulmerton Road,
Clearwater, Fla. 33520.

G.S.I.
Natural gas systems
5361 Production Drive,
Huntington Beach, C.A. 92649.

Hood
Sails and furling gear
Box 928, Little Harbour Way,
Marblehead, Mass. 01945.

Hyde Products
Self-furling gear
810 Sharon Drive,
Cleveland, Ohio 44145.

Hydrographer of the Navy
Admiralty charts
Taunton, Somerset, England.

Hydrovane
Self steering
117 Bramcote Lane, Chilwell,
Nottingham NG9 4EU, England.

I.M.I.
Auto helms
40 Signal Road,
Stamford, CT. 06902.

Ideal Windlass Co.
P.O. Box 430,
E. Greenwich, R.I. 02818.

Imta
Flexible tanks
151C Mystic Avenue,
Medford, Mass. 02155.

Jay Stuart Haft
Catalog sales
P.O. Box 11210,
Bradenton, Fla. 33507.

Kenyon
All spars
P.O. Box 308,
Guilford, C.T. 06437.

K. Foster
Solar cells
1742 Dowd,
St. Louis, M.O. 63136.

Lewmar
Winches
Southmoor Lane, Havant,
Hampshire PO9 1JJ, England.

Luger
Boat kits
3800 West Highway 13,
Burnsville, M.N. 55337.

Lumic
Wind generators
24 Worthington Crescent,
Poole, Dorset, England.

Marine Buyers Co-op
314 Lincoln Street,
M.A. 02043.

Marine Center Catalog
2130 Westlake Avenue,
P.O. Box 9968,
Seattle, W.A. 98109.

Marlow
Ropes
Hailsham, East Sussex, England.

Marlow
Running rigging
151 Mystic Avenue,
Medford, Mass. 02155.

Max Prop.
Feathering props.
PYI 749 N. 81 Street,
Seattle, WA. 98103.

Merriman
All sorts of marine gear
P.O. Box 405,
Millersville, M.D. 21108.

M. L. Condon
Boat lumber
240 Ferris Avenue,
White Plains, N.Y. 10603.

Murray Winches
Bottom handle winches
S.P.A. 3827 Stone Way N.,
Seattle, W.A. 98103.

New England Ropes
Running rigging
Popes Island,
New Bedford, MA. 02740.

N.F.M.
Bronze marine hardware
240 Airport Road,
Port Townsend, W.A. 98368.

Nicro Fico
Marine hardware
2065 West Avenue 140th,
San Leandro, CA. 94577.

Norseman
First-class rigging ware
Station Road, Lawford,
Manningtree, Essex CO11 2LN.

North Sails
All over the place.

Nautech
Electronic self steering
The Airport, Eastern Road,
Portsmouth, Hants PO3 5QF, England.

Navik
Autopilots
Plastimo Manufacturing.
School Lane, Chandlers Ford I.E.,
Eastleigh, Hants. SO5 3NB.

Navtec
Rigging
527 Great Road,
Littleton, MA. 01460.

Quality Woods Ltd.
Teak ply and lumber
Box 205,
Lake Hiawatha, N.J. 07034.

Para-anchors
Sea anchors
Box 19,
Summerland C.A. 93067.

P.D.C. Labs
Solarcharger
Box 603,
El Segundo C.A. 90245.

Pettit Paints
36 Pine Street,
P.O. Box 378,
Rockway, N.J. 07866.

Ratsey & Lapthorne
Sailmakers
34 Medina Road, Cowes,
Isle of Wight.

Red Wing Generators
Wind or water powered generators
4151 Charles,
La Mesa, CA. 92041.

Ritchie
Compasses, instruments
Oak Street,
Pembroke, MA. 02359.

Sails U.S.A.
Silver Street,
Portland, M.E. 04112.

Seemann
Fiberglass planking
Box 13704,
New Orleans, L.A. 70185.

Simpson Lawrence
Instruments and hardware
218 Edminston Drive,
Glasgow G51 2YT, Scotland.

Steiner
Binoculars
Pioneer & Co.,
216 Haddon,
Westmont, N.J. 08108.

Tamaya
Sextant and computers
5-8 3-chome, Ginza,
Chuo-ku, Tokyo, Japan.

Tiller-master
Autopilot
774 W. 17th,
Costa Mesa, C.A. 92627.

Vega Instruments
Barographs
75 Main Avenue, Bush Hill Park,
Enfield, Middx, England.

Whale
First-class bilge pumps
151 Mystic Avenue,
Medford, MA. 02155.

Westlawn
School of yacht design
733 Summer Street,
Stamford, CT. 06904.

Yachtmail
Mail-order hardware
Cornwall Crescent,
London W11 1PH, England.

Index